1001
Kitchen Appliance
RECIPES

BEEKMAN HOUSE
New York

Contents

Introduction

Kitchens today are equipped with a variety of time-saving, space-saving, and energy-saving appliances that allow even the busiest cook to prepare an elegant meal. This cookbook is filled with over 1,000 recipes geared specifically toward the most useful kitchen appliances.

You'll learn how to prepare a complete meal—including appetizers, main courses, vegetables, breads, and desserts—using a crepe pan, crock pot, food processor, microwave oven, pressure cooker, skillet, toaster oven, and wok.

These appliances are invaluable tools for the cook who has limited time but the desire to prepare exciting meals. The crock pot cooks all day, or all night, on low heat, so that your food can be prepared while you are at work or sleeping. It's a handy, inexpensive, and energy-saving way to prepare meals ahead of time. The microwave oven allows foods to be defrosted and cooked quickly— even if you are away from home all day, you'll have time to prepare a roast for dinner. The pressure cooker too is a time-saving device that allows food to cook more quickly.

The food processor not only saves you a great deal of time in grating, chopping, slicing, and puréeing, it helps you prepare more complex dishes with less effort. Many of the recipes can also be adapted for use in a blender or mixer, if a food processor is not available. Keep in mind, however, that some of the time-saving steps will have to be done manually.

Another appliance that makes once-difficult dishes easy to prepare is the crepe pan. Crepes are now quick and easy to make and can turn leftovers into an elegant meal.

The skillet and wok are useful in preparing a variety of foods, including one-pot meals that reduce cleaning-up time afterwards. Foods can be sautéed quickly in a skillet or wok, keeping them crispy and sealing in the nutrients.

The many recipes in this book will help familiarize you with all of these appliances and will help you prepare sophisticated dishes with a minimum of effort.

Crepe Pan

Successful Crepes

Common Problems in Crepe-making

1) Serving crepes inside out: The inside of a crepe is seldom attractive and it detracts from your table setting to stack crepes with the inside most prominent.

2) Serving burned crepes: Displaying burned crepes also detracts from your table setting. Such burning results from extreme heat and excessive cooking time. These crepes were held on high heat too long.

3) Batter too thick: It becomes impossible to coat the bottom of the crepe pan evenly before cooking begins.

4) Pan too hot: The crepe cooks quickly, resulting in lumpiness and gaps.

5) Insufficient batter: The bottom of the crepe pan is not evenly covered with batter, and oddly shaped crepes result.

6) Fragmented crepes: These usually result from insufficient batter in an overheated or improperly seasoned pan.

7) Soggy crepes: These result from prefolding crepes around a juicy or greasy filling too long before serving. It is far better to serve separately a stack of crepes and the filling and permit the diner to fold his or her own.

8) Spongy crepe: Topping a folded crepe with fruit results in the juice being absorbed, leading to dry fruit and a spongy crepe.

Special Tips for Perfect Crepes

1) If batter is lumpy, strain through sieve.

2) Make batter and store in refrigerator up to 3 days. Bring to room temperature before using.

3) Practice making thinner more delicate crepes by using less batter.

4) Use a small measuring cup to dip up batter when making crepes.

5) Brush spatula with melted butter or oil to prevent it from sticking to crepes while turning.

6) Makes crepes ahead of time. Stack, wrap, and refrigerate 1 to 2 days. Freeze up to 2 months.

7) If flaming crepes, ignite slightly warm alcohol with a long wooden match. Slowly pour over food.

8) Use high-proof liqueur for flaming.

Different Ways to Serve Crepes

Some popular ways of serving crepes are:

1) Stack or Gateau: Crepes are stacked with filling between each layer. Place crepes, best side up, on a board or plate. Spread filling over each crepe, leaving about ¼-inch border around edge. Stack one filled crepe on another to desired height. Usually it is easier to spread each one before stacking; but, if filling is runny or hard to handle, you can spread each crepe after it is added to the stack.

2) Crepe Suzette Fold: Place crepe, best-looking side down, on board or plate.

Spoon filling on center of crepe. Fold in half. Fold in half again, forming a triangle four layers thick. Excellent for creamy or butter-filled recipes.

3) Blintz or Pocket Fold: Place crepe, best-looking side down, on board or plate. Spoon filling on center of crepe. Fold bottom of crepe over almost half of filling. Fold right side over slightly more than half the filling. Then fold left side of crepe over filling, slightly overlapping right side. Fold top of crepe down over both sides, almost to center. A popular variation of this fold is to fold both sides over filling, then fold bottom and top. This fold keeps the filling inside the crepe—especially good for any recipe to be sautéed or deep-fried.

4) Roll-Up: Place crepe, best-looking side down, on board or plate. Spread filling over other side, leaving about ¼-inch border around edge. Starting at one side, roll up like a jelly roll. This is a good shape for most fillings that can be spread over crepes. Appetizers in this form are easy to cut into bite-size pieces.

5) Fold-Over: Place crepe, best-looking side down, on board, plate, or in pan. Spoon or spread filling along center of crepe. Fold one side over, covering most of the filling. Fold over opposite side, overlapping first fold. This shape is popular because it is easy to make and shows off the filling.

6) Half-Fold: Place crepe, best-looking side down, on board or plate. Place filling on half of the lighter side of the crepe. Fold crepe in half. This is a handy fold for Crepewiches when the filling is too large for other shapes.

7) Burrito Roll: Place crepe, best-looking brown side down, on board or plate. Spread filling over light side, leaving about ½-inch border around edge, or spoon filling into center of crepe. Fold right and left sides over filling. Starting at the bottom of the crepe, roll up. Make sure the folded sides are included in the roll. This is handy for fillings that may become runny when heated. The folded sides help keep the mixture inside the crepe.

Batter Recipes

Basic Batter

Yield: 24 to 26 crepes

1½ cups flour
1 teaspoon sugar (for dessert crepes)
⅛ teaspoon salt
3 eggs
1½ cups milk
2 tablespoons butter or oil, melted or cooled

Sift the dry ingredients into a bowl. Break the eggs into another bowl and mix until yolks and whites are blended. Pour the beaten eggs into a reservoir in the middle of the dry ingredients. (The mixing is more difficult if you break the eggs right into the dry ingredients.)

Stir the flour mixture into the eggs little by little. It may be necessary to add a little milk (or whatever liquid is used in the recipe) to incorporate all the flour. Mix the liquid in thoroughly a spoonful at a time before adding more. When the mixture becomes easy to work (when about half of the liquid has been used), the remainder can be added in two portions.

Add melted butter (and flavorings if indicated). Mix again, cover and set aside for at least an hour but not more than 6 hours at room temperature. Crepe batter can be held overnight in the refrigerator. If necessary, the crepe batter can be cooked immediately, but the "resting" time allows the flour to absorb more liquids, makes the batter easier to handle and gives the crepes more flavor. Since flours vary in their ability to absorb liquid, if the crepe batter seems too thick when you are ready to cook it, a small amount of extra liquid can be added at this time. The consistency should be at least as thin as heavy cream.

Mixer or whisk method: In medium mixing bowl, combine eggs and salt. Gradually add flour, alternating with milk, beating with an electric mixer or whisk until smooth. Beat in melted butter.

Blender method: Combine ingredients in blender jar; blend for about 1 minute. Scrape down sides with rubber spatula and blend for another 15 seconds or until smooth.

Richer Batter

Yield: 30 to 35 crepes

4 eggs
¼ teaspoon salt
2 cups flour
2 cups milk
½ cup melted butter

Mixer or whisk method: In medium mixing bowl, combine eggs and salt. Gradually add flour, alternating with milk, beating with electric mixer or whisk until smooth. Beat in melted butter.

Blender method: Combine ingredients in blender jar; blend for about 1 minute. Scrape down sides with rubber spatula and blend for another 15 seconds or until smooth.

This is a thick batter. You may want to add 1 or 2 tablespoons of milk or water for thinner crepes. Refrigerate at least 1 hour before using.

Instant Flour Batter

Yield: 16 to 20 crepes

3 eggs
¼ teaspoon salt
1 cup instant flour
⅔ cup milk
⅔ cup water
1 tablespoon cooking oil

Mixer or whisk method: In medium mixing bowl, combine eggs and salt. Gradually add flour, alternating with milk and water, beating with electric mixer or whisk until smooth. Beat in oil.

Blender method: Combine ingredients in blender jar; blend for about 1 minute. Scrape down sides with rubber spatula and blend for another 15 seconds or until smooth.

This batter does not have to be refrigerated before using. You can use it right away. Be sure to stir batter occasionally, as flour has a tendency to sink.

Basic Dessert Crepe Batter

Yield: 20 to 25 crepes

4 eggs
1 cup flour
2 tablespoons sugar
1 cup milk
¼ cup water
1 tablespoon melted butter

Mixer or whisk method: In medium mixing bowl, beat eggs. Gradually add flour and sugar alternating with milk and water, beating with electric mixer or whisk until smooth. Beat in melted butter.

Blender method: Combine ingredients in blender jar; blend for about 1 minute. Scrape down sides with rubber spatula and blend for another 15 seconds or until smooth.

Refrigerate batter at least 1 hour before use.

Chocolate Dessert Crepe Batter

Yield: 18 to 22 crepes

3 eggs
1 cup flour
2 tablespoons sugar
2 tablespoons cocoa
1¼ cups buttermilk (or add 1 tablespoon lemon juice to 1¼ cups regular milk)
2 tablespoons melted butter

Mixer or whisk method: In medium mixing bowl, beat eggs. Add flour, sugar, and cocoa, alternating with buttermilk, beating with electric mixer or whisk until smooth. Beat in melted butter.

Blender method: Combine ingredients in blender jar; blend for about 1 minute. Scrape down sides with rubber spatula and blend for another 15 seconds or until smooth.

Refrigerate batter for at least 1 hour before use.

Calorie-Counters Crepe Batter

Yield: 18 to 22 crepes

3 eggs
1 cup flour
¼ cup instant nonfat dry milk
1 cup water
⅛ teaspoon salt

Combine ingredients in medium mixing bowl. Beat with electric mixer, blend in a blender, or whisk until smooth. Refrigerate 1 hour or more. If batter separates, stir gently before cooking. Cook on upside-down crepe griddle or in traditional pan.

Sauces for Crepes

Spiced Apricot Sauce

Yield: 1 cup

1 10-ounce jar apricot preserves
Rind and juice of 1 lemon
Pinch of cinnamon
Pinch of cloves
1 teaspoon arrowroot or 1 teaspoon cornstarch dissolved in
1 tablespoon cold water

Melt the apricot preserves in a small heavy saucepan, adding the juice and rind of a lemon and the spices. Strain the contents of the pan and return the clear liquid into a clean saucepan. Dissolve the arrowroot or cornstarch in the water and add to the sauce. As the sauce comes to the boiling point, it will thicken. This sauce can be used hot or cold.

Note: Arrowroot is used in preference to cornstarch to make a clearer more shiny sauce. However, if you are not able to find any arrowroot, cornstarch is a good substitute.

Chocolate Sauce

Yield: 1 cup

6 ounces semisweet chocolate pieces
3 tablespoons cold water
⅓ cup heavy cream
1 tablespoon butter
1 tablespoon dark rum

Melt the chocolate in the water and add the remaining ingredients. Serve hot or cold. The sauce will thicken as it cools and will require reheating and thinning out with a little more cream or water if it is taken right from the refrigerator.

Handmade Hollandaise Sauce

Yield: 1 cup

1¾ sticks of butter
3 egg yolks
1 tablespoon cold water
Juice of 2 lemons
¼ teaspoon salt
Dash cayenne pepper

Melt 1½ sticks of butter. Have 2 separate tablespoons of cold butter on the counter.

In a heavy saucepan, beat the egg yolks with a wire whisk until slightly thickened. Add the water, lemon juice, salt and cayenne pepper. Put the pan on a gentle heat and add the first tablespoon of cold butter. Stir rapidly with a wire whisk. Allow the butter to melt but not completely disappear, then add the second tablespoon of cold butter. When the butter has almost melted, remove the pan from the heat. Gradually add the hot butter, still stirring rapidly and constantly. The egg yolks will combine with the hot butter and thicken off the heat into a beautiful smooth sauce. Check the seasoning, adding more lemon juice or salt if necessary.

Marmalade Sauce

Yield: 1 cup

1 cup orange, lemon or lime marmalade
Juice of 1 orange, lemon or lime
Pinch of ground ginger
(1 teaspoon prepared horseradish for shrimp or crab crepes)
(¼ teaspoon cloves and ¼ teaspoon cinnamon for apricot crepes)

Put the above ingredients in the blender for 10 seconds.

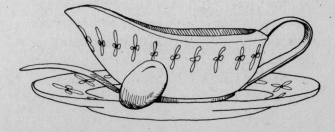

Blender Hollandaise Sauce

Yield: 1 cup

3 egg yolks
Juice of 1 lemon
Dash cayenne pepper
Pinch of salt
1 stick of butter

Put the egg yolks, lemon juice, cayenne pepper and salt into the blender. Heat the butter until hot and bubbling but not browned.

Turn on the blender and pour in the hot butter in a slow continuous stream. Blend for 10 seconds and turn off the motor. Taste and add more lemon juice or salt to your taste. Serve immediately or reheat by standing the sauce in a basin of hot but not boiling water. This sauce will keep for 2 or 3 days in the refrigerator.

Note: Hollandaise does not need to be boiling hot. The food on which it is served will heat it up a little. By trying to get it as hot as possible the risk of curdling is greatly increased.

Lemon Sauce

Yield: 1 cup

1 cup water
1 tablespoon butter
½ cup sugar
2 whole eggs
Juice of 1 lemon
1 tablespoon cornstarch
1 teaspoon vanilla

Melt the butter in the water with half of the sugar. In a separate bowl combine the eggs and the remaining sugar with the juice of the lemon. Add 1 tablespoon cornstarch.

Pour the boiling water, sugar and melted butter into the eggs, sugar, lemon juice and cornstarch and stir over a gentle heat until thickened. Add 1 teaspoon vanilla.

Handmade Melba Sauce

Yield: 1 cup

2 cups fresh raspberries or strawberries
2 tablespoons water
2 tablespoons sugar
Juice of ½ lemon
1 teaspoon arrowroot
1 tablespoon cold water

Wash berries and place in a small saucepan with the 2 tablespoons water, sugar, and lemon juice. Simmer together gently for 5 minutes and press through a fine sieve. Return to a clean saucepan and thicken with 1 teaspoon arrowroot dissolved in 1 tablespoon cold water. Chill before serving.

Blender Melba Sauce

Yield: 1 cup

1 package frozen raspberries
3 tablespoons sugar
Juice of ½ lemon
1 tablespoon Framboise, cognac, or
    kirsch, optional
1 or 2 teaspoons arrowroot or
    cornstarch, optional
1 tablespoon cold water, optional

Defrost the raspberries and place in the blender with the remaining ingredients. Turn on the motor for 10 seconds and pass the liquid through a fine sieve to remove the tiny seeds. This and all fruit sauces may be thickened, if desired, with 1 or 2 teaspoons arrowroot or cornstarch dissolved in 1 tablespoon cold water. Bring the sauce to the boil and add the thickening. It will thicken immediately, leaving no taste.

Mornay Sauce

Yield: 1 cup

1 tablespoon butter
1 tablespoon flour
1 cup milk
3 tablespoons grated Swiss or Gruyére cheese
1 tablespoon grated Parmesan cheese
½ teaspoon mild prepared mustard, preferably of the Dijon type

Melt the butter in a small saucepan. Remove from the heat and add the flour, stirring with a wire whisk. Return to a moderate heat. Add the milk gradually, stirring the mixture constantly until the sauce is thickened. Add the remaining ingredients, and salt and pepper to taste.

Peach Sauce

Yield: 4 or more cups

2 cups water
1 cup sugar
2 strips lemon rind
Juice of ½ lemon
6 ripe fresh peaches or ½ pound dried peaches soaked overnight in water

Make a syrup by combining the sugar and water. Add the lemon juice and rind. Simmer the peaches in the syrup for 10 minutes. Remove the peaches and press through a sieve or blender, adding a little of the syrup in which the peaches were poached to correct the consistency of the sauce.

Pineapple Sauce

Yield: 1 cup

Juice from a 1-pound 4-ounce can crushed pineapple
1 tablespoon butter
2 whole eggs
1 tablespoon sugar
1 tablespoon cornstarch
¼ teaspoon almond extract
1 tablespoon kirsch

Melt the butter in the pineapple juice. In a separate bowl combine the eggs, 1 tablespoon sugar and 1 tablespoon cornstarch. Pour the boiling pineapple juice into the contents of the bowl and stir over gentle heat until thickened. Remove from the heat and add almond extract and kirsch.

White Sauce

Yield: 1 cup

1 tablespoon butter
1 cup flour
1 cup milk

Melt the butter in a small saucepan. Remove from the heat and add the flour, stirring with a wire whisk. Add the milk gradually, stirring the mixture constantly until the sauce has thickened. Season with salt and pepper.

Tomato Sauce

Yield: 1 cup

3 medium-size ripe tomatoes, sliced
½ small onion
1 bay leaf
½ cup chicken stock or chicken broth
1 tablespoon butter
1 tablespoon flour
1 cup flavored tomato juices from
     above
1 teaspoon sugar
¼ teaspoon rosemary or ¼ teaspoon
     basil or ¼ teaspoon oregano
½ teaspoon tomato paste, optional

Melt the butter and add the flour. Add the strained tomato juices gradually, stirring the sauce with a wire whisk until thickened. Add the sugar and herbs and simmer the sauce for 5 minutes. Correct the seasoning with salt and pepper.

Note: It may be necessary to add the optional tomato paste in the winter months when the tomatoes have less flavor. This is an excellent sauce for spaghetti as well as other foods.

Veloute Sauce

Yield: 1 cup

1 tablespoon butter
1 tablespoon flour
1 cup chicken stock or chicken broth
1 egg yolk
1 to 2 tablespoons whipping cream

Melt the butter in a small saucepan. Remove from the heat and add the flour, stirring with a wire whisk. Add the chicken stock gradually, stirring constantly over a moderate heat. In order to enrich the sauce and give it a more beautiful color, combine the yolk and the cream.

Add about 3 tablespoons of the hot sauce into the combined egg yolk and cream and stir together. Return it to the remaining hot sauce. Do not let the sauce boil after the egg yolk and cream have been added.

Appetizers

Appetizer wedges

Yield: 8 servings

1 8-ounce package cream cheese,
     softened
2 teaspoons milk
1 tablespoon grated onion
½ teaspoon garlic salt
¼ teaspoon black pepper
½ cup sour cream
⅓ cup bacon bits or 6 strips bacon,
     fried and crumbled
¼ cup finely chopped green pepper
12 cooked crepes
½ cup chopped pecans

In a small mixing bowl mix cream cheese with milk, onion, garlic salt, pepper, and sour cream until smooth. Stir in bacon and green pepper. Spread 2 tablespoons cheese mixture over each crepe. Make 2 stacks, each 6 crepes high. Sprinkle tops with chopped pecans. Refrigerate until firm—1 hour or more. Cut into wedges for serving.

Crepes with Fillings

Yield: 6 servings

1-pound package bacon strips, cut in half
1 pound fresh mushrooms
1 small green pepper
1 small red pepper
12 warm crepes

Fry bacon until crisp. Drain on paper towels. Wash mushrooms and fry until browned. Clean peppers and cut into strips. Serve with crepes and let guests fill their own.

Cheesy Dipping Chips

Yield: 10 servings (72 to 96 dippers)

6 cooked crepes
Melted butter
Grated Parmesan cheese

Brush crepes with butter; sprinkle with grated cheese. Bake at 325°F for 6 to 9 minutes or until crispy. (Use Italian seasoning or garlic salt for variations.)

Cheese-Olive Snack

Yield: 12 servings (80 to 95 appetizers)

2 cups grated sharp cheddar cheese
15 stuffed green olives, chopped
2 tablespoons finely chopped green onions
1 cup mayonnaise
16 crepes
Bacon bits or bacon, cooked and crumbled

Combine cheese with olives, onions, and mayonnaise. Spread on crepes. Broil until cheese bubbles. Sprinkle with bacon bits and cut each crepe into 5 or 6 wedges. Serve immediately.

Cheese and Beef Rolls

Yield: 8 to 10 servings (60 appetizers)

½ pound sharp cheddar cheese
1 small onion, chopped
1 2½-ounce package dried beef, finely chopped
1 teaspoon dry mustard
½ teaspoon Worcestershire sauce
2 teaspoons mayonnaise
16 crepes
Melted butter

Put cheese and onion through a food grinder or blender (a little at a time). Stir in dried beef, mustard, Worcestershire sauce and mayonnaise. Form into several rolls about ½ inch in diameter and 12 to 14 inches long. Cut each roll into pieces about 4 to 5 inches long. Place one cheese log in center of each cooked crepe. Roll up and refrigerate until just before serving. Place on broiler pan; brush with melted butter. Broil until cheese bubbles. Cut each crepe into 4 or 5 crosswise pieces. Serve warm.

Dried Beef Appetizers

Yield: 8 to 10 servings

1 8-ounce package cream cheese,
  softened
¼ cup grated Parmesan cheese
1 tablespoon prepared horseradish
⅓ cup stuffed green olives
2 to 3 ounces dried beef, finely
  chopped
8 crepes
Stuffed olives for garnish

Combine cheeses, horseradish, olives, and dried beef. Spread on crepes and roll up. Chill until ready to serve. Cut each crepe into 3 or 4 pieces. Place on a toothpick with a stuffed olive and serve.

Bouillon with Crepes

Yield: 6 servings

4 cups beef bouillon or clarified stock
Slivered raw beef or leftover rare roast
  beef (about ¼ pound)
4 crepes
1 tablespoon chopped parsley

Bring the bouillon to a boil. Add slivered beef and simmer for 1 to 2 minutes. Add the crepes. Cut in strips. Add parsley and serve at once.

Chicken Consommé with Crepes

Yield: 4 servings

4 cups clarified chicken broth or
  bouillon
1 cup chopped raw chicken (or ¼
  pound)

6 crepes
Watercress for garnish, chopped

Heat broth or bouillon. Cut chicken into very thin slivers and simmer for 2 or 3 minutes in the liquid. Cut crepes into long thin strips. Add crepes to broth and heat through. Float watercress on top.

Crepes with Chicken-Liver Pâté

Yield: 6 servings

2 tablespoons butter
½ pound chicken livers
2 eggs, hard-cooked
2 packages (3-ounce size) soft cream
  cheese
1 tablespoon finely chopped parsley
1 teaspoon salt
⅛ teaspoon pepper
1 tablespoon cognac
12 crepes
1 tablespoon melted butter

Heat butter in frying pan. Add chicken livers and cook, stirring occasionally, over medium heat for 10 minutes or until tender. Drain.

Chop livers and eggs in a food grinder or blender (add a little at a time). With spoon, work cream cheese until light and fluffy. Mix cheese into liver mixture along with all remaining ingredients except melted butter.

Put 2 spoonfuls along the center of each crepe; roll and turn seam side down in a buttered baking dish. Brush with melted butter and bake at 375°F for 15 to 20 minutes. These may be served hot as a first course or sliced and served cold as an hors d'oeuvre.

Crepes with Bacon Quiche

Yield: 18 servings

8 ounces cream cheese
½ cup heavy cream
1 egg
1 egg yolk
⅛ teaspoon black pepper
2 tablespoons chopped chives
4 tablespoons Swiss cheese, grated
4 strips bacon, cooked and crumbled
18 small crepes—about 5 inches

Soften cream cheese at room temperature for 1 hour before starting. Gradually blend in the heavy cream, whole egg, and egg yolk until the mixture is smooth and thick. Add black pepper, chives and grated cheese and mix well.

Bake in 3 muffin tins. Place a crepe over one opening, add a few bits of bacon and a spoonful of cheese mixture in the center. Gently push crepe into muffin cup. Repeat until all crepes are filled. The crepes will act as pastry shells. Bake for 30 minutes in a 375°F oven.

Deviled-Ham Crepes

Yield: 8 servings

2 4½-ounces cans deviled ham
10 chopped stuffed green olives
1 tablespoon prepared mustard
1 3-ounce package cream cheese, softened
2 teaspoons milk
8 crepes

Combine ham, olives, and mustard. Add cream cheese and milk and mix well. Spread on crepes. Place in hot oven (425°F) for 3 minutes or until bubbly. Cut into wedges and serve.

Crepes with Caviar

Yield: 4 to 6 servings

8 to 10 warm crepes
½ cup red caviar
½ cup black caviar
8 to 10 lemon wedges

Have the above foods available and allow guests to make their own delicious crepes. These crepes would be perfect for an informal yet elegant cocktail party.

Tuna Pâté Crepes

Yield: 12 servings

1 8-ounce package cream cheese, softened
2 tablespoons chili sauce
2 tablespoons minced parsley
1 chopped green onion
½ teaspoon bottled hot pepper sauce
2 7-ounce cans tuna, drained
12 crepes

Blend cream cheese, chili sauce, parsley, onion, and hot sauce. Add tuna and mix well. Spread on crepes and roll up. Chill until ready to use. Cut each crepe into 3 or 4 pieces. Place a toothpick in each piece and serve.

Curried Crab Appetizers

Yield: 6 to 8 servings

1 can crab meat, drained
¼ teaspoon salt
½ teaspoon curry powder
3 tablespoons mayonnaise
1 teaspoon lemon juice
1 teaspoon instant minced onion
6 crepes
Paprika

Shred crab meat and add salt, curry powder, mayonnaise, lemon juice, and onion. Spread on crepes in a thin layer. Roll up and chill. When ready to use, cut each crepe into 3 or 4 pieces. Sprinkle with paprika and serve.

Deviled-Crab Crepes

Yield: 6 to 8 servings

2 tablespoons butter
2 tablespoons onion, minced
2 tablespoons green pepper, minced
1 tablespoon celery, minced
2 teaspoons cornstarch
½ cup heavy cream
2 egg yolks
1 teaspoon prepared mustard
½ teaspoon paprika
Salt and pepper to taste
Cayenne if desired
½ pound crab meat, shredded (canned or fresh)
8 warm crepes

Melt butter and sauté the onions, green pepper, and celery until soft—about 5 minutes. Stir the cornstarch into the cream, add egg yolks and beat well. Add mustard, paprika, salt and pepper and cayenne if desired. Add the crab meat to the vegetables and cook for 1 to 2 minutes over high heat. Reduce heat and add cream-egg yolk mixture, stirring thoroughly. Spread over half the crepes and top with remaining crepes. Place on a greased cookie sheet and bake at 400°F for about 20 minutes. Cut into wedges and serve with cocktails.

Smoked Oyster Crepes

Yield: 4 servings

1 3-ounce package cream cheese, softened
2 tablespoons mayonnaise
1 tablespoon finely chopped green onions
1 teaspoon finely chopped pimiento
1 3½-ounce can smoked oysters, drained and chopped
8 cooked crepes

Combine cream cheese with mayonnaise, green onions, pimiento, and oysters. Spread on crepes and roll up. Broil until bubbly and serve hot for first course.

Crabby Crepes

Yield: 8 to 10 servings (64 wedges)

1 teaspoon chopped chives
⅛ teaspoon tarragon
2 teaspoons chopped parsley
⅛ teaspoon chervil
6 ounces crab meat
1 cup mayonnaise
8 crepes

Combine herbs and crab meat with mayonnaise. Refrigerate for 1 hour to blend flavors. Spread on crepes. Cut each crepe into 8 wedges. Roll up like a crescent roll and serve on toothpicks.

Vegetable Crepes

Asparagus and Egg Crepes

Yield: 8 servings

2 pounds fresh asparagus
4 eggs, hard-cooked and sliced
8 crepes
½ teaspoon salt
⅛ teaspoon pepper

Hollandaise Sauce

3 egg yolks
¼ teaspoon salt
½ teaspoon dry mustard
1 tablespoon lemon juice
½ cup butter

Cook asparagus in salted water until tender. Drain. Arrange eggs and asparagus on crepes. Season with salt and pepper. Fold crepes and place in a shallow baking dish. Cover with a foil top. Heat at 350°F for 10 minutes or until warm.

To make sauce, place yolks, salt, mustard and lemon juice in blender. Cover and blend until eggs are well-mixed. Heat butter until bubbling hot and immediately pour butter in a tiny stream through small opening in top of blender, keeping blender on low until mixture is thickened. Spoon sauce over warm crepes. Serve immediately.

Green Crepes

Yield: 4 servings

Basic crepe batter
½ package frozen chopped spinach
½ teaspoon chervil, crumbled
2 tablespoons chopped chives

Thaw the spinach. Add spinach, chervil, and chives to batter. Mix thin crepes. Serve with a cup of hot bouillon, seasoned if desired with chives.

Cauliflower Crepes with Mornay Sauce

Yield: 8 servings

1 small head cauliflower
3 tablespoons butter
3 tablespoons flour
½ cup light cream
½ cup milk
½ teaspoon salt
8 crepes
½ cup dry bread crumbs
1 tablespoon melted butter
¼ cup grated Parmesan cheese

Break cauliflower in small pieces and cook in salted water until soft. Drain. Melt butter; stir in flour and add cream, milk and salt. Cook over low heat until thickened, stirring continuously. Add cauliflower. Fill crepes; fold over and place in greased baking dish. Mix bread crumbs with butter and cheese. Sprinkle on tops of crepes. Bake at 350°F for 15 minutes or until lightly browned.

Egg and Zucchini Crepes

Yield: 4 to 6 servings

1 cup dry bread crumbs
½ cup butter
⅓ cup minced onion
1 large zucchini, cut into julienne strips
3 eggs, lightly beaten
½ teaspoon salt
⅛ teaspoon pepper
3 tablespoons minced parsley
12 crepes
⅓ cup grated Parmesan cheese
⅓ cup grated Gruyère cheese

Sauté bread crumbs in half the butter, tossing them until lightly toasted. Remove from pan and reserve. Add rest of butter to pan and sauté onion and zucchini until the vegetables are tender. Add the eggs, salt and pepper and with a fork very lightly scramble the mixture over low heat. Add the egg mixture to the bread crumbs. Stir in parsley and divide the mixture between the crepes. Roll up and arrange seam side down in a buttered shallow baking dish. Sprinkle crepes with cheeses and bake at 375°F for 10 minutes or until hot and cheese is golden.

Green Beans in Cheese Crepes

Yield: 6 servings

1 tablespoon butter
1 tablespoon flour
¼ teaspoon salt
1 teaspoon minced onion
⅛ teaspoon pepper
½ teaspoon grated lemon peel
¼ cup water
½ cup dairy sour cream
1 10-ounce package frozen French-style green beans, cooked and drained
6 crepes
¼ cup grated cheddar cheese
1 tablespoon melted butter
¼ cup dry bread crumbs

In saucepan, melt 1 tablespoon butter and stir in flour, salt, onion, pepper, and lemon peel. Add water and cook over medium heat until thick and bubbly. Stir in sour cream and green beans. Divide mixture between crepes; fold over. Mix cheese with melted butter and bread crumbs. Sprinkle over filled crepes. Broil until cheese melts.

Ratatouille Crepes

Yield: 4 servings

2 tablespoons olive oil
1 onion, finely chopped
1 clove garlic, crushed
1 green pepper, chopped
1 zucchini or 1 cucumber, diced
3 slices of eggplant or 1 very small
   eggplant, diced
2 medium tomatoes, peeled, seeded,
   and chopped
¼ teaspoon basil
¼ teaspoon oregano
2 tablespoons tomato purée
1 teaspoon cornstarch
1 tablespoon water
Salt and pepper
8 crepes
Chopped parsley
Tomato wedges
Pitted black olives
Grated Parmesan

Heat the oil and add the onion and garlic. Cook until soft and translucent. Add the green pepper, zucchini or cucumber, and eggplant. Cover and simmer over a gentle heat for 15 minutes. Add the tomatoes and the herbs and continue cooking uncovered for another 10 minutes.

Drain the vegetables and put into another bowl. To the pan juices, add tomato purée and 1 teaspoon cornstarch dissolved in 1 tablespoon water. Cook until thick. Adjust the seasoning, adding salt and pepper.

Place 2 tablespoons of the ratatouille in each crepe. Roll the crepes and place in a buttered oven-proof dish. Bake for 10 minutes in an oven preheated to 400°. Pour the sauce over the crepes. Garnish the dish with chopped parsley, tomato wedges and pitted black olives.

Ratatouille is an excellent vegetable dish on its own. Sprinkle with a little grated Parmesan and run under the broiler before serving.

Crepes Madrilene

Yield: 6 servings

1 onion, sliced
1 tablespoon vegetable oil
4 tomatoes, peeled and cut in wedges
1 teaspoon dried thyme
1 green pepper, sliced in strips
1 red pepper, sliced in strips
Several pitted black olives
Several pitted green olives
1 clove garlic, crushed
½ teaspoon salt
¼ teaspoon pepper
6 crepes

Heat oil and sauté the onion until soft. Add tomatoes, thyme, peppers, olives, garlic, salt and pepper. Simmer for a few minutes to soften tomatoes and peppers. Spoon over crepes, and garnish.

Crepes with Fresh Mushrooms

Yield: 4 servings

½ pound fresh mushrooms
2 tablespoons butter
½ teaspoon salt
1 bouillon cube, crumbled
2 tablespoons sherry
¼ cup dairy sour cream
1 tablespoon minced chives
8 crepes
1 recipe tomato sauce

Slice mushrooms. Sauté in hot butter for several minutes. Add salt, bouillon cube and sherry. Cook until simmering. Stir in sour cream and chives. Heat until warm through. Spoon mixture onto center of crepes; fold and serve with tomato sauce spooned over the top.

Creamed-Mushroom Crepes

Yield: 4 servings

2 tablespoons butter
2 tablespoons chopped green onions
1 pound fresh mushrooms, sliced
1 cup heavy cream
½ teaspoon salt
⅛ teaspoon pepper
2 tablespoons flour
2 tablespoons water
½ cup grated Gruyère cheese
8 crepes
Chopped parsley

Cook onions and mushrooms in hot butter until mushrooms are done. Add cream, salt, and pepper. Remove mushrooms with slotted spoon and reserve. Dissolve flour in water; stir into creamy mixture in pan. Simmer until thickened, stirring often. Add cheese and heat through. Fill crepes with mushrooms, roll up and place in greased baking pan. Spoon creamy sauce over crepes. Heat at 350°F for 10 to 15 minutes. Garnish with parsley.

Main-Dish Crepes

Cheese, Bacon and Onion Crepes

Yield: 6 servings

1 pound thinly sliced bacon
10 green onions, with tops, chopped
2 tablespoons butter
2 cups grated American cheese
12 crepes

Fry bacon until crisp. Drain and crumble. Pour off bacon fat from fry pan. Add butter, and heat. Stir in onions and cook for 3 minutes, until soft.

In each crepe, place a small amount of onions, and spoonfuls of bacon and cheese. Reserve enough cheese to sprinkle tops. Roll up each crepe and place in a buttered baking dish. Sprinkle tops with cheese. Bake at 400°F for 15 minutes.

Crepes with Cottage Cheese

Yield: 4 to 6 servings

8 ounces cottage cheese
Batter for 12 crepes

Mix ½ cup cottage cheese into batter before frying crepes. As crepes are cooked, lay in a lightly greased oven-proof dish and sprinkle each layer with cottage cheese. Bake at 325°F for 10 minutes. Serve the warm crepes with a tossed salad.

Crepes with Welsh Rarebit Sauce

Yield: 4 servings

1 tablespoon cornstarch
2 cups grated sharp cheddar cheese
¾ cup milk
1 teaspoon dry mustard
1 egg, well-beaten
8 crepes
¼ cup bacon bits or 8 strips bacon, cooked and crumbled
1 tomato, chopped

In mixing bowl combine cornstarch and cheese. Add milk and mustard. Heat until cheese melts. Stir often. Add a small amount of hot mixture to egg; return to hot mixture. Cook and stir over low heat until mixture thickens and is creamy. In shallow baking pan, fill crepes with bacon bits and half of the rarebit sauce; fold crepes over. Pour remaining sauce over all and top with tomatoes. Broil until sauce is bubbly.

Beef Burgundy Crepes

Yield: 4 to 6 servings

1 pound round or sirloin steak
2 strips bacon
2 tablespoons butter
8 small white onions, peeled
1 cup red wine
1 cup beef bouillon
½ teaspoon thyme
½ teaspoon salt
⅛ teaspoon pepper
½ pound mushrooms, quartered
2 tablespoons cornstarch
3 tablespoons cold water
12 crepes

Cut the steak into bite-size pieces. Dice the bacon and fry in hot butter. When crisp, remove and set aside. Add onions and brown outsides. Set aside. Add meat and brown. Drain fat. Add wine, bouillon, bacon, onions, thyme and salt and pepper. Cover and simmer for 2 hours. Add the mushrooms. In a small bowl, add cornstarch to 3 tablespoons cold water. Mix well and stir into meat mixture. Cook until mixture thickens.

Put a spoonful or two in the center of each crepe. Roll and place seam side down in a baking dish. Spread remaining sauce over tops of crepes or brush with melted butter. Bake at 375°F for 20 minutes.

Beef and Blue Cheese Crepes

Yield: 6 servings

1 pound ground beef (ground chuck or
  ground round)
½ cup chopped onions
2 tablespoons vegetable oil
½ cup finely chopped olives
½ cup blue cheese (or Roquefort)
1 cup dairy sour cream
1 egg, beaten
Salt and pepper to taste
12 crepes
2 tablespoons melted butter

Brown beef and onions in hot oil. Drain. Add olives. Crumble cheese and mix with sour cream and egg. Mix into beef mixture and cook over low heat for 5 minutes, stirring occasionally. Season to taste. Cool. Place 2 spoonfuls of the beef mixture along the center of each crepe; roll. Place in greased baking dish with seam side down. Brush tops of crepes with butter and bake at 375°F for 20 minutes.

Beef Stroganoff Crepes

Yield: 4 to 6 servings

1 pound boneless sirloin
1 tablespoon flour
½ teaspoon salt
2 tablespoons butter
¼ pound mushrooms, chopped
1 small onion, chopped
½ cup beef bouillon
1 cup dairy sour cream
1 tablespoon tomato paste or catsup
Sour cream for topping, optional
12 crepes

Cut sirloin into ¼-inch strips. Combine flour and salt and coat meat. Heat butter and brown meat on both sides. Add mushrooms and onion and cook 3 or 4 minutes, until onion is tender. Add bouillon and cook for 3 minutes longer. Mix the tomato paste into the sour cream and stir into the meat mixture on low heat. Season to taste.

Divide mixture between crepes. Roll and turn seam side down in a greased baking dish. Top with more sour cream if desired and bake at 375° for 20 minutes.

Crepes with Hamburger Stroganoff

Yield: 6 servings

1 small onion, chopped
1 tablespoon vegetable oil
1 pound lean ground beef
1 can cream of mushroom soup,
  undiluted
½ teaspoon salt
2 tablespoons catsup
1 4-ounce can mushrooms, drained
½ cup sour cream
12 crepes
2 tablespoons melted butter

Sauté onion in oil, add ground beef, and cook until browned. Pour off fat. Mix in soup, salt, catsup and mushrooms. Heat to boiling. Remove from heat and stir in sour cream. Fill crepes with mixture and fold over. Place in shallow baking pan. Brush with butter. Heat in 350° oven for 15 minutes.

Crepes with Swedish Meatballs

Yield: 6 servings

1 pound lean ground beef
1 cup soft bread crumbs
½ cup chopped onion
1 egg, slightly beaten
2 tablespoons chopped parsley
⅛ teaspoon ginger
⅛ teaspoon nutmeg
⅛ teaspoon pepper
1 tablespoon vegetable oil
2 tablespoons flour
1 bouillon cube, crumbled
½ cup milk
1 cup dairy sour cream
½ teaspoon salt
12 warm crepes

Combine beef with bread crumbs, onion, egg, parsley, ginger, nutmeg, and pepper. Form meatballs. Heat oil and add meatballs. Cook over moderate heat, turning several times, until done. Remove meatballs and keep warm. Stir flour and bouillon cube into meat juices. Add milk and stir over low heat until thickened. Mix in sour cream and salt and heat but do not boil. Divide meatballs between crepes and fold over. Spoon sauce over filled crepes and serve.

Beef and Bean Sprout Crepes

Yield: 8 servings

1½ pounds flank steak
1 16-ounce can bean sprouts
¼ cup butter
1 green pepper, cut in 1-inch strips
1 cup beef bouillon
2 tablespoons soy sauce
16 crepes

Slice steak in paper thin strips and then into bite-size pieces. Drain bean sprouts. Brown meat in hot butter. Add the bean sprouts, green pepper, bouillon and soy sauce. Cook together for 2 to 3 minutes, until steak is just done.

Fill crepes with mixture and roll up. Place seam side down in a greased baking dish. Pour extra pan liquid over crepes. Bake at 375°F for 20 minutes.

Beef and Snow Peas Crepes

Yield: 6 servings

1 pound flank steak, sliced as thin as possible
¼ cup soy sauce
2 tablespoons sherry
2 teaspoons cornstarch
2 green onions, thinly sliced
3 tablespoons vegetable oil
1 package frozen snow peas (pea pods), defrosted
½ cup chicken bouillon
12 crepes

Marinate steak in a mixture of soy sauce, sherry, cornstarch, and onions for 30 minutes. Brown the meat quickly in 2 tablespoons of hot vegetable oil over high heat. Stir continuously. Remove from pan. Add rest of vegetable oil. When hot, stir in snow peas and cook until pods are beginning to soften. Return steak to pan and add chicken bouillon. Cook for 2 to 3 minutes.

Fill warm crepes and serve immediately.

Crepes with Veal

Yield: 4 servings

1 pound thin slices of veal, cut into
   1-inch squares
2 tablespoons flour
3 tablespoons vegetable oil
1 clove garlic, minced
2 tablespoons onions, chopped
1 tablespoon parsley
½ teaspoon basil
2 tomatoes, chopped
¼ cup heavy cream
Salt and pepper to taste
12 crepes

Dredge veal with flour. Heat oil and fry the veal until lightly brown. Move meat to side of pan and sauté the minced garlic, onions, and parsley. Add the basil and tomatoes. Cook over medium heat until the tomatoes are soft. Break up with a fork and add cream, salt and pepper and cook over low heat until thoroughly heated. Cool.

Place a spoonful or two of filling in each crepe. Roll up and place seam side down in a greased baking dish. Bake at 350°F for 30 minutes.

Other buffet dishes include: stuffed cabbage leaves, stuffed tomatoes, roast chicken, beet greens, quiche, cannelloni, fillet of veal, pork stuffing, and spinach.

Ham and Asparagus Crepes

Yield: 6 servings

12 thin slices boiled ham
1 pound asparagus
Mornay or Hollandaise sauce
12 crepes
2 tablespoons butter

Peel the lower third of each asparagus spear and simmer, uncovered, in plenty of lightly salted water for about 15 minutes or until tender.

Spread out the crepes and cover each crepe with a slice of ham. Over the ham place 2 or 3 asparagus spears and roll up the crepes. Place the crepes in a buttered ovenproof dish. Dot the surface of the crepes with butter and bake in a preheated 400°F oven for 15 minutes. Cover with Mornay or Hollandaise sauce.

Ham and Beef Crepes

Yield: 4 servings

½ pound ground beef
1 cup chopped leftover ham
¼ cup flour
1 cup beef bouillon
¼ cup mushrooms, sliced
1 tablespoon butter
1 tablespoon flour
1 cup milk
3 tablespoons grated Swiss cheese
1 tablespoon grated Parmesan cheese
½ teaspoon prepared mustard
8 crepes

Cook ground beef over medium heat until slightly brown. Drain fat. Add ham and stir in ¼ cup flour. Add bouillon and sliced mushrooms. Bring to a simmer, stirring often. Cover and simmer for 30 minutes.

Meanwhile melt butter in a small saucepan. Remove from heat and add the flour, stirring with a wire whisk. Over a moderate heat, add the milk gradually, stirring the mixture constantly until the sauce is thickened. Add remaining ingredients, and salt and pepper to taste.

Fill crepes with meat mixture. Roll up and place in an oven-proof dish. Pour sauce over top. Bake at 375°F for 25 minutes or until golden brown.

Mushroom Crepes with Ham

Yield: 4 servings

3 tablespoons butter
3 green onions or ½ onion, finely
    chopped
1½ cups mushrooms, thinly sliced
2 tablespoons lemon juice
½ cup chicken broth
8 thin slices of boiled ham
½ cup grated Swiss or Gruyère cheese
¼ cup heavy cream
Salt and pepper
1 tablespoon cornstarch dissolved in 2
    tablespoons cold water
8 crepes
2 tablespoons butter

Sauté the onion in the butter until soft. Add the mushrooms. Spinkle the mushrooms with lemon juice to prevent discoloration. Cook the mushrooms for 1 minute. Add the chicken broth and cook over a high heat, uncovered, for 1 more minute. Lower the heat and add the grated cheese and cream. Do not heat the cheese too quickly or it will spin into threads. Add the cornstarch dissolved in water and the mixture will thicken immediately. It should be thick enough to hold its shape in the rolled crepe. Adjust the seasoning, adding salt and pepper to taste.

Lay a piece of boiled ham on each crepe. Put about 3 tablespoons of the mushroom mixture over the ham and roll the crepes. Place in a buttered oven-proof dish and dot the crepes with butter. Bake in a preheated 400°F oven for 15 minutes and serve immediately.

Spinach and Ham Crepes

Yield: 4 servings

1 pound spinach
1 cup boiled ham, finely chopped
3 tablespoons heavy cream
Pinch of salt
Pinch of nutmeg
(1 tablespoon cornstarch)
(2 tablespoons cold water)
2 tablespoons butter
8 crepes
Pieces of ham or bacon for garnish

Discard the stems and heavy veins of the spinach and wash it to remove grains of sand. Cook spinach about 5 minutes in plenty of boiling water. Drain the spinach.

Chop the ham finely and place half of it in the blender. Add the spinach, cream, salt and nutmeg. Turn on the motor. You may need to add a little more cream if the blades of the blender become jammed. Return the mixture to a clean saucepan and add the remainder of the chopped ham. Stir over a low heat. If the purée appears too thin, add 1 tablespoon cornstarch dissolved in 2 tablespoons cold water and it will thicken immediately. Spread the ham and spinach purée on a crepe. Fold the crepe into a triangle and place in a buttered oven-proof dish. Dot the crepes with butter. Heat for 15 minutes in a preheated 400°F oven. Garnish with pieces of ham or bacon. May be served with a Mornay or Hollandaise sauce.

21

Hot Dogs in Crepes

Yield: 5 to 6 servings

6 long hot dogs
Sauerkraut
Swiss cheese, grated

Cook the hot dogs and sauerkraut together and roll each hot dog with some sauerkraut into a crepe. Top the rolled crepes with the grated Swiss cheese and place in an oven-proof dish. Heat at 425°F until the cheese browns. Serve hot.

Curried-Lamb Crepes

Yield: 6 servings

1½ pounds boneless lamb, cut into
    bite-size pieces
2 tablespoons butter
½ cup sliced onions
1 clove garlic, peeled
1½ cups milk
1 slice fresh ginger or ½ teaspoon
    ground ginger
2 teaspoons curry powder
½ teaspoon salt
½ teaspoon pepper
2 tablespoons lemon juice
Grated rind of 1 lemon
½ cup heavy cream
3 teaspoons cornstarch
1 tablespoon melted butter
2 ounces slivered almonds
12 crepes

Brown lamb in butter and onions and whole clove of garlic. Sauté over low heat for 15 to 20 minutes. Remove garlic and add milk, ginger, curry powder, salt, pepper, lemon juice and grated lemon rind. Cook for 15 minutes. Mix cream with cornstarch. Add to curry mixture and stir until thickened.

Divide curry mixture between crepes; roll and place in a greased baking dish. Brush with melted butter and sprinkle with almonds. Bake at 400°F for 12 minutes.

Chicken-Filled Crepes

Yield: 4 servings

White Sauce
3 tablespoons butter
¼ cup flour
¼ teaspoon salt
1 cup milk

Filling
1 tablespoon sherry or 1 teaspoon
    lemon juice
1½ cups finely diced cooked chicken
¼ cup finely chopped almonds
1 tablespoon finely minced onion
⅓ cup mayonnaise
1 egg white stiffly beaten
2 tablespoons grated Parmesan cheese
8 crepes

Prepare white sauce by melting butter and blending in flour and salt. Add milk all at once. Cook quickly, stirring constantly, until the mixture thickens and bubbles.

Combine white sauce, sherry, chicken, almonds and onion. Divide the mixture between the crepes, spreading it on each one. Roll up and place 2 rolls in individual serving dishes. Fold mayonnaise into the egg white and spread over crepes. Sprinkle with cheese. Bake at 375°F for 10 minutes.

Chicken Crepe Soufflé

Yield: 6 servings

5 cups chicken, minced
1 pound mushrooms, chopped
1 lemon, juiced
2 egg yolks
½ cup cream

Bechamel Sauce

2 tablespoons butter
¼ cup flour
2 cups cold milk
½ teaspoon salt
⅛ teaspoon white pepper

To make sauce, melt butter and blend in flour. Cook for 3 minutes, stirring constantly. Add the milk, salt and pepper and cook until thickened. Add the chicken, mushrooms, lemon juice, egg yolks and cream to the sauce. Mix well.

Butter a round soufflé mold or an oven-proof bowl and place crepes on the bottom and sides. Fill with chicken mixture and place crepes on top. Bake in a moderate oven (350°F) for 30 minutes. Unmold on a warm platter and serve with extra Bechamel Sauce. It is delicious and unusual.

Quick Chicken Divan Crepes

Yield: 6 servings

1 10-ounce package frozen chopped broccoli
1 can cream of chicken soup (undiluted)
½ teaspoon Worcestershire sauce
¾ cup grated Parmesan cheese

2 cups cooked chicken, cut into small strips
12 crepes
⅓ cup mayonnaise
1 tablespoon milk

Cook broccoli according to package directions; drain. Combine with soup, Worcestershire sauce, ½ cup of the cheese, and chicken. Divide mixture between crepes, roll up, and place in a shallow baking dish. Combine mayonnaise with milk; spread over crepes. Sprinkle with ¼ cup cheese and broil until cheese bubbles.

Chicken in White Wine Crepes

Yield: 6 servings

3 tablespoons butter
3 tablespoons minced green onions
3 cups chicken, diced
1 cup cooked ham, diced
½ teaspoon salt
⅛ teaspoon pepper
½ teaspoon tarragon
½ cup dry white wine
½ cup canned mushrooms
1 hard-cooked egg, diced
A double recipe Veloute sauce
12 crepes
2 tablespoons melted butter

Sauté onions in hot butter for 1 minute. Stir in chicken, ham, salt, pepper and tarragon. Stir mixture on high heat for 2 minutes. Pour in wine and boil down until the liquid has almost disappeared. Mix in mushrooms and egg. Fold in Veloute sauce. Divide mixture between crepes and roll up. Place in a greased baking dish and brush tops with melted butter. Heat at 350°F for 10 minutes.

Crepes with Cashew-Chicken Filling

Yield: 6 servings

3 tablespoons butter
½ cup cashew nuts, coarsely chopped
2 cups uncooked chicken, chopped
1 cup thinly sliced broccoli
1 onion, sliced
1½ cups chicken bouillon
2 tablespoons cornstarch
2 tablespoons soy sauce
12 warm crepes

Heat butter and cook cashews until lightly toasted. Remove nuts from pan. In remaining butter, stir in chicken and broccoli; cook about 5 minutes, turning mixture often. Add onions and bouillon. Cover and cook for 6 to 8 minutes. Dissolve cornstarch in soy sauce; stir into chicken mixture. Stir over medium heat until thickened. Add cashews. Fill crepes and serve immediately.

Crepes with Hot Chicken Salad

Yield: 6 servings

2 cups diced cooked chicken
2 cups celery, chopped
3 tablespoons onion, minced
½ teaspoon salt
½ teaspoon pepper
½ cup pecans, chopped
¾ cup mayonnaise
1 small can sliced mushrooms, drained
1 can cream of chicken soup
12 warm crepes

Mix all filling ingredients. Divide between crepes and roll up. Place in large greased oven-proof baking dish or in 6 individual baking dishes. Cook at 300° for 30 minutes.

Hawaiian Crepes

Yield: 6 servings

2 tablespoons butter
1 medium onion, sliced
1 green pepper, cut into small strips
1 8-ounce can pineapple chunks with syrup
1 tablespoon honey
1 tablespoon vinegar
1 tablespoon soy sauce
2 tablespoons cornstarch
1 cup chicken bouillon
2 cups cooked chicken, cut in small pieces
¼ cup cashews, chopped
12 crepes

Melt butter and cook onion and green pepper until soft. Add pineapple, honey, vinegar and soy sauce. Dissolve cornstarch in bouillon and add to pineapple mixture. Cook, stirring, until thickened. Stir in chicken and cashews. Heat. Fill warm crepes and fold. Serve immediately.

Chicken and Oyster Crepes

Yield: 6 servings

1 pint oysters
1 cup milk
1 teaspoon butter
¼ teaspoon oregano
2 cups cooked chicken cut into small pieces

½ cup cooked diced potatoes
1 tablespoon butter
1 tablespoon flour
Salt
Dash of cayenne pepper
1 egg yolk
1 teaspoon heavy cream
Finely chopped parsley for garnish
12 crepes

Put the oysters with their liquor into a small saucepan with ½ cup milk and 1 teaspoon butter.

Add ¼ teaspoon oregano. After the milk has reached simmering point, continue to cook at a gentle simmer for 6 minutes.

Drain the oysters and put in a bowl with the shredded chicken and diced potatoes.

Melt 1 tablespoon butter and when foaming remove from the heat and add 1 tablespoon flour. Gradually add the liquor in which the oysters were cooked. Continue to cook over a gentle heat until the sauce has thickened. Check the seasoning and add salt and a dash of cayenne pepper to taste.

Enrich the sauce by combining 1 egg yolk with 1 teaspoon cream. Add 2 tablespoons of the hot sauce to the egg yolk and cream and return to the sauce in the saucepan. This will improve the color and the taste of the sauce. Add 3 tablespoons of the thick sauce to the chicken, oysters and potatoes. Put 2 tablespoons of the mixture into each crepe. Roll the crepes and place in a buttered oven-proof dish to cook at 400° for 15 minutes. Pour the remaining sauce over the crepes. Sprinkle some finely chopped parsley over the sauce just before serving.

Chicken-Liver Crepes in Madeira Sauce

Yield: 4 servings

1 tablespoon butter plus 1 tablespoon butter for sauce
4 green onions or 1 small onion finely chopped
2 pounds chicken livers
1 teaspoon paprika
2 tablespoons flour
¼ cup chicken stock or chicken broth
¼ cup heavy cream
2 tablespoons Madeira
8 crepes
Parsley for garnish

Heat the butter until foaming. Add the onion and cook until softened. Wash and cut chicken livers in half. Add the livers to the pan. Cook until lightly browned but still soft and tender. Remover the livers and onion from the pan.

In a clean saucepan melt the remaining 1 tablespoon butter and add paprika and flour. Add the juices from the chicken livers, the stock, cream and finally the Madeira. Cook over a moderate heat until thickened, stirring with a wire whisk.

Add 3 tablespoons of the sauce to the chicken livers and onions. Fill each crepe with 2 tablespoons of the chicken livers. Place in a buttered oven-proof pan and heat in a preheated oven at 400° for 15 minutes. Pour the rest of the sauce over the crepes just before serving. Sprinkle with finely chopped parsley.

Easy Turkey-Spinach Crepes

Yield: 4 servings

1 cup diced cooked turkey (or chicken)
½ cup cooked chopped spinach, drained
¼ cup dry bread crumbs
⅓ cup grated Parmesan cheese
1 tablespoon minced onion
1 can cream of chicken soup (undiluted)
8 crepes
½ cup milk
¼ cup slivered almonds

Mix turkey, spinach, bread crumbs, cheese, onion, and ½ can condensed soup. Fill crepes and roll up. Place in a shallow baking dish. Combine rest of soup with milk and pour over crepes. Sprinkle with almonds. Heat at 350° for 15 minutes.

Flaming Shellfish Crepes

Yield: 4 servings

4 tablespoons butter
3 drops Tabasco sauce
⅛ teaspoon salt
Dash pepper
2 cups milk
2 egg yolks
3 tablespoons sherry
½ pound cooked crab meat
1 pound cooked, deveined shrimp
1 small can mushroom pieces, drained
8 crepes
Brandy

Make white sauce by adding butter, Tabasco sauce, and seasonings to milk. Add beaten egg yolks and cook over low heat un-til thickened. Blend in remaining ingredients except brandy. Place crepes in single-serving baking dishes. Fill cavity with shrimp-crab mixture. Bake at 350° for 5 to 10 minutes. Sprinkle with warmed brandy and ignite. Serve immediately.

Crab Crepes with Tomatoes and Herbs

Yield: 4 servings

12-ounce can or ¾ pound fresh crab meat
2 medium tomatoes, skinned and seeds removed
1 green pepper, diced
3 green onions
Mornay sauce
Juice of 1 lemon
1 tablespoon butter
¼ cup heavy cream
1 tablespoon chives combined with parsley, finely chopped
8 crepes

Clean the crab and set aside. Remove the skin and seeds from the tomatoes. Melt the butter and sauté the green onions and green pepper over a moderate heat for about 4 minutes.

Prepare a Mornay sauce.

In a bowl, combine the crab meat, tomatoes, and green pepper-onion mixture. Add the lemon juice, cream, and herbs. Add about ½ of the prepared sauce. Place 2 tablespoons of the mixture in each crepe. Place the crepes in a buttered oven-proof dish and spoon the remainder of the sauce over the crepes. Heat in a preheated oven at 400° for 15 minutes, until the sauce is golden brown and bubbling. Sprinkle with chives and parsley.

Creamed-Crab in Crepes

Yield: 6 servings

2 tablespoons butter
3 tablespoons minced green onions
1½ cups crab meat, shredded
½ teaspoon salt
⅛ teaspoon pepper
¼ cup dry white wine
2 tablespoons cornstarch
2 tablespoons milk
1½ cups heavy cream
½ cup grated Swiss cheese
12 crepes
¼ cup grated Swiss cheese
2 tablespoons butter

Heat butter and stir in onions and crab meat. Stir over high heat for 1 minute. Season and add white wine. Boil mixture until wine has almost evaporated. Remove mixture and reserve.

Blend cornstarch with milk and add to skillet with cream. Simmer for 2 minutes and blend in cheese. Stir continuously until cheese is melted. Blend half the sauce with crab mixture.

Divide mixture between crepes and roll up. Place in a buttered baking dish and spoon rest of sauce over tops of crepes. Sprinkle with cheese and dot with butter. Bake at 425°F for 6 to 8 minutes or until cheese is lightly browned.

Creamed-Oyster Crepes

Yield: 4 servings

1 pint oysters
2 tablespoons butter
2 tablespoons flour
1 cup oyster liquor (add cream to make
   1 cup)

½ teaspoon salt
½ teaspoon curry powder
1 teaspoon lemon juice
8 warm crepes
Chopped parsley for garnish

Drain oysters and pat dry with paper towels. Save the liquor. Melt butter and blend in flour. Stir in oyster liquor slowly. Add salt and curry powder. Heat to simmer temperature and add oysters. Heat oysters thoroughly but do not boil. Season with lemon juice. Divide between warm crepes and roll up. Add parsley garnish.

Down-East Lobster Crepes

Yield: 4 servings

¼ cup butter
2 tablespoons flour
1½ cups light cream
3 egg yolks, beaten
½ pound cooked lobster, chunked
¼ teaspoon paprika
¼ teaspoon salt
⅛ teaspoon pepper
¼ cup dry white wine
8 crepes
Parsley to garnish

Melt butter and blend in flour. Add cream and cook over low heat, stirring constantly, until thickened. Stir 2 tablespoons hot mixture into egg yolks; then place egg yolks in pan. Cook over low heat, stirring constantly, until thickened. Add lobster, paprika, salt, pepper, and wine. Place crepes in shallow baking pan. Fill crepes with lobster mixture and fold over. Pour remaining sauce over crepes. Heat in 350°F oven for 15 minutes or until hot. Garnish with parsley.

Lobster Crepes (Fruit of the Sea Crepes)

Yield: 4 servings

1 4½-pound lobster or 2 cups of cooked shrimp, flounder, and scallops in any proportion
1 tablespoon tomato paste
Mornay sauce
2 tablespoons butter
8 crepes

Poach the fish in salted water held at simmering point. The lobster will cook in 20 minutes. Other seafoods will cook in 8 to 10 minutes.

Cut the fish into small pieces and place in a bowl with the tomato paste.

Prepare a Mornay sauce.

Combine half of the sauce with the lobster or combination of seafoods.

Place about 2 to 3 tablespoons of the seafood in each crepe. Roll the crepes. Place the crepes in a buttered oven-proof dish. Dot the surface of the crepes with butter and bake in a preheated 400°F oven for 15 minutes. Serve with the remainder of the sauce. Garnish the dish with lobster tails or shrimp, parsley, and lemon wedges.

Salmon Crepes

Yield: 4 servings

2 tablespoons butter
2 tablespoons flour
¼ teaspoon salt
1 cup milk
1 small can pink or red salmon, drained and flaked
8 warm crepes
Salad garnish, optional

Melt butter in saucepan over low heat. Blend in flour and salt. Mix well. Add milk all at once. Cook over moderate heat, stirring constantly, until mixture thickens and bubbles. Add salmon; heat thoroughly. Spoon on crepes; roll up.

Crepes Romaine

Yield: 4 servings

1 tablespoon onion, chopped
1 tablespoon butter
1 tablespoon flour
1 cup light cream
4 ounces smoked salmon, diced
3 hard-cooked eggs, chopped
1 to 2 tablespoons capers
½ teaspoon chopped dill
½ teaspoon fresh lemon juice
2 tablespoons grated cheese
1 tablespoon butter
8 warm crepes

Fry onion in butter until soft. Stir in flour. Add cream a little at a time. Let simmer for 3 to 4 minutes and then add rest of ingredients. Season to taste. Place a heaping tablespoon on each crepe, roll up and place in a buttered oven-proof dish. Sprinkle with grated cheese, dot with butter, and bake in a preheated oven (400°F) for 5 to 8 minutes or until the cheese has melted and crepes are hot throughout.

Smoked Salmon and Cream Cheese Crepes

Yield: 6 servings

8 ounces cream cheese
3 tablespoons cold Bechamel (white) sauce

½ pound smoked salmon
1 tablespoon butter
6 crepes
Parsley sprigs

Soften the cream cheese with the cold white sauce and spread 2 tablespoons of the cheese on each crepe. Lay the smoked salmon over the cheese and fold or roll the crepes. Lay in a buttered oven-proof dish, dot with butter, and reheat in a preheated 400°F oven for 15 minutes. Serve with Bechamel sauce and garnish with smoked salmon rolls and sprigs of parsley.

Shrimp Crepes with Veloute Sauce

Yield: 8 servings

1 pound small shrimp, cooked, peeled
   and deveined
4 egg whites
½ cup heavy cream
½ teaspoon salt
¼ teaspoon pepper
16 crepes
Double recipe Veloute sauce

Chop half the shrimp into 4 or 5 pieces each. Beat egg whites until stiff. Beat cream until stiff. Combine cream and egg whites; add seasonings and chopped shrimp. Divide mixture between crepes. Roll and turn seam side down in a buttered baking dish. Pour sauce over the tops of the crepes. Bake at 350°F for 20 minutes. During last three minutes, add rest of shrimp for garnish and heat only to warm.

Shrimp and Water Chestnut Crepes

Yield: 6 servings

2 scallions, thinly sliced
2 tablespoons butter
1 pound shrimp, cooked and peeled
¼ pound mushrooms, finely chopped
1 can water chestnuts, chopped
3 tablespoons butter
3 tablespoons flour
¼ teaspoon salt
1 cup milk
¼ cup heavy cream
1 lemon, sliced
12 warm crepes

Sauté scallions in butter for 2 minutes. Reserve several shrimp for garnish. Slice the rest of the shrimp into ⅓-inch slices. Add shrimp and mushrooms to scallions and cook 2 minutes. Add water chestnuts and remove from heat while preparing the cream sauce.

Melt butter in saucepan over low heat. Blend in flour and salt. Mix well. Add milk all at once. Cook over moderate heat, stirring constantly, until mixture thickens and bubbles. Add cream a little at a time, blending thoroughly. Stir into shrimp mixture.

Fill crepes and roll. Turn seam side down in a buttered baking dish. Bake 10 to 15 minutes in a 375°F oven. Garnish with reserved shrimp and lemon slices. Can be served with pork chops and orange sauce.

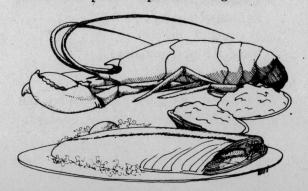

29

Tuna with Herbs Crepes

Yield: 4 servings

1 6½-ounce can tuna, drained
3 hard-cooked eggs, peeled and
    chopped
½ cup mayonnaise
1 teaspoon prepared mustard
¼ teaspoon salt
⅛ teaspoon pepper
1 tablespoon sweet pickle relish
1 tablespoon chopped parsley
½ teaspoon dried tarragon
½ teaspoon dried chervil
8 crepes
2 tablespoons melted butter

Break tuna into small chunks. Combine tuna, eggs, mayonnaise, mustard, salt, pepper, relish, parsley, tarragon, and chervil. Divide mixture between crepes and roll up. Brush tops with butter. Heat at 350°F for 20 minutes or until crepes are hot throughout.

Crispy Tuna-Noodle Crepes

Yield: 4 servings

⅓ cup chopped onion
⅓ cup chopped green pepper
2 tablespoons butter
⅓ cup mayonnaise
1 tablespoon prepared mustard
¼ cup milk
1 7-ounce can tuna
¼ teaspoon salt
¼ teaspoon pepper
1 can Chinese noodles
12 warm crepes

Cook onion and green pepper in hot butter until tender. Mix mayonnaise, mustard, and milk; stir until smooth. Add tuna, salt, pepper, onion and green pepper to mayonnaise mixture. Just before serving, fold in the Chinese noodles; fill warm crepes, and roll. Serve immediately.

Imitation Chinese Egg Rolls

Yield: 6 servings

1 cup chopped cooked pork
1 16-ounce can Chinese vegetables,
    drained
¼ cup minced green onions
½ teaspoon ground ginger
2 teaspoons soy sauce
1 teaspoon sugar
12 warm cooked crepes
Hot oil for deep-fat frying

Mix pork with Chinese vegetables, onions, ginger, soy sauce, and sugar. Place about 2 tablespoons mixture on each crepe, fold over sides, and roll up. Seal edges with leftover crepe batter or a little flour-water mixture. Cook in hot oil at 375° until golden brown. Drain. Serve hot.

Chinese Spring Rolls Fried in Oil

Yield: 4 servings

Batter for 16 crepes
Vegetable oil for deep-fat frying
1 can bean sprouts
6 ounces pork, minced (about ¾ cup)
1 large onion, minced
1 can bamboo shoots, sliced thin
1½ tablespoons soy sauce
1 teaspoon freshly ground black pepper
1 egg white or 2 tablespoons flour and
    ¼ cup water

Rinse bean sprouts in cold water; drain well. Heat 1½ tablespoons vegetable oil in pan and fry pork and onion for about 4 minutes. Add bean sprouts, bamboo shoots, soy sauce and pepper. Fry for 2 minutes while stirring.

Make crepes, frying on one side only. Distribute the filling on the fried side of the crepes. Fold in sides and roll up like small parcels. Seal with egg white or with flour stirred in a small amount of water. Deep fat fry in oil at 400°F until golden brown. Drain on paper towels. Serve immediately with soy sauce and a large green salad.

Baked Chinese Spring Rolls with Cabbage

Yield: 4 to 6 servings

9 ounces white cabbage
2 tablespoons vegetable oil
1 tablespoon soy sauce
1 teaspoon salt
¼ teaspoon pepper
9 ounces pork, minced (about 1 cup)
1 green onion, minced
Batter for 12 to 16 crepes

Slice the cabbage into fine strips and fry in oil until partially soft. Add the soy sauce, salt, and pepper, and cook 2 minutes more. In a separate pan fry the pork with the green onion until done. Mix with cabbage.

Fry crepes on one side only. When done, place filling on browned side of crepes. Wrap up like a parcel. Place crepes in a lightly greased oven-proof dish and brush with soy and oil. Bake in oven at 400°F for about 15 minutes.

Oriental Beef and Pepper Crepes

Yield: 6 servings

1½ pounds sirloin steak, sliced into ⅛-inch slivers
2 green peppers, sliced into rings
3 tablespoons vegetable oil
3 cups thinly sliced onions
¾ teaspoon salt
1 clove garlic, crushed
3 green onions, thinly sliced
1½ teaspoons sugar
⅓ cup sherry
½ teaspoon ginger
¾ beef bouillon
3 tablespoons cornstarch
¾ cup water
2 tablespoons soy sauce
12 crepes

Heat oil in fry pan. Add green pepper rings, onion slices, salt, garlic, and green onions. Cook, stirring over high heat, for 3 minutes. Add beef slivers and cook, stirring over high heat, for 2 minutes. Stir in sugar, sherry, and ginger. Cook for 1 minute. Add bouillon and bring mixture to a boil.

In a small bowl, combine cornstarch, water and soy sauce. Stir into beef mixture and cook until sauce is thickened.

Divide mixture between warm crepes, roll up and serve. Pour any remaining juices over tops.

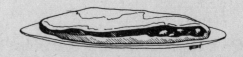

Italian Meat Crepes

Yield: 6 servings

1 pound ground beef
6 ounces Italian sausage
¾ teaspoon Italian seasoning
4 ounces shredded mozzarella
3 cups spaghetti sauce
12 to 14 crepes
Parmesan cheese for topping

Brown meat and sausage. Add seasoning, cheese, and 1 cup spaghetti sauce. Fill crepe with 2 to 3 tablespoons of meat mixture. Roll up, and place seam side down in shallow baking dish with a thin layer of sauce. Pour and cover crepes with sauce and sprinkle with Parmesan cheese. Bake in moderate oven until bubbly—about 25 minutes.

Cannelloni Crepes

Yield: 4 servings

1 medium onion, finely chopped
2 tablespoons vegetable oil
¾ pound ground beef
2 tablespoons tomato sauce
½ cup flour
1 beef bouillon cube dissolved in 1 cup
    boiling water
⅓ cup mushrooms, sliced
½ teaspoon salt
⅛ teaspoon pepper
2 tablespoons butter
1¼ cups milk
⅓ cup cheddar or Parmesan cheese,
    grated
8 warm crepes
Watercress

Fry onions in hot vegetable oil for 5 minutes. Add meat and cook for 5 minutes.

Remove from heat and stir in tomato sauce and ¼ cup flour. Add bouillon, sliced mushrooms, and seasonings. Cover and simmer for 45 minutes. Meanwhile, melt butter in a separate small pan. Stir in ¼ cup flour and cook for 2 minutes. Remove from heat and gradually stir in 1¼ cups milk. Bring to a boil while stirring. Blend in ¼ cup cheese. Remove from heat; leave cover on.

Fill warm crepes with ground beef mixture and roll up. Place them in a baking dish and pour the sauce over them. Sprinkle with remaining cheese and broil for about 3 minutes or until golden. Serve at once. Garnish with watercress.

Manicotti Crepes

Yield: 6 to 8 servings

3 eggs
½ teaspoon salt
2 pounds ricotta cheese
¾ cup Parmesan or Romano cheese
¼ teaspoon pepper
½ pound Mozzarella, cut into 12 strips
12 to 14 crepes
3 cans (8 ounces each) tomato sauce

Mix eggs, salt, ricotta, ¼ cup Parmesan, and pepper. Place about 2 tablespoons of filling and a strip of Mozarella on each crepe and roll up.

Pour 1 can tomato sauce into a large baking dish. Place crepes, seam side down in sauce and sprinkle with ½ cup Parmesan cheese. Cover crepes with remaining 2 cans of sauce. Bake in preheated 350°F oven for 45 minutes.

Crepes with Spaghetti Sauce

Yield: 4 to 5 servings

Prepare 2 cups of a favorite recipe of spaghetti sauce. Add meat, sausage, or mushrooms. If sauce is runny, add enough tomato paste to thicken. Fill 8 to 10 crepes, roll and place in baking dish. Spread extra sauce over the tops of crepes and sprinkle with grated Parmesan cheese. Bake at 400°F for 15 minutes.

Pizza Crepes

Yield: 6 servings

6 crepes
1 tablespoon vegetable oil
½ cup tomato sauce
½ teaspoon oregano
¼ teaspoon basil
¼ cup pepperoni, cut into thin slices
¼ cup sliced mushrooms
¾ cup grated Mozzarella cheese
¼ cup grated Parmesan cheese

Brush crepes with oil and spread with tomato sauce. Sprinkle with herbs and top with pepperoni, mushrooms and cheese. Broil open-face until bubbly.

Desserts

Crepes Suzettes

Yield: 6 servings

6 cubes of sugar
2 oranges
1 lemon
1 stick soft sweet butter
¼ cup Grand Marnier, Curacao,
    Benedictine, Cointreau or Triple Sec
12 dessert crepes
¼ cup brandy

Rub 6 cubes of sugar over the rind of the oranges and lemon and combine it on a plate with 1 stick of soft sweet butter.

Place the flavored butter in the chafing dish and add the juice of 1 orange and 1 lemon and ¼ cup of one of the above liqueurs.

When the contents of the pan are hot and bubbling, add the crepes one at a time. Coat each crepe with the sauce, fold it into a triangle, and push it to the side of the dish. When all the crepes are coated with sauce, arrange them over the surface of the dish and allow them to heat through. Flame the crepes with ¼ cup brandy and serve immediately.

Easy Crepes Suzette

Yield: 6 servings

½ cup sweet butter, softened
¼ cup sugar
2 teaspoons orange peel, grated
½ cup orange juice
¼ cup curacao
1 small orange, sliced
1 small lemon, sliced
2 tablespoons brandy
12 warm dessert crepes

Cream butter and beat in sugar. Add orange peel, juice, and curacao. Spread orange butter on each crepe. Fold into fourths. Decorate with orange and lemon slices. Pour brandy over and serve. (If flaming dessert is desired, heat brandy in small pan, pour over crepes and ignite.)

Stacked Crepes Suzettes

Yield: 4 servings

½ pound unsalted butter, softened
½ cup sugar
1 teaspoon lemon juice
½ cup orange juice
¼ cup orange liqueur
16 dessert crepes
1 tablespoon sugar
2 tablespoons orange liqueur
2 tablespoons cognac

Beat butter with ½ cup sugar until thoroughly mixed. Add lemon juice, orange juice and ¼ cup liqueur while continuing to beat. Heat orange butter until bubbly. Dip crepes in hot orange butter and stack. Sprinkle top with 1 tablespoon sugar. Heat liqueur and cognac. Pour over stacked crepes and ignite. Spoon sauce over crepes until flames die. Cut and serve immediately.

Citrus Crepes

Yield: 6 to 8 servings

12 small sugar cubes
1 orange
2 lemons
6 tablespoons butter
¾ cup Cointreau
16 warm dessert crepes
2 tablespoons sugar
Lemon slices for garnish

Rub sugar cubes over skin of orange to absorb oil. Squeeze orange and lemons; reserve juice. Melt 3 tablespoons butter in chafing dish. Drop in sugar cubes, and press to crush. Add rest of butter, juice, and ½ cup Cointreau. Heat, stirring, until well-mixed. Dip each crepe in sauce, and roll. Sprinkle with sugar. Add ¼ cup Cointreau and tilt pan toward flame to ignite. Garnish with lemon slices.

Fresh-Fruit Dessert Crepes

Yield: 6 servings

½ cup commercial sour cream
2 3-ounce packages of cream cheese, softened
3 tablespoons sugar
1 pint sliced strawberries or 2 cups sliced peaches
12 dessert crepes

Blend sour cream, cream cheese, and sugar well; then whip until smooth and fluffy. Sweeten fruit with sugar and set aside. Top dessert crepe with 2 or 3 tablespoons of cream cheese mixture and roll up. Spoon fresh fruit over top. Serve cold or warm.

Mixed-Fruit Crepes with Whipped Cream

Yield: 6 servings

3 bananas
2 tablespoons heavy cream
1 tablespoon sugar
1 pound fresh or canned peaches
1 pound fresh or canned pears
12 dessert crepes
2 tablespoons butter

Mash the bananas with cream and sugar and cover the surface of each crepe. Cut the peaches and pears into small pieces and lay over the bananas. Roll or fold the crepes. Place the crepes in a buttered oven-proof dish, dot with butter and bake in a preheated 400°F oven for 15 minutes. Serve with a melba sauce or whipped cream.

Tangy Apple Crepes

Yield: 4 servings

3 tablespoons margarine
5 medium tangy apples, peeled, cored and sliced ½ inch thick
1½ tablespoons lemon juice
¾ teaspoon lemon peel
¼ teaspoon cinnamon
⅛ teaspoon allspice
½ cup sugar
8 crepes

Melt margarine over medium heat in a large pan. Gently cook apples, mixed with lemon juice, peel, and spices about 8 minutes or until apples are just tender. Cook 2 to 3 minutes longer after sprinkling with sugar. Cool to room temperature.

Roll up about 3 tablespoons filling in crepes and place seam side down in baking dish. Cover with remaining filling. Tightly cover dish with foil and bake at 325°F for about 25 minutes.

Baked-Apple Crepe Cake

Yield: 6 servings

2 pounds apples, sliced (about 6 medium apples)
⅓ cup sugar
¼ cup melted butter
12 crepes
6 stale macaroons, crumbled
1 tablespoon melted butter
1 tablespoon sugar

Spread apples in a baking pan and sprinkle with sugar and butter. Cook at 350°F for 15 minutes or until apples are tender. Place 2 crepes side by side in a greased baking dish and spread with layers of apple slices and sprinkle with macaroons. Place 2 crepes on top and continue with apple filling. Top with crepes. Brush with melted butter and sprinkle with sugar. Bake at 375°F until bubbly.

Apple Strudel Crepes

Yield: 6 servings

1 16-ounce can applesauce
12 dessert crepes
½ cup butter
2 tablespoons sugar
3 tablespoons confectioner's sugar
2 teaspoons cinnamon

Spread applesauce over each crepe and roll up. Melt butter in a hot frying pan or chafing dish. Place crepes in pan or chafing dish and brush tops with butter. Sprinkle with 2 tablespoons sugar. Heat until lightly browned on all sides. Sprinkle with confectioner's sugar and cinnamon. Serve.

Apple Crepes with Roquefort Cheese

Yield: 4 servings

2 pounds cooking apples
2 tablespoons butter
1 tablespoon sugar
½ pound Roquefort cheese
1 to 2 tablespoons heavy cream
8 dessert crepes
1 tablespoon butter

Peel, core, and cut the apples into thin slices. Melt 2 tablespoons butter in a frying pan. Add the apples. Sprinkle the apples with sugar and cook until the apples are lightly browned but not soft.

Put the cheese in a bowl; add the cream and work into a paste, using the back of a wooden spoon.

Spread out the crepes and cover the surface of each crepe with the Roquefort cheese. Put 1 to 2 tablespoons sautéed apple slices in each crepe and roll or fold the crepes into envelopes.

Lay the crepes on a buttered oven-proof dish, dot with 1 tablespoon butter and bake in a preheated 400°F oven for 15 minutes. Decorate the dish with apple slices.

Brandied Apricot Crepes

Yield: 4 to 6 servings

12 dessert crepes
½ cup apricot jam
3 tablespoons sugar
2 tablespoons melted butter
⅓ cup apricot brandy

Spread jam over crepes. Roll up and arrange in buttered baking dish. Sprinkle with sugar and melted butter. Broil for a minute or two to brown tops. Heat brandy in a small pan. Pour over crepes and ignite with long match. Serve.

Apricot Soufflé Crepes

Yield: 6 servings

2 cups dried apricots
1 cup water
6 eggs, separated
⅔ cup sugar
2 cups egg custard or 1 package egg custard mix
Slivered toasted almonds
12 warm dessert crepes

Prepare apricot purée by simmering apricots in water until tender. Sieve or purée in blender. Reserve.

Beat egg yolks and sugar until thick. In separate bowl, beat egg whites until stiff. Fold ½ cup apricot purée into beaten yolks and fold this mixture into egg whites.

Spread crepes with a little of the remaining apricot purée, then divide egg mixture between crepes. Lightly fold crepes over soufflé and place in baking dish. Cook in very hot oven (450°F) for 4 minutes or until puffy. Pour warm custard over crepes; sprinkle with almonds and serve.

Banana Crepes

Yield: 8 servings

⅓ cup butter
½ cup orange marmalade
2 tablespoons sugar
1 tablespoon cornstarch
3 large bananas, sliced
2 tablespoons confectioner's sugar

Nutmeg, if desired
8 warm dessert crepes

Heat butter and marmalade until the marmalade melts. In a separate container mix sugar and cornstarch. Gradually stir into butter-marmalade mixture. Cook over medium heat, stirring constantly, until mixture bubbles. Remove from heat and gently stir in bananas. Divide between warm crepes and roll. Sprinkle tops with confectioner's sugar and nutmeg, if desired.

Blueberry Crepes

Yield: 6 servings

2 pints blueberries
½ cup red wine
½ cup orange juice
¼ cup red currant jelly
1 tablespoon arrowroot
2 tablespoons cold water
12 dessert crepes
2 tablespoons butter
Confectioner's sugar
Whipped cream or sour cream

Wash the blueberries and put them in a bowl. Combine the wine, orange juice, and red currant jelly. Bring to the boiling point in a small saucepan. Dissolve 1 tablespoon arrowroot in 2 tablespoons cold water and add to the boiling liquid. It will thicken immediately. Remove from the heat and combine the sauce with the blueberries.

Put 2 to 3 tablespoons blueberries in each crepe. Roll the crepes and place in a buttered oven-proof dish. Dot the crepes with butter and bake in a preheated 400° oven. Cook for 15 minutes. When they are removed from the oven, dust the crepes heavily with sifted confectioner's sugar. Serve with whipped or sour cream.

Cherry and Apple Crepes

Yield: 6 servings

6 cooking apples
¾ cup sugar
⅛ teaspoon cinnamon
¼ cup water
1 16-ounce can cherry pie filling
½ cup sugar
6 warm rich dessert crepes

Peel, core, and slice the apples. Place in a pan with the ¾ cup sugar, cinnamon and ¼ cup water. Cover and cook over a low heat for 15 minutes or until the apples are just cooked. Heat the cherry pie filling. Drain apples and spoon apples into the center of each crepe. Spoon pie filling at each end. Carefully roll up each crepe. Sprinkle on ½ cup sugar. Heat 2 skewers over gas or electric burner until very hot. Using an oven mitt to hold skewer, place a skewer diagonally over the sugared crepes. Repeat with the second skewer, placing it at the opposite angle. Repeat until all the crepes are decorated in this way. Serve at once while crepes are hot. For a special occasion, serve with whipped cream.

Date-Nut Crepes

Yield: 8 servings

1 cup chopped dates
1 cup chopped pecans
½ cup light-brown sugar
1 cup dairy sour cream
8 warm dessert crepes

Mix dates, pecans, brown sugar, and sour cream. Fill and roll up or allow guests to help themselves.

George Washington Crepes

Yield: 8 servings

2 cups sour cream
4 tablespoons sugar
1 teaspoon almond extract
1 can cherry pie filling
16 dessert crepes
2 tablespoons butter

Blend sour cream, sugar, and almond extract. Spoon 1 tablespoon sour cream mixture and 1 tablespoon pie filling on each crepe; roll up. Cover and refrigerate until serving time. When ready to serve, melt butter in blazing pan of chafing dish over direct high heat. Heat crepe, turning to heat evenly. Spoon remaining pie filling over crepes; heat carefully to avoid scorching, and serve.

Black-Cherry Crepes

Yield: 4 servings

2 pounds pitted black Bing cherries
¼ teaspoon ground cinnamon
¼ cup sugar
Rind and juice of 2 oranges
1 tablespoon kirsch
1 teaspoon arrowroot
8 dessert crepes
2 tablespoons confectioner's sugar
1 tablespoon butter
Toasted almonds or whipped cream

Drain the cherries and reserve the juice. Simmer the cherries in a covered saucepan over moderately low heat with the cinnamon, sugar and orange rind. There will be enough juice still clinging to the cherries to prevent them from burning. Dissolve the arrowroot in the orange juice and add to the

pan of hot cherries and continue cooking until a thick sauce is formed around the cherries. Add 1 tablespoon kirsch. If the sauce appears too thin, add another teaspoon arrowroot dissolved first in 1 tablespoon reserved cherry juice. If the sauce is too thick, thin it out a little with more juice. Butter an oven-proof dish. Put 2 tablespoons of the cherry filling in each crepe and roll the crepe. Dot the surface of the crepes with 1 tablespoon butter and heat in a preheated oven at 400° for 15 minutes.

Sprinkle the surface of the heated crepes with sifted confectioner's sugar and serve with toasted almonds over the confectioner's sugar or with whipped cream.

Crepes with Grape Filling

Yield: 8 servings

4 cups blue grapes
¾ cup sugar
1½ tablespoons lemon juice
1 tablespoon grated orange rind
1 tablespoon quick-cooking tapioca
8 warm dessert crepes
Confectioner's sugar

Remove pulp from grape skins. Reserve skins and cook pulp until the seeds become loose. Press through a colander to remove seeds. Combine pulp and skins. Add sugar, lemon juice, orange rind and tapioca. Simmer for 20 minutes. Cool slightly and spread on warm dessert crepes. Roll up and sprinkle with the sugar.

Lemon Dessert Crepes

Yield: 6 servings

3 tablespoons sweet butter
4 tablespoons unsifted all-purpose flour
½ cup hot milk
3 eggs, separated
3 tablespoons sugar
3 tablespoons lemon juice
1 teaspoon dried lemon peel
Salt
12 dessert crepes

Preheat oven to 400°F. Melt butter over low heat, blend in flour, and continue cooking and stirring 1 to 2 minutes. Remove from heat and beat in milk. Return to heat and stir continuously until mixture boils and thickens. Transfer to a bowl before beating in egg yolks one at a time. Stirring thoroughly, blend in 3 tablespoons sugar, lemon juice, and lemon peel. In another bowl, whip egg whites with ⅛ teaspoon salt until they form soft peaks; continue beating until whites form stiff peaks. Gently fold in a small amount of whites to lemon mixture; then add remaining whites to the mixture.

Add 1 tablespoon of lemon mixture on dessert crepe and fold the crepes in half and in half again. Place in shallow, buttered baking dish side by side, and bake 10 minutes.

Mandarin-Cream Crepes

Yield: 6 servings

2 small cans mandarin oranges
3 tablespoons apricot jam, sieved
½ cup heavy cream
Candy orange slices
6 warm dessert crepes

Drain mandarin oranges; mix them with jam. Lightly whip the cream until thick but not buttery. Place in a pastry bag with small star nozzle. Spoon mandarin mixture into the center of each crepe and roll up. Pipe a line of cream on each pancake and decorate with candy orange slices.

Peach Dessert Crepes

Yield: 6 servings

2 16-ounce cans sliced peaches
1 15- to 16-ounce can red cherries
¼ cup golden syrup
6 warm dessert crepes

Drain fruit. Set aside 15 cherries and 15 peach slices. Cut these cherries in half and slice peaches. Chop rest of fruit. Mix chopped fruit with syrup. Warm mixture on low heat. Fill warm crepes with mixture and roll up. Decorate.

Peach-Nut Flambé

Yield: 4 servings

⅓ cup butter
1 16-ounce can sliced peaches
½ cup chopped pecans
1 teaspoon grated orange peel
1 tablespoon sugar
¼ cup brandy
8 warm dessert crepes

Melt butter in chafing dish. Drain peaches and pour juice into pan with butter. Simmer about 5 minutes. Stir in peaches and pecans. Sprinkle with orange peel and sugar. Warm brandy in a small pan and add. Ignite with a long match. Spoon sauce over crepes.

Danish Prune Crepes

Yield: 4 servings

¾ cup dried prunes
3 tablespoons sugar
¼ teaspoon ground cardamom
½ teaspoon vanilla
⅛ teaspoon salt
4 warm dessert crepes
2 tablespoons confectioner's sugar

Add enough water to cover prunes. Bring to a boil; then reduce heat and simmer, covered, for 30 minutes. Drain prunes, reserving 3 tablespoons liquid. Cool, pit and chop. Combine prunes, prune liquid, sugar, and cardamom. Cook, stirring continuously, for 5 minutes or until mixture is thick. Add vanilla and salt.

Divide between warm crepes and roll. Sprinkle with sugar and serve.

Strawberry Cream Crepes

Yield: 6 servings

4 cups fresh strawberries, sliced
2 tablespoons sugar
1 14-ounce can sweetened condensed milk
¼ cup lemon juice
½ cup heavy cream, whipped
12 dessert crepes
Whipped cream for garnish
12 whole strawberries for garnish

Sprinkle strawberries with sugar and set aside. Beat condensed milk with lemon juice until thick. Fold in strawberries and whipped cream. Divide between crepes and fold. Garnish with additional whipped cream and a strawberry centered on cream.

Strawberry-Banana Crepes

Yield: 8 servings

¾ cup water
2 cups strawberries, crushed
2 cups strawberries, halved
¼ cup sugar
2 tablespoons cornstarch
½ cup Curacao or other orange liqueur
3 medium bananas, quartered
8 warm dessert crepes

In a medium saucepan add ¾ cup water to 2 cups crushed strawberries. Bring to a boil and cook 2 minutes. Strain. Combine sugar and cornstarch and gradually stir into hot strawberry mixture. Cook over medium heat, stirring constantly, until mixture thickens and bubbles. Remove from heat. Stir in liqueur and set aside 1 cup of glaze. Stir half of the strawberry halves into remaining glaze. Spread 3 tablespoons glaze on each crepe and roll up. Place in chafing dish or large fry pan with the rest of strawberry halves and quartered bananas. Pour reserved glaze over top; cover and heat through. Serve warm.

Strawberry and Orange Crepes

Yield: 4 servings

1 pint strawberries
2 oranges
2 tablespoons kirsch
1 tablespoon Grand Marnier
4 tablespoons red currant jelly
8 dessert crepes
2 tablespoons butter

Wash and slice the strawberries. Peel an orange and chop the peel into the smallest possible pieces. Put the peel in a saucepan of boiling water and simmer the peel for 15 minutes. Drain the peel. Cut the oranges into segments, cutting between the membranes.

Combine the sliced strawberries, orange segment, and peel. Sprinkle with 2 tablespoons kirsch and 1 tablespoon Grand Marnier. Spread each crepe with red currant jelly. Fill the crepes with 2 to 3 tablespoons combined fruits and roll into shape. Place the crepes in a buttered oven-proof dish and dot with butter. Bake in a preheated 400° oven for 15 minutes. Serve with a fruit sauce, lemon sauce or whipped cream.

Sour Cream-Strawberries Crepes

Yield: 8 servings

2 cups commercial sour cream
4 tablespoons sugar
1 pint sliced strawberries
1 tablespoon butter
16 dessert crepes
Powdered sugar

Blend sour cream and sugar. Roll up crepes with a filling of 1 tablespoon sour cream mixture and 1 tablespoon strawberries. Refrigerate, covered, until serving time. In pan or blazing pan of chafing dish melt butter over direct high flame. Turn crepes to heat evenly. Add strawberries; heat. Sprinkle with powdered sugar.

Blintzes

Yield: 4 servings

12 ounces cottage cheese
1 egg yolk
1 teaspoon butter, softened

1 teaspoon vanilla
18 crepes, cooked only on 1 side
2 teaspoons butter
2 teaspoons vegetable oil
2 tablespoons sugar
1 tablespoon cinnamon
Dairy sour cream to pass

Mix cheese, egg yolk, butter, and vanilla. Divide filling between the crepes on cooked side and roll up. Melt butter and oil in a large fry pan. Place half of crepes in pan and fry until golden brown, turning once. Repeat with rest of crepes. Add more butter and oil if necessary. Sprinkle each serving with sugar and cinnamon. Pass sour cream.

Cream-of-Almond Crepes

Yield: 6 servings

12 to 15 dessert crepes
2 tablespoons butter
2 tablespoons flour
1 cup milk
3 ounces almond extract
3 egg yolks
1 cup sugar
½ teaspoon salt
½ cup Grand Marnier liqueur or rum

Melt butter and blend in flour. Cook for 1 minute and add cold milk. Bring to a simmer and cook 2 to 3 minutes, stirring constantly. Remove from heat. Add almond extract, egg yolks, sugar and salt. Beat. Adjust sweetness to your taste and add the Grand Marnier liqueur. Refrigerate until cold. Divide the mixture between the crepes and roll up package style. Place crepes in an oven-proof dish and dot with butter. Sprinkle tops with sugar. Place under broiler for 3 to 4 minutes, until sugar is browned.

Chocolate and Nut Crepes

Yield: 6 servings

2 tablespoons cocoa
⅓ cup cornstarch
¼ cup sugar
2½ cups milk
½ cup chopped walnuts
6 warm dessert crepes

Blend the cocoa, cornstarch, and sugar with a small amount of milk. Bring the rest of the milk to a boil and blend into cocoa mixture. Return to the pan and bring to a boil, stirring constantly, until thick. Reserve ¼ cup of the chocolate sauce and 1 tablespoon of the chopped walnuts. Mix the rest of the sauce with the nuts. Fill warm crepes with the mixture and roll up. Spoon the remaining sauce on top of crepes and sprinkle with reserved nuts. Serve at once.

Crepes with Chocolate Mousse

Yield: 8 servings

6 ounces semisweet chocolate pieces
1 teaspoon sugar
1 teaspoon vanilla
⅓ cup boiling water
4 eggs, separated
8 dessert crepes
Whipped cream to garnish

In a blender grind chocolate pieces until powdery; loosen pieces from corners so all chocolate is ground. Add sugar, vanilla and boiling water and blend until chocolate is smooth. Add the egg yolks to blending chocolate. Beat the egg whites until stiff peaks are formed. Fold chocolate into whites and

blend. Chill at least 1 hour before filling crepes. Divide mixture between crepes and roll. Garnish tops with whipped cream.

Chocolate-Coconut Crepes

Yield: 8 servings

8 ounces sweet chocolate
½ cup water
1 tablespoon butter
½ cup heavy cream
1 cup coconut
8 crepes

Melt chocolate, water, and butter over low heat. Slowly mix in cream to make sauce. Stir in coconut. Divide between crepes and roll up.

Flaming Crepes d'Angers

Yield: 8 servings

1 cup heavy cream
½ cup and 2 tablespoons orange
  liqueur
2 tablespoons sugar
Grated semisweet chocolate
16 crepes

Whip cream and add 2 tablespoons orange liqueur. Fold crepes in quarters and arrange in heated serving pan. Sprinkle with sugar. Add ½ cup orange liqueur, warm, and ignite. Spoon liqueur over crepes. Top each crepe with whipped cream and a sprinkle of chocolate.

Coffee Crepes Flambé

Yield: 6 servings

12 crepes
¼ cup brown sugar, packed
⅛ teaspoon cinnamon
⅓ cup heavy cream
6 tablespoons coffee-flavored liqueur, heated
Whipped cream for garnish

Fold crepes in quarters. In chafing dish combine brown sugar, cinnamon, and cream. Heat to simmer, stirring continuously. Add folded crepes and coat with sauce. With a long match, ignite liqueur. Pour into chafing dish while flaming and spoon over crepes. Garnish with whipped cream before serving.

Hot-Fudge Crepes

Yield: 6 servings

½ cup butter
1 cup sugar
1 teaspoon instant coffee powder
2 tablespoons rum
⅓ cup cocoa
1 cup heavy cream
1 teaspoon vanilla
12 crepes
12 small scoops chocolate ice cream
Whipped cream for garnish

Melt butter in saucepan and blend in sugar, coffee powder, rum, and cocoa. Add cream and heat to simmer temperature. Cook about 5 minutes, stirring occasionally. Remove from heat and add vanilla. Fill crepes with ice cream and pour fudge sauce over filled crepes. Top with whipped cream.

Hot Ice-Cream Crepes

Yield: 4 servings

12 cold dessert crepes
1 pint coffee ice cream
Chocolate or melba sauce

Preheat oven to 475°. Divide ice cream between the crepes and roll up. Place in an oven-proof dish. Bake in hot oven for about 2 to 3 minutes. Serve with cold chocolate sauce or melba sauce.

Ice Cream Crepes with Raspberry Sauce

Yield: 8 servings

1 10-ounce package frozen raspberries
½ cup sugar
1 tablespoon cornstarch
¼ teaspoon nutmeg
1 tablespoon lemon juice
8 crepes
Vanilla ice cream
½ cup whipped cream

Thaw berries. In a saucepan combine sugar, cornstarch, and nutmeg. Stir in berries and lemon juice. Cook, stirring, until thickened. Cool 5 to 10 minutes. Fill crepes with ice cream. Fold over and spoon warm sauce over tops. Garnish with whipped cream.

Fondue Chips

Yield: 4 to 6 servings

6 dessert crepes
Powdered sugar

Chocolate fondue

10 ounces milk chocolate
½ cup heavy cream
2 tablespoons kirsch or cognac

Cut each crepe into 12 or 16 pieces. Place on a cookie sheet and bake at 400° for 6 to 8 minutes or until crisp. Remove from oven and sprinkle with sugar. Use with chocolate fondue.

To make the chocolate fondue, break chocolate into pieces about 1 inch square and combine with other ingredients in fondue pot over low heat. Stir until chocolate is melted and mixture is smooth. Dip fondue chips into sauce.

Meringue Crepes

Yield: 6 servings

4 egg whites
¾ cup sugar
½ cup and 2 tablespoons Cointreau or orange liqueur
½ cup chopped almonds
16 crepes

Beat egg whites until soft peaks are formed. Slowly beat in sugar until whites are stiff. Fold in 2 tablespoons Cointreau or orange liqueur. Divide meringue between crepes, sprinkle with 1 tablespoon almonds, and roll up. Place in heated serving pan. Sprinkle with rest of almonds. Add ½ cup Cointreau, warm and ignite. Spoon over crepes.

Russian Crepes

Yield: 6 servings

12 warm dessert crepes
¾ cup cottage cheese
½ cup sugar
Pinch of cardamom
2 eggs, separated
¼ teaspoon salt
⅓ cup candied cherries, chopped
4 egg whites
⅓ cup raisins
⅓ cup candied orange peel, chopped
1 tablespoon lemon peel

Drain the cottage cheese. Mix with the sugar, egg yolks, cardamom, and salt until it resembles a thick paste. Add all the fruit, including the lemon peel. Whip the 6 egg whites to stiff peaks and fold into cheese mixture. Divide the mixture between the crepes and roll up. Place in oven-proof dish and sprinkle a little sugar over the tops. Place under broiler for 3 to 4 minutes to brown sugar and warm filling. Serve immediately.

Whipped-Cream Filled Crepes

Yield: 6 servings

½ pint heavy cream, chilled
Sugar and vanilla to taste
1 pint fresh raspberries or strawberries
6 warm dessert crepes

Whip chilled cream until thick. Add sugar and vanilla to taste. Divide whipping cream between crepes; fill and roll. Garnish with berries and sprinkle sugar over tops for a beautiful but simple dessert. (A filling of sour cream would be a delicious variation.)

Crock Pot
Breakfast Foods

Hot Oatmeal

Yield: 4 servings

1½ cups old-fashioned oatmeal (not quick oats)
3 cups cold water
1 teaspoon salt

Combine ingredients in the slow cooker at bedtime. Cook on low 8 to 10 hours or overnight. Serve hot in the morning with milk and a dash of nutmeg.

Variations: Add 1 cup grated carrots before cooking or add 2 or 3 tablespoons brown sugar before cooking.

Cinnamon Oatmeal and Fruit

Yield: 4 servings

3 cups cold water
1½ cups old-fashioned oatmeal
½ teaspoon cinnamon
¼ cup raisins
1 apple, cored, peeled, and cut into
  ½-inch cubes
1 teaspoon salt

Combine all ingredients in the slow cooker at bedtime. Cook on low overnight, 8 to 10 hours. Serve with milk.

Hot Rolled Wheat

Yield: 4 servings

Rolled wheat makes an interesting change from oatmeal. You can find it in most natural-food stores.

1½ cups rolled wheat
3 cups cold water
1 teaspoon salt

Rolled wheat makes an interesting change from oatmeal. You can find it in most natural-food stores.

Combine ingredients in the slow cooker at bedtime. Cook on low overnight, 8 to 10 hours. Serve from the pot in the morning with honey or brown sugar and milk.

Crunchy Granola

Yield: About 5 cups

4 cups rolled oats
⅔ cup wheat germ
¼ cup sesame seeds
¼ cup shredded coconut
¼ cup vegetable oil
⅔ cup honey
1 teaspoon vanilla
½ cup raisins

Combine all ingredients except the raisins in the slow cooker. Heat on low with lid slightly ajar for about 4 hours. Stir occasionally. Let cook and add raisins. Store in a tightly covered container. Use within 1 to 2 weeks.

Honey-Wheat Granola

Yield: About 5 cups

1 cup rolled wheat (available from
  natural-food stores)
3 cups rolled oats
½ cup wheat germ
½ cup honey
½ cup hulled sunflower seeds
¼ cup vegetable oil
1 teaspoon vanilla
¼ teaspoon salt
¼ cup chopped dried apricots or dates

Combine all ingredients except the dried fruit in the slow cooker. Cook on low with lid slightly ajar for about 4 hours, stirring occasionally. Cook, add dried fruit, and store in an airtight jar. Use within 1 to 2 weeks.

Cinnamon-Cocoa Granola

Yield: 5 cups

4 cups rolled oats
1 cup bran flakes
1 cup wheat germ
2 tablespoons cocoa
¾ cup honey
¼ cup vegetable oil
1 teaspoon cinnamon
½ cup sesame seeds

Combine all ingredients in the slow cooker. Cook on low heat with lid slightly ajar about 4 hours, stirring occasionally. Cool and store in airtight jars. Use within 1 to 2 weeks.

The Ultimate Granola

Yield: About 6 cups

3 cups rolled oats
1 cup wheat germ
1 cup shredded coconut
½ cup sesame seeds
½ cup coarsely chopped cashews
½ cup coarsely chopped almonds
⅔ cup honey
¼ cup vegetable oil
Dash cinnamon and nutmeg
½ cup raisins
½ cup chopped dates

Combine all ingredients except the raisins and dates in the slow cooker. Cook on low with lid slightly ajar for about 4 hours, stirring occasionally. Cool and add fruit. Store in airtight jars. Use within 1 to 2 weeks.

Meat

Beef Stew

Yield: 6 servings

No need for last-minute thickening of the gravy with the technique used here. A good, hearty stew.

2 pounds lean beef (round, chuck,
  sirloin tip, rump), cut into 1-inch
  cubes
⅓ cup all-purpose flour
2 tablespoons vegetable oil
4 potatoes, cut into 1-inch cubes
6 carrots, cut into 1-inch slices
1 onion, chopped

2 cups water
⅓ cup all-purpose flour in ⅓ cup cold
    water, mixed to a paste
2 teaspoons salt
½ cup frozen defrosted peas
Fresh parsley leaves

Toss beef cubes in flour; shake off excess. Brown in hot oil in a large skillet for about 10 minutes.

Place meat in slow cooker with potatoes, carrots, and onion.

Drain accumulated fat from skillet. Add water, flour-water mixture, and salt to skillet. Bring to a boil, stirring constantly, until thickened. Add mixture to meat and vegetables in slow cooker. Cover and cook on low for 8 to 10 hours.

Add peas last 10 minutes of cooking to heat through. Serve hot, garnished with parsley leaves.

Variations to beef stew: To the gravy, add one of the following: ¼ cup tomato paste; 1 teaspoon oregano and 1 teaspoon basil; 1 tablespoon Worcestershire sauce or soy sauce.

Red-Wine Stew

Yield: 6 to 8 servings

3 to 4 slices bacon, cubed
2 pounds lean beef and pork, cut into
    1-inch cubes (or use all beef)
1 whole onion
4 whole cloves
3 onions, chopped
1 bay leaf
2 carrots, sliced

1½ teaspoons salt
1½ cups dry red wine
2 hot dogs
1 cup green beans, peas, or chopped
    green pepper
2 tomatoes, quartered
Fresh parsley leaves
Flour-water paste, optional

Brown bacon in a large skillet; add beef and pork cubes and brown well on all sides.

Place meat in slow cooker along with a whole onion studded with the cloves, chopped onions, bay leaf, carrots, and salt.

Pour accumulated fat from skillet and add some of the red wine. Stir to pick up the browned bits.

Add to slow cooker along with remaining wine. Cover and cook on low about 8 hours.

Add hot dogs the last ½ hour and the green vegetable and tomatoes the last 10 minutes of cooking.

Before serving, remove whole onion and cloves. Garnish with parsley.

Gravy may be thickened in a saucepan with a flour-water paste if desired.

Beef Stew with Apples and White Wine

Yield: 6 servings

2½ pounds lean beef, cut into 1-inch
    cubes
2 tablespoons vegetable oil or olive oil
2 cloves garlic
2 carrots, cut into 1-inch cubes
2 onions, cut into wedges
1 teaspoon salt
¾ cup dry white wine
¾ cup apple cider
2 apples, peeled, cored, and cut into
    1-inch cubes
¼ cup all-purpose flour in ¼ cup cold
    water, mixed to a paste

Brown beef in hot oil in a large skillet.
Place meat in slow cooker with garlic,
carrots, onions, salt, and wine.

Add cider to the skillet and stir to pick
up the browned bits.

Add cider to slow cooker. Cover and
cook on low about 8 hours. Add apples the
last 3 hours of cooking.

Pour accumulated juice into a saucepan.
Add flour-water paste. Heat, stirring constantly, until mixture boils and is thickened.

Return mixture to meat and vegetables.
Serve at once.

Hungarian Kettle Stew

Yield: 4 servings

1 pound lean beef, cut into 1-inch
    cubes
2 tablespoons vegetable oil or bacon fat
1½ cups water
2 medium onions, chopped
1 clove garlic, minced

4 potatoes, cut into 1-inch cubes
1 teaspoon salt
1 tablespoon tomato paste
1 tablespoon paprika
1 teaspoon caraway seeds
2 tomatoes, coarsely chopped
2 green peppers, cubed
3 tablespoons all-purpose flour in 3
    tablespoons cold water, mixed to a
    paste
½ cup sour cream
Parsley for garnish, optional

Brown beef in hot oil in a large skillet.
Place in slow cooker.

Pour off accumulated fat. Add some of
the water to the skillet and stir to pick up
the browned bits. Add to the meat along
with remaining water, onions, garlic, potatoes, salt, tomato paste, paprika, and caraway seeds. Cover and cook on low about 8
hours.

Add tomatoes and green peppers the last
5 minutes of cooking.

Pour accumulated gravy into a saucepan,
add flour-water mixture, and bring to a boil,
stirring constantly, until thickened. Stir in
sour cream and return mixture at once to
meat and vegetables. Serve immediately in
hot bowls. Garnish with parsley leaves, if
you wish.

Panamanian Stew

Yield: 4 to 6 servings

1 pound lean beef, cut into ¾-inch
    cubes
8 ounces lean pork, cut into ¾-inch
    cubes
2 tablespoons vegetable oil or bacon fat
3 cups water
2 carrots, sliced into ¼-inch slices

1 beet, peeled and cut into ½-inch cubes
2 stalks celery, cut into ¾-inch cubes
2 medium potatoes, cut into ¾-inch cubes
2 onions, sliced
½ small head cabbage, shredded
2 teaspoons salt
2 tomatoes, peeled and quartered
1 cup frozen, defrosted green beans
2 tablespoons fresh parsley leaves, chopped
½ teaspoon basil or thyme

Brown beef and pork in oil in a large skillet. Place meat in slow cooker.

Add some of the water to the skillet and stir to pick up the browned bits. Add to the meat along with remaining water, carrots, beet, celery, potatoes, onions, cabbage, and salt. Cover and cook on low about 8 hours or until vegetables are tender.

Add tomatoes, green beans, parsley, and basil the last 10 minutes of cooking. Serve stew hot in large bowls with crusty Italian rolls.

Carbonnade of Beef 'n Beer

Yield: 6 servings

2 to 3 pounds lean beef, cut into 1-inch cubes
2 tablespoons vegetable oil
3 onions, sliced
2 cloves garlic
12 black peppercorns
1 bay leaf
1 teaspoon thyme
1½ teaspoons salt
1 tablespoon sugar

1 12-ounce can beer
4 tablespoons all-purpose flour in 4 tablespoons cold water, mixed to a smooth paste
6 thin slices bread
French mustard

Brown beef in hot oil in a skillet. Place in slow cooker with onions, garlic, peppercorns, bay leaf, thyme, salt, and sugar.

Drain fat from skillet and add beer and the flour-water paste. Heat and stir until mixture comes to a boil and is thickened. Add to slow cooker. Cover and cook on low 8 to 10 hours.

Pour stew into a shallow casserole dish. Spread each slice of bread with mustard. Place the slices mustard-side-down over the stew. Press to imbed lightly in gravy. Place in 350°F oven 15 to 20 minutes to brown the bread. Serve at once.

Beef Short Ribs with Spiced Fruit

Yield: 6 servings

3 pounds beef short ribs
2 cups water
2 tablespoons salt
⅛ teaspoon pepper
1 11-ounce package mixed dried fruit
¼ cup sugar
1 stick cinnamon
2 tablespoons lemon juice

Brown short ribs in a large skillet. Drain away accumulated fat. Place meat in slow cooker. Add remaining ingredients. Cover and cook on low about 8 hours. Serve meat with fruit and accumulated juices.

Beef Paprika

Yield: 6 servings

Lamb may be substituted for beef in this recipe with excellent results. A very good dish.

    2 to 3 pound lean beef, cut into 1-inch cubes
    2 tablespoons bacon fat or vegetable oil
    2 to 3 tablespoons water
    1 6-ounce can tomato paste
    2 cloves garlic
    1½ tablespoons paprika
    1 teaspoon salt
    2 green peppers, cut into 1-inch strips
    1 cup sour cream

Brown beef in hot fat in a large skillet. Place meat in slow cooker.

Pour off accumulated fat and add water to skillet. Stir to pick up browned bits. Add to meat along with tomato paste, garlic, paprika, and salt. Cover and cook on low about 8 hours. Add green peppers the last 10 minutes of cooking.

Just before serving, lightly fold in the sour cream. It need not be uniformly distributed. Serve immediately.

Hearty Steak Roll-ups

Yield: 4 servings

Filling

    3 slices bacon, cooked and crumbled
    1 medium onion, chopped
    4 ounces fresh or canned mushrooms, coarsely chopped
    1 tomato, peeled and chopped
    2 tablespoons fresh parsley leaves, chopped

    ½ teaspoon salt
    ⅛ teaspoon pepper

Steak rolls

    4 4-ounce beef sandwich steaks (very thinly sliced beef round)
    Salt and pepper
    2 tablespoons vegetable oil
    1 onion, chopped
    2 tablespoons tomato paste
    1 cup water

Gravy

    2 tablespoons all-purpose flour and 2 tablespoons cold water, mixed to a smooth paste.
    ½ cup heavy cream or sour cream

Combine filling ingredients. Place steaks on a flat surface, season lightly with salt and pepper, and place ¼ of the filling mixture on each. Roll up, jelly-roll fashion, and fasten with string. Brown rolls lightly in hot oil and place in slow cooker. Add onion, tomato paste, and water. Cover and cook on low 6 to 8 hours. Remove beef rolls to a warm platter.

Pour accumulated gravy into a saucepan; add flour-water paste and bring to boil, stirring constantly until thickened. Stir in cream and serve at once over hot beef rolls.

Chinese Red-Stewed Beef

Yield: 6 servings

Red-stewing is the Chinese method of preparing less-tender cuts of meat.

    3 pound lean pot roast (chuck, round, rump , or sirloin tip)
    ½ cup soy sauce
    ¼ cup sherry

4 slices fresh gingerroot
3 scallions
1 clove garlic
2 tablespoons brown sugar
½ teaspoon anise seeds
1 cup water

Place pot roast in slow cooker and add remaining ingredients. Cover and cook on low about 10 hours. Slice meat and cover with cooking sauce as it is served.

Marinated Beef Pot Roast

Yield: 6 servings

Marinade

1 cup tomato juice
3 tablespoons prepared mustard
4 tablespoons Worcestershire sauce
1 teaspoon basil
1 teaspoon oregano
1 teaspoon onion powder
1 teaspoon garlic salt
¼ teaspoon freshly ground black pepper

3 pounds lean beef pot roast (chuck or round)
2 tablespoons bacon fat or vegetable oil
Flour-water paste, optional

Combine marinade ingredients and pour over pot roast in a shallow bowl. Cover and refrigerate overnight or for 24 hours. Remove meat from marinade and pat with paper towels to dry.

Heat bacon fat in large skillet and brown meat on all sides. Place in slow cooker. Cover and cook on low 8 to 10 hours. Serve with accumulated gravy. (This may be thickened in a saucepan with a flour-water paste if you wish.)

Beef Pot Roast with Red Wine

Yield: 6 servings

2 pounds very lean beef pot roast (rump, round, or sirloin tip)
¼ cup all-purpose flour
2 tablespoons vegetable oil
¼ cup water
1 cup dry red wine
¼ cup all-purpose flour in ¼ cup cold water, mixed to a paste
1 teaspoon salt
3 bay leaves
1 dozen whole black peppercorns
1 lemon, sliced

Dredge beef with flour and brown in hot oil in a large skillet. Remove, cut into thick slices, and place in slow cooker.

Drain accumulated fat from skillet and add water. Stir to loosen browned bits. Add wine, flour-water mixture, and salt. Bring to a boil, stirring constantly until thickened. Pour over meat in the slow cooker and add remaining ingredients. Cover and cook on low 8 to 10 hours. Serve with boiled potatoes.

Lemon slices added the last hour of cooking will retain their shape and color.

51

Barbecued Pot Roast

Yield: 6 servings

1 teaspoon salt
2 pounds lean beef pot roast (rump, round, or chuck)
½ cup tomato paste
24 peppercorns
1 small onion, chopped
1 teaspoon Worcestershire sauce

Sprinkle salt over pot roast and place in slow cooker. Spread tomato paste over meat; imbed peppercorns in paste; top with onions and Worcestershire sauce. Cover and cook on low 8 to 10 hours. Serve meat with accumulated gravy.

Easy Pot Roast

Yield: 6 servings

Surface of meat will brown while the meat cooks.

4 potatoes, cut into 1-inch cubes
8 carrots, cut into 1-inch slices
1 onion, chopped
3 pounds lean beef pot roast (chuck, round, rump)
1 teaspoon salt
½ teaspoon pepper
3 tablespoons all-purpose flour in 3 tablespoons cold water, mixed to a paste

Place vegetables in bottom of the slow cooker. Season meat with salt and pepper. Place on top of vegetables. Cook on low 10 to 12 hours.

Pour accumulated juice into a saucepan; skim off fat. Add flour-water mixture. Bring to a boil, stirring constantly until thickened.

Return to meat and vegetables. Serve at once.

German Sauerbraten

Yield: 8 servings

3 pounds lean beef (bottom of the round)

Marinade

1 cup dry red wine
½ cup red wine vinegar
1 cup water
1 medium onion, thinly sliced
1 bay leaf
3 whole cloves
6 whole black peppercorns
3 tablespoons vegetable oil or bacon fat
2 onions, chopped
1 stalk celery, chopped
1 carrot, chopped
1 teaspoon salt

Gravy

3 tablespoons all-purpose flour in 3 tablespoons cold water, mixed to a paste
Salt and pepper
½ cup light or heavy cream, optional

Place meat in a glass bowl. Combine all marinade ingredients in a saucepan. Bring to a boil, remove from heat, and allow to cool. Pour over meat. Cover and refrigerate for 2 days. Turn meat occasionally in the marinade.

Remove meat from marinade. Strain marinade and reserve 1 cup. Brown meat on all sides in hot oil in a skillet. Place in slow cooker.

Add some of the marinade to the skillet and stir to pick up the browned bits. Add to the slow cooker along with remaining marinade, onions, celery, carrot, and salt. Cover and cook on low about 10 hours. Remove meat, slice, and keep it warm.

Strain cooking liquid into a saucepan. Add flour-water paste. Bring to a boil, stirring constantly until thickened. Season with salt and pepper. Stir in cream if desired. Pour some of the gravy over the meat. Serve remainder separately.

Sauerbraten with Raisin Sauce

Yield: 6 to 8 servings

Marinade

1 cup vinegar
1 cup water
1 bay leaf
6 black peppercorns
½ teaspoon mustard seeds
1 medium onion, thinly sliced

3 pounds lean beef pot roast (bottom of the round)
2 tablespoons vegetable oil
2 tablespoons dry red wine

Raisin Sauce

2 ounces crushed ginger snaps
2 tablespoons all-purpose flour in
    2 tablespoons cold water, mixed to a paste
⅓ cup raisins
¼ cup heavy cream or sour cream, optional
Salt to taste

In a large glass bowl combine marinade ingredients. Add meat, cover, and refrigerate for 3 days. Turn meat in marinade occasionally.

After 3 days remove meat. Strain and reserve marinade. Brown meat in oil in a large skillet and place in slow cooker.

Add wine and ¼ cup of the reserved marinade to the skillet and stir to pick up the browned bits. Add to meat. Cover and cook on low 8 to 10 hours.

Pour accumulated juices into a saucepan; skim off fat. Add crushed ginger snaps, flour-water mixture, and raisins. Bring to a boil, stirring constantly until thickened. Add cream if you wish. Add salt to taste. Serve gravy over hot, sliced beef.

New England Corned-Beef and Cabbage Dinner

Yield: 6 servings

4 carrots, cut into 1-inch slices
4 potatoes, cut into 1-inch cubes
1 small head cabbage, shredded
1 onion, sliced
3 pounds corned-beef brisket, fat trimmed away
1 cup water

Place vegetables in slow cooker. Add beef and water. Cover and cook on low 8 to 10 hours. Remove and slice beef. Serve with vegetables.

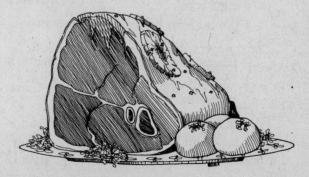

Corned Beef with Horseradish

Yield: 6 to 8 servings

3 pounds corned-beef brisket
2 cups water
1 bay leaf
4 whole cloves
8 black peppercorns
½ teaspoon mustard seeds
½ teaspoon thyme

Horseradish Roll

½ cup whipping cream, whipped
2 tablespoons horseradish

Place corned beef in slow cooker with water, herbs, and spices. Cover and cook on low 8 to 10 hours.

Combine whipped cream and horseradish. Freeze in a 2-inch roll.

When meat is done, slice it into ½-inch slices. Arrange on a hot platter with hot cubed beets, potatoes, sliced carrots, or other vegetables. Garnish with slices of the horseradish roll.

Mexican Chili Con Carne

Yield: 4 servings

½ pound kidney beans
4 cups water
1 pound lean beef or veal, cut into
    1-inch cubes
2 tablespoons vegetable oil or bacon fat
1 16-ounce can tomatoes or 2 fresh
    tomatoes, peeled and cubed
1 teaspoon salt
1½ tablespoons chili powder
1 tablespoon paprika

Soak beans in water in slow cooker overnight. Do not drain. Cover and cook on high 2 to 3 hours or until tender. Drain; reserve liquid.

Brown beef in oil or bacon fat and add to beans along with remaining ingredients. Add sufficient reserved liquid to barely cover beans. Cover and cook on low 8 to 10 hours. Serve with rice.

Cabbage Rolls in Beer

Yield: 8 rolls; 4 servings

1 small onion, finely chopped
1 stalk celery, minced
2 tablespoons fresh parsley leaves,
    minced
1 pound extra-lean ground beef
1 cup cooked rice
½ teaspoon salt
¼ teaspoon pepper
8 large cabbage leaves, boiled 3 to 5
    minutes, stems and thick veins
    removed

Sauce

¾ cup beer
¾ cup chili sauce
1 teaspoon Worcestershire sauce
½ teaspoon salt

Combine onion, celery, parsley, beef, rice, salt, and pepper. Place ⅛ of this mixture in the center of each cabbage leaf. Fold the sides in toward the center and roll tightly. Place in slow cooker.

Combine sauce ingredients and pour over rolls. Cover and cook on low 7 to 8 hours. Serve rolls with sauce ladled over each.

Spinach Rolls

Yield: 4 to 6 servings

1 pound extra-lean ground beef
3 slices bread torn into crumbs
2 onions, chopped
1 egg
1 teaspoon salt
⅛ teaspoon pepper
½ teaspoon marjoram
⅛ teaspoon nutmeg
16 to 20 large spinach leaves, boiled
    2 to 3 minutes
1 cup beef broth
2 tablespoons butter or margarine

Combine beef, bread crumbs, onions, egg, and seasonings. Place 1 heaping tablespoon of this mixture on each spinach leaf. Fold ends in toward center and roll tightly. Place rolls in slow cooker. Add broth and dot with butter. Cover and cook on low 6 to 8 hours.

Garlic Meatballs in Lemon Sauce

Yield: 6 servings

Meatballs

1½ pounds extra-lean ground beef
3 slices bread, torn into soft crumbs
4 cloves garlic, minced
2 tablespoons fresh parsley leaves,
    chopped
2 tablespoons fresh mint leaves,
    chopped
1 teaspoon paprika
1 teaspoon salt
Pepper to taste
2 eggs

Lemon Sauce

1 8-ounce can tomato sauce
Grated rind from 2 lemons
¼ cup lemon juice
Salt and pepper to taste
1 tablespoon fresh mint leaves, minced

Combine all ingredients for the meatballs and form into walnut-sized balls. Place in slow cooker. Combine sauce ingredients and pour over meatballs. Cover and cook on low 4 to 6 hours. Serve with rice.

Italian Meat Loaf

Yield: 4 servings

Meat Loaf

1 pound extra-lean ground beef
2 slices rye bread, torn into soft crumbs
1 onion, chopped
2 tablespoons chopped fresh parsley
    leaves
¼ cup grated Parmesan cheese
1 egg
1 teaspoon salt
½ teaspoon freshly ground black
    pepper

Gravy

1 8-ounce can tomato sauce
1 teaspoon oregano
Garlic salt to taste

Combine ingredients for meat loaf and gently form into a round loaf. Place in slow cooker on a trivet or small rack. Cover and cook on low 6 to 8 hours.

Serve with gravy prepared by combining and heating gravy ingredients in a saucepan.

Veal Stew with Rice

Yield: 6 to 8 servings

Beef may be substituted successfully for veal in this recipe.

4 slices bacon, cubed
2 pounds veal, cut into 1-inch cubes
2¼ cups water
2 onions, coarsely chopped
2 cloves garlic, minced
6 carrots, sliced
1 cup converted rice (you must use converted rice)
1½ teaspoons salt
4 tomatoes, peeled and quartered
2 green peppers, cut into strips
Dash Tabasco sauce
2 tablespoons fresh parsley leaves, chopped

Cook bacon in a large skillet until transparent. Add veal and brown well. Place in slow cooker.

Add some of the water to the skillet and stir to pick up the browned bits. Add to veal along with remaining water, onions, garlic, carrots, rice, and salt. Cover and cook on low about 8 hours.

Add tomatoes, green peppers, and Tabasco sauce the last 10 minutes of cooking. Serve sprinkled with chopped parsley.

Hungarian Veal Goulash

Yield: 4 servings

1 pound lean veal, cut into 1-inch cubes
2 tablespoons bacon fat
2 medium onions, chopped
½ cup tomato paste
1 teaspoon salt
1 tablespoon paprika
2 green peppers, cut into ¼-inch strips
Dash Tabasco sauce

Brown veal in hot bacon fat in a large skillet. Place in slow cooker with onions and tomato paste. Sprinkle with salt and paprika. Cover and cook on low about 8 hours.

Add green peppers and Tabasco sauce 10 minutes before serving.

Lamb and Carrot Stew

Yield: 6 servings

2 pounds lean lamb
2 cups water
5 whole black peppercorns
1 whole onion
4 potatoes, cubed
1 pound carrots, cut into ½-inch slices
½ pound kohlrabi, cut into 1-inch cubes
2 teaspoons salt
½ teaspoon caraway seeds
1 leek or 3 scallions, cut into ½-inch slices
Chopped fresh parsley
Flour-water paste, optional

Place lamb, water, peppercorns, onion, potatoes, carrots, kohlrabi, salt, and caraway seeds in slow cooker. Cover and cook on low about 10 hours.

Add leek and parsley the last ½ hour of cooking. Remove meat; cut into 1-inch cubes and return to vegetables. Serve very hot in bowls.

Gravy may be poured into a saucepan and thickened with a flour-water paste if a thickened gravy is desired. It will not, however, be brown, as meat was not browned before cooking.

Mint Sauce for Lamb Stews

Yield: 1⅓ cups

⅓ cup mint jelly
½ pint sour cream
Fresh mint leaves

Melt mint jelly over low heat and stir into sour cream. Place in a bowl and garnish with fresh mint leaves. Serve with slow-cooked lamb stews or pot roasts.

Lemon Lamb Pot Roast

Yield: 6 servings

3 pounds shoulder roast of lamb, fat trimmed away
3 tablespoons vegetable oil
1 onion, thinly sliced
1 lemon, thinly sliced
1 bay leaf
1 teaspoon salt
½ teaspoon pepper
¼ teaspoon allspice
3 tablespoons lemon juice
3 egg yolks, lightly beaten
⅓ cup sliced black olives
¼ cup fresh parsley leaves

Brown lamb on all sides in hot oil in a large skillet. Place lamb, onion, lemon, bay leaf, and seasonings in slow cooker. Cover and cook on low 8 to 10 hours.

Place 1½ cups of the accumulated stock in a saucepan. Add lemon juice.

Spoon about ¼ cup warm stock into egg yolks, then stir diluted yolks back into stock. Heat gently, stirring constantly, until mixture thickens; do not boil.

Slice lamb, cover with thickened stock, and garnish with olives and parsley.

Herbed Lamb with Squash

Yield: 6 to 8 servings

¾ pound Italian sausage, cut into 1-inch slices
1½ pounds lean lamb, cut into 1-inch cubes
1 cup dry red wine
1 8-ounce can tomato sauce
1 bay leaf
1 teaspoon each thyme, basil, paprika, black pepper, ginger, and oregano
1½ teaspoons salt
1 onion, chopped
1 small butternut squash, cut into 1-inch cubes
2 zucchini squash, cut into ½-inch slices
½ cup sliced mushrooms, browned in butter
Fresh mint leaves

Brown sausage pieces in large skillet. Place in slow cooker.

Brown lamb in accumulated fat. Place in slow cooker.

Drain fat from skillet and add wine. Stir to pick up browned bits, then pour into slow cooker along with all remaining ingredients except the mushrooms and mint leaves. Cover and cook on low about 8 hours.

Just before serving, add mushrooms. Garnish with fresh mint leaves.

Pork with Apples

Yield: 6 servings

2½ pounds lean pork, cut into 1-inch cubes
2 tablespoons vegetable oil
1 tablespoon sugar
1½ teaspoons salt
2 teaspoons paprika
1½ cups apple cider
4 tart apples, peeled, cored, and cut into 1-inch cubes
¼ cup all-purpose flour in ¼ cup cold water, mixed to a paste
2 scallions, thinly sliced
Freshly ground black pepper

Brown pork in hot oil in a large skillet. Drain away accumulated fat. Place meat in slow cooker with sugar, salt, and paprika.

Add some of the cider to the skillet and stir to pick up the browned bits. Add to slow cooker. Cover and cook on low about 8 hours.

Add apples the last 3 hours of cooking.

Pour off juice and thicken in a saucepan with flour-water paste. Return to stew. Garnish with scallions and black pepper.

Pork Chops with Raisins and Oranges

Yield: 6 servings

6 lean pork chops, about 1 inch thick, well-trimmed
Flour, salt, and pepper
2 tablespoons vegetable oil
2 oranges, sections removed from membranes
¼ cup raisins

Sauce

1 cup water
2 tablespoons cornstarch in 2 tablespoons cold water, mixed until smooth
2 tablespoons lemon juice
2 tablespoons sugar
¼ teaspoon allspice

Dredge pork chops with flour that has been seasoned with salt and pepper. Brown in hot oil on both sides in a large skillet. Place in slow cooker with orange sections and raisins.

Combine sauce ingredients in a saucepan. Stir and heat until sauce boils and is thickened. Pour over pork and fruit in slow cooker. Cover and cook on low 5 to 6 hours. Spoon fruit and accumulated cooking liquid over chops when served.

Poultry

Oriental Chicken

Yield: 4 servings

1 2- to 3-pound frying chicken, cut up
⅓ cup soy sauce
2 tablespoons dry sherry
2 tablespoons brown sugar
1 teaspoon ginger or 2 slices fresh gingerroot
1 clove garlic, minced
2 tablespoons cornstarch in 2 tablespoons cold water, stirred until smooth
¼ cup slivered almonds

Place chicken in the slow cooker.

Combine soy sauce, sherry, brown sugar, ginger, and garlic. Pour over chicken. Cover and cook on low about 8 hours.

Pour cooking liquids into a measuring cup. Prepare gravy by combining 1 cup of the accumulated cooking liquid with the cornstarch mixture in a saucepan. Bring to a boil, stirring constantly until thickened. Serve over chicken. Garnish with slivered almonds.

Chicken in Orange Sauce with Cashews

Yield: 4 servings

1 2- to 3-pound frying chicken, cut up
⅓ cup frozen orange-juice concentrate
1 small onion, sliced thin
1 teaspoon salt
10 black peppercorns
3 tablespoons all-purpose flour in
    3 tablespoons cold water, mixed to a
    smooth paste
¼ cup cashew nuts, chopped

Place chicken in the slow cooker. Combine orange juice, onion, salt, and peppercorns. Pour over chicken. Cover and cook on low about 8 hours.

Remove chicken and pour juices into a saucepan. Add flour-water mixture. Heat and stir until mixture boils and is thickened. Serve over chicken. Garnish with cashew nuts.

Chicken Tarragon

Yield: 4 servings

1 3- to 4-pound frying chicken
2 tablespoons soft butter or margarine
1 teaspoon garlic salt

1 teaspoon tarragon
1 tablespoon dried parsley
⅛ teaspoon freshly ground black
    pepper
3 tablespoons vinegar

Gravy

2 tablespoons cornstarch in 2
    tablespoons cold water, stirred until
    smooth
1 cup accumulated cooking liquid

Rub chicken with butter; place in the slow cooker. Combine seasonings and herbs and sprinkle evenly over chicken. Add vinegar. Cover and cook on low about 8 hours. Do not remove lid during this time. Remove chicken to a hot platter.

Prepare the gravy by combining the cornstarch mixture and 1 cup of accumulated liquid in a saucepan. Heat and stir until mixture boils and is thickened. Serve over hot chicken.

Easy Chicken and Mushrooms

Yield: 4 servings

1 2- to 3-pound frying chicken, cut up
2 tablespoons vegetable oil
1 10¾-ounce can cream of mushroom
    soup

Brown chicken in hot oil in a large skillet. Place in slow cooker. Add mushroom soup. Cover and cook on low about 8 hours. Serve chicken with accumulated gravy.

Chicken Stew with Rice

Yield: 4 servings

2 stalks celery, cut into ¼-inch slices
4 carrots, cut into ¼-inch slices
¾ cup converted rice
1 2- to 3-pound frying chicken
2 cups water
1½ teaspoons salt
1 cup frozen, defrosted peas
Fresh parsley leaves

Place celery, carrots, and rice in the bottom of the slow cooker. Add chicken, water, and salt. Cover and cook on low about 8 hours.

Add peas the last 10 minutes of cooking.

Remove skin and bones from the chicken, cube the meat, and return it to the vegetables and rice. Ladle stew into bowls and garnish with fresh parsley leaves.

Chicken and Lentil Stew

Yield: 4 servings

½ pound dried lentils
2 carrots, diced
2 leeks or 3 scallions, sliced
1 teaspoon salt
½ teaspoon sage
¼ teaspoon pepper
1 slice lemon
1 2- to 3-pound frying chicken, cut up
2 to 3 tablespoons bacon fat or
    vegetable oil
2 cups water
¼ cup sour cream

Place the lentils, carrots, leeks, seasonings, and lemon slice in slow cooker.

Brown chicken in bacon fat or oil in a large skillet. Drain away excess fat. Place chicken in slow cooker on top of vegetables.

Add the water to the skillet and stir to loosen the browned bits. Pour into slow cooker. Cover and cook on low about 8 hours. Stir in sour cream and serve at once.

Mandarin Chicken with Almonds

Yield: 4 servings

Chicken

1 teaspoon salt
2 teaspoons paprika
3-pound frying chicken, cut up
3 tablespoons vegetable oil
1 clove garlic
2 tablespoons raisins
½ cup dry red wine

Gravy

1 cup accumulated cooking liquid
2 tablespoons cornstarch in 2
    tablespoons cold water, mixed to a
    smooth paste
2 tablespoons soy sauce
½ teaspoon ground ginger
1 11-ounce can mandarin oranges,
    drained
½ cup heavy cream or sour cream
2 to 4 tablespoons sliced almonds

Combine salt and paprika and rub chicken pieces with the mixture. Brown chicken on all sides in hot oil in a heavy skillet, about 10 minutes. Place in the slow cooker with garlic and raisins.

Add the red wine to the skillet and stir to pick up the browned bits. Add to the chicken. Cover and cook on low about 8 hours.

Pour off accumulated cooking juices, reserving 1 cup. Place this in a saucepan with the cornstarch mixture, soy sauce, and ginger. Bring to a boil, stirring constantly until thickened. Add mandarin oranges. Blend in cream. Pour at once over chicken arranged on a hot platter. Garnish with almonds. Serve at once with rice.

Pasta and Sauces

Beef Enchiladas

Yield: 4 servings

8 to 10 corn tortillas

Filling

1 pound extra-lean ground beef (sausage meat may be substituted for half of the beef)
¼ 8-ounce can tomato sauce
¼ 10-ounce can mild enchilada sauce
1 teaspoon salt
1 medium onion, chopped
½ cup raisins
3 tablespoons chopped, roasted, and peeled green chilies (available canned)
4 ounces cheddar cheese, shredded

Sauce

¾ 8-ounce can tomato sauce
¾ 10-ounce can mild enchilada sauce
2 ounces cheddar cheese, shredded

Brown the beef in a skillet and drain well. Add the tomato and enchilada sauces and salt. Simmer 3 to 4 minutes, until thickened.

Place some of the meat mixture down the center of each tortilla. Sprinkle with chopped onions, raisins, chilies, and cheese. Roll and place, flap-side-down, in slow cooker.

Combine the remaining sauces and pour over the rolled tortillas. Top with cheese. Cover and cook on low about 1 to 1½ hours or until heated through. Serve at once with a cool beverage and a tossed salad.

Chicken Enchiladas

Yield: 3 or 4 servings

8 corn tortillas

Filling

2 cups coarsely chopped cooked chicken
¼ cup black olives, sliced
4 ounces mozzarella cheese, diced
½ cup sour cream
½ teaspoon salt

Sauce

1 10-ounce can mild enchilada sauce
1 8-ounce can tomato sauce
Salt to taste
2 ounces mozzarella cheese, shredded

Combine filling ingredients and place some of the filling down the center of each tortilla. Roll, and place flap-side-down in the slow cooker.

Combine tomato and enchilada sauces and salt. Pour over the tortillas. Top with cheese. Cover and cook on low 1 to 1½ hours, until heated through. Serve at once.

Lasagna

Yield: 4 or 5 servings

This luscious oven dish can be prepared in your slow cooker. Serve with a tossed salad, hearty red wine, and toasted garlic bread.

8 lasagna noodles, cooked according to package directions
8 ounces ricotta cheese
1 tablespoon dried parsley leaves
¼ cup grated Parmesan cheese
8 ounces mozzarella cheese, thickly sliced

Sauce

½ pound ground beef, browned in a skillet (optional, beef may be omitted)
1 6-ounce can tomato paste
2 ounces pepperoni, sliced
¾ cup water
2 teaspoons oregano
¾ teaspoon garlic salt
¼ teaspoon freshly ground black pepper
Parmesan cheese for topping (about 2 tablespoons)

Place half of the noodles in the bottom of the slow cooker. Spread with half the ricotta cheese, parsley, Parmesan cheese, mozzarella cheese, and sauce made by stirring together the sauce ingredients. Repeat. Top with additional Parmesan cheese. Cook on high 1 hour. Turn to low to keep warm if necessary. Serve hot.

Manicotti

Yield: 4 servings

Make it this way and you won't have to heat the oven.

8 to 10 manicotti macaronis

Filling

1 pound ricotta cheese
8 ounces mozzarella cheese, cut into ½-inch cubes
¼ cup grated Parmesan cheese
1 egg
¼ teaspoon salt or garlic salt
½ teaspoon oregano
1 tablespoon fresh parsley leaves, minced

Sauce

1 6-ounce can tomato paste
1 cup water
2 teaspoons oregano
½ teaspoon garlic salt
1 tablespoon olive oil

Cook manicotti macaronis according to package directions; drain well.

Combine ingredients for the filling. Place about 3 tablespoons of this mixture inside each cooked manicotti. Place filled manicotti in slow cooker.

Combine ingredients for the sauce and pour over manicotti. Top with additional Parmesan cheese. Cover and cook on high 1¼ hours. Serve at once with Italian bread, tossed salad, and a dry red wine.

Ricotta and Frijole Casserole with Chili Peppers

Yield: 4 to 6 servings

2 cups cooked brown rice*
2 cups cooked black beans*
½ teaspoon garlic salt
8 ounces ricotta cheese
1 tablespoon dried parsley leaves
8 ounces mozzarella cheese, sliced
About 3 tablespoons canned chopped
    roasted chili peppers (available in
    the Mexican food section of your
    supermarket)
¼ cup grated Parmesan cheese

Combine rice, beans, and garlic salt. Place ⅓ of this mixture in slow cooker. Top with half of the ricotta cheese, parsley, mozzarella slices, and chili peppers. Repeat, ending with a layer of the bean-rice mixture. Top with Parmesan cheese. Heat on high for 1 hour.

Keep casserole warm for a short time, if necessary on low. Serve hot with a tossed salad. Dish may be garnished with parsley leaves or chopped tomatoes.

*Note: 1 cup black beans, soaked overnight, combined with 1 cup uncooked brown rice may be cooked in 5 cups water on high 2 to 3 hours, until tender. Drain away excess water before using in this recipe.

Ziti al Forno

Yield: 6 to 8 servings

1 pound ziti (extra-large macaroni),
    cooked according to package
    directions
1 cup ricotta cheese

1 16-ounce jar of your favorite
    prepared spaghetti sauce
8 ounces mozzarella cheese, cut into
    ½-inch cubes
Salt and pepper to taste
½ cup grated Parmesan cheese

Drain ziti well. Place in slow cooker. Gently combine with ricotta cheese and spaghetti sauce. Add mozzarella cheese, salt, and pepper. Toss lightly. Top with Parmesan cheese. Cover and cook on low about 1 hour, until heated through and mozzarella cheese is completely melted.

Italian Spaghetti Sauce

Yield: 4 or 5 servings

1 pound extra-lean ground beef,
    browned and drained
1 12-ounce can tomato paste
2½ cups water
1 tablespoon oregano
1 teaspoon thyme
¼ teaspoon black pepper
1 teaspoon salt
2 tablespoons fresh parsley leaves,
    chopped
2 cloves garlic
¼ teaspoon fennel seed
12 ounces spaghetti noodles, cooked
    according to package directions

Combine all ingredients except the spaghetti in the slow cooker. Cover and cook on low 3 to 4 hours. Longer cooking diminishes the flavor. Serve sauce hot over prepared spaghetti noodles.

Fresh Tomato Pasta Sauce

Yield: About 1 quart sauce, to serve 4

An excellent way to use an abundant supply of garden-ripened tomatoes.

2 scallions, minced
1 clove garlic, minced
2 tablespoons butter
2 tablespoons olive oil
6 large tomatoes, skinned and coarsely chopped (about 4 cups)
2 teaspoons oregano
¼ teaspoon freshly ground pepper
Salt to taste
Fresh parsley for garnish

Sauté scallions and garlic in a mixture of butter and olive oil in a small skillet until soft, about 3 minutes. Place in slow cooker along with all remaining ingredients. Cover and cook on low about 3 hours or until heated through. Serve at once over hot pasta. Garnish with parsley if you wish.

Bolognese Sauce

Yield: About 1 quart sauce

A traditional Italian spaghetti sauce to serve over your favorite pasta.

3 slices bacon
½ pound chicken livers
2 onions, chopped
1 carrot, chopped
1 stalk celery, chopped
1 pound extra-lean ground beef or veal
1 6-ounce can tomato paste
1½ cups dry white wine
1½ cups beef stock or bouillon

1 teaspoon oregano
½ teaspoon nutmeg
½ teaspoon freshly ground black pepper
Salt to taste

Brown the bacon and remove it from skillet. Lightly brown the chicken livers in the bacon fat. Remove and chop them; chop cooked bacon. Place both in slow cooker.

Add onions, carrot, and celery to skillet. Cook about 3 minutes, until soft. Place in the slow cooker.

Brown beef in skillet; drain and place in slow cooker. Add remaining ingredients to slow cooker. Cover and cook on low about 3 to 4 hours to blend flavors. Serve sauce over hot, well-drained pasta. Garnish with grated Parmesan cheese.

Vegetables

Artichokes

Yield: 4 servings

4 small artichokes
Juice of ½ lemon
2 cups boiling water
1 teaspoon salt
Melted butter

Wash each artichoke; trim off the base. Cut about a 1-inch slice off the top. Using scissors, cut about ¼-inch from the tip of each leaf. Separate leaves and scoop out the hairy white choke with a spoon. Finally, rub the artichokes with lemon juice and place in slow cooker. Add water and salt, cover, and cook on low about 5 hours.

Serve with small bowls of melted butter. Only the lower thick parts of the leaves and the artichoke hearts are edible.

Boston Baked Beans

Yield: 6 to 8 servings

1 pound dried navy beans
6 cups water
4 ounces salt pork, cut into 1-inch cubes
2 teaspoons dry mustard
2 teaspoons salt
½ teaspoon freshly ground black pepper
¾ cup molasses

Soak beans in water in the slow cooker overnight. Do not drain. Cover and cook on high 2 to 3 hours, until tender. Drain, reserving liquid. Add remaining ingredients and sufficient reserved liquid (about ¾ cup) to barely cover beans. Cover and cook on low 10 to 12 hours. Serve hot.

Cassoulet

Yield: 8 servings

1 pound dried navy beans
6 cups water
8 ounces chicken meat, cubed
4 ounces pepperoni, sliced
1 tablespoon bacon fat
1 bay leaf
3 cloves garlic
1 onion, chopped
1 carrot, thinly sliced
1 8-ounce can tomato sauce
½ cup dry red wine
1½ teaspoons salt

1 scallion, cut into ½-inch slices
2 tablespoons bread crumbs

Soak beans overnight in water in slow cooker. Do not drain. Cover and cook on high 2 to 3 hours, until tender. Drain; reserve liquid.

Brown chicken and pepperoni in hot bacon fat in a skillet; drain away excess fat. Add to beans along with the bay leaf, garlic, onion, carrot, tomato sauce, wine, and salt. Add sufficient reserved bean cooking liquid to barely cover beans. Cover and cook on low 10 to 12 hours. Stir in sliced scallion and bread crumbs just before serving.

Apple-Nut Beans with Honey and Butter

Yield: 6 to 8 servings

1 pound dried navy beans
6 cups water
2 slices fresh gingerroot
2 teaspoons salt
4 apples, cored, peeled, and cut into ¾-inch cubes
½ cup honey
¼ cup butter or margarine
½ cup, or more, coarsely chopped walnuts

Soak beans overnight in water in slow cooker. Do not drain. Cover and cook on high 2 to 3 hours, until tender. Drain; reserve liquid. Add ginger, salt, apples, honey, and sufficient reserved liquid to barely cover beans. Cover and cook on low about 8 hours.

Remove and discard ginger slices. Stir in butter and nuts just before serving.

Pork and Beans in Tomato Sauce

Yield: 6 to 8 servings

1 pound dried kidney beans or pink beans
6 cups water
1 pound smoked ham hocks
1 8-ounce can tomato sauce
⅓ cup molasses
1 teaspoon dry mustard
1 teaspoon Worcestershire sauce
2 teaspoons salt

Soak beans overnight in water in the slow cooker. Do not drain. Cover and cook on high 2 to 3 hours, until tender. Drain; reserve liquid. Add remaining ingredients and enough reserved liquid to barely cover beans. Cover and cook 10 to 12 hours on low. Remove ham, chop meat, and return meat to beans. Serve hot.

Barbecue Beans with Burgundy Wine

Yield: 6 to 8 servings

These beans have a wonderful smoky flavor.

1 pound dried kidney beans
6 cups water
1 pound smoked ham hocks
2 teaspoons salt
2 tablespoons sugar

2 teaspoons chili powder
2 teaspoons Worcestershire sauce
1 cup dry Burgundy
1 8-ounce can tomato sauce
1 onion, chopped

Soak beans overnight in water in the slow cooker. Do not drain. Cover and cook on high 2 to 3 hours, until tender. Drain; reserve liquid. Add remaining ingredients and enough reserved liquid (about ¾ cup) to barely cover beans. Cover and cook 10 to 12 hours on low.

Remove ham, chop it, and return meat to beans. Serve hot.

Italian Bean and Cheese Casserole

Yield: 4 servings

1 16-ounce can kidney beans (1½ cups cooked)
2 large onions, chopped
2 cloves garlic, finely minced
5 teaspoons dried basil
1 teaspoon oregano
2 teaspoons salt
2 carrots, coarsely grated
1 large stalk celery, chopped
2 tomatoes, chopped
1 cup (4 ounces) grated cheddar cheese

Combine beans, onions, garlic, herbs, and salt in slow cooker. Cover and heat on high 1 hour.

Stir in carrots, celery, and tomatoes. Top with cheese. Heat on high 10 minutes longer. Serve hot.

Sour-Cream Limas

Yield: 6 to 8 servings

Try these with pork or ham.

1 pound dried baby lima beans
6 cups water
2 teaspoons salt
1 scant cup sour cream
1 green onion, sliced thin
1 teaspoon basil
¼ cup fresh parsley leaves, chopped
Freshly ground black pepper to taste

Soak beans overnight in water in the slow cooker. Do not drain. Add salt, cover, and cook 2 to 3 hours on high until tender. Drain.

Gently stir in remaining ingredients. Cook on low 1 hour. Serve while hot.

Romanian Bean Pot

Yield: 6 to 8 servings

¼ pound dried pinto beans
½ pound dried great northern or navy beans
3 cups water
4 slices bacon, cubed
1 large onion
1 clove garlic
½ teaspoon thyme
1 teaspoon salt
½ pound green beans, cut into 1-inch pieces
½ pound wax beans, cut into 1-inch pieces
2 teaspoons lemon juice

Place dried beans in slow cooker. Add water and soak overnight. Do not drain. Add bacon, onion, garlic, thyme, and salt. Cover

and cook on high 2 to 3 hours, until beans are tender.

Add green beans and wax beans. Cover and cook on low about 20 minutes, until fresh beans are tender. Add lemon juice just before serving.

Pizza Beans

Yield: 4 servings

1 15-ounce can soy beans, undrained
1 cup canned tomatoes, drained
1 small onion, finely chopped
⅓ green pepper, chopped
1 clove garlic, minced
1 teaspoon salt
½ teaspoon oregano
¼ teaspoon rosemary
8 ounces mozzarella cheese, cut into ½-inch cubes
2 slices salami, cut into ¼-inch strips
3 tablespoons Parmesan cheese

Combine vegetables, spices, herbs, and mozzarella cheese in the slow cooker. Top with salami strips and sprinkle with Parmesan cheese. Cover and heat on high for 1 hour. Serve with tossed greens and garlic bread.

Chick Peas and Ham

Yield: 6 to 8 servings

1 pound dried chick peas
6 cups water
½ pound lean ham, cut into ½-inch
   cubes
2 teaspoons marjoram
1 bay leaf
2 onions, chopped
2 carrots, cut into ½-inch cubes
2 potatoes, cut into ½-inch cubes
1 leek or 2 scallions, sliced
2 teaspoons salt
Chopped fresh parsley for garnish

Soak peas in water in the slow cooker overnight. Do not drain. Cover and cook on high 2 to 3 hours, until tender. Drain, reserving liquid.

Add all remaining ingredients, except parsley. Add enough reserved liquid barely to cover beans. Cover and cook on low about 8 hours. Serve in hot bowls garnished with parsley.

Eggplant Parmesan

Yield: 4 to 6 servings

2 eggs
1 teaspoon salt
1 large eggplant, pared and cut into
   ⅓-inch slices
Olive oil or vegetable oil
2 8-ounce cans tomato sauce
2 teaspoons oregano
Garlic salt to taste
½ cup grated Parmesan cheese
½ pound sliced mozzarella cheese

Combine eggs and 1 teaspoon salt. Dip eggplant slices in this mixture and sauté in hot oil until golden brown on both sides.

Combine tomato sauce, oregano, and garlic salt.

Place half the eggplant slices in the bottom of the slow cooker. Top with half the Parmesan cheese and half the mozzarella cheese. Cover with half the tomato-sauce mixture. Repeat. Cover; cook on low about 1 hour, until heated through.

Sauerkraut and Knockwurst

Yield: 4 servings

1 16-ounce can sauerkraut, drained,
   and rinsed several times in cold
   water
2 apples, cored, peeled, and cut into
   ½-inch cubes
1 onion, sliced
¼ teaspoon caraway seeds
¼ cup water
4 knockwursts

Combine sauerkraut, apples, onion, and seasonings in slow cooker. Add knockwurst; cook on low 4 to 5 hours.

Acorn Squash Stuffed with Sausage and Apples

Yield: 4 servings

The combination of spicy sausage and apples in the stuffing is quite good with the mild squash. This dish is best for four persons, as more halved stuffed squashes will not fit inside a 3½-quart cooker.

1 pound sausage meat
1 small onion, chopped
2 apples, cored and chopped
½ teaspoon oregano
Salt to taste
2 acorn squashes, halved, seeds
   removed
¼ cup water

Brown sausage meat well and break into small pieces. Drain well. Combine meat with onion, apples, oregano, and salt. Generously fill each squash half with the mixture and arrange filled halves in the slow cooker in staggered layers. Pour about ¼ cup water into the bottom of the cooker. Cover and cook on low for 6 to 8 hours, until squash is tender. Serve at once.

Baked Butternut Squash and Fruit

Yield: 6 servings

1 2-pound butternut squash, quartered,
   seeded, peeled, and cut into ¼-inch
   slices
3 apples, cored and cut into ¼-inch
   round slices

¼ cup raisins
½ lemon, cut into 4 round slices
½ cup brown sugar
1 teaspoon salt
½ teaspoon cinnamon
4 tablespoons butter or margarine

Combine squash, apples, and raisins in slow cooker. Arrange lemon slices on top. Sprinkle with sugar, salt, and cinnamon. Dot with butter. Cover and cook on low 4 to 6 hours. Serve hot in small bowls with the rich, zesty sauce.

Zucchini-Squash Bake

Yield: 4 to 6 servings

2 large zucchini squashes, unpeeled,
   cut into ½-inch slices
1 cup canned tomatoes, well-drained
1 tablespoon olive oil
1 small onion, chopped
1 clove garlic, minced
½ teaspoon salt
½ teaspoon basil
¼ teaspoon freshly ground black
   pepper
2 tablespoons grated Parmesan cheese

Combine all ingredients except cheese in the slow cooker. Cover and cook on low 4 to 5 hours. Sprinkle with cheese just before serving.

Soups

House Bean Soup

Yield: 8 servings

A simple-to-make, filling soup served every day in the United States House of Representatives' cafeteria. Try the Senate Bean Soup also.

1 pound dried navy beans
7 or 8 cups water
1 pound smoked ham hocks
Salt and freshly ground pepper to taste

Soak beans in water overnight in the slow cooker. Do not drain. Cover and cook on high about 3 hours, until tender.

Add ham and seasonings. Cover and cook on low 10 to 12 hours.

Remove ham, chop meat, and return it to soup. Add more water if you wish, and adjust seasonings. Serve hot for lunch.

Senate Bean Soup

Yield: 8 servings

Your soup will have more meat in it, otherwise this is the hearty soup served every day in the United States Senate's cafeteria.

1 pound dried navy beans
7 or 8 cups water (approximately)
1 pound smoked ham hocks
2 onions, finely chopped
4 stalks celery with leaves, finely chopped
1 clove garlic, minced

¼ cup fresh parsley leaves, finely chopped
Salt and freshly ground black pepper to taste

Soak beans in the water overnight in the slow cooker. Do not drain. Cover and cook on high about 3 hours, until very tender.

Add remaining ingredients, except salt and pepper, cover, and cook on low 10 to 12 hours.

Remove ham, chop meat, and return it to soup. Season to taste with salt and pepper. More water may be added if soup seems too thick. Serve piping hot in large soup bowls—a meal in itself!

Bean Soup with Frankfurters

Yield: 6 to 8 servings

1 pound dried great northern or navy beans
7 or 8 cups water
1 carrot, diced
1 stalk celery with leaves, diced
1 large onion, chopped
2 teaspoons salt
¼ teaspoon pepper
2 or 3 frankfurters, sliced
2 tablespoons fresh parsley leaves, chopped

Soak beans overnight in water in the slow cooker. Do not drain. Cover and cook on high about 3 hours, until tender.

Add vegetables and seasonings. Cover and cook on low 10 to 12 hours.

Add frankfurters the last 30 minutes of cooking. Stir to mash some of the beans and thicken the soup. Serve hot, garnished with fresh parsley.

French Bean and Potato Soup

Yield: 6 servings

½ pound dried great northern or navy beans
6 cups water
½ cup dry red wine
12 ounces lean salt pork or smoked ham, cut into 1-inch cubes
3 potatoes, cubed
2 cloves garlic
1½ teaspoons salt
¼ teaspoon black pepper
1 10-ounce package frozen green beans, defrosted
3 tomatoes, peeled and cubed
Fresh parsley, chopped

Soak beans in water overnight in the slow cooker. Do not drain. Add wine, pork, potatoes, garlic, salt, and pepper. Cover and cook on high about 3 hours, until beans and potatoes are tender.

Add green beans and tomatoes and continue cooking on high 10 minutes longer. Serve at once garnished with fresh parsley.

Homestyle Lentil Soup

Yield: 8 servings

1 pound dried lentils
6 cups water
2 medium onions, chopped
4 carrots, sliced, cubed, or trimmed in the shape of round balls
1 teaspoon thyme
1 bay leaf
1 teaspoon salt
2 tablespoons sugar
10 whole black peppercorns

4 to 5 ounces heavily cured ham or Canadian bacon, cut into ½-inch cubes
½ cup dry red wine

Combine all ingredients, except for the wine, in the slow cooker. Cover and cook on low 6 to 8 hours.

Just before serving, stir in the red wine. Adjust seasonings, if necessary. Additional water may be added for a thinner consistency.

Chunky-style Split-Pea Soup with Ham

Yield: 8 servings

1 pound dried split peas
6 cups hot water
1 pound smoked ham hocks
3 carrots, cut into ½-inch cubes
2 potatoes, cut into ½-inch cubes
1 onion, chopped
2 stalks celery, chopped
2 teaspoons salt
12 peppercorns
Parmesan cheese, grated, for garnish

Combine all ingredients except cheese in the slow cooker. Cover and cook on low 5 to 6 hours. Turn heat to high and cook an additional 1 to 1½ hours or until peas and vegetables are tender.

Remove ham; cube meat and return it to soup. Stir to mash some of the peas and thicken soup. Add additional water if you wish to thin the consistency. Garnish with grated Parmesan cheese when served.

Spinach Soup with Beef

Yield: 6 servings

1½ pounds lean beef with bones
6 cups water
1½ teaspoons salt
6 medium potatoes, cubed
3 onions, sliced
1½ pounds fresh spinach, washed and
    coarsely chopped
4 tomatoes, peeled and cut into wedges
Nutmeg and freshly ground black
    pepper

Combine beef, water, salt, potatoes, and onions in slow cooker. Cover and cook on low about 8 hours.

Add spinach and tomatoes the last 10 minutes of cooking.

Remove meat from soup, cut it into 1-inch cubes, and return it to soup. Season with nutmeg and pepper. Add additional salt if desired.

Julienne Vegetable Soup

Yield: 6 servings

2 medium onions, sliced
½ pound carrots, cut into julienne
    strips
2 celery stalks, cut into julienne strips
2 leeks, sliced
3 kohlrabi or turnips, cut into julienne
    strips
5 cups Brown Beef Broth (see next
    recipe) or bouillon
1½ teaspoons salt
1 teaspoon dried chervil
⅛ teaspoon pepper
Fresh parsley leaves

Combine all ingredients, except the chervil, pepper, and parsley, in the slow cooker. Cover and cook on low 4 to 5 hours or until vegetables are tender.

Add chervil and pepper 10 minutes before soup is done. Ladle into large bowls and garnish with parsley.

Brown Beef Broth or Bouillon

Yield: 6 cups

2 pounds beef shanks (or 2 pounds
    beef—about ⅓ should be bones)
2 tablespoons vegetable oil
6 cups water
4 whole black peppercorns
2 carrots, quartered
2 onions, quartered
1½ teaspoons salt

Brown meat on all sides in a large skillet. Place meat in the slow cooker.

Add some of the water to the skillet and stir to pick up the browned bits. Add to the meat along with remaining water, vegetables, and salt. Cover and cook on low about 10 hours.

Strain broth before using in soups or other recipes.

Chicken Broth or Stock

Yield: 6 cups

2 pounds chicken with bones, cut up
6 cups water
1 small onion, chopped
1 large stalk celery with leaves,
    chopped
4 whole black peppercorns
1½ teaspoons salt

Combine all ingredients in slow cooker. Cover; cook on low about 10 hours.

Strain broth before using in other recipes.

This broth may be used whenever a recipe calls for white stock. It is good also for use in the gravy of Oriental stir-fry dishes.

Consommé

Yield: 6 cups

This is a clear soup usually made from two kinds of meat or meat and poultry.

1 pound lean beef, cut into 1-inch cubes
1 pound lean veal, cut into 1-inch cubes (1 pound cut-up chicken with bones may be substituted)
6 cups water
1 carrot, chopped
1 stalk celery with leaves, chopped
1 onion, chopped
4 whole black peppercorns
2 whole cloves
1 teaspoon dried herbs (your favorite)
1½ teaspoons salt

Combine all ingredients in slow cooker. Cover and cook on low about 10 hours.

Clarify soup by pouring it through several layers of cheesecloth. Skim off fat. Serve very hot.

Barley Soup with Beef and Vegetables

Yield: 6 to 8 servings

½ pound lean beef, cut into ½-inch cubes
1 tablespoon vegetable oil
6 cups water

4 carrots, cut into ½-inch cubes
2 stalks celery with leaves, cut into ½-inch cubes
4 green onions, cut into ¼-inch slices
¼ cup fresh parsley leaves, chopped
1 tomato, peeled and chopped
½ cup barley
1½ teaspoons salt
½ teaspoon whole peppercorns
½ teaspoon thyme

Brown meat in hot oil in a skillet. Add a little of the water to the skillet and stir to pick up browned bits.

Pour into slow cooker. Add remaining water and all other ingredients except the thyme. Cover and cook on low 4 to 6 hours, until vegetables and barley are tender. Add thyme just before serving.

Neopolitan Minestrone

Yield: 4 to 6 servings

4 cups Brown Beef Broth (see Index)
2 tablespoons olive oil
1 clove garlic
1 green pepper, cubed
2 zucchini, cubed
6 black olives, chopped
2 anchovies, mashed
2 cups cooked rice
4 mint leaves
½ teaspoon basil
½ teaspoon oregano
½ cup tomato paste
Grated Parmesan cheese

Place all ingredients except cheese in slow cooker. Cover and cook on high about 30 minutes or until all ingredients are heated through.

Remove garlic clove. Serve hot, garnished with Parmesan cheese.

Beef Soup with Dumplings

Yield: 4 or 5 servings

1 pound lean beef, cut into 1-inch cubes or smaller
2 tablespoons vegetable oil
5 cups water
1 teaspoon salt
2 stalks celery with leaves, chopped
1 onion, chopped
2 carrots, cut into ½ × 1½-inch sticks
1 leek or 3 scallions, sliced
Fresh parsley leaves, chopped

Dumplings

1 cup all-purpose flour
1½ teaspoons baking powder
½ teaspoon salt
2 tablespoons vegetable oil
1 egg
⅓ cup milk
2 tablespoons fresh parsley leaves, minced

Brown beef in hot oil in a large skillet. Add a little of the water and stir to loosen the browned bits. Pour into the slow cooker. Add remaining water, salt, celery, onion, carrots, and leek. Cover and cook on low 4 to 6 hours or until vegetables are tender. Turn heat to high and prepare dumplings.

To prepare dumplings, sift together the flour, baking powder, and salt. Stir together the oil, egg, milk, and parsley leaves. Add all at once to the dry ingredients and stir just until blended. Drop small amounts from a tablespoon into the hot soup. Cover and continue to cook on high for 20 to 30 minutes, until dumplings rise to the surface and are cooked through. Serve at once garnished with fresh parsley leaves.

Beef-Vegetable Noodle Soup

Yield: 6 to 8 servings

2 pounds beef shanks with bones
2 tablespoons vegetable oil
4 to 5 cups water
1 16-ounce can tomatoes
2 carrots, cut into ½-inch cubes
2 stalks celery with leaves, sliced
1 leek or 3 scallions, sliced
2 cloves garlic
2 potatoes, cut into ½-inch cubes
1½ teaspoons salt
1 cup frozen, defrosted peas
6 ounces egg noodles, cooked according to package directions and drained

Brown beef shanks in vegetable oil in a large skillet. Drain off accumulated fat and place meat in slow cooker.

Add a little of the water to the skillet and stir to pick up the browned bits. Add to the meat in the slow cooker along with remaining water, carrots, celery, leek, garlic, potatoes, and salt. Cover and cook on low about 8 hours.

Remove meat, cube it, and return it to soup. Add peas, cover, and continue to cook 10 to 15 minutes.

Add cooked noodles. Serve at once.

Italian Minestrone

Yield: 6 servings

1 pound lean beef, cut into ½-inch cubes
5 cups water
2 medium onions, chopped
1 stalk celery, chopped

4 carrots, cut into small bite-size sticks
2 turnips, cubed
1 medium potato, cubed
1 clove garlic
1 teaspoon salt
½ small head cabbage, finely shredded
2 ounces macaroni, cooked according
  to package directions and drained
½ cup cooked rice, optional
2 or 3 peeled tomatoes, cut into small
  wedges
Chopped fresh parsley
Grated Parmesan cheese

Combine beef, water, onions, celery, carrots, turnips, potato, garlic, and salt. Cover and cook on low about 8 hours.

Turn heat to high the last 20 minutes of cooking and add cabbage.

Add the cooked macaroni, rice, and tomatoes the last 10 minutes of cooking on high.

Ladle at once into bowls and serve with parsley and grated Parmesan cheese or Pesto Sauce (see Index).

Swiss Minestrone

Yield: 6 to 8 servings

1½ pounds beef shanks
2 tablespoons vegetable oil
5 cups water
4 medium potatoes, diced
5 carrots, sliced
3 stalks celery, sliced
1 cup cubed pumpkin, if available
1 onion, chopped
2 scallions, sliced
½ pound cabbage, shredded
1 8-ounce can tomato sauce
1½ teaspoons salt
1 cup cooked rice

1 10-ounce package frozen green beans,
  defrosted
¼ teaspoon rosemary
¼ teaspoon sage
Chopped parsley

Brown beef shanks in hot oil in a large skillet. Place in slow cooker.

Add some of the water to the skillet and stir to pick up the browned bits. Add to the slow cooker along with the potatoes, carrots, celery, pumpkin, onion, scallions, cabbage, tomato sauce, and salt. Cover and cook on low about 8 hours.

Remove meat, cube, and return it to soup. Add cooked rice, beans, rosemary, and sage. Cover and continue cooking on high about 10 minutes. Serve soup hot, garnished with parsley.

Pesto Sauce for Minestrone Soups

Yield: About 1 cup

Stir a little of this sauce into any vegetable or minestrone soup just before serving.

1 cup fresh basil leaves or fresh parsley
  leaves
½ cup grated Parmesan cheese
¼ cup olive oil
1 clove garlic

Place all ingredients in a blender and blend at high speed until smooth. Use at once or cover and refrigerate no more than a week.

Scottish Lamb Soup

Yield: 4 servings

1 pound lean lamb, cut into 1-inch
  cubes
2 tablespoons vegetable oil
6 cups water
1½ teaspoons salt
2 carrots, sliced
3 parsnips, sliced
3 leeks, sliced
1 pound small potatoes, peeled
½ cup barley
1 tablespoon sugar
1 tablespoon dried mint leaves
Tarragon vinegar to taste
Fresh parsley leaves

Brown lamb in a large skillet in hot oil.
Place in slow cooker.

Add some of the water to the skillet and
stir to pick up the browned bits. Add to
meat with remaining water, salt, vegetables,
barley, sugar, and mint leaves. Cover and
cook on low about 6 hours. Season to taste
with a little tarragon vinegar. Serve very hot
garnished with parsley.

Lamb and Vegetable Soup

Yield: 5 to 6 servings

1 pound lean lamb, cut into bite-size
  cubes
2 tablespoons vegetable oil
5 cups water
2 tablespoons tomato paste
1 medium onion, chopped
2 stalks celery with leaves, sliced
4 carrots, sliced
2 potatoes, cut into ½-inch cubes
1 leek, sliced, optional

½ small head cabbage, coarsely
  shredded
Salt and pepper to taste
1 10-ounce package frozen cauliflower,
  defrosted
1 cup frozen green beans, defrosted
1 cup fresh spinach leaves, torn into
  bite-size pieces
2 tablespoons fresh parsley leaves,
  chopped

Brown lamb in hot oil in a large skillet.
Add a little of the water and stir to pick up
the browned bits. Pour into the slow cooker
along with remaining water, tomato paste,
onion, celery, carrots, potatoes, leek, cabbage, salt, and pepper. Cover and cook on
low about 8 hours.

Turn heat to high and add cauliflower
and green beans. Cook 10 to 15 minutes
longer. Just before serving, stir in spinach
and parsley. Serve at once.

Shrimp Soup

Yield: 4 or 5 servings

4 ounces cooked ham, cubed
2 slices bacon, cubed
4 cups hot water or beef broth
⅓ cup tomato paste
3 tablespoons catsup
½ cup converted rice
3 tomatoes, peeled and cubed
12 green olives, coarsely chopped
1 tablespoon capers
½ teaspoon oregano
¼ teaspoon coriander
10 ounces frozen or fresh cleaned and
  deveined shrimp
Salt and pepper to taste

Brown ham and bacon in a skillet. Place in slow cooker with water, tomato paste, catsup, rice, and tomatoes. Cover and cook on low about 3 hours or until rice is tender.

Turn heat to high. Add remaining ingredients and cook on high 5 to 10 minutes or just until shrimp has heated through. Serve at once.

Fish Chowder with White Wine

Yield: 5 or 6 servings

2 slices bacon
2 medium onions, chopped
1 clove garlic
¼ cup tomato paste
2 cups beef broth
1 cup dry white wine
4 tomatoes, peeled and cubed
2 teaspoons paprika
Salt to taste
1 tablespoon lemon juice
1 to 1½ pounds fish fillets, cut into bite-size pieces
Chopped fresh parsley leaves

Brown bacon in a large skillet. Remove, crumble, and place in slow cooker. Brown onions and garlic in the accumulated bacon fat. Pour into slow cooker along with all remaining ingredients except the fish and parsley. Cover and cook on high for 1 hour.

Add fish and continue to cook on high 10 to 15 minutes or until fish is tender.

Serve at once or keep warm on low for about an hour. Overcooking will make fish tough. Garnish with chopped parsley.

Yugoslavian Apple Soup

Yield: 4 servings

6 tart apples, cored, peeled, and sliced
2 cups water
1 cup dry white wine
2 tablespoons sugar
1 teaspoon cinnamon
Juice of half a lemon
3 tablespoons butter
Croutons for garnish

Combine apples, water, wine, sugar, cinnamon, and lemon juice in slow cooker. Cover and cook on low about 6 hours or until apples are very soft.

Add butter. Puree in a food mill. Serve hot, garnished with croutons.

Breads

Swedish Limpa Round Rye Bread

Yield: 1 loaf

This loaf has an orange-licorice flavor and complements ham and cheese slices well.

In the recipe for Light Rye Bread (see page 78), add to the dissolved yeast mixture:

1 teaspoon anise seeds
Grated rind of 1 orange
3 tablespoons of sugar in place of the molasses

Follow recipe directions as given.

Boston Brown Bread

Yield: 1 5-cup loaf or 3 15-ounce can loaves

Serve this with Boston Baked Beans (see Index). Note: You will need 3 empty 15- or 16-ounce vegetable cans for the small loaves.

1 tablespoon vegetable oil
1 egg
½ cup molasses
1 cup buttermilk (or 1 cup milk plus
    ½ tablespoon vinegar)
½ cup raisins
1 cup rye flour
½ cup whole-wheat flour
⅓ cup cornmeal
1 teaspoon baking soda
1 teaspoon salt

Turn the slow cooker high. Butter a 5-cup mold or 3 15- or 16-ounce vegetable cans. Boil about 2 cups water and set aside.

Combine liquid ingredients and raisins.

Stir together the dry ingredients. Stir the wet ingredients into the dry ingredients all at once just until blended. Do not overmix. Pour immediately into a prepared mold or cans (fill only ⅔ full). Cover mold or cans with aluminum foil and tie it on with string. Place in the slow cooker. Add boiling water to come halfway up the sides of the molds. Cook on high 2 to 3 hours.

Remove from slow cooker and cool 10 minutes. Invert mold or cans to remove bread. Cool completely on a wire rack. Serve with butter or cream cheese.

Round Light Rye Sandwich Bread

Yield: 1 loaf

1 package active dry yeast
1 cup warm water (105-115°F)
1 tablespoon molasses
2 tablespoons vegetable oil
1 tablespoon caraway seeds
1½ cups all-purpose flour
1½ cups rye flour
1½ teaspoons salt

Dissolve yeast in warm water in a large bowl. Add molasses, oil, seeds, and all-purpose flour. Stir vigorously until smooth. Cover bowl and let stand in a warm place for ½ hour.

Stir in the rye flour and salt. Knead on a lightly floured surface until smooth, about 1 to 2 minutes.

Pat into a greased 48-ounce fruit-juice can, trimmed to barely fit under the lid of the covered slow cooker. Place can in slow cooker. Cover and cook on high for 2 hours. Do not remove lid even if the loaf rises and touches it. Loaf is done when a skewer inserted into loaf comes out clean.

Cool bread in can about ½ hour. Invert and shake to loosen. Cool on a wire rack. Serve warm.

Apricot-Nut Bread

Yield: 1 round loaf

½ cup chopped dried apricots
½ cup water
1 egg
2 tablespoons vegetable oil
1 cup sugar

½ cup orange juice
¾ teaspoon salt
1 cup walnuts, chopped
2 cups sifted all-purpose flour
3 teaspoons baking powder
¼ teaspoon baking soda

Soak apricots in the water for 30 minutes.

Combine egg, oil, sugar, orange juice, and salt. Beat until light and fluffy. Stir in apricot-water mixture and nuts.

Sift together the flour, baking powder, and soda. Stir into the beaten mixture only until well-blended.

Pour into a greased 7- to 8-cup mold or 3-pound shortening can. Cover loosely with aluminum foil. Place in slow cooker and cook on high 2 to 3 hours or until a long skewer inserted into bread comes out clean.

Cool 10 to 20 minutes in can and invert on a wire rack. Cool completely before slicing.

Round Pumpernickel Sandwich Bread

Yield: 1 loaf

1 package active dry yeast
¾ cup lukewarm water
2 tablespoons molasses
1¼ teaspoons salt
2 tablespoons vegetable oil
1¼ cups all-purpose flour
1¼ cups rye flour
1 tablespoon caraway seeds

Dissolve yeast in warm water in a large bowl. Add molasses, salt, oil, and the all-purpose flour. Stir vigorously until smooth. Cover and let stand in a warm place for ½ hour.

Stir in the rye flour and caraway seeds. Knead on a lightly floured surface about 2 minutes, until smooth. Pat into a greased 48-ounce fruit-juice can trimmed to barely fit under the lid of the covered slow cooker.

Place can in slow cooker. Cover and cook on high about 2 hours, until a skewer inserted into the loaf comes out clean.

Allow loaf to cool in can about ½ hour. Invert and shake gently to loosen loaf. Cool on a wire rack. Slice when cool.

Pumpkin Tea Bread

Yield: 1 round loaf

1 cup sugar
½ cup butter
2 eggs
¾ teaspoon cinnamon
½ teaspoon nutmeg
½ teaspoon cloves
½ teaspoon salt
1 cup pureed cooked pumpkin
   (canned may be used)
2 cups sifted all-purpose flour
1½ teaspoons baking powder
½ teaspoon baking soda

Combine sugar, butter, eggs, spices, and salt. Beat until light and fluffy. Add pumpkin and beat only until combined.

Sift together the flour, baking powder, and baking soda. Stir into the beaten mixture.

Pour into a greased 3-pound shortening can or other 7- to 8-cup mold. Cover loosely with aluminum foil. Place in slow cooker. Cover and cook on high 2 to 3 hours or until a long skewer inserted into bread comes out clean.

Cool 10 to 20 minutes, then invert mold on a rack. Slice and serve with whipped

Round Raisin Whole-Wheat Bread

Yield: 1 round loaf

Note: A 3-pound shortening can or 6- to 8-cup mold is needed.

    1 cup buttermilk
    1 egg
    ¼ cup molasses
    2 tablespoons vegetable oil
    2 tablespoons sugar
    ¾ cup raisins, cut up
    ¼ cup chopped nuts
    1 cup whole-wheat flour
    1 cup sifted all-purpose flour
    1 teaspoon baking powder
    1 teaspoon baking soda

Combine buttermilk, egg, molasses, oil, and sugar. Beat until well-blended. Add raisins and nuts.

Stir together the flours, baking powder, and baking soda. Add the buttermilk mixture and stir only until the dry ingredients are moistened.

Pour into a greased 3-pound shortening can or other 6- to 8-cup mold. Cover loosely with aluminum foil. Place in slow cooker. Cover and cook on high 2 to 3 hours or until a skewer inserted into bread comes out clean.

Cool in mold 10 to 20 minutes. Invert and cool on wire rack. Cool completely before slicing.

Round Whole-Wheat Sandwich Bread

Yield: 1 loaf

Begin this at 9 o'clock in the morning and serve it for lunch. Perfect for round lunch-meat slices. Bread rises and cooks in the slow cooker.

    1 package active dry yeast
    1 cup warm water (105-115°F)
    1 tablespoon sugar
    2 tablespoons vegetable oil
    1½ cups whole-wheat flour
    1½ cups all-purpose flour
    1 teaspoon salt

Dissolve yeast in warm water in a large bowl. Add sugar, oil, and whole-wheat flour. Stir vigorously until smooth. Cover and let stand in a warm place for ½ hour.

Stir in all-purpose flour and salt. Knead on a lightly floured surface 1 to 2 minutes, until smooth. Pat into a greased 48-ounce fruit-juice can trimmed to barely fit under the lid of the covered slow cooker.

Place can in slow cooker. Cover and cook on high about 2 hours, until a skewer inserted into the loaf comes out clean.

Allow loaf to cool in can about ½ hour. Invert and shake gently to loosen. Cool on a wire rack. Serve while warm. Loaf will rise and touch lid during cooking; do not take lid off until loaf has cooked the full 2 hours.

Desserts

Baked Apples with Cranberry Sauce

Yield: 4 servings

4 large apples, cored but not through
   the bottom
8 tablespoons whole cranberry sauce
1 tablespoon butter
4 tablespoons sugar

Fill the cored apples with cranberry sauce. Dot with butter. Place in slow cooker, not touching the sides. Stack, if necessary. Cover and cook on low 3 to 4 hours.

Remove to small dishes. Serve hot or cold. Sprinkle with sugar just before serving.

Apples Baked in Wine with Rum

Yield: 6 servings

2 tablespoons chopped walnuts
2 tablespoons chopped dates
1 tablespoon chopped candied cherries
2 tablespoons confectioners' sugar
6 large apples, cored but not through
   the bottom
1 cup dry white wine
3 tablespoons rum
Whipped cream for a garnish

Combine walnuts, dates, cherries, and sugar. Fill the cored apples with the mixture. Arrange filled apples in the slow cooker, not touching the sides, where they may burn. Apples may be stacked upon one another if staggered. Pour wine around apples. Cover and cook on low 3 to 4 hours.

Remove to dessert dishes and ladle the wine and accumulated cooking juices around each. Pour rum over fillings and garnish with whipped cream.

Baked Apples with Assorted Fillings

Yield: 6 apples

6 apples, cored but not through the
   bottom
Brown sugar and cinnamon
Raisins
Honey

Stuff the cored apples with either the raisins, brown sugar, or honey. Arrange in the slow cooker, not touching the sides, where they may burn. Apples may be stacked if staggered in layers. Water is not necesssary unless you wish to add about ½ cup to serve with the apples when they are done. Cook on low 3 to 4 hours, until soft. Serve hot or chilled.

Apple Slump

Yield: 4 or 5 servings

A favorite recipe of Louisa May Alcott, author of *Little Women,* is adapted here for your slow cooker. She was so fond of this dessert, she named her Concord, Massachusetts, home "Apple Slump" after it. You'll find it to be a hearty fruit dessert.

6 cups apple slices
½ cup sugar
1 teaspoon cinnamon
½ cup water

Dumplings

1 cup sifted all-purpose flour
1½ teaspoons baking powder
½ teaspoon salt
2 tablespoons butter or margarine
½ cup milk

Nutmeg Sauce

Scant ½ cup sugar
½ tablespoon all-purpose flour
½ cup water
½ tablespoon butter
½ tablespoon nutmeg

Place apples, sugar, cinnamon, and water in slow cooker. Cover and cook on low 4 to 6 hours, until apples are tender. Turn heat on high and prepare dumplings.

To prepare dumplings, sift together the flour, baking powder, and salt. Cut in butter; stir in the milk. Drop from a tablespoon on top of hot apples. Cover and continue to cook on high for about 30 minutes without removing the lid.

Meanwhile, prepare Nutmeg Sauce. Combine sugar and flour in a saucepan. Stir in water; bring to a boil, stirring constantly until thickened. Stir in butter and nutmeg.

Place hot apples and dumplings in dessert bowls and spoon hot Nutmeg Sauce over each.

Fruits and Honey Dessert

Yield: 4 servings

2 peaches, peeled and cubed
2 cups fresh or frozen pineapple cubes
2 apples, peeled, cored, and cut into rings
1¼ cups water or pineapple juice
¼ cup honey
2 lemon slices
1 stick cinnamon
1 banana, sliced lengthwise then in half
2 tablespoons sliced blanched almonds
½ cup heavy cream, whipped
4 cherries

Combine all but the last 4 ingredients in the slow cooker. Cover and cook on low about 2 to 3 hours. Add banana. Divide into 4 portions.

Serve warm, garnished with almonds, whipped cream, and cherries.

Pears in Wine

Yield: 6 servings

6 pears, cored and halved lengthwise
¾ cup brown sugar
1 cup dry red wine
4 lemon slices
4 whole cloves
1 stick cinnamon
Sweetened heavy cream, whipped

Place pears in slow cooker. Combine sugar, wine, lemon, and spices. Pour over pears. Cover and cook on low for 3 to 4 hours. Cool and serve with whipped cream.

Stewed Plums

Yield: 8 servings

3 pounds plums
Water
4 whole cloves
1 stick cinnamon
Outer peel of 1 lemon
Sugar to taste
Sour cream

Wash plums and poke a few holes into each with a toothpick. Place in slow cooker. Add water to half the depth of the fruit. Add cloves, cinnamon, and lemon peel. Cover and cook on low 3 to 4 hours or until tender. Add sugar to sweeten.

Serve warm or cold with a dollop of sour cream.

Mixed Stewed Fruit

Yield: 4 to 6 servings

A fruit compote with a light, delicately spiced, slightly sweet, citrus-flavored sauce.

1 11-ounce package mixed dried fruits
2 apples, peeled, cored, and sliced into ½-inch-thick rings
⅓ cup raisins, golden preferred
2 lemon slices
¼ cup orange juice
¼ cup sugar
1 stick cinnamon
2 cups water

Combine all ingredients in the slow cooker. Cover and cook on low 2 to 3 hours. Serve warm or chilled.

Variations: Soft fruits such as sliced bananas, canned pineapple, fresh strawberries, or seedless grapes can be added just before serving.

Pink Cinnamon – Vanilla Custard

Yield: 4 servings

A quick and nourishing dessert. The slow cooker is used here in place of your oven.

2 cups milk
¼ cup sugar
2 eggs
1 teaspoon vanilla
Generous dash cinnamon
Few drops red food coloring

Whisk together all ingredients in a 1-quart mold until well-blended. Cover mold with aluminum foil and set on a trivet in the slow cooker. Add boiling water to a depth of about 1 inch. Cover and cook on high about 1¼ hours or until a knife inserted 1 inch from the mold sides comes out clean.

Serve warm or chilled. Serve alone or spooned over sliced fresh fruit. Do not overcook, or the network of egg and milk proteins will contract and water will separate out.

Variation: Make Honey-Vanilla Custard by omitting cinnamon and using ⅓ cup honey in place of ¼ cup sugar in preceding recipe.

Jolly Madame

Yield: 4 small servings

A dessert that is a little different—not quite a pudding, not really a cake.

4 egg yolks
¼ cup sugar
Pinch salt
Fresh bread crumbs from 3 slices bread
4 egg whites
½ cup heavy cream
2 tablespoons brown sugar
2 tablespoons finely chopped almonds

Caramel Sauce

3 tablespoons sugar
6 tablespoons water

Beat yolks, sugar, and salt together in a small bowl until light and lemon-colored. Add bread crumbs.

Beat egg whites until stiff.

Whip cream.

Fold yolk-crumb-sugar mixture, beaten whites, and whipped cream together.

Butter a 4-cup mold; sprinkle with brown sugar and almonds. Fill with prepared batter and cover tightly with aluminum foil.

Place mold on a trivet in the slow cooker. Add boiling water to come halfway up sides of mold. Cover and cook on high 1 hour.

Remove mold, cool, and invert to remove pudding. Serve with Caramel Sauce.

To make the sauce, melt and brown sugar over low heat in a skillet. Add water, bring to a rapid boil, remove from heat, and pour at once over pudding.

Zwieback Pudding

Yield: 4 servings

¼ cup butter
¼ cup sugar
4 egg yolks
10 pieces zwieback (4 ounces), crushed to fine crumbs
3 ounces ground almonds
½ cup raisins
Grated rind of lemon
1 cup milk
½ teaspoon salt
4 egg whites
2 tablespoons bread crumbs

Cream butter and sugar; gradually beat in yolks until mixture is light. Blend in zwieback crumbs, almonds, raisins, lemon peel, milk, and salt.

In a separate bowl, beat egg whites until stiff. Carefully fold into egg-yolk mixture. Pour into a 1-quart mold that has been buttered and sprinkled with bread crumbs. Cover mold with aluminum foil and place on a trivet in a slow cooker. Add boiling water to come about halfway up the sides of the mold. Cover and cook on high about 1 hour or until a toothpick inserted into pudding comes out clean.

Remove mold, let rest for 5 minutes, then turn out onto a platter. Serve warm.

English Plum Pudding

Yield: 6 servings

1 cup raisins
1½ cups currants (or raisins if currants are unavailable)
½ cup chopped mixed candied fruit (citron, orange peel, lemon peel)

½ cup chopped almonds or walnuts
2 cups soft bread crumbs
¾ cup brown sugar
½ teaspoon nutmeg
½ teaspoon cinnamon
Dash ginger
2 ounces chopped or ground suet
⅓ cup milk
1 egg
3 tablespoons orange juice or 4
    tablespoons brandy

Combine all ingredients and mix well. Pack into a well-greased 1-quart mold. Cover with aluminum foil and fasten on with string. Place mold on a trivet in the slow cooker and add about 3 inches of boiling water. Cover and cook on high 5 to 6 hours.

Remove mold and let stand 15 minutes. Loosen pudding with a knife around edges. Unmold and serve with Hard Sauce (recipes follow).

Pudding may be cooled at room temperature in mold, refrigerated, and rewarmed by steaming in slow cooker for an hour before serving.

Assorted Hard Sauces for Plum Pudding

Yield: ½ cup each

Orange Hard Sauce

1 cup confectioners' sugar
¼ cup soft butter or margarine
1 tablespoon orange juice
1 teaspoon grated orange rind

Combine all ingredients and beat until light. Serve chilled or at room temperature with steamed pudding.

Brandy Hard Sauce

Substitute 1 tablespoon brandy for the orange juice and rind.

Blueberry Hard Sauce

Beat in ½ cup blueberries, a few at a time. Omit orange juice and rind.

Beverages

Spiced Tea

Yield: 6 cups

5 cups boiling water
5 tea bags
¾ cup sugar
¼ cup strained orange juice
½ cup strained lemon juice
6 cloves
1 stick cinnamon

Pour boiling water over tea bags in slow cooker; let steep 1 to 2 minutes. Remove tea bags. Add remaining ingredients, cover, and hold on low for 2 to 3 hours.

Ladle directly from the crock pot into warm cups. Tea may be garnished with thin orange or lemon slices.

Coffee Copenhagen

Yield: 8 servings

8 cups hot coffee
1 cup rum
¾ cup sugar
2 sticks cinnamon or 1 teaspoon
   ground cinnamon
12 whole cloves

Combine all ingredients in slow cooker.
Cover and keep warm on low for up to 2
hours. Ladle into mugs or tall, heavy glasses.

Tea Punch

Yield: 8 cups

3 cups strong black tea
3 cups dry red wine
¾ cup orange juice
1 cup rum
3 whole cloves
1 stick cinnamon
¾ cup sugar
6 to 8 lemon slices as a garnish

Combine all ingredients except lemon
slices in slow cooker. Cover and hold on low
2 to 3 hours.
Ladle hot into mugs. Garnish with lemon
slices.

Hot Fruit Punch

Yield: About 2 quarts

3 cups orange juice
1 quart cranberry juice
1 12-ounce can light beer
2 apples, cored, peeled, and sliced thin
½ cup brown sugar
1 stick cinnamon

½ teaspoon ginger
½ teaspoon nutmeg
4 slices orange as a garnish

Combine all ingredients except orange
slices in slow cooker. Cover and cook on low
1 hour. Garnish with orange slices. Serve
hot.

Lamb's Wool

Yield: 8 servings

8 apples, peeled, cored, and coarsely
   chopped
¼ cup butter
2 quarts beer or ale
1 cup sugar
½ teaspoon nutmeg
½ teaspoon ginger

Combine all ingredients in slow cooker.
Cover and cook on low 2 to 3 hours.
Remove apples, mash or sieve, and return
to beer mixture. Serve very hot from slow
cooker.

Mulled Cider

Yield: 2 quarts

2 quarts cider
1 orange, sliced
1 lemon, sliced
2 sticks cinnamon
8 whole cloves

Combine all ingredients in slow cooker.
Cover and heat on low for 1 hour. Ladle
into punch cups.

Hot Cider Cocktail

Yield: 6 cups

4 cups water
1 cup rum
⅓ cup curaçao
Sugar to taste
4 whole cloves
Lemon slices for garnish

Combine all ingredients in slow cooker. Cover and cook on low 2 to 3 hours. Remove apples, mash or sieve, and return to beer mixture. Serve very hot from slow cooker.

Swedish Glogg

Yield: About 2 quarts

1 bottle port (4/5 quart)
1 bottle claret (4/5 quart)
½ cup apricot brandy
½ cup raisins or currants
6 dried apricot halves, chopped
12 blanched almonds
4 whole cloves
2 sticks cinnamon
4 whole cardamom

Combine all ingredients in the slow cooker. Cover and cook on low for 1 to 2 hours. Serve hot.

Wassail Bowl

Yield: About 2 quarts

2 cups sugar
1 teaspoon nutmeg
1 teaspoon ginger
½ teaspoon mace
8 whole cloves
8 whole allspice
1 stick cinnamon
2 quarts dry sherry
6 eggs, separated
½ cup brandy

Combine sugar, spices, and sherry in slow cooker. Cover and cook on low for 1 hour, stirring occasionally. Whisk in the egg yolks and brandy.

Beat the egg whites until soft peaks form. Fold into the sherry mixture. Serve warm. Do not allow the mixture to boil, or the eggs will curdle.

Food Processor
Appetizers

Camembert Spread

Yield: About 1¼ cups

Spread

⅓ cup cold butter, cut into 4 pieces
8 ounces Camembert cheese
1 teaspoon paprika
1 small onion
8 blades of chives, cut into 1-inch
pieces

Garnish

Small pretzels
Circle of pumpernickel bread
Radish rose

Place ingredients for spread in processor bowl and process with metal blade until onions are minced. Arrange on a plate and garnish with pretzels. Place bread circle in center and top with the radish. Serve with crackers or thinly sliced dark bread.

Surprise Cheese Puffs

Yield: About 24

Prepare these in advance and heat just before serving.

4 ounces sharp cheddar cheese,
shredded with the shredding disk
¼ cup cold butter, cut into 4 pieces
½ cup sifted all-purpose flour
¼ teaspoon salt
½ teaspoon paprika
24 olives, or cocktail onions, or cubes
of cooked ham, etc.

Place shredded cheese, butter, flour, salt, and paprika in processor bowl. Process with metal blade until smooth.

Form a teaspoonful of the mixture around each olive, onion, or piece of ham. Place on an ungreased baking sheet and refrigerate.

Just before serving, bake in a 400°F oven for 10 to 15 minutes or until golden.

Champagne — Fruit Cocktail

Yield: 6 servings

⅔ cup fresh pineapple, cut into 1-inch
cubes
1 peeled orange, sliced, seeds removed
⅔ cup fresh strawberries
3 tablespoons sugar
1 bottle champagne, chilled

Place fruit and sugar in processor bowl and process with metal blade until finely chopped.

Place some of the mixture in each of 6 chilled champagne glasses. Fill with champagne and serve at once.

Cocktail Cream Puffs

Yield: 24

2 dozen small Cream Puff Shells
(see Index)
½ pint sour cream
2 (or more) tablespoons caviar

Prepare small Cream Puff Shells as recipe directs. Cut off tops.

Combine sour cream and caviar. Fill shells. Replace tops. Serve at once.

Cream puffs may also be filled with many of the Sandwich Spreads (see Index) and used as appetizers.

Mushroom Cocktail

Yield: 4 to 6 servings

½ pound fresh mushrooms
2 tablespoons vinegar
1 teaspoon horseradish
¾ cup catsup
Lettuce cups

Wedge mushrooms sideways in the tube and slice into "T" shapes with the slicing disk.

Combine vinegar, horseradish, and catsup. Add mushrooms. Chill and serve in lettuce cups with crackers.

Olive – Nut Hors d'Oeuvres

Yield: 8 hors d'oeuvres

Use small olives, if you wish, and you can make more.

3 ounces cream cheese, cut into 4 pieces
¼ cup almonds
1 teaspoon milk
8 large stuffed olives, patted dry
Paprika, optional

Place cheese, almonds, and milk in processor bowl and process with metal blade until almonds are minced.

Form mixture around each of the 8 olives. Chill. Serve on toothpicks.

These can be rolled in paprika, more chopped almonds, or parsley chopped with the metal blade, for added color and interest.

Steak Tartare

Yield: About 2 cups

½ pound fresh beef, cut into 1-inch cubes
1 teaspoon Worcestershire sauce
2 teaspoons cognac
1 egg yolk
Dash Tabasco sauce
½ teaspoon paprika
Salt and pepper to taste

Garnishes

Olives
Cocktail onions
Anchovy fillets with capers
Sliced gherkins
Onion, chopped finely with the metal blade
Crackers or thin slices of dark rye or pumpernickel snack bread

Place beef, Worcestershire sauce, cognac, egg yolk, Tabasco sauce, and paprika in processor bowl. Process with metal blade until beef is finely chopped. Place mixture in a bowl set in cracked ice. Place garnishes in small bowls. Guests spread meat on crackers or bread and top with a garnish.

Cocktail Meatballs in Beer Sauce

Yield: 20 to 30

1½ pounds lean beef, cut into 1-inch
    cubes
2 teaspoons salt
½ teaspoon pepper
Vegetable oil for browning
½ cup beer
½ cup chili sauce
1 teaspoon soy sauce
1 teaspoon sugar

Process the beef with the metal blade, one cup at a time, until finely chopped. Season with salt and pepper and form into firm 1-inch balls. Brown in oil in a skillet. Place in a chafing dish or fondue pot with remaining ingredients. Heat.

Guests serve themselves directly from the chafing dish with toothpicks.

Herring in Sour Cream

Yield: 2 cups

2 6-ounce cans herring fillets
1 medium onion, sliced with the
    slicing disk
24 whole black peppercorns
2 crushed bay leaves
1 cup sour cream
3 tablespoons sauterne

Cut fillets into bite-size pieces. Combine in a bowl with onion, pepper, and bay leaves.

Mix sour cream and wine and stir into fillet mixture. Cover and refrigerate 4 to 8 hours before serving. Keeps for 1 or 2 days.

Shrimp or Scallop Cocktail

Yield of sauce: About 1 cup

Chilled, cooked shrimp or scallops
Lettuce

Cocktail Sauce

¼ cup catsup
⅓ cup lemon juice
½ teaspoon Worcestershire sauce
1 teaspoon salt
1 tablespoon prepared horseradish
1 small stalk celery, minced with the
    metal blade.

Arrange shrimp over lettuce in cocktail glasses. Combine sauce ingredients and serve over shrimp.

Chips & Dips

Banana Chips

Yield: 1 or more cups chips

Vegetable oil for frying
2 to 3 green bananas
Salt

Heat oil in a deep pan to 390°F. Peel and slice the bananas crosswise with the slicing disk. Fry the slices a few at a time until light brown, 1 to 2 minutes. Remove from fat and drain on paper towels. Sprinkle with salt while still warm.

Corn Chips

Yield: Varies with number of tortillas used

6 to 12 tortillas
Vegetable oil for frying
Salt or garlic salt

Heat tortillas in oven until warm. After heating, cut them into wedges with a knife or pizza cutter. Let dry at room temperature overnight.

Heat oil to 375°F and drop in several chips at a time. Fry until lightly browned, 1 or 2 minutes. Drain on paper towels. Sprinkle with salt while still warm.

Pumpkin Chips

Yield: Varies with amount of pumpkin used

Fresh pumpkin, seeded, pared, and cut into 2 × 4-inch sections
Vegetable oil for frying
Salt or garlic salt

Slice the pumpkin sections with the slicing disk. Soak slices in water for 1 hour. Remove and pat dry. Fry in oil at 360°F, a few slices at a time, for about 2 minutes or until lightly browned. Drain on paper towels. Sprinkle with salt or garlic salt or a mixture of salt, ginger, and nutmeg. A mixture of garlic salt and curry powder is also good.

Potato Chips

Yield: Varies with number of potatoes used

With a food processor, homemade potato chips are easily prepared. The potatoes can be sliced uniformly and thinly enough for professional looking chips that you know are fresh and tasty.

Fresh potatoes, peeled, and trimmed to fit the processor tube
Vegetable oil for frying
Salt

Slice the potatoes with the slicing disk. Rinse slices in cold water to remove excess surface starch. Drain and pat dry. Fry a few slices at a time in oil at 375°F until very lightly browned. Drain on paper towels. Sprinkle with salt while still warm.

Baked Bean and Ham Dip

Yield: 1½ cups

1-pound can baked beans in molasses sauce
3 ounces cooked ham, cut into 5 pieces
1½ tablespoons horseradish
1 tablespoon Worcestershire sauce
½ medium onion, cut into 4 pieces
1 or 2 drops Tabasco sauce

Place all ingredients in the food processor bowl and process with the metal blade until smooth. Serve chilled.

Clam Dip

Yield: 1½ cups

1 8-ounce package cream cheese, cut
  into 8 pieces
1 2-inch piece scallion
1 teaspoon Worcestershire sauce
2 8-ounce cans minced clams, drained

Process the cream cheese, scallion, and
Worcestershire sauce with the metal blade
until the scallion is minced, about 15 seconds. Add clams and process by turning
blade on and off quickly 2 or 3 times to
blend. Serve chilled with crackers, chips, or
vegetable dippers.

Cucumber Green Goddess Dip

Yield: 1⅓ cups

2 3-ounce packages cream cheese, each
  cut into 4 pieces
2 slices onion
½ teaspoon salt
¼ teaspoon cumin or oregano
½ unpeeled cucumber, cut into 6
  pieces

Place cream cheese, onion, salt, and
cumin in processor bowl. Process with metal
blade until smooth, about 15 seconds. Add
cucumber, and process by turning on and off
quickly until cucumber is minced. Serve
chilled with chips or vegetable dippers.

Fish Dip

Yield: 2 cups

Use fish in season: flounder, mackerel,
cod, etc.

1 cup sour cream
1 3-ounce package cream cheese, cut
  into 4 pieces
1 scallion, cut into 1-inch pieces
1 tablespoon horseradish
½ teaspoon salt
8 ounces cooked fish
2 hard-cooked eggs, quartered

Place first five ingredients in processor
bowl. Process with metal blade until cheese
is blended and scallion is minced, about 15
seconds. Add fish and eggs. Process by turning on and off quickly 4 or 5 times, until fish
and eggs are finely chopped. Serve cold with
chips or vegetable dippers.

Guacamole Dip

Yield: 1 cup

1 ripe avocado, peeled and pitted
¼ onion
1 teaspoon lemon juice
½ teaspoon salt
⅛ teaspoon freshly ground black
  pepper
¼ teaspoon ascorbic or citrus acid
  mixture, optional

Place all ingredients in food processor
bowl and process with metal blade until
smooth, about 15 seconds. Serve at once
with chips or vegetable dippers.

Dip darkens quickly and cannot be stored. To delay darkening, ¼ teaspoon ascorbic or citric acid mixture may be added during processing.

Pink Ham Dip

Yield: 1¾ cups

1 8-ounce package cream cheese
½ cup mayonnaise
2 tablespoons catsup
1 3-inch stalk celery
2 ounces cooked ham, cut into 3 pieces
2 tablespoons fresh parsley leaves
Salt if necessary
8 to 10 small olives

Place all ingredients except olives in the food processor bowl and process with the metal blade until smooth, about 15 seconds. Add olives and process until finely chopped. Serve chilled with crackers or vegetable dippers.

Spinach Dip

Yield: 1 cup

3 scallions, cut into 1-inch pieces
2 cups mayonnaise
1 10-ounce package frozen spinach, thawed, lightly drained, large stems removed
Garlic salt and pepper to taste

Place scallions and mayonnaise in processor bowl. Process with metal blade until scallions are minced. Add spinach, and process by turning blade on and off quickly to

blend. Season to taste with garlic salt and pepper. Chill and serve with vegetable dippers.

Herb Butters

Béarnaise Butter

Yield: About ½ cup

½ cup (1 stick) cold butter, cut into 6 pieces
1 teaspoon dried tarragon
1 tablespoon dry white wine
1 teaspoon vinegar

Combine all ingredients in the processor bowl and process with the metal blade until light. Serve with poultry, steaks, or fish.

Garlic Butter (Snail Butter)

Yield: ½ cup

½ cup (1 stick) cold butter, cut into 6 pieces
1 or 2 cloves garlic
1 tablespoon fresh parsley leaves
½ teaspoon salt

Place butter and garlic in processor bowl and process with the metal blade until garlic is very finely minced, about 10 seconds. Add parsley and salt and process until parsley is finely chopped, about 5 seconds. Serve with vegetables or snails.

Ginger – Green Onion Butter

Yield: ½ cup

½ cup (1 stick) cold butter, cut into 6 pieces
1 slice fresh gingerroot, ¼ inch thick
1 scallion, cut into 1-inch pieces
½ teaspoon salt

Place butter and ginger in processor bowl and process with the metal blade until ginger is finely minced. Add scallion and salt and process until scallion is finely chopped. Serve with fish.

Lemon Butter

Yield: About ½ cup

½ cup (1 stick) cold butter, cut into 6 pieces
3 tablespoons fresh parsley leaves
1 tablespoon lemon juice
⅛ teaspoon freshly ground black pepper

Place all ingredients in processor bowl and process with metal blade until parsley is minced, about 15 seconds. Serve with potatoes, fish, or in poultry sandwiches.

Parsley Butter

Yield: About ½ cup

½ cup (1 stick) cold butter, cut into 6 pieces
3 tablespoons fresh parsley leaves
⅛ teaspoon freshly ground black pepper

Place all ingredients in the processor bowl and process with the metal blade until parsley is finely chopped. Use with potatoes or other vegetables.

Pesto Sauce

Yield: About 1½ cups

Not truly a butter, but used in the same way on vegetables, rice, or pasta.

2 cups fresh basil leaves (or fresh parsley)
1 cup Parmesan cheese
½ cup olive oil

Place all ingredients in processor bowl and process with the metal blade until basil is minced. Serve with pasta or vegetables. Store covered in the refrigerator. Stir before using.

Creative Fines Herbes Butter

Yield: Yield: ½ cup

Use your favorite herbs and process with one stick of butter. Use 3 tablespoons fresh chives, rosemary, chervil, tarragon, dillweed, or coriander for each stick of butter.

Wonderful if you have an herb garden! Use 1 or 2 teaspoons dried herbs per stick of butter if fresh herbs are not available.

Main Dishes

Banana Meat Loaf

Yield: 4 or 5 servings

Cooked carrots, frankfurters, or small pickles may be used in place of the bananas.

1 pound lean beef, cut into 1-inch cubes
2 onions, each cut into quarters
2 tablespoons fresh parsley leaves
2 eggs
1 teaspoon salt
¼ teaspoon freshly ground pepper
2 cups cooked rice
2 bananas, peeled

Process half the beef, onions, parsley, eggs, salt, and pepper at a time in the processor bowl, using the metal blade, turning it on and off quickly, until the beef and onions are coarsely chopped.

Add this mixture to the rice and mix well. Place half of mixture in the bottom of a 9 x 5-inch loaf pan. Place bananas on top. Cover with remaining meat mixture. Bake at 350°F for about 1 hour. Serve at once.

Swiss Cheese Fondue

Yield: 4 servings

The food processor is a great help during the preparation of cheese fondues. Often a large quantity of cheese must be grated, and this step is done rapidly with the shredding disk.

1 pound Swiss cheese, shredded with the shredding disk
1½ cups dry white table wine
1 clove garlic
2 tablespoons cornstarch
Dash of freshly ground black pepper
Dash of nutmeg
2 tablespoons kirsch
1-inch cubes of stale French or Italian bread

Combine cheese, wine, garlic, cornstarch, pepper, and nutmeg in a fondue or chafing dish. Heat gently, stirring occasionally, just until mixture thickens and begins to bubble. Remove garlic clove and discard. Stir in kirsch. Spear bread cubes on fondue forks and dunk bread into fondue. Keep heat under fondue low to prevent coagulation of the cheese.

Calzone Italiana

Yield: 4 or 5 servings

Follow the recipe for Calzone alla Napoli (see page 96) and use the following filling in place of the ham-and-cheese filling.

1 pound mild Italian sausage, casing removed
2 teaspoons oregano
1 8-ounce can tomato sauce
8 ounces mozzarella cheese, shredded with the shredding disk
1 cup grated Parmesan cheese

Brown the sausage in a skillet. Drain well. Add oregano and tomato sauce. Spread on turnovers, top with cheeses, seal, and bake as directed.

Calzone Alla Napoli (Ham and Cheese Turnovers)

Yield: 10 rolls, to serve 4 or 5

Serve these with wine and a tossed salad for a light supper.

Dough

1 recipe White Bread dough or 1 10 ounce can refrigerated Parker House rolls

Filling

8 ounces mozzarella cheese
½ pound cooked ham, cut into 1-inch cubes
10 green olives, pitted
Salt and pepper to taste
1 egg white
1 to 2 tablespoons milk

Divide dough into 10 pieces. Roll out each on a floured surface to 5-inch-round circles.

Grate cheese with shredding disk. Chop ham and olives with metal blade. Combine ham, olives, and cheese. Season with salt and pepper. Place mixture on half of each dough circle to within ¼ inch of edge. Brush edges with egg white. Fold plain half over and seal. Place on a greased baking sheet; brush each turnover with milk. Bake at 400°F for 15 to 20 minutes. Serve at once.

Italian Beans

Yield: 4 servings

2 large onions, quartered
2 cloves garlic
2 tablespoons vegetable oil
1 large stalk celery, cut into 3-inch lengths
⅔ cup fresh parsley leaves
2 tomatoes, quartered
2 carrots
1½ cups canned kidney beans (1 pound) and half the can liquid
5 teaspoons dried basil
1 teaspoon oregano
2 teaspoons salt
Pepper to taste
4 ounces cheddar cheese

Insert the metal blade in the processor bowl and coarsely chop the onions. Finely chop the garlic. Sauté both in vegetable oil until tender.

Separately chop the celery, parsley leaves, and tomatoes coarsely with the metal blade.

Grate the carrots with the shredding disk. Add these vegetables, beans and liquid, spices, salt and pepper to the onion and garlic. Heat. Vegetables should remain rather crisp. Sprinkle with cheese, shredded with the shredding disk. Serve at once with boiled brown rice.

Stuffed Chicken Breasts

Yield: 4 to 8 servings

5 ounces lean veal
5 ounces lean pork
3 ounces chicken giblets or liver
1 slice stale bread, torn in quarters
3 eggs
½ teaspoon salt
2 tablespoons fresh parsley leaves
4 ounces canned mushrooms, drained
4 whole chicken breasts
Butter for frying
½ cup water

½ cup sour cream
1 tablespoon cornstarch

Coarsely chop veal, pork, and giblets with the metal blade. Remove to a large bowl.

Combine bread, eggs, salt, parsley, and mushrooms in processor bowl. Process with metal blade until mushrooms are finely chopped. Add to meat.

Bone the chicken breasts, keeping each breast in one piece. Fill the breasts with the meat mixture. Sew or fasten with skewers to close. Fry in butter until browned on all sides. Add water, cover, and cook 30 minutes. Remove chicken and keep it warm.

Add sour cream and cornstarch to drippings. Heat until thick. Serve over chicken on a bed of sauerkraut.

Teriyaki Meatballs

Yield: 4 servings

Meatballs
¼ cup fresh parsley leaves
2 stalks celery with leaves, cut into 1-inch pieces
1 slice bread, torn into 4 pieces
½ teaspoon salt
1 egg
1 pound cubed lean beef, chopped 1 cup at a time, using the metal blade

Gravy
⅓ cup cold water mixed with 1 tablespoon cornstarch
¼ cup soy sauce
½ teaspoon paprika
1 teaspoon sugar
¼ teaspoon ground ginger
2 tablespoons candied fruit

Place parsley, celery, bread, salt, and egg in processor bowl. Process with metal blade until celery is finely chopped.

Add to meat and form mixture into walnut-sized balls. Brown in hot oil in skillet for 5 minutes. Drain.

Heat ingredients for gravy in a saucepan until mixture boils and is clear. Pour over meatballs. Serve hot with boiled rice. Garnish with celery leaves.

Turkish Meatball Kabobs

Yield: 4 servings

1 pound lean beef or lamb cut into 1-inch cubes
2 small boiled potatoes, peeled
2 small onions, each cut into quarters
1 small green pepper, seeded and cut into 8 pieces
4 sprigs fresh parsley leaves
1 teaspoon salt
1 teaspoon prepared mustard
1 teaspoon curry powder, optional
Flour for rolling
Vegetable oil for frying

Process half of the ingredients at a time in the processor bowl with the metal blade, turning it on and off quickly, until meat and vegetables are coarsely chopped.

Form plum-size meatballs. Roll in flour. Fry in a small amount of oil in a skillet, or deep fry in oil at 375°F until done. Remove and drain well. Serve on 4 wooden skewers.

California Stuffed Breast of Veal

Yield: 6 servings

Stuffing

1 pound fresh spinach, large stems removed
1 medium onion, quartered
3 tablespoons butter or margarine
⅔ cup raisins, plumped in boiling water, then drained
¼ cup bread crumbs (or 1 slice dry bread, quartered, and chopped with the metal blade)
1 teaspoon salt
1 teaspoon basil
1 teaspoon parsley
1 egg yolk

Veal Breast

1 4- to 4½- pound breast of veal
Salt and pepper
3 to 4 tablespoons vegetable oil
½ cup dry white wine
2 bay leaves
4 whole cloves
¼ cup hot beef broth, if needed

Prepare the stuffing. Wash spinach well and shred with the slicing disk. Chop the onion with the metal blade. Sauté the onions in butter in a large skillet until soft. Add the spinach and sauté until just wilted. Remove from heat. Add raisins, bread crumbs, seasonings, and the egg yolk. Toss until combined.

Prepare the veal breast. Remove breastbone, ribs, and cartilage from veal breast with sharp knife. Cut pocket in meat, season with salt and pepper, and fill with stuffing. Close pocket with toothpicks. Heat oil in a large skillet. Brown stuffed breasts on all sides for about 15 minutes. Lower heat and add wine, bay leaves, and cloves. Cover and simmer over low heat for about 2 hours. Add broth if necessary to replenish liquid in bottom of pan. Baste meat occasionally.

Serve at once on a hot platter. Remove toothpicks and slice the meat.

Scalloped Fish

Yield: 4 servings

4 baking shells or ramekins

Fish

1 tablespoon lemon juice
1 pound fish fillets
2 bay leaves
4 whole cloves
6 whole peppercorns
1 small onion, sliced

Bechamel Sauce

2 tablespoons butter
1 onion, chopped with the metal blade
2 tablespoons flour
1 cup fish broth
½ teaspoon salt
⅛ teaspoon nutmeg
¼ teaspoon paprika
⅛ teaspoon pepper
4 blades chives, cut into ¼-inch pieces
½ cup light cream

Garnish

4 tablespoons Parmesan cheese
1 slice stale bread, crumbled with the metal blade
2 tablespoons butter

Sprinkle lemon juice over fish; let stand for 10 minutes. Place fish in a wire basket and poach in simmering water to cover with the bay leaves, cloves, peppercorns, and onion for about 10 to 15 minutes. Remove fish and let it drain, reserving broth. Place fish in processor bowl and process with metal blade by turning on and off quickly until fish is coarsely chopped.

Prepare the sauce. Place butter in a skillet and cook the onion until it is soft. Add flour and blend with butter until no lumps remain. Add 1 cup of the reserved fish broth gradually, stirring constantly. Add salt and spices. Bring to a boil. Add chives and cream.

Fill shells or ramekins with fish. Pour sauce over each. Sprinkle with Parmesan cheese and bread crumbs; dot with butter. Bake at 400°F for about 15 minutes. Serve at once.

Seafood Tempura

Yield: 6 to 8 servings

Frying Batter

1 large egg
¾ cup water
1 cup sifted all-purpose flour
½ teaspoon salt
1 teaspoon rosemary
1 teaspoon basil

Seafood

Vegetable oil for deep-fat frying
½ pound sliced eel
½ pound shrimp
½ pound mussels
½ pound fish fillets, rolled and
    fastened with toothpicks

Combine ingredients for batter in processor bowl and process with metal blade just until smooth. Let batter stand for 1 hour, or refrigerate it overnight. This thickens the batter and softens the flour.

Heat oil to 400°F. Using tongs, dip seafood pieces into batter, drain briefly, and drop gently into hot fat. Deep-fry until brown, about 3 or 4 minutes, depending on size of seafood pieces. Remove from oil as done and drain on paper toweling. Serve with assorted dips for seafood.

Stuffed Zucchini

Yield: 4 servings

4 medium zucchini
Salt and pepper
1 pound cubed lamb, chopped with the
    metal blade 1 cup at a time
2 tomatoes, coarsely chopped with
    metal blade
¼ cup frozen, defrosted peas
½ cup boiled rice
1 cup hot beef broth or bouillon
4 ounces Swiss cheese, shredded with
    the shredding disk

Wash and trim ends from zucchini. Cook in boiling water 5 minutes. Halve lengthwise and scoop out seeds with a spoon. Season halves with salt and pepper.

Brown the lamb in a skillet. Drain, and add tomatoes, peas, and rice. Season to taste with salt and pepper. Fill zucchini halves with mixture. Place in a casserole dish. Add broth, and cover. Bake at 350°F for 20 minutes. Uncover. Top with cheese and bake 10 minutes longer, uncovered. Serve at once.

Vegetables

Baked Butternut Squash and Apples

Yield: 6 servings

1 small (2-pound) butternut squash, pared, seeded, and cut into pieces to fit tube
2 apples, cored and cut into quarters
½ cup brown sugar
¼ cup cold butter or margarine, cut into 5 pieces
1 tablespoon flour
1 teaspoon salt
¼ teaspoon cinnamon
¼ teaspoon nutmeg

Slice squash and apples with the slicing disk, using firm pressure on the pusher. Place in a rectangular baking dish.

Process remaining ingredients with metal blade until blended. Sprinkle over apples and squash. Cover with foil and bake at 350°F until tender, about 50 minutes.

Pureed Pumpkin and Roasted Pumpkin Seeds

Yield: About 3 or 4 cups pureed pumpkin

Remove the seeds and strands from an 8-inch pumpkin and set aside. Cut pumpkin into 3-inch squares and peel outer skin from each. Steam, using a small amount of water, for 30 minutes or until pieces are very tender. Drain well.

Place pumpkin in processor bowl and process with metal blade until smooth.

To roast seeds, remove strands from seeds and discard. Do not wash or rinse seeds. Spread on a baking sheet and sprinkle with salt. Bake at 350°F for 20 minutes; stir occasionally.

Sliced Carrots with Honey and Parsley

Yield: 4 servings

6 medium carrots, scraped
2 tablespoons fresh parsley leaves
2 tablespoons butter or margarine
2 tablespoons honey

Wedge the carrots into the tube and slice with the slicing disk, using firm pressure on the pusher. Chop the parsley with the metal blade.

Place carrots and parsley in a saucepan with a small amount of water. Dot with butter and dribble with honey. Steam over moderate heat until tender.

To prepare in a microwave oven, use a small glass casserole dish and cook for 5 minutes.

Baked Potatoes with Sour Cream and Caviar

Yield: 6 to 8 servings

6 to 8 medium baking potatoes, baked
½ pint sour cream
1 small pickle, cut into 1-inch pieces
1 small onion, quartered
1 sprig fresh dillweed or parsley
⅛ teaspoon freshly ground black pepper

½ teaspoon salt
Caviar for garnishing

Cut crisscross across the top of the baked potatoes. Press the sides to split the cross open and expose the insides of the potatoes.

Place sour cream, pickle, onion, dill, pepper, and salt in processor bowl and process with metal blade until pickle and onion are coarsely chopped. Spoon mixture onto potatoes. Garnish with caviar and additional sprigs of dill or parsley.

Mashed Potatoes

Yield: 4 servings

4 boiled, skinned potatoes
2 tablespoons butter or margarine
Salt and freshly ground pepper to taste
¼ cup milk

Place all ingredients in processor bowl and process with metal blade until smooth. Serve at once, garnished with parsley leaves and paprika.

Scalloped Potatoes

Yield: 4 or 5 servings

4 medium potatoes, peeled, and sliced
  with the slicing disk
1 medium onion, sliced with the
  slicing disk
Salt and freshly ground black pepper
About 2 cups milk
2 tablespoons butter or margarine

Layer the potato and onion slices in a greased baking dish. Season each layer with salt and pepper. Add milk to within ½ inch from the top. Dot with butter and bake, uncovered, at 350°F for 1¼ hours.

Golden Sweet Potatoes

Yield: 4 to 6 servings

A must for Thanksgiving dinner, these sweet potatoes are laced with sherry and orange juice. Leftovers freeze well. Double the recipe for a large group and process half at a time.

2 pounds sweet potatoes (4 medium)
1 teaspoon cinnamon
1 teaspoon salt
2 tablespoons brown sugar
2 tablespoons butter or margarine
3 tablespoons dry sherry
3 tablespoons orange juice

Boil sweet potatoes until easily pierced with a fork. Slip off and discard skins. Place potatoes in processor bowl with remaining ingredients. Process with metal blade until smooth; scrape down sides and break up large pieces with spatula, if necessary.

Heap into a 1-quart casserole dish. Dot with additional butter and bake at 350°F until reheated. This dish may be prepared in advance and refrigerated.

If serving this with turkey, rewarm it in the oven with the turkey for about 20 to 25 minutes.

Fondue Dips, Sauces & Relishes

Avocado Fondue Dip

Yield: About 1 cup

2 ripe avocados, pitted and peeled
2 tablespoons mayonnaise
1 tablespoon lemon juice
1 teaspoon prepared mustard
Garlic salt and pepper to taste

Combine all ingredients in processor bowl and process with metal blade until smooth. Garnish with strips of lemon peel. Serve with beef, seafood, or poultry fondue.

Mushroom Fondue Dip

Yield: About ¾ cup

½ cup mayonnaise or sour cream
1 teaspoon lemon juice
Dash Tabasco sauce
Salt and pepper to taste
¼ cup canned mushrooms, drained, or
½ cup fresh chopped mushrooms
browned in butter
Salt and pepper to taste

Place all ingredients in processor bowl and process with metal blade until mushrooms are coarsely chopped. Garnish with whole mushrooms.

Onion – Parsley Fondue Dip

Yield: About ¾ cup

¼ cup vegetable oil
1 tablespoon lemon juice
1 teaspoon prepared mustard
2 medium onions, quartered
1 tablespoon prepared horseradish
¼ cup fresh parsley leaves
½ teaspoon sugar
Salt and pepper to taste

Place all ingredients in processor bowl and process with metal blade until onion is finely chopped. Garnish with additional parsley. Especially good for beef fondue.

Paprika Fondue Dip

Yield: 1 cup

½ cup mayonnaise
1 tablespoon paprika
Salt and pepper to taste
½ green or red pepper, cut into
4 pieces

Place all ingredients in processor bowl and process with metal blade until pepper is minced. Garnish with additional chopped green pepper. Serve with seafood or poultry fondue.

Sour Cream – Chive Fondue Dip

Yield: About 1 cup

½ pint sour cream
1 teaspoon lemon juice
1 teaspoon prepared mustard

5 blades chives, cut into 1-inch pieces
Dash sugar
1 tablespoon catsup
Salt and pepper to taste

Place all ingredients in processor bowl and process with metal blade until chives are just minced. Serve with beef fondue.

Béarnaise Sauce

Yield: 1½ cups

2 tablespoons dry white wine (Chablis)
1 tablespoon white vinegar
2 teaspoons chopped onion
½ teaspoon dried tarragon
1 cup butter (½ pound)
3 egg yolks
1 tablespoon water
Dash cayenne pepper

Combine the wine, vinegar, onion, and tarragon in a saucepan. Heat and reduce to 1 tablespoon. Add butter and heat until bubbly; do not brown.

Place egg yolks, water, and pepper in processor bowl. Process with the metal blade until light, about 15 seconds. Dribble the hot butter (it must be hot or it will not thicken the egg yolks) through the tube with the motor running. Add slowly, drop by drop, at first. Then add remainder in a scant, steady stream. Serve at once while warm, or chill and serve cold with steak or pot roast.

Cambridge Sauce

Yield: About ⅔ cup

½ cup sour cream or mayonnaise
2 hard-cooked egg yolks

2 teaspoons prepared mustard
2 anchovy fillets
1 tablespoon fresh parsley leaves
¼ teaspoon tarragon
3 blades chives, cut into 1-inch pieces
Salt and pepper to taste
Dash wine vinegar

Place all ingredients in processor bowl and process with metal blade just until anchovy fillets are coarsely chopped. Garnish with parsley or other fresh herbs and additional anchovy fillets. Serve with meat, poultry, or beef fondue.

Hollandaise Sauce

Yield: 1 cup

An indispensable sauce for broccoli, asparagus, and eggs benedict.

2 tablespoons lemon juice
3 egg yolks
¼ teaspoon salt
½ cup butter

Place lemon juice, egg yolks, and salt in the processor bowl. Process with metal blade until blended, about 15 seconds.

Heat butter in saucepan until bubbly; do not brown. With processor running, add the hot butter through the tube, drop by drop at first. Then add remainder in a scant, steady stream. The butter must be hot to thicken the yolks. Serve at once, or chill and serve cold over well-drained vegetables.

Gloucester Sauce

Yield: About 1 cup

½ cup yogurt
½ cup mayonnaise
Salt and pepper to taste
½ teaspoon sugar
1 teaspoon lemon juice
Dash Worcestershire sauce

Place all ingredients in processor bowl and process with metal blade until smooth. Garnish with a little grated lemon rind. Serve with meat, fish, poultry, or beef fondue.

Horseradish Sauce

Yield: About ⅔ cup

½ cup mayonnaise
1 tablespoon prepared horseradish
2 tablespoons dry white wine
½ teaspoon sugar
Salt and pepper to taste
1 peeled tomato, quartered, and
    coarsely chopped with metal blade

Combine all ingredients except tomatoes in processor bowl. Process with metal blade until smooth. Fold in tomato pieces and reserve a few for a garnish. Serve with meat or beef fondue.

Mayonnaise

Yield: 1¼ cups

1 egg
1 tablespoon vinegar or lemon juice
½ teaspoon salt or a mixture of garlic
    and onion salt (use less if
    mayonnaise is to be used with salty
    ingredients, such as tuna)

¼ teaspoon dry mustard
1 cup vegetable oil

Place the egg, vinegar, salt, and dry mustard in processor bowl. Process with metal blade 4 or 5 seconds. With the motor running, pour oil through the feed tube, drop by drop at first, then in a scant, steady stream. (Let it run down the edge of the bowl next to the handle.) Refrigerate in a covered jar. Use within 1 to 2 weeks.

If the mayonnaise should separate, place another egg in the processor bowl and add the separated mixture very slowly through the tube with the blades running. It will re-emulsify.

Tartar Sauce

Yield: About ⅔ cup

1 hard-cooked egg
½ cup mayonnaise
1 teaspoon prepared mustard
¼ cup fresh parsley leaves
1 teaspoon chervil
1 teaspoon tarragon
½ teaspoon sugar
2 teaspoons lemon juice
Salt and pepper to taste

Place all ingredients in processor bowl and process with metal blade until parsley is minced. Garnish with chopped chives. Serve with meat, fish, or beef fondue.

Tomato — Wine Sauce

Yield: About 1 cup

½ cup sour cream or mayonnaise
¼ cup tomato paste
2 tablespoons dry white wine

2 teaspoons lemon juice
Salt and pepper to taste
Dash Worcestershire sauce

Place all ingredients in processor bowl and process with metal blade until smooth. Serve with beef, pork, fish, or with seafood or beef fondue.

Speedy Chutney

Yield: 2 cups

½ small lemon, seeded, and cut into
  4 pieces
1 small onion, quartered
2 apples, cored, unpeeled, and cut into
  6 pieces
½ cup raisins
2 tablespoons candied citron or mixed
  candied fruit
½ cup vinegar
⅔ cup brown sugar
½ teaspoon salt
½ teaspoon ginger
¼ teaspoon cinnamon
⅛ teaspoon cloves

Place lemon in processor bowl and process with metal blade until finely chopped. Add onion and process until coarsely chopped; add apples and process until very coarsely chopped. Place this mixture in a saucepan with remaining ingredients. Simmer for about 1 hour. Refrigerate until ready to serve.

Carrot – Lemon Relish

Yield: 1 cup

A tangy relish to serve with poultry.

2 medium carrots, scraped and cut into
  1-inch pieces
½ small lemon, seeded and cut into
  quarters
3 tablespoons sugar

Place all ingredients in processor bowl and process with the metal blade until very finely chopped, about 20 seconds. Stop and scrape down sides twice. Store in a covered jar in the refrigerator. Serve cold.

Cranberry – Orange Relish

Yield: 2 cups

Delicious with chicken or turkey at Thanksgiving! The apple tones down the sharp cranberry-tangerine flavor.

½ pound cranberries (2 cups)
1 apple, cored, unpeeled, and cut into
  6 pieces
½ tangerine or orange, seeds removed,
  skin left on, cut into 4 pieces
¾ cup sugar

Place cranberries, apple, and tangerine in processor bowl. Process with metal blade until mixture is chopped fine, about 30 seconds. Stop and scrape sides as needed. Add sugar and process until blended. Make 2 or 3 days before needed and refrigerate in a covered jar. Serve cold.

Stuffings

Basic Bread Stuffing

Yield: Stuffing for an 8- to 12-pound turkey

The food processor reduces the usual preparation time by about two-thirds.

8 slices stale, but not hard, white or
    whole-wheat bread, torn in quarters
2 tablespoons fresh parsley leaves
1 medium onion, quartered
2 stalks celery with leaves, cut into
    2-inch pieces
1 teaspoon salt
¼ teaspoon freshly ground black
    pepper
½ cup melted butter or margarine

Process bread, four slices at a time, with the parsley. Turn metal blade on and off quickly just until bread is very coarsely chopped. Empty into a large bowl.

Process onion and celery with the metal blade until coarsely chopped. Add to the bread with the seasonings.

Melt butter and pour over mixture; toss well. Pack loosely into neck and body cavities of poultry. Place any extra stuffing in a pie pan, cover with aluminum foil, and bake 30 to 40 minutes.

Remove stuffing from bird immediately after cooking. Immediately chill that amount not served.

For larger birds, add 1 cup for each additional pound of bird, halve recipe for a 4-pound chicken.

Wild Rice and Mushroom Stuffing

Yield: Stuffing for a 12-pound turkey

2½ cups wild rice
⅓ pound sausage meat
⅓ cup butter or margarine
¾ pound mushrooms, coarsely
    chopped with the metal blade
2 medium onions, coarsely chopped
    with the metal blade
1½ teaspoons salt
½ teaspoon freshly ground black
    pepper

Wash, then cook rice in 5 cups boiling water until tender, about 30 minutes. Drain well.

Brown the sausage meat, add the margarine, mushrooms, and onions. Cook over low heat 3 to 4 minutes. Stir in rice and seasonings. Fill neck and body cavities of the turkey.

Stuffing Variations

Apple Stuffing

Add 2 cooking apples, chopped with the metal blade, to the Basic Bread Stuffing.

Apricot Stuffing

Add 1 cup apricots, coarsely chopped with the metal blade, and ½ cup coarsely chopped nuts to the Basic Bread Stuffing.

Brown-Rice Stuffing

Substitute 4 cups cooked brown rice for bread in the Basic Bread Stuffing.

Chestnut Stuffing

Add 1 cup boiled, skinned chestnuts, chopped with the metal blade, to the Basic Bread Stuffing.

Corn-Bread Stuffing

Substitute corn bread for white bread in the Basic Bread Stuffing.

Date-Pumpkin-Seed Stuffing

Add ½ cup shelled pumpkin seeds and 1 cup dates, coarsely chopped with the metal blade, to the Basic Bread Stuffing.

Herb Stuffing

Add the following seasonings to the Basic Bread Stuffing: 1 teaspoon thyme or 1 teaspoon sage or 1 teaspoon savory, ½ teaspoon basil, ½ teaspoon thyme, ½ teaspoon marjoram or 2 more tablespoons parsley, 1 teaspoon tarragon, and ½ cup almonds, chopped with the metal blade.

Mixed Dried-Fruit Stuffing

Add 1 cup assorted dried fruit, coarsely chopped with the metal blade, and ½ cup chopped nuts to the Basic Bread Stuffing.

Mushroom Stuffing

Add ½ pound chopped or sliced mushrooms cooked in the butter to the Basic Bread Stuffing.

Orange Stuffing

Add outer peel of an orange, finely minced with the metal blade, to the Herb Stuffing.

Oyster Stuffing

Add 1 cup drained, chopped oysters to the Basic Bread Stuffing.

Raisin-Walnut Stuffing

Add 1 cup chopped raisins, ½ cup chopped walnuts, and 1 teaspoon sage to the Basic Bread Stuffing.

Omelettes

Herb and Cheese Omelette

Yield: 3 servings

2 tablespoons butter or margarine
1 small pickle, cut into several pieces
5 blades chives, cut into 1-inch pieces
2 tablespoons fresh dillweed or
 ½ tablespoon dried dillweed
6 eggs, lightly beaten with a fork
1 teaspoon savory
6 ounces cheese, grated with the
 shredding disk
Salt and pepper to taste
1 peeled tomato, cut into wedges

Melt butter in a large skillet.
Chop pickle, chives, and dill with metal blade in processor bowl.
Pour eggs into skillet; add chopped ingredients, herbs, cheese, salt, and pepper. Cook over low heat without stirring. When bottom of mixture sets, lift edges and allow uncooked mixture to run underneath. When omelette is completely set, fold and roll out of pan. Garnish with tomato wedges and finely sliced chives.

Bacon and Potato Omelette

Yield: 3 servings

3 slices bacon, cut into small pieces
2 small potatoes, peeled, and sliced
  with the slicing disk
8 fresh spinach leaves, stems removed,
  and sliced with the slicing disk
6 eggs, lightly beaten with a fork
Salt and pepper to taste

In 1 10-inch skillet, heat bacon briefly. Add potatoes and fry until bacon is crisp and potatoes are lightly browned; add spinach and remove mixture to a small bowl.

Pour eggs, salt, and pepper into skillet. Distribute potato mixture evenly over them. Cook over low heat without stirring. As eggs set on bottom, lift edges and allow uncooked mixture to run underneath. When the omelette is set, fold with a fork and serve immediately.

Chinese Omelette

Yield: 4 servings

Tomato Sauce

1 8-ounce can tomato sauce
1 tablespoon olive oil
1 clove garlic
2 tablespoons soy sauce
1 slice fresh gingerroot or ¼ teaspoon
  ground ginger

Omelette

1 small leek, sliced with the slicing
  disk
2 small onions, sliced with the slicing
  disk
Several dark-green celery leaves

3 tablespoons vegetable oil
8 eggs, lightly beaten with a fork
4 ounces canned lobster tails, coarsely
  chopped with the metal blade or by
  hand
Salt and pepper to taste
½ cup cooked small peas

Simmer together the ingredients for the tomato sauce, about 10 minutes. Remove garlic clove and ginger slice before serving.

Stir-fry the leek, onions, and celery leaves in vegetable oil in a large skillet. Pour in eggs; add lobster, salt, and pepper. Cook over low heat without stirring. As eggs set on bottom, lift edges to allow uncooked mixture to run underneath. When omelette is set, serve at once. Garnish with peas and serve with tomato sauce.

Parsley and Chive Omelette

Yield: 2 servings

½ cup fresh parsley leaves
4 or 5 eggs
¼ teaspoon salt
Pepper to taste
4 blades of chives, cut into ¼-inch
  pieces
1 tablespoon butter
Tomato slices for garnish

Place parsley, eggs, and seasonings in processor bowl. Process with metal blade until parsley is finely chopped. Add chives.

Heat butter in a 10-inch skillet. Pour in the egg mixture. Cook over low heat without stirring. As eggs cook on bottom, lift edges and allow uncooked mixture to run underneath. When all the mixture is set, loosen with a spatula and roll onto a hot dish. Serve at once. Garnish with tomato slices.

Salads & Dressings

Fresh Fruit Salads

Use the slicing disk to slice assorted fruits:

Apples
Bananas
Peaches
Pineapple wedges
Strawberries

Arrange on a platter or toss with:

Slivered almonds
Blueberries
Flaked coconut
Pitted dates, halved
Grapes
Salted nuts
Orange segments
Pineapple chunks
Raisins
Raspberries

Sprinkle with pineapple or orange juice and honey, or serve with Low Calorie Fruit Salad Dressing.

Cranberry — Apple Molded Salad

Yield: 8 servings

Serve this with a chicken or turkey dinner.

2 cups whole cranberries
½ cup water
1 package cherry-flavored gelatin
1 cup boiling water
1 tablespoon lemon juice
1 unpeeled apple, cored and cut into
6 pieces
¼ cup walnuts
¼ cup mayonnaise

Place cranberries and water in a saucepan. Bring to a boil and simmer 4 to 5 minutes, until tender or until the skins pop. Strain, reserve juice, and set berries aside in a large bowl.

Dissolve gelatin in ½ cup reserved juice. Add boiling water and lemon juice. Chill until the consistency of egg white.

Process apple and walnuts with metal blade until coarsely chopped and add to the cranberries in the large bowl.

Place thickened gelatin and mayonnaise in processor bowl and process with metal blade until fluffy. Add this mixture to apples, nuts, and cranberries. Stir until combined, and pour into a 1-quart mold. Chill 4 hours or overnight. Unmold and serve on a bed of lettuce.

Fresh Vegetable Salads

Select a favorite assortment and toss together or assemble a salad bar with each vegetable in a separate bowl.

Use the slicing disk to slice:

Beets
Red cabbage
White cabbage
Carrots
Cauliflower florets
Celery
Cucumbers
Fresh mushrooms
Olives
Pepperoni for an Italian salad
Radishes
Scallions
Yellow squash
Zucchini (excellent raw)

Use the chopping disk to chop:

Cooked bacon
Cauliflower
Cooked chicken or turkey
Hard-cooked eggs
Green pepper, cut into 8 pieces
Olives
Onions
Parsley
Tomatoes, cut into quarters
Walnuts

Use the shredding disk to grate:

Carrots
Cheese

Add:

Anchovy fillets
Bean sprouts
Capers
Seasoned croutons
Garbanzo beans
Slivers of cooked ham, chicken, or
    turkey
Red kidney beans
Broken lettuce
Salted nuts
Poppy seeds
Crumbled Roquefort or feta cheese
Slivers of salami or other luncheon
    meats
Toasted sesame seeds
Sunflower seeds

Serve with your favorite dressing, Garlic Salad Dressing, or Vegetable Salad Dressing. Many of the Dips (see Contents) may be used as salad dressings.

Cucumber — Radish — Sour Cream Salad

Yield: 4 to 6 servings

Home-grown cucumbers do not need to be peeled before using, as they are not coated with wax, as commercially grown ones are, to prevent dehydration.

2 large cucumbers, peeled and cut into
    quarters lengthwise
16 to 24 radishes
½ cup sour cream
Salt to taste

Slice the cucumbers and radishes with the slicing disk. Remove from processor bowl and combine with sour cream and salt. Serve at once.

Peanut — Sunflower Waldorf Salad

Yield: 4 to 6 servings

4 apples, cored, cut into quarters
2 stalks celery, cut into 3-inch pieces
½ cup peanuts
½ cup sunflower seeds
¼ cup raisins
Mayonnaise
Lettuce leaves

Chop the apples, two at a time, very coarsely with the metal blade. Chop the celery. Chop the peanuts coarsely.

Combine the apples, celery, peanuts, sunflower seeds, and raisins in a large bowl. Add sufficient mayonnaise to moisten. Serve cold in lettuce cups.

Tossed Russian Salad with Walnut Dressing

Yield: 4 servings

Salad

1 peeled cucumber, quartered lengthwise, and sliced with the slicing disk
2 stalks celery, sliced with the slicing disk
1 tomato, seeds removed, and diced
Salt to taste

Dressing

½ cup walnuts
1 clove garlic
Dash cayenne
½ teaspoon ground coriander or 1 tablespoon fresh coriander leaves
1 tablespoon vinegar

3 tablespoons water
½ medium onion
2 tablespoons fresh parsley leaves
Lettuce leaves

Combine salad ingredients. Process walnuts, garlic, and cayenne with metal blade until nuts have formed a paste. Add remaining dressing ingredients and process with metal blade until onion is minced. Pour over salad ingredients and toss lightly. Serve in lettuce cups.

Stuffed Tomatoes

Yield: 4 servings

4 large ripe tomatoes
1 tablespoon vegetable oil
1 teaspoon vinegar
1 teaspoon Worcestershire sauce
Salt and pepper
1 6½-ounce can tuna, well drained
4 anchovy fillets
2 hard-cooked eggs, quartered
1 teaspoon capers
4 blades of chives, cut into 1-inch pieces
2 tablespoons fresh parsley leaves
¼ cup mayonnaise
¾ cup yogurt
1 tablespoon lemon juice
1 teaspoon celery salt

Cut tops off tomatoes and scoop out pulp. Brush insides with a mixture of oil, vinegar, and Worcestershire sauce. Season with salt and pepper. Let stand one hour.

Place remaining ingredients in processor bowl. Process with metal blade, turning on and off quickly 2 or 3 times, just until eggs are coarsely chopped.

Drain Worcestershire sauce mixture from tomatoes and fill with tuna mixture. Place tops on tomatoes. Serve at once.

Low Calorie Fruit Salad Dressing

Yield: 1½ cups

1 cup yogurt
½ cup fresh strawberries or raspberries
1 tablespoon honey (or more, to taste)

Place all ingredients in processor bowl and process with metal blade until strawberries are finely chopped. Serve with fruit salad. Delicious alone as a snack!

Garlic Salad Dressing

Yield: About 1 cup

1 cup sour cream
1 clove garlic
2 tablespoons fresh parsley leaves
2 blades chives, cut into 1-inch pieces
½ teaspoon freshly ground black
    pepper
Salt to taste

Place all ingredients in processor bowl and process until parsley is minced. Serve with vegetable salads.

Vegetable Salad Dressing

Yield: About 1½ cups

½ cup sour cream or yogurt
½ cup cottage cheese
½ cucumber, cut into 4 pieces
8 radishes
1 scallion, cut into 1-inch pieces
Salt or seasoned salt to taste
Fresh herbs to taste: dill, parsley,
    tarragon, basil, etc.

Place all ingredients in processor bowl and process with metal blade until vegetables are finely chopped. Serve with vegetable salads.

Sandwiches & Spreads

Baked Bean Spread

Yield: 1 cup

1 cup baked beans
1 small onion, cut into 6 pieces
1 stalk celery, cut into 2-inch pieces
1 tablespoon lemon juice
¼ teaspoon salt

Combine all ingredients in the processor bowl. Process with the metal blade until ingredients are well blended. Chill and use as a spread for whole-wheat sandwiches. Top the filling with chopped tomatoes, shredded lettuce, and grated cheese. Or, top with crumbled bacon and parsley.

Chicken Salad Spread

Yield: 1¼ cups

1 cup cooked chicken (or more), cut
    into 1-inch cubes
1 stalk celery with leaves, cut into
    1-inch pieces
1 small onion, cut in half
3 tablespoons mayonnaise
Salt to taste

Chicken Salad Spread Variations

Add one or more of these ingredients:

½ cup cooked ham and 2 teaspoons
mustard or horseradish
4 slices crisp bacon, broken into 1-inch
pieces
½ cup slivered almonds
½ cup water chestnuts and 1
tablespoon soy sauce
3 tablespoons fresh parsley leaves
1 tablespoon catsup
4 gherkins, halved
8 small black or green olives
1 small apple, cored and cut into
6 pieces
½ teaspoon curry powder
1 teaspoon lemon juice

Place all ingredients in food processor
bowl and process with metal blade until
coarsely chopped. Chop finely for canapés.

Cocktail Spread aux Fines Herbes

Yield: About 1 cup

This spread is nearly identical in flavor to
that of a popular brand name French spread.
Try it! It's less expensive when you prepare it
yourself.

¼ cup cold butter, cut into 3 pieces
2 small cloves garlic
1 8-ounce package cream cheese, cut
into 6 pieces
¼ cup fresh parsley leaves
½ teaspoon salt (or more)
Cracked peppercorns, optional

Process butter and garlic with metal blade
until garlic is finely minced, about 30 seconds. Add remaining ingredients, except
pepper, and process until parsley is minced.

Shape mixture into a flattened ball. Roll
in cracked peppercorns, wrap tightly, and
chill for several hours, until firm. Serve with
assorted crackers.

Cream Cheese Spread

Yield: 1 cup

Cream cheese is half fat and should not
be used routinely as a substitute for meat or
cheese in sandwiches for children unless
other good sources of protein are present in
the meal.

¼ cup nuts (or more)
1 8-ounce package cream cheese, cut
into 6 pieces

Cream Cheese Spread Variations

Add one of the following:

½ cup canned crushed pineapple,
drained
Omit nuts and add ½ cup olives, a few
slices onion, and a dash Tabasco
sauce
2 cups watercress, cut into 1-inch
pieces

Place nuts and cheese in processor bowl
and process with metal blade until nuts are
coarsely chopped. Tint cheese with food
coloring if spread is to be used for canapés.

Egg Salad Spread

Yield: 1½ cups

6 hard-cooked eggs, cut into quarters
2 stalks celery, cut into 1-inch pieces
½ teaspoon salt
¼ teaspoon freshly ground black
   pepper
3 tablespoons mayonnaise

Egg Salad Spread Variations

Add one of these combinations:

1 tablespoon catsup and 3 gherkins,
   halved
½ cucumber, peeled and cut into
   1-inch pieces, and 2 tablespoons
   fresh parsley leaves
½ cup cooked chicken and
   ½ teaspoon curry powder
½ cup cooked chicken and 8 small
   olives
4 slices crisp bacon, crumbled
½ cup cheddar cheese, shredded with
   the shredding disk, and 1 teaspoon
   prepared mayonnaise
½ green pepper, cut into 1-inch
   pieces, and several slices onion
2 tablespoons chili sauce and several
   slices onion
4 ounces cooked chicken livers and
   several slices onion
4 anchovy fillets and 1 teaspoon lemon
   juice
2 teaspoons lemon juice and 3
   tablespoons fresh parsley leaves
½ cup ham, cut into 1-inch cubes,
   and 8 small black or green olives
4 anchovy fillets and ½ teaspoon
   paprika
2 4½-ounce cans deviled ham and
   1 teaspoon prepared mustard

Place all ingredients in processor bowl
and process with metal blade until coarsely
chopped. Process finer if spread is to be used
for canapés.

Ham Salad Spread

Yield: 1¼ cups

1 cup cooked ham, cut into 1-inch
   cubes
3 tablespoons mayonnaise
1 stalk celery, cut into 1-inch pieces

Ham Salad Spread Variations

Add one or more of the following
ingredients:

2 hard-cooked eggs, quartered, and
   ½ teaspoon garlic powder
1 small onion, halved
8 small black or green olives
4 gherkins, halved, or 2 tablespoons
   relish
2 tablespoons orange marmalade and
   ½ teaspoon prepared mustard
2 teaspoons prepared mustard and
   2 tablespoons fresh parsley leaves

Place all ingredients in food processor
bowl and process with metal blade until
coarsely chopped. Chop finely for canapés.

Peanut Butter

Yield: About 1 cup

Peanuts (12-ounce bag of raw shelled
   and blanched peanuts, baked at
   350°F for 15 to 20 minutes; or
   ½ pound very fresh roasted peanuts
   in the shell, shelled and skinned;
   or 1 to 2 cups salted peanuts)
Honey to taste

Salt to taste
Vegetable oil, if needed

Process the peanuts with the metal blade, 1 to 2 cups at a time, until a ball forms on the blades, about 1 to 2 minutes. Commercially made peanut butter usually contains sugar, and you may wish to add about a tablespoon of honey. Process until blended. Taste and add salt to your liking if unsalted peanuts were used.

Occasionally, the peanuts will not form a spread, even after processing for 2 minutes. Correct by dribbling small quantities of vegetable oil in through the tube and processing until a paste is formed.

Mock Pizzas

Yield: 8 4-inch pizzas

2 ripe tomatoes, quartered
¼ green pepper, cut into 3 pieces
1 teaspoon oregano
½ teaspoon garlic salt
1 tablespoon olive oil
6 to 8 ounces cheddar cheese, shredded with the shredding disk
4 English muffins, halved

Place tomatoes, pepper, oregano, garlic salt, and olive oil in processor bowl. Process with metal blade until coarsely chopped. Add cheese and process just until blended. Spread mixture on muffin halves and broil until cheese melts and surface is brown.

Salmon Spread

Yield: About 1¼ cups

1 7¾-ounce can salmon, drained
1 stalk celery with leaves, cut into 1-inch pieces
½ green pepper, cut into 1-inch cubes
¼ cup mayonnaise

Place all ingredients in processor bowl and process with metal blade until coarsely chopped. Process longer if spread is to be used for canapés.

Tuna Salad Spread

Yield: About 1 cup

1 6½-ounce can tuna, well drained
1 stalk celery with leaves, cut into 1-inch pieces
3 tablespoons mayonnaise

Tuna Salad Spread Variations

Add one or more of the following ingredients:

½ green pepper, cut into 1-inch pieces
2 tablespoons chutney and 1 hard-cooked egg, quartered
1 small onion, halved, 2 hard-cooked eggs, and 1 teaspoon lemon juice

Place in food processor bowl and process with metal blade until coarsely chopped. Process longer if spread is to be used for canapés.

Curried Turkey Spread

Yield: 1½ cups

1 cup cooked turkey, cut into 1-inch
  cubes
1 stalk celery with leaves, cut into
  1-inch pieces
1 teaspoon lemon juice
1 teaspoon curry powder
½ teaspoon salt
¼ teaspoon freshly ground black
  pepper
1 small apple, cored and cut into
  6 pieces
Few slices onion
3 to 4 tablespoons mayonnaise

Combine all ingredients in processor bowl and process with the metal blade until coarsely chopped.

Soups

Avocado Soup

Yield: About 4 cups

2 ripe, soft avocados, pitted and peeled
1 cup chicken broth
1 cup light cream
½ cup yogurt
½ cup dry white wine
1 teaspoon lemon juice
Salt and pepper to taste

Reserve a few slices of avocado for a garnish and place remaining avocado in processor bowl and process with metal blade until smooth.

Warm broth slightly, add avocado and remaining ingredients. Stir to blend. Serve cold, or heat over moderate heat and serve warm. Garnish with reserved avocado slices.

Red Bean Soup

Yield: 3 cups

1 medium onion
1 large stalk celery with leaves
½ green pepper
2 tablespoons vegetable oil
1 cup cooked kidney beans
1 cup kidney bean liquor
1 cup tomato juice
Thin lemon slice
Parsley leaves

Chop the onion, celery, and green pepper coarsely with the metal blade. Sauté in the oil until soft. Place sautéed vegetables and beans in the processor bowl and process with the metal blade until smooth, about 15 seconds.

Add mixture to bean liquor and tomato juice in a saucepan and heat thoroughly. Serve hot garnished with a thin slice of lemon and a few parsley leaves.

Russian Borscht

Yield: 4 cups

1 No. 2½ can beets, liquid reserved
1 can condensed cream of chicken
  soup
1 clove garlic
1 can condensed beef consommé
½ teaspoon tarragon
½ teaspoon chervil
½ teaspoon dried parsley
Sour cream

Process the beets, cream of chicken soup, and garlic with the metal blade until smooth. Combine with the consommé, herbs, and reserved beet liquid in a 1½-quart container. Chill. Serve cold, garnished with a spoonful of sour cream.

New England-style Clam Chowder

Yield: 5 cups

2 medium onions, cut into quarters
3 tablespoons butter or margarine
2 medium potatoes, peeled and cut into several pieces
1 10½-ounce can clams, broth reserved
1 cup boiling water and reserved clam broth
½ teaspoon salt
⅛ teaspoon pepper
1 tablespoon flour
2 tablespoons cold water
1 pint whole milk

Chop onions finely with the metal blade and sauté in butter in a large skillet until soft.

Chop potatoes very coarsely with the metal blade and add to the onions in the skillet. Add the boiling water and broth and salt and pepper. Simmer 30 minutes. Add more hot water if necessary.

Combine flour and cold water and stir until smooth. Add to potato-clam mixture and heat until thickened. Add milk and heat through. Serve at once with chowder crackers.

Swiss Fondue Soup

Yield: 4 to 6 servings

This soup is thickened with bread crumbs and laced with shredded cheese and wine.

8 dry, white bread slices, each torn in quarters
½ pound Swiss cheese, shredded with shredding disk
3 cups hot chicken broth
1 cup dry white wine
10 blades of chives, sliced fine
1 teaspoon fresh parsley leaves or dillweed, chopped
Salt and pepper to taste

Garnish

1 small onion, sliced with the slicing disk
4 slices bacon, halved

Process bread with the metal blade, four slices at a time, until coarsely chopped. Add bread and cheese to hot broth. Let stand 10 minutes. Process half at a time in processor bowl with the metal blade until smooth. Place in a saucepan and bring to a boil. Add wine, chives, and parsley. Season to taste with salt and pepper. Keep warm.

In a skillet, brown onion rings and bacon until onion is glazed. Serve soup at once, garnished with bacon and onion.

Gazpacho

Yield: About 4 to 5 cups

There are countless variations to this flavorful cold soup. You can adjust the ingredients according to vegetables available or in season. Those given here are a suggested assortment. Herbs and parsley also may be added.

1 medium onion, peeled and quartered
1 clove garlic
2 green peppers, seeded and quartered
4 tomatoes, peeled, seeds removed if you wish, quartered
1 cucumber, peeled and cut into 6 pieces
Salt and pepper to taste
⅓ cup olive oil
¼ cup lemon juice
2 or more cups tomato juice
1 tablespoon dry sherry

Chop each of the vegetables separately until coarse in the processor bowl, with the metal blade. Remove to a large jar. Add salt and pepper, olive oil, lemon juice, tomato juice, and sherry and chill well. Serve cold with a dollop of sour cream on top.

Hearty Lentil Soup

Yield: 5 to 6 cups

Lentils, unlike other dried beans, do not have to be soaked prior to cooking.

1½ cups lentils
1 medium onion, quartered, and chopped with the metal blade
2 large stalks celery with leaves, cut into 3-inch sections, and chopped with the metal blade

4 cups water
⅓ pound smoked pork neck bones with meat attached
Salt and pepper

Place beans, onion, celery, and water in saucepan with neck bones. Simmer 45 to 60 minutes or until beans are tender. Remove bones and trim off meat.

Process soup 1 to 2 cups at a time with the metal blade until smooth. Add meat and rewarm if necessary. Season to taste. Serve hot.

Cream of Mushroom Soup

Yield: 4 servings

1 small onion, quartered
1 stalk celery, cut into 3-inch pieces
4 to 6 tablespoons butter or margarine
1 pound fresh mushrooms
3½ cups whole milk
¼ cup all-purpose flour
Salt
Fresh parsley sprigs

Chop onion and celery coarsely with metal blade. Cook over low heat in butter in a large skillet until soft.

Slice the mushrooms into "T" shapes with the slicing disk (by wedging them into the tube sideways) and add to onions and celery. Cook 2 to 3 minutes. Add 3 cups of the milk to the mushrooms in the skillet.

Shake ½ cup cold milk in a jar with the flour until no lumps are present. Add to the skillet. Heat and stir over moderate heat until soup is thickened and begins to boil. Salt to taste. Serve at once garnished with parsley sprigs.

Parisian Onion Soup

Yield: 5 to 6 cups

3 tablespoons vegetable oil
3 cups onions, quartered, and coarsely
   chopped a few at a time with metal
   blade
4 cups rich beef stock
½ cup vermouth
Slices of dry French bread
Swiss cheese, grated with shredding
   disk
Grated Parmesan cheese

Place oil and onions in a frying pan;
cover, and cook over low heat until soft,
about 10 minutes. Remove lid, turn up heat
and brown onions until they are a rich, ma-
hogany brown, about 10 minutes or longer.
Stir every 2 to 3 minutes and do not burn.
Add stock and simmer 1 hour. Stir in
vermouth.
   Place soup in bowls. Add a slice of
French bread to each and sprinkle with a
mixture of Swiss and Parmesan cheeses.
Place bowls in a hot oven or under broiler
until cheese melts. Serve immediately.

Indian Pea Soup

Yield: About 5 cups

1 1-pound can peas, drained, liquid
   reserved
3 cups chicken broth or bouillon
2 teaspoons curry powder
1 teaspoon sugar
¼ cup all-purpose flour shaken in a jar
   with ⅓ cup cold water until lump-
   free
¼ cup slivered almonds
¼ cup raisins
½ cup light cream
Salt and pepper to taste

Place drained peas in processor bowl and
process with metal blade until smooth. Place

in saucepan with reserved liquid, broth,
curry, sugar, and flour mixture. Bring to a
boil, stirring constantly. Add almonds and
raisins. Simmer 5 minutes. Remove from
heat and add cream. Season to taste with salt
and pepper. Serve at once.

Nut Breads & Quick Breads

Banana – Orange Nut Bread

Yield: 1 9 × 5-inch loaf

1 cup sugar
½ cup hydrogenated shortening
2 eggs
½ teaspoon salt
Skin of ½ tangerine or peeled outer
   rind of 1 small orange
2 bananas, each broken into 8 pieces
½ cup walnuts
2 cups sifted all-purpose flour
1½ teaspoons baking powder
½ teaspoon baking soda

Insert metal blade in processor bowl. Add
sugar, shortening, eggs, salt, and rind. Process until light and the rind is finely chopped,
about 15 seconds. Add bananas; process 4 or
5 seconds. Scrape down sides and break up
any remaining large pieces. Add walnuts,
process 1 second.
   Stir together the flour, baking powder,
and soda. Add to the bowl and process by
turning on and off quickly 4 or 5 times or
just until blended. Do not overprocess.
   Pour into a greased 9 × 5-inch loaf pan
and bake at 350°F for 55 to 60 minutes.
Cool on a rack and serve warm. Top with a
little whipped cream or cream cheese if you
are not too concerned with calories.

Apple – Raisin Bread

Yield: 1 9 × 5-inch loaf

¾ cup brown sugar
½ cup cold butter or margarine, cut
    into 6 pieces
2 eggs
1 teaspoon cinnamon
¼ teaspoon cloves
½ teaspoon salt
2 large apples, peeled, cored, and each
    cut into 8 pieces
½ cup raisins
2 cups sifted all-purpose flour
¼ teaspoon baking soda
2 teaspoons baking powder
½ cup walnuts, optional

Place sugar, butter, eggs, spices, and salt in the processor bowl. Process with the metal blade until light, about 15 seconds. Add apples and process until finely chopped. Add raisins; process 2 seconds.

Stir together the flour, soda, and baking powder. Add to the processor bowl. Turn blade on and off quickly 4 or 5 times, until flour is blended in. Do not overprocess.

Pour into a 9 × 5-inch loaf pan and bake at 350°F for 55 to 60 minutes. Cool on a wire rack. If you like nuts, ½ cup walnuts may be added with the flour.

Cream Puff Shells

Yield: 8 to 12 large puffs
24 to 36 small puffs

1 cup water
½ cup butter or margarine
¼ teaspoon salt
1 cup sifted all-purpose flour
4 eggs

Place the water, butter, and salt in a saucepan. Heat to boiling but do not evaporate. Add the flour all at once and stir vigorously. Cook, stirring continuously, until the mixture forms a ball and no longer clings to the sides of the pan, about 1 to 2 minutes. Remove from heat and let stand for 5 minutes.

Insert metal blade in processor bowl. Add the batter and process 15 seconds. Add the eggs and process until dough is smooth and shiny, about 30 seconds.

Drop the mixture from a teaspoon or tablespoon, depending on size desired, onto a greased baking sheet. Or press through a star-shaped tip of a cookie press. Leave 2 inches between each to allow for spreading.

Bake in a preheated 450°F oven for 15 minutes. Reduce the heat to 325°F and continue baking 25 minutes longer. Remove from baking sheet with a spatula and cool on a wire rack.

Shortly before serving time, cut off the tops and fill with pudding, whipped cream, berries, or other desired dessert filling. Or, fill with tuna or chicken salads and serve as a main dish or the small ones as appetizers. Serve at once after filling.

Date – Nut – Carrot Whole-Wheat Bread

Yield: 1 9 × 5-inch loaf

2 medium carrots, cleaned and scraped
¾ cup brown sugar
½ cup cold butter or margarine, cut
    into 6 pieces
2 eggs
½ teaspoon salt
¼ cup orange juice
½ cup pitted dates, halved

¾ cup flaked coconut, optional
½ cup walnuts
1 cup sifted all-purpose flour
1 cup whole-wheat flour
2 teaspoons baking powder
¼ teaspoon baking soda

Grate the carrots with the shredding disk. Remove from the bowl and set aside. Insert the metal blade in the food processor bowl. Add the sugar, butter, eggs, and salt. Process until light, about 15 seconds. Add orange juice. Process until it is combined. Add grated carrots, dates, coconut, and walnuts. Process by turning on and off quickly 3 or 4 times. Scrape down sides twice.

Stir together the flour, baking powder, and soda. Add to the bowl. Process by turning blade on and off quickly 4 or 5 times, until ingredients are combined. Do not over-process, or cake will be tough and nuts and fruits pulverized.

Pour into a greased 9 × 5-inch loaf pan and bake at 350°F for about 55 minutes. Remove from pan and cool on a wire rack. Slice when completely cool.

Fruit Muffins

Yield: 12

1 cup milk
1 egg
2 tablespoons vegetable oil
2 tablespoons sugar
1 teaspoon salt
About 1 cup dates, apples, or bananas
    cut into 1-inch pieces, or blueberries
2 cups sifted all-purpose flour
3 teaspoons baking powder

Place milk, egg, oil, sugar, salt, and the desired fruit in the processor bowl. Process with the metal blade until the fruit is coarsely chopped.

Sift together in a large mixing bowl the flour and baking powder. Pour in the liquid-fruit mixture and stir just until the dry ingredients are moistened.

Fill greased muffin pans ⅔ full. Bake at 425°F for 15 to 20 minutes. Remove from pan at once and serve hot with butter.

Variations. *Cheese Muffins:* Follow directions for Fruit Muffins, but substitute 1 cup grated cheese, grated with the shredding disk, for the fruit. *Whole-Wheat Muffins:* Use the Fruit Muffins recipe, but substitute 1 cup whole-wheat flour for 1 cup of the all-purpose flour.

Popovers

Yield: 8 or 9

Hollow, mushroom shapes to be served piping hot with butter.

1 cup sifted all-purpose flour
½ teaspoon salt
1 tablespoon vegetable oil
2 eggs
1 cup milk

Place all ingredients in the processor bowl and process with the metal blade until smooth, about 10 seconds.

Lightly grease muffin pans or custard cups. Fill cups ½ full with the batter. Bake at 450°F for 15 minutes; reduce heat to 325°F and bake another 30 minutes. Serve at once.

Yeast Breads

Cottage Cheese – Dill Bread

Yield: 1 loaf

1 package active dry yeast
¼ cup lukewarm water (105-115°F)
1 tablespoon sugar
2 tablespoons vegetable oil
1 egg, room temperature
1 teaspoon salt
1 small onion, peeled and quartered
1 cup creamed cottage cheese, warmed
    to lukewarm so it will not delay
    rising
2½ cups all-purpose flour
1 tablespoon dillseeds

Dissolve yeast in warm water in the processor bowl. Add sugar, oil, egg, salt, onion, and cheese. Process with the metal blade for 15 seconds or until the onion is finely minced. Add 1¼ cups of the flour and process until smooth, about 15 seconds. Let rise in processor bowl 20 to 30 minutes. Add remaining flour and dillseeds. Process until a ball forms on the blades or the motor begins to stall, about 5 seconds.

Knead on a floured surface 1 to 2 minutes, until smooth. Pat dough into a well-greased 8½ × 4½-inch loaf pan. Cover and let rise in a warm (80-85°F) place, about 45 minutes or until doubled in bulk.

Bake at 375°F for 30 to 35 minutes. Cool loaf on a wire rack and serve warm.

French Bread

Yield: 1 loaf

The shaped loaf is brushed with water and baked in a steamy oven to form a crisp, crunchy crust. Serve this with a bottle of wine and an assortment of your favorite cheese for Saturday's lunch.

1 package active dry yeast
1 scant cup lukewarm water
    (110-115°F)
2 tablespoons vegetable oil
1¼ teaspoons salt
3 cups all-purpose flour

Dissolve yeast in lukewarm water in the processor bowl. Add oil, salt, and 1½ cups of the flour. Process with the metal blade about 15 seconds. Let dough rise in the covered processor bowl for about 30 minutes. Add remaining flour and process until a ball forms or the blades slow down and the motor begins to stall.

Remove dough and knead on a floured board for about 2 minutes. Shape dough into a long roll about 2 inches in diameter. Place on a greased baking sheet, cover with a damp towel, and let it rise in a warm place (80-85°F) until doubled in bulk, about 45 minutes.

Slash the top of the loaf with a sharp knife diagonally ⅛ to ¼-inch deep every 1½ inches. Brush the loaf with cold water and place on the top oven shelf. On the second shelf beneath the loaf, place 1 cup of boiling water in a cake pan. Turn the oven on to 400°F and bake loaf 30 to 40 minutes.

After 10 minutes of baking, brush or spray loaf with cold water. Repeat again in 15 minutes. Cool loaf on a rack and serve at once.

Light Rye Bread

Yield: 1 loaf

1 package active dry yeast
¾ cup lukewarm water (105-115°F)

122

1 tablespoon sugar
1 teaspoon salt
2 tablespoons vegetable oil
1¼ cups all-purpose flour
1¼ cups rye flour
1 tablespoon caraway seeds (optional)
1 egg, lightly beaten

Dissolve yeast in the lukewarm water in the processor bowl. Add sugar, salt, oil, and the all-purpose flour. Process with the metal blade for 15 seconds. Let rise in the processor bowl for 20 to 30 minutes. Add the rye flour and caraway seeds. Process until a ball forms on the blades, about 5 seconds.

Knead dough on a lightly floured surface for 1 to 2 minutes, until smooth and elastic. Form into a loaf about 8 inches long, with tapered ends, and place on a greased baking sheet. Cover and let rise in a warm place (80-85°F) until doubled in bulk, about 45 to 60 minutes.

Brush crust with lightly beaten egg and sprinkle with additional caraway seeds. Bake in a preheated 375°F oven for 30 to 40 minutes. Cool on a wire rack. Serve at once. Loaf is compact and moist.

White Bread

Yield: 1 loaf

¾ cup lukewarm water (105-115°F)
1 package active dry yeast
2 tablespoons sugar
½ teaspoon salt
2 tablespoons vegetable oil
2½ cups all-purpose flour

Place water in the food processor bowl, add yeast and allow it to dissolve. Add sugar, salt, oil, and 1½ cups of the flour. Process with the metal blade for 15 seconds. Let rise in the processor bowl for 20 to 30 minutes. Add the remaining 1 cup of flour. Process only until a ball of dough forms on the blades.

Remove and knead dough on a floured surface for 1 to 2 minutes, until smooth and elastic. Shape into a loaf and press into a well-greased 8 × 4-inch loaf pan. Cover and rise in a warm (80-85°F) place for 30 to 45 minutes, until doubled in bulk.

Place in a preheated 375°F oven and bake for 30 minutes. Remove from pan immediately and cool on a wire rack. Serve at once.

Salt Sticks

Yield: 12 rolls

1 recipe White Bread
Caraway seeds
Kosher (coarse) salt
1 egg beaten with 1 tablespoon water

Prepare yeast dough and knead as directed. Roll dough into a 12-inch circle and cut with a sharp knife or pizza cutter into 12 pie-shaped wedges. Begin with the wide end and roll each wedge tightly. Moisten the point and seal to the roll. Curve each roll to form a crescent and place on a greased baking sheet. Let rise in a warm (80-85°F) place until doubled in bulk.

Brush each roll with the egg mixture, sprinkle with caraway seeds and a little salt. Bake in a preheated 400°F oven for 12 to 15 minutes. Serve at once.

Dark German Rye Bread

Yield: 1 loaf

Very dark in color, sweet, and moist.

1 package active dry yeast
¾ cup lukewarm water (105-115°F)
3 tablespoons molasses
1 tablespoon cocoa
1 teaspoon salt
2 tablespoons vegetable oil
1¼ cups all-purpose flour
1¼ cups rye flour
1 tablespoon caraway seeds
1 egg, lightly beaten

Dissolve yeast in lukewarm water in the processor bowl. Add molasses, cocoa, salt, oil, and the all-purpose flour. Process with the metal blade for 15 seconds. Let rise in the food processor bowl for 20 to 30 minutes. Add rye flour and caraway seeds. Process until a ball forms on the blades, about 5 seconds, or until motor begins to stall.

Remove dough and knead on a floured surface 1 to 2 minutes, until smooth. Shape into an 8-inch oblong loaf. Place on a greased baking sheet. Cover and let rise in a warm (80-85°F) place about 45 minutes or until doubled in bulk.

Brush with highly beaten egg and sprinkle with additional caraway seeds. Bake in a preheated 375°F oven for 30 to 40 minutes. Cool on a wire rack. Slice and serve at once.

Sweet-Roll Dough

Yield: see following recipes

1 package active dry yeast
½ cup lukewarm water (105-115°F)
¼ cup sugar
½ teaspoon salt

¼ cup butter or margarine, cut into
    4 pieces
1 egg, room temperature
2½ cups all-purpose flour

Dissolve yeast in warm water in the processor bowl. Add sugar, salt, butter, egg, and 1½ cups flour. Process 15 seconds. Let rise in the processor bowl for 20 minutes. Add remaining cup of flour and process until a ball forms on the blades, about 5 seconds.

Remove dough and knead on a floured surface for 1 to 2 minutes. Shape, rise, and bake as directed in the following recipes.

Rising time for sweet-roll dough is longer than for bread dough because sugar slows the growth of the yeast.

Apple – Crumb Coffee Cake

Yield: 1 8-inch-square coffee cake

1 recipe Sweet-Roll Dough
2 apples, peeled, cored, quartered, and
    sliced with the slicing disk
⅓ cup brown sugar
¼ cup all-purpose flour
1 teaspoon cinnamon
3 tablespoons cold butter, cut into
    3 pieces

Prepare Sweet-Roll Dough as recipe directs. After kneading, pat dough into a greased 8 × 8 × 2-inch-square baking pan. Arrange apple slices over the dough.

Place the sugar, flour, cinnamon, and butter in the processor bowl and process with the metal blade until the mixture is crumbly, about 10 seconds. Sprinkle over apples. Let rise in a warm (80-85°F) place until doubled in bulk, 45 to 60 minutes.

Bake in a preheated 375°F oven for 35 to 40 minutes. Cool in pan 15 minutes. Remove to a rack. Serve warm.

Bugnes

Yield: About 50

Bugnes (pronounced buns) are sweet fritters with an unusual shape.

1 recipe Sweet-Roll Dough
Vegetable oil for deep-fat frying
1 cup confectioner's sugar
1 teaspoon cinnamon
1 teaspoon nutmeg

Prepare Sweet-Roll Dough as recipe directs. Roll out dough to 1/16-inch thickness on a floured surface. Cut into 1- by 3-inch rectangles with a fluted pastry wheel. Make a 1½-inch lengthwise slit down the center of each rectangle. Push one end through slit and pull back. Let pieces rise for about 30 minutes.

Drop a few at a time into oil at 375°F. Fry until lightly browned on both sides. Remove with a slotted spoon and drain on paper towels.

Combine sugar and spices and sprinkle over Bugnes.

Brioche Rolls

Yield: 8 to 10

Rich, golden, French rolls with a top-knot. In France these delicate rolls are most often served at breakfast.

1 package active dry yeast
¼ cup lukewarm water (105-115°F)
¼ cup sugar
½ teaspoon salt
2 eggs, room temperature
2½ cups all-purpose flour
½ cup cold butter, cut into 6 pieces

Dissolve yeast in lukewarm water in the processor bowl. Add 1 tablespoon of the sugar, salt, eggs, and 1¼ cups flour. Process 20 seconds. Let rise in processor bowl for 20 to 30 minutes. Add butter and remaining sugar. Process until blended, about 15 seconds. Add remaining ¼ cups of flour and process until a ball forms on the blades or motor begins to stall.

Knead lightly 1 to 2 minutes. Set aside ¼ of the dough. Cut the remaining ¾ into 8 to 10 pieces. Roll each into a smooth ball and place in greased muffin tins or fluted brioche-tart molds, if you have them.

Cut reserved dough into 8 or 10 pieces; roll in balls. Make an indentation in the center of each large ball. Moisten, and press the small ball into the dent. Let rise in a warm (80-85°F) place for 30 to 45 minutes, until doubled in bulk. Brush each brioche with beaten egg.

Bake at 375°F for about 15 to 20 minutes. Serve warm with sweet butter or marmalade.

Scandinavian Bear-Track Doughnuts

Yield: 24

1 package active dry yeast
½ cup lukewarm water (105-115°F)
¼ cup sugar
½ teaspoon anise seeds
¼ cup cold butter cut into 3 pieces
1 egg, room temperature
2½ cups all-purpose flour
Vegetable oil for deep-fat frying

Dissolve yeast in the lukewarm water in the processor bowl. Add sugar, anise, butter, egg, and 1¼ cups of the flour. Process with the metal blade for 15 seconds and let rise in the processor bowl for 20 to 30 minutes. Add remaining flour and process until a ball of dough forms on the blades, about 5 seconds.

Remove and knead for 1 to 2 minutes. Roll out dough to a 6 × 12-inch rectangle. Cut into 12 3 × 1-inch strips. Cover and let rise in a warm place (80-85°F) until doubled in bulk.

Slice the edges of each strip into "fingers" by making 4 cuts along the long edge of each strip, cutting through past the middle.

Deep-fry "tracks" in oil at 375°F a few at a time until a very light golden color. Drain on paper towels. Coat each with sugar by shaking in a paper bag containing sugar. Serve warm.

Soft Pretzels

Yield: 8 to 10 soft pretzels

These pretzels are like those you can buy from pretzel stands on city street corners in many cities.

1 package active dry yeast
⅔ cup lukewarm water (105-115°F)
1 tablespoon vegetable oil
2 tablespoons sugar
½ teaspoon salt
1 egg, lightly beaten and divided in half
2¼ cups all-purpose flour
1½ teaspoons lye (handle with care!) dissolved in 2 cups cold water in a stainless-steel pan (This very dilute mixture of lye is harmless and gives pretzels their characteristic flavor.) or
2 teaspoons baking soda dissolved in 2 cups water may be used in place of the lye mixture. (Flavor is similar to, but not the same as, the dilute lye solution.)
Kosher (coarse) salt
1 tablespoon cold water

Dissolve the yeast in the warm water in the processor bowl. Add the oil, sugar, plain salt, ½ the beaten egg, and 1¼ cups flour. Process with the metal blade for 20 seconds and let rise in the processor bowl for 30 minutes. Add remaining flour and process until a ball forms on the blades.

Knead the dough on a lightly floured surface for 1 to 2 minutes. Cut the dough into 8 or 10 pieces. Roll each piece into a 16-inch long rope. Dip into the lye or baking-soda solution. Form into a pretzel. Seal ends well. Place on a lightly greased baking sheet. Let rise slightly, but not until doubled in bulk or the texture will be spongy rather than crisp (about 15 minutes).

Combine remaining ½ egg with 1 tablespoon cold water and brush the pretzels with the mixture. Sprinkle with coarse salt.

Bake in a preheated 400°F oven for about 15 minutes. Cool on a wire rack. Serve warm.

Pizza Dough with Whole Wheat Flour

Yield: 12 × 15-inch pizza or 12- to 14-inch round pizza

1 package active dry yeast
⅔ cup lukewarm water (105-115°F)
2 teaspoons sugar
½ teaspoon salt
1 tablespoon vegetable or olive oil
1½ cups all-purpose flour
1 cup whole-wheat flour

Dissolve yeast in warm water in the processor bowl. Add sugar, salt, oil, and all of the all-purpose flour. Process with the metal blade for 15 seconds. Let rise for 30 minutes in the processor bowl. Add whole-wheat flour and process until a ball forms on the blades.

Remove dough and knead on a floured surface for 1 minute. Roll out into a large circle or rectangle to the desired thickness, about ⅛ to ¼ inch thick. Pinch up a rim around the edge.

Spread with the prepared Pizza Sauce mixture, shredded cheese, and desired toppings.

Bake in a preheated 400°F oven for 15 to 20 minutes, depending on thickness of crust. Cut into wedges and serve immediately with a cool beverage or wine and a tossed salad.

Variation. Pizza Dough with Enriched Flour: Substitute all-purpose flour for the whole-wheat flour.

Pizza Sauce and Toppings

Yield: Sauce for 1 12- to 14-inch round pizza.

1 6-ounce can tomato paste
3 ounces (½ can) water
½ teaspoon garlic salt
2 teaspoons oregano
⅛ teaspoon freshly ground black pepper
1 to 2 tablespoons olive oil
4 ounces mozzarella cheese, shredded with shredding disk
2 tablespoons grated Parmesan cheese

Additional Toppings

Fresh mushrooms, chopped coarsely with metal blade or sliced with the slicing disk
Pitted black olives, sliced or chopped with the metal blade
Green peppers, chopped with the metal blade
Onion, chopped with the metal blade or sliced with the slicing disk
Pepperoni, sliced with the serrated slicing disk (What a joy it is to use the processor for this tedious task!)
Fresh parsley, chopped with the metal blade
Cooked ground beef
Cooked sausage
Anchovy fillets
Slivered ham
Fresh tomato slices or wedges

Combine tomato paste with water and spread on prepared pizza dough. Sprinkle with seasonings and oil. Top with cheese and desired toppings.

Desserts

Apple – Almond – Rum Bars

Yield: 20 bars, each about 2 inches square

2 eggs
1 cup sugar
2 tablespoons water
1 apple, peeled, cored, and cut into 6 pieces
1 teaspoon rum flavoring
2 teaspoons cinnamon
¼ teaspoon ground cloves
⅓ cup semisweet chocolate bits, optional
¼ cup candied fruit
4 ounces almonds
2 cups sifted all-purpose flour
1 teaspoon baking powder

Glaze

1 cup confectioners' sugar
1½ tablespoons water
½ teaspoon rum flavoring

Place eggs, sugar, and water in processor bowl. Process with the metal blade for 10 seconds. Add apple, flavoring, and spices; process 10 seconds. Add chocolate bits; process 5 seconds. Add fruit and almonds; process 5 seconds.

Stir together the flour and baking powder. Add to the mixture in the processor bowl and process just until blended, about 5 seconds.

Spread in a greased 9 × 13-inch baking pan. Bake at 350°F for 20 minutes.

Combine confectioners' sugar, water, and flavoring. Glaze bars while warm. Cool and cut into squares.

Apple Crisp

Yield: 4 servings

3 apples, peeled, cored, and cut into quarters
½ cup brown sugar
½ cup whole-wheat flour
¼ cup cold butter or margarine, cut into 4 pieces
½ teaspoon cinnamon
⅓ cup granola or quick-cooking oats

Slice the apples with the metal slicing disk and toss with ½ of the brown sugar in a 1-quart casserole dish.

Place remaining sugar, flour, butter, cinnamon, and granola in processor bowl and process with the metal blade until crumbly. Sprinkle this mixture evenly over the apples. Bake in a 375°F oven for 30 to 40 minutes, until apples are tender. Serve warm.

No-cook Applesauce

Yield: 3 or 4 servings

4 apples, peeled, cored, and each cut into quarters
3 to 4 tablespoons sugar
1 teaspoon lemon juice
Dash cinnamon, optional
¼ teaspoon antioxidant mixture (optional if eaten quickly) such as "Fruit Fresh" or "ACM"

Place all ingredients in processor bowl and process with metal blade until smooth. Serve at once.

If apples are very large, process 2 or 3 initially and add remaining pieces through the tube as machine is running.

Bourbon or Rum Balls

Yield: 4 dozen

5 dozen vanilla wafers, broken
  (2½ cups crumbs)
1 cup walnuts
1 cup confectioners' sugar
⅓ cup bourbon or rum
3 tablespoons corn syrup
Confectioners' sugar for coating

Process vanilla wafers a few at a time with the metal blade until they are finely crushed. Remove to a mixing bowl and repeat until all are crushed.

Chop walnuts coarsely with the metal blade. Add to crushed wafers along with remaining ingredients. Mix well and form into 1-inch balls. Roll in confectioners' sugar and store in an airtight container for a week or two before using.

Cannelloni Alla Siciliana

Yield: About 12

Shells

2 tablespoons butter, melted
3 cups sifted all-purpose flour
3 tablespoons sugar
¼ teaspoon salt
1 egg
½ cup dry white wine

Filling

1 pound ricotta cheese
1 cup confectioners' sugar
½ teaspoon vanilla
¼ cup candied fruit
¼ cup chocolate bits
1 egg white for sealing
Vegetable oil for deep-fat frying
Cannelloni molds or aluminum foil

Place ingredients for shells in the processor bowl and process with the metal blade until a ball forms on the blades. Remove and knead on a floured surface for 1 to 2 minutes. Cover, and refrigerate for 1 hour.

Place ingredients for filling in processor bowl and process with the metal blade until fruit and nuts are coarsely chopped. Refrigerate for 20 to 30 minutes.

Roll out dough on a floured surface to about ⅛ inch thick. Cut with a pastry cutter into 4- or 5-inch squares. Wrap each square diagonally around a cannelloni form or a roll of aluminum foil. Seal corners with egg whites.

Deep-fry in oil at 375°F for about 3 minutes or until golden brown. Drain on paper towels and cool about 15 minutes with foil or forms still inside. Remove foil. Fill with cheese mixture and serve at once.

Cream Puffs with Fruit and Whipped Cream

Yield: 12

2 cups heavy whipping cream, very
  cold
⅓ cup sugar
12 large Cream Puff Shells (see Index)
1 small can mandarin oranges, drained
¼ cup nuts, chopped with the metal
  blade

Combine cream and sugar and whip until soft peaks form. (The metal blade does not whip air into cream well; use a mixer or whisk for greatest volume.)

Cut tops off cream puff shells and fill with the whipped-cream mixture. Garnish with mandarin oranges and chopped nuts. Serve immediately.

Cassata Alla Siciliana

Yield: 8 to 10 servings

2 pounds ricotta cheese
1⅔ cups sugar
1 teaspoon vanilla
¼ cup your favorite liqueur
¼ cup chocolate bits
¼ cup diced candied fruit
30 ladyfingers, halved lengthwise

Place cheese, sugar, vanilla, and liqueur in processor bowl. Process with metal blade until smooth and light, about 30 seconds. Add chocolate and fruit and process 2 or 3 seconds.

Line the sides and bottom of a 1½-quart casserole dish or springform pan with ladyfinger halves. Pour in one-third of the cheese mixture and cover with a layer of ladyfinger halves. Repeat two more times, ending with ladyfinger halves. Refrigerate overnight or for 4 to 6 hours. Carefully invert to remove from mold or remove sides from springform pan. Garnish with more candied fruit or cherries. Heavenly!

Nurnberger Lebkuchen

Yield: 3 dozen

Spicy German cookies.

4 eggs
1⅓ cups sugar
⅓ cup candied fruit
½ cup almonds
1 teaspoon cinnamon
¼ teaspoon cloves
¼ teaspoon nutmeg
¼ teaspoon cardamom
½ teaspoon baking soda
2¼ cups sifted all-purpose flour

Place eggs and sugar in processor bowl and process with the metal blade for 1 minute. Add fruit, nuts, spices, and baking soda. Process 3 seconds. Add flour; process 5 seconds. Do not overprocess or the nuts and fruits will be pulverized. Refrigerate mixture 3 or 4 hours.

Spread mixture with a moistened knife into 1½ × 2½-inch bars, ¼ inch thick, on a well-greased and floured baking sheet. Let dry at room temperature overnight. Bake at 350°F for 20 minutes.

These will be hard at first and are best when served after storing for 2 weeks in covered containers.

Russian Tea Cookies

Yield: 3 to 4 dozen

Be sure to use *butter* in these. Margarine will not give the same flavor.

1 cup cold butter, cut into 8 pieces
½ cup confectioners' sugar
1 teaspoon vanilla
½ teaspoon salt
2 cups sifted all-purpose flour
¾ cup walnuts
Confectioners' sugar for coating

Combine butter, sugar, vanilla, and salt in processor bowl. Process with metal blade until light, about 15 seconds. Add flour and process until a ball forms on the blades. Scatter the walnuts over the dough and process a few seconds or until nuts are distributed.

Remove dough and return one-quarter. Process until walnuts are coarsely chopped. Remove and repeat with remaining quarters.

Roll dough into 1-inch balls and place on an ungreased baking sheet. Bake at 400°F on the top oven shelf for 10 minutes, until set but not brown. Roll at once in confectioners' sugar. Cool on a wire rack and roll again in more sugar.

Zimtsterne (Cinnamon Stars)

Yield: 4 dozen

Be sure to use an electric mixer to whip the egg whites. The food processor does not incorporate sufficient air into them.

1 pound shelled almonds, blanched or
  unblanched
4 egg whites
¼ teaspoon salt
3 cups confectioners' sugar (stirred and
  spooned into the measuring cup)
1 tablespoon lemon juice
1½ tablespoons cinnamon

Process the almonds, half at a time, with the metal blade until they are finely ground, about 30 to 45 seconds.

Beat the egg whites with a mixer until soft peaks form; add salt, and gradually beat in the sugar. Set aside ½ cup of this mixture for a glaze. Stir the almonds, lemon juice, and cinnamon into the beaten egg whites and sugar mixture. Let stand for 20 to 30 minutes to allow almonds to soften.

Roll out small portions of the mixture to ¼ inch thick on a board sprinkled with confectioners' sugar. Cut into star shapes. (Or roll into walnut-sized balls and flatten.) Place on a greased and floured baking sheet and let dry at room temperature 3 to 4 hours.

Spread glaze on top of each. Bake at 300°F for 25 minutes. The glaze should remain light in color. Cool on a wire rack and store in an airtight container.

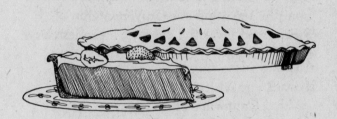

Microwave Oven
Appetizers

Swiss Fondue

Yield: 8 servings

Though either Swiss or Gruyère can be used for making fondue, the imported cheese from the mountainous Gruyère region of Switzerland gives the deepest, creamiest, and richest flavor.

1 cup white wine (Chablis or
   California white wine)
2 whole cloves garlic, peeled
¾ pound (3 cups) grated Gruyère or
   Swiss cheese
3 tablespoons flour
Freshly ground black pepper
3 tablespoons kirsch
3 tablespoons butter
¼ cup heavy cream
1 teaspoon salt

Pour the wine into a 1½-quart earthenware pot, a clay pot, or a glass casserole. Add the garlic. Cook uncovered on "simmer" setting for 5 minutes. Discard the garlic cloves.

Combine the cheese, flour, and pepper and stir into the hot wine. Simmer for 3 minutes. Stir in the kirsch, butter, and cream. Simmer for 4 more minutes. Season with salt.

Serve immediately with cubes of fresh, crusty French bread and chilled white wine. Spear the bread cubes with fondue forks and swirl into the hot fondue.

Mushroom caps, quickly fried in hot butter, as well as salami, carrot sticks, and cauliflower sprigs, make delicious contrasts of taste and texture with the fondue. In Switzerland there is also a bowl of pickled onions and potatoes boiled in their jackets to eat with the fondue.

Paté Maison

Yield: 10 servings

This paté is as good as any you will eat anywhere. Serve on freshly made toast with cocktails or for a first course. French cornichons or small gherkins and tiny onions browned in butter are good accompaniments.

½ pound ground raw pork
1 pound ground raw veal
1 pound ground raw calves liver
2 cloves garlic, finely chopped
¾ teaspoon thyme
¼ teaspoon nutmeg
1 teaspoon salt
Freshly ground black pepper
2 tablespoons brandy
2 tablespoons Madeira
½ cup heavy cream
2 eggs, lightly beaten
4 chicken livers, cut in half
6 slices bacon

Combine all ingredients except the chicken livers and bacon in a large bowl. Do not stir too much or the mixture becomes heavy.

Place half of the mixture in a 9 × 5 × 2½-inch glass loaf pan. Arrange the chicken livers in a row down the length of the pan and cover with the remaining mixture. Arrange the bacon in overlapping slices on top of the paté.

Cook on "roast" setting for 25 minutes. Rotate the pan one-quarter of a turn after 10 minutes.

Cool the paté. Cover with aluminum foil and weight the paté with 3 1-pound cans of food so it can be sliced without crumbling. Chill for 48 hours before serving.

Meatball Appetizers

Yield: 30 1-inch meatballs

Meatballs are cooked so quickly in the microwave oven that they remain moist but will not fall apart. Serve them with toothpicks and dip into mustard.

1 egg
1 teaspoon soy sauce
Freshly ground black pepper
½ teaspoon thyme
1 tablespoon oil
1 pound ground lean chuck steak
¼ cup fine fresh bread crumbs
½ small onion, finely chopped
1 tablespoon meat sauce such as A-1
¼ cup milk

Place all ingredients except the oil in a bowl and stir lightly with a fork until just combined. Do not overmix or the meatballs will become heavy. Form the mixture into 1-inch balls.

Heat a ceramic plate on the highest setting for 4 minutes. Add the oil. Cook 10 meatballs at a time for 1 minute on each side. Rotate the dish one-quarter of a turn after the first minute.

Marinated Steak Kabobs

Yield: 6 servings

These appetizers are marinated in wine, cooked at the last moment, and served sizzling hot, tender, and juicy.

1 pound sirloin steak, weighed without the bone
½ cup red wine
2 tablespoons oil
1 tablespoon soy sauce
1 clove garlic, finely chopped
2 tablespoons cracked black pepper
2 tablespoons oil

Cut the steak into bite-size cubes and place in a bowl. Add the wine, 2 tablespoons oil, soy sauce, and garlic. Marinate the steak for 2 hours. Remove and dry on paper towels. Press the cracked pepper onto the surface of the beef.

Heat the ceramic browning plate on the highest setting for 4 minutes. Add the remaining 2 tablespoons oil. Add the steak cubes and cook for 2 minutes on each side. They should be rare in the center. Serve with toothpicks.

Note: A ceramic browning plate is supplied with some models of microwave ovens. If your oven does not have one, use a shallow Corning® skillet.

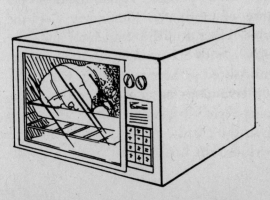

Chicken Terrine

Yield: 8 servings

A 1½-quart clay or earthenware dish can be used for preparing this dish, or use a deep glass or ceramic casserole. Serve as an appetizer or lunch dish with a salad.

1 3-pound cooked chicken
1 pound raw pork sausage meat
½ pound sliced boiled ham, diced
2 cloves garlic, finely chopped
2 eggs, lightly beaten
1 teaspoon tarragon
1 tablespoon finely chopped parsley
¼ cup brandy
½ teaspoon salt
Freshly ground black pepper
½ cup butter, softened
½ pound sliced bacon

Discard the skin and bone and cut the chicken into small pieces. Leave to one side. Stir together all remaining ingredients except the bacon.

Line a glass or ceramic casserole with half the bacon slices. Cover with one-third of the sausage mixture and top with half the chicken. Continue forming layers, top with the sausage mixture, and cover with the remaining bacon.

Cook in the microwave oven on "roast" setting for 25 minutes. Rotate the dish one-quarter of a turn after 15 minutes. Cool the terrine. Place it in the refrigerator and weight it with 3 1-pound cans of food so it can be sliced without crumbling. Chill 12 hours before serving.

Coquilles Saint-Jacques

Yield: 4 servings

1 pound bay scallops (sea scallops may also be used; cut them into smaller pieces)
¼ cup white vermouth
1 cup water
¼ teaspoon tarragon
2 tablespoons finely chopped parsley
2 tablespoons butter
4 mushrooms, thinly sliced
2 tablespoons flour
2 egg yolks
¼ cup heavy cream
4 tablespoons freshly grated Parmesan cheese
2 tablespoons butter

Place the scallops, vermouth, water, tarragon, and parsley in a small glass or ceramic casserole. Cover and cook on the highest setting for 2 minutes. Drain the scallops and reserve the liquid.

Heat 2 tablespoons of butter in a small bowl. Add and cook the mushrooms for 2 minutes. Stir in the flour and the reserved liquid. Stir in the egg yolks and whipping cream. Combine with the scallops and place in scallop shells or ramekins.

When ready to serve, reheat in the microwave oven on "reheat" setting for 2 minutes. Sprinkle with cheese, dot with butter, and place under the preheated broiler of a conventional oven for 3 minutes, until the cheese is lightly browned.

Scallops in Lime Juice

Yield: 8 servings

The success of this almost-instant appetizer is entirely dependent on the freshness of the scallops. Naturally tender enough to be eaten raw, when scallops are cooked briefly, they absorb the flavor of the other ingredients. They are also superb in a cold mixed-seafood salad.

 1 pound bay scallops (sea scallops may also be used; cut them into smaller pieces.)
 1 paper-thin slice fresh gingerroot, minced
 1 teaspoon sugar
 Juice of 1 lime
 ¼ teaspoon salt

Toss all ingredients except the salt together in a shallow glass dish. Cook on the highest setting for 2 minutes. Stir once so that the scallops cook evenly. Season with salt.

The scallops can be served immediately or chilled for 4 hours and served with small pieces of avocado, pimiento, or chopped tomato. A few pitted green and black olives make an attractive garnish.

Garlic Shrimp

Yield: 4 servings

This is a Spanish recipe and very good to serve with drinks before dinner. Use large, fresh shrimp.

 1½ pounds shrimp, peeled and deveined
 4 cloves garlic, peeled and left whole
 4 tablespoons olive oil
 1 tablespoon lemon juice
 ½ teaspoon tarragon

Place the shrimp in a shallow glass or ceramic baking dish with all the remaining ingredients.

Cook 8 minutes on highest setting, until shrimp are pink. Turn the shrimp and rotate the dish one quarter of a turn after 4 minutes. Serve hot, using toothpicks to pick up the shrimp.

Shrimp with Tarragon

Yield: 6 servings

 1 pound jumbo shrimp, shelled, but with the tails left on
 1 tablespoon oil
 2 tablespoons chopped scallions
 1 clove garlic, finely chopped
 ½ teaspoon tarragon
 ½ cup white vermouth
 Salt and pepper

Devein the shrimp and cut lengthwise in half, keeping the tail attached.

Heat a ceramic plate on highest setting for 4 minutes. Add the oil, scallions, garlic, tarragon, and white vermouth and cook for 1 minute. Add the shrimp and continue cooking for 3 minutes. Turn the shrimp once and rotate the dish one-quarter of a turn to ensure that all the shrimp are cooked evenly. Serve hot, seasoned with salt and pepper.

Salted Shrimp

Yield: 4 servings

Nothing could be simpler, but this appetizer is always a huge success. Give each person a finger bowl of warm water, and float a slice of lemon in each bowl.

1 pound jumbo shrimp with the shells on
2 tablespoons oil
Kosher or coarse salt

Rinse and dry the shrimp on paper towels. Heat the oil on a ceramic plate for 1 minute on the highest setting. Spread the shrimp on the plate and cook for 3 minutes on the same setting, until the shells are bright pink. Stir and turn the shrimp once to be sure all are cooked evenly. Immediately roll the shrimp in salt and serve hot.

Soups

Jerusalem Artichoke Soup

Yield: 6 servings

1 pound Jerusalem artichokes
1 tablespoon lemon juice
3 cups chicken broth
2 tablespoons butter
2 tablespoons flour
1 cup milk
1 cup light cream
1 teaspoon salt
Freshly ground black pepper
½ cup freshly grated Parmesan cheese

Peel the artichokes and place them in a 2-quart glass saucepan. Add the lemon juice and enough water to cover. Cover and cook on the highest setting for 15 minutes, until very tender. Drain the artichokes and place in the blender with 1 cup of chicken broth. Purée until smooth.

Heat the butter on the highest setting for 30 seconds, and stir in the flour. Stir in the remaining chicken broth, artichoke purée, milk, cream, salt, and pepper. Cook uncovered for 6 minutes. Sprinkle with Parmesan cheese at the table.

Cream of Broccoli Soup

Yield: 6 servings

All cream soups are made in a similar way. Cream of asparagus soup can be made by substituting asparagus for broccoli.

1½ pounds broccoli
1 onion, finely chopped
1 carrot, sliced
2 stalks celery with the leaves
2 potatoes, peeled and chopped
1 teaspoon salt
3 cups chicken broth
1 cup light cream
½ cup thinly sliced boiled ham, diced
½ cup sour cream

Discard the lower third of the broccoli stems and chop the remaining part into small pieces. Place in a 2-quart glass or ceramic casserole with the onion, carrot, celery, potatoes, salt, and chicken broth. Cover and cook on the highest setting for 10 minutes, until the broccoli is tender.

Purée the soup in a blender. Add the cream and ham and heat (highest setting) for 5 minutes, until very hot. Serve with a spoonful of sour cream.

Chicken Soup

Yield: 4 servings

1 2½-pound chicken, cut into serving
   pieces
4 cups water
1 onion or 2 leeks, chopped
2 carrots, diced
3 chicken bouillon cubes
1 cup fresh peas
2 tablespoons chopped parsley
Salt and pepper

Place the chicken in a 2-quart glass or ceramic casserole. Add 2 cups of water, the onion or leeks, and carrots. Cover and cook on the highest setting for 30 minutes.

Cool the chicken and discard the skin and bones. Cut the meat into small pieces and place to one side. Skim the fat from the surface of the broth in the casserole. Add the remaining 2 cups of water, the bouillon cubes, peas, and parsley. Cook for 2 minutes. Add the chicken pieces and season with salt and pepper. Continue cooking, uncovered, for 2 more minutes, until the soup is hot.

Cream of Corn Soup

Yield: 4 servings

A traditional early American soup that is equally good served hot or cold.

3 cups chicken broth
1 onion, finely chopped
1 potato, peeled and cut into small
   pieces
2 stalks celery, finely chopped
1 cup freshly shucked corn kernels or
   1 cup canned cream-style corn
1 cup light cream
2 egg yolks
Salt and pepper

Place the chicken broth, onion, potato, and celery in a 2-quart glass or ceramic casserole. Cover and cook on the highest setting for 6 minutes, until the potato and celery are very tender. Purée the soup in a blender. Add the corn.

Add ¾ cup cream and heat to simmering point for 2 minutes. Stir the remaining ¼ cup of cream with the egg yolks and add to the soup. Cook uncovered for 30 seconds. Season with salt and pepper.

Crab Soup

Yield: 6 servings

1½ pounds tomatoes
1 onion, finely chopped
1 cup chicken broth
1 cup clam broth
2 teaspoons tomato paste
2 tablespoons flour
¼ cup Madeira or dry sherry
1 cup heavy cream
½ teaspoon salt
Freshly ground black pepper
1 pound crab meat

Cut the tomatoes into wedges and place in a 2-quart glass or ceramic casserole with the onion. Add the chicken broth, clam broth, and tomato paste. Cook uncovered at the highest setting for 30 minutes. Transfer the soup to a blender and add the flour. Purée the soup until smooth, and strain to remove the tomato skins and seeds. Stir in the Madeira and cream. Season with salt and pepper and heat uncovered for 5 minutes. Add the crab and cook another 5 minutes. Serve hot.

Crab and Corn Soup

Yield: 4 servings

3 tablespoons butter
⅓ cup flour
2 cups milk
2 cups cold water
1 6-ounce can crab meat
12-ounce can whole-kernel corn
½ teaspoon salt
⅛ teaspoon pepper
¼ cup table cream
Slices of tomato, optional
Watercress, optional

Melt the butter in a 1½-quart glass or ceramic casserole for 30 seconds on the highest setting. Stir in flour with a wire whisk. Gradually stir in milk and water. Cook for 5 minutes or until thickened. During cooking stir twice with whisk to make a smooth sauce.

Drain crab and corn. Break crab meat into pieces, removing cartilage. Stir crab meat and corn into the sauce. Season with salt and pepper. Cover casserole and cook for 5 minutes on "simmer" setting. Remove from oven and stir in cream. Garnish with slices of tomato and watercress.

Goulash Soup

Yield: 6 servings

This soup has no added thickening, as the potato and the other ingredients give it body.

2 tablespoons butter
2 tablespoons oil
3 medium-size onions, sliced
1 clove garlic, finely chopped
2 teaspoons paprika
½ pound veal, ground
¼ pound pork, ground
4 cups stock (can be made with 4 bouillon cubes and 4 cups boiling water)
Salt and pepper
2 medium-size potatoes, sliced
3 small tomatoes, chopped
6 thin slices French bread

Heat butter and oil in a 3-quart glass or ceramic casserole on the highest setting for 20 seconds. Add onions and garlic and fry for 2 minutes. Add paprika and cook for 30 seconds. Stir in the ground meats, and cook for 2 minutes.

Gradually add the stock, and season to taste. Cover and cook on highest setting for 5 minutes. Add potato and tomato, and cook covered for 8 minutes longer, until the potatoes are soft. Toast bread in toaster or in a broiler until crisp and brown. Serve with the soup.

Peanut Soup

Yield: 6 servings

1½-pound chicken
1 large onion, peeled and thinly sliced
1 teaspoon salt
6 whole black peppercorns
2 tablespoons unsalted butter
4 ounces salted peanuts
3 ounces dry sherry
1¼ cups milk
½ cup whipping cream

Cut the chicken into 3 or 4 pieces, removing the fat, and place in a 2½-quart glass or ceramic casserole with half the onion slices. Add salt, pepper, and 6 cups of water.

Cover and cook on the highest setting for 30 minutes. Cool stock.

Heat butter in a 2-quart glass or ceramic casserole for 20 seconds. Add the remaining onions and cook for 2 minutes to soften. Rub the peanuts in a cloth to get rid of the salt. Place the peanuts, onion slices, and butter in the blender. Blend until the nuts are finely chopped. Strain the cooled stock; skim off fat. Add nuts and onions to the stock. Place in a saucepan. Cover and simmer for 15 minutes. Taste, and add more seasoning if necessary. Stir in the sherry and milk, and cook for 4 minutes.

Cover pan and refrigerate overnight. Just before serving, add the cream. Heat to simmering point but do not allow the soup to boil. Serve garnished with chopped parsley and finely chopped peanuts.

Scottish Hot Pot

Yield: 6 servings

2 pounds lamb shoulder
6 cups beef bouillon
1 teaspoon salt
½ teaspoon pepper
2 onions, sliced
2 tablespoons butter
2 teaspoons flour
1 stalk celery, diced
2 carrots, diced
1 turnip, diced
1 scallion, white and green parts, thinly sliced
1 small cauliflower divided into florets
1 10-ounce package frozen peas
½ cup sherry
2 tablespoons finely chopped parsley

In a 3-quart glass or ceramic casserole place meat, bouillon, salt, pepper, and onions. Cook on "simmer" setting for 30 minutes. Remove from oven. Cut meat into serving pieces. Heat 2 tablespoons butter in a 1-quart glass bowl at highest setting for 20 seconds. Brown meat in butter for 3 minutes and sprinkle with flour. Return meat to the stock and add celery, carrots, turnip, and scallion. Continue cooking for 15 minutes. Add cauliflower and peas to soup and cook for 8 minutes. Before serving, correct seasoning and sprinkle with parsley.

Tomato Soup

Yield: 6 servings

Homemade soups are so quickly made in the microwave oven that you can have a different one every day. Tomato soup is at its best in the summer months when the tomatoes are bursting with red, ripe flavor.

2 pounds Italian plum tomatoes or about 6 medium-size tomatoes
1 onion, chopped
1 stalk celery, chopped
2 cups chicken broth
1 tablespoon tomato paste
1 teaspoon basil or oregano
Freshly ground black pepper
1 teaspoon salt
1 cup yogurt, or sour cream, or heavy cream (optional)

Cut the plum tomatoes in half or cut larger tomatoes into wedges to release the juice. Place in a 3-quart glass or ceramic casserole with the onion and celery. Add the chicken broth, tomato paste, and basil or oregano and season with black pepper.

Cook uncovered on the highest setting for 20 minutes. Season with salt. Strain to remove the tomato skins and seeds. Garnish with spoonfuls of yogurt or sour cream or stir in whipping cream.

Shrimp and Mushroom Soup

Yield: 6 servings

Creamy and full of textures and flavors, this soup is equally fine served hot or cold.

¾ pound small mushroom caps
1 small onion, finely chopped
½ small cucumber, peeled and chopped into pieces the size of the mushroom caps
1 tablespoon lemon juice
2 tablespoons white vermouth
2 tablespoons oil
1 pound small fresh shrimp with shells on
2 tablespoons butter
2 tablespoons flour
2½ cups milk
1 cup light cream
Salt and pepper

Place the mushroom caps, onion, cucumber pieces, and lemon juice in a small glass bowl. Add the white vermouth. Cover and cook on the highest setting for 2 minutes. Oil a plate. Place the shrimp on the plate. Sprinkle with oil and cook for 2 minutes (highest setting used throughout). Stir the shrimp to rearrange them after 1 minute. Peel the shrimp.

Heat the butter for 30 seconds. Stir in the flour and cook for 20 seconds. Stir in the milk and cream. Cook for 4 minutes. Stir briskly with a wire whisk. Add the mushroom mixture and the shrimp. Season with salt and pepper. Serve hot (reheat if necessary), or chill for 4 hours before serving.

Vichyssoise

Yield: 6 servings

Vichyssoise is the cold summer soup that was created in 1910 by chef Louis Diat to honor the gala opening of the roof garden at the Ritz Carlton Hotel in New York City. The soup was an instant success and is still as popular as it was in the first public unveiling of the masterpiece.

2 pounds potatoes (about 4 medium-size potatoes)
6 leeks or 3 yellow onions, finely chopped
6 cups chicken broth, hot
1 cup heavy cream
1 teaspoon salt
Chopped chives
Freshly ground black pepper

Peel the potatoes, cut into small pieces, and place in a 2-quart glass or ceramic casserole. Slice the white part and the lower third of the green part of the leeks. Wash in plenty of cold water to remove sand from the leeks. Add the leeks or onions to the potatoes along with the hot chicken broth. Cover and cook on the highest setting for 10 minutes, until the potatoes are very soft. Purée the soup in a blender. Add the cream and salt and chill for 4 hours before serving. Garnish with chopped chives and black pepper.

Note: Cold soups need more salt than hot soups.

Watercress and Potato Soup

Yield: 4 servings

1 bunch watercress
2 tablespoons butter

1 onion, finely chopped
1 stalk celery, chopped
2 medium-size potatoes, peeled and cut
    into small pieces
3 cups chicken broth
1 tablespoon lemon juice
½ teaspoon salt
Freshly ground black pepper
½ cup heavy cream

Wash the watercress. Reserve ½ cup of the leaves and chop the remaining leaves and stems into small pieces. Using the highest setting throughout this recipe, heat the butter in a 2-quart glass or ceramic casserole for 20 seconds. Add the onion and celery and cook uncovered for 2 minutes. Add the watercress, potatoes, chicken broth, lemon juice, salt, and pepper. Cover and cook for 15 minutes. Purée these ingredients in the blender and return to the pan. Add the cream and heat for 2 minutes, until very hot. Add the reserved watercress leaves and serve hot or cold.

Eggs

Eggs with Mustard Sauce

Yield: 4 servings

A quick brunch to serve either alone or with crisp bacon and freshly made buttered toast.

6 hard-boiled eggs
2 tablespoons butter
2 tablespoons flour
1¼ cups beef or chicken broth
2 teaspoons Dijon mustard
2 tablespoons finely chopped parsley

Slice the eggs and place in a shallow buttered glass or ceramic baking dish. Heat the butter in a glass measuring cup on the highest setting. Stir in the flour. Add the broth and return to the oven for 2 minutes, until hot. Stir in the mustard and parsley.

Pour the sauce over the eggs and cook on "roast" setting for 2 minutes.

Deviled Eggs Mornay

Yield: 4 servings

2 tablespoons butter
2 tablespoons flour
1¼ cups milk
½ teaspoon salt
¼ teaspoon pepper
1½ cups grated cheddar cheese
1 cup cooked pasta shells
6 hard-boiled eggs
1 teaspoon dry mustard
½ teaspoon curry powder
2 tablespoons butter, melted
3 or 4 green olives, sliced
3 or 4 tablespoons cream

Melt the butter in a 1-quart measuring glass for 20 seconds on the highest setting. Stir in flour with a wire whisk. Stir in milk gradually. Cook for 3 minutes or until thick. During cooking stir twice with whisk to give a smooth sauce. Season with salt and pepper. Add ½ cup of grated cheese and the cooked pasta. Place in an ovenproof dish and keep it warm in a conventional oven. Cut eggs in half lengthwise and remove yolks. Mix yolks with mustard, curry powder, melted butter, and salt and pepper to taste. Put mixture into egg-white halves. Cover with Mornay sauce. Arrange sliced olives on top of the sauce. Top with and sprinkle with remaining cheese. Cook uncovered on highest setting for 2 minutes to melt cheese. Serve immediately.

Spanish Eggs

Yield: 4 servings

This simple brunch or supper dish is a good way to use up leftovers. Chicken can be used instead of pork.

1 tablespoon oil
¼ small onion, finely chopped
1 clove garlic, finely chopped
½ green pepper, finely chopped
½ cup cooked pork, diced
½ cup cooked ham, diced
2 tablespoons flour
¾ cup chicken broth
½ teaspoon basil
1 tomato, peeled, seeded, and chopped
Salt and pepper
2 tablespoons butter
4 eggs

Heat the oil in an 8-inch glass pie plate. Add the onion, garlic, and green pepper and cook on the highest setting for 1 minute. Add the pork and ham. Stir in the flour and add the chicken broth and basil. Cook 3 minutes. Add the tomato and cook 1 minute. Season with salt and pepper.

Heat the butter on a plate. Break the eggs onto the plate and cut a cross in the yolks with a fork. Cook the eggs on "roast" setting for 4 minutes, until set. Slide the eggs on top of the pork mixture and decorate the edges of the plate with parsley if you wish.

Meat

Beef Stewed in Red Wine

Yield: 6 servings

1½ pounds boneless chuck steak, cut into 1½-inch cubes
2 tablespoons butter
1 tablespoon oil
1 large turnip, cut into 1-inch pieces
1 rutabaga, cut into 1-inch pieces
1 pound small white onions, peeled
1 pound carrots, cut into 1-inch pieces
3 tablespoons flour
1 cup beef bouillon
1 cup red wine
Dash of Worcestershire sauce
½ teaspoon peppercorns
3 bay leaves

Heat butter and oil in a 3-quart glass or ceramic casserole for 20 seconds. Brown beef, turnip, rutabaga, onions, and carrots for 4 minutes. Add flour, stir, and cook for another 2 minutes. Add bouillon, wine, Worcestershire sauce, peppercorns, and bay leaves. Cover and cook at "simmer" setting for 50 minutes. Leave overnight and reheat next day.

Corned Beef Hash

Yield: 4 servings

Corned beef hash made from leftover corned beef is ready to eat very quickly when it is made in the microwave oven. Cook the fried eggs separately and place on top of the hot hash.

1 pound ground or finely chopped
    corned beef
2 cups finely chopped cabbage (use a
    meat grinder or food processor if you
    have one), parboiled for 6 minutes
1 onion, finely chopped
2 boiled potatoes, diced
¼ cup tomato purée
½ teaspoon salt
Freshly ground black pepper
2 tablespoons oil
2 eggs, fried, optional

Combine all ingredients except the oil. Pour the oil into a shallow 9-inch glass baking dish and heat for 30 seconds on the highest setting. Add the hash ingredients and cook 2 minutes. Stir the hash and cook 3 minutes. Top with fried eggs if you wish.

Ground Beef and Noodles

Yield: 4 servings

It is very easy to inadvertently overcook ground beef dishes in the microwave oven because they cook very quickly. Taste the beef after 5 minutes and let it rest for 5 minutes. Taste it again and return it to the oven for another minute only if you are really sure it needs additional time.

1 pound ground chuck steak
1 tablespoon oil
1 onion, finely chopped
1 clove garlic, finely chopped
1 green pepper, finely chopped
½ teaspoon oregano
¼ cup beef broth
¾ cup sour cream
1 tablespoon tomato paste
2 tomatoes peeled, seeded, and
    chopped

1½ cups cooked noodles or macaroni
½ teaspoon salt
Freshly ground black pepper

Preheat a ceramic browning plate on the highest setting for 4 minutes. Add the beef and oil and cook for 2 minutes. Drain off any accumulated fat and transfer to a 2-quart glass or ceramic casserole. Add the onion, garlic, and green pepper to the casserole and cook for 2 minutes. Add all the remaining ingredients. Cover and cook for 5 minutes. Stir the mixture once and rotate the dish one-quarter of a turn after 3 minutes. Taste the beef and season with salt and pepper.

Pork Chops Bagatelle

Yield: 4 servings

Stacked or skewered foods can be cooked in a microwave oven if wooden hibachi skewers are used instead of metal skewers.

8 pork chops
8 slices Gruyère cheese
4 slices ham
2 eggs, beaten
Bread crumbs
¼ cup butter

Stack in sequence and skewer 1 pork chop, 1 slice cheese, ½ slice ham, a second slice of cheese, and another pork chop. Repeat for other 3 skewers. Coat with egg and dip into bread crumbs. Heat butter in a glass baking dish on highest setting for 20 seconds. Add chops and cook on each side for 1 minute. Cover and cook on "roast" setting for 12 to 15 minutes or until pork is thoroughly cooked.

Casserole of Pork and Apples

Yield: 6 servings

Pork is at its best when it is cooked slowly, so prepare this casserole on the "roast" setting. It will be ready to eat in half the conventional cooking time. Cumin gives the pork an unusually good flavor. Serve with cauliflower and crusty bread.

3 pounds boneless pork loin cut into
    1½-inch cubes
2 tablespoons oil
4 leeks, washed and sliced, or 2
    onions, sliced
2 green cooking apples, peeled, cored,
    and sliced
1 teaspoon cumin powder or curry
    powder
2 tablespoons flour
1¼ cups apple cider
¼ cup apple brandy or white vermouth
1 teaspoon salt
Freshly ground black pepper

Brown the pork in hot oil in a skillet and transfer the cubes to a casserole. Cook the leeks or onions and apples in the same oil for 3 minutes until softened. Stir in the cumin or curry powder and cook 1 minute. Stir in the flour and all the remaining ingredients. Transfer to a 2-quart glass or ceramic casserole. Cover and cook in the microwave oven for 1 hour on "roast" setting. Rotate the dish one-quarter of a turn after 30 minutes. Allow to rest 10 minutes before serving.

Pork and Orange Casserole

Yield: 4 servings

3 tablespoons oil
2 onions, finely chopped
1½ pounds lean pork, cut into
    1½-inch cubes
½ cup seasoned flour
Grated rind and juice of 1 orange
11-ounce can mandarin oranges
1 cup water
1 chicken bouillon cube
1 green pepper, sliced

Heat the oil in a 2-quart glass or ceramic casserole on the highest setting for 20 seconds. Add the onions and cook for 2 minutes. Add pork coated in seasoned flour. Cook in hot fat for a few seconds to seal in juices. Toss to seal. Grate rind. Squeeze the orange. Drain the mandarin oranges. Mix the syrup from the can with the fresh juice. Combine syrup and juice with water, rind, bouillon cube, and sliced pepper in a small glass or ceramic bowl. Cook on "simmer" setting for 5 minutes. Add to pork. Cover and cook for 20 minutes on "roast" setting. Rotate dish one-quarter of a turn after 10 minutes. Add the mandarin oranges during last 5 minutes. Let stand 10 minutes before serving.

Pork Roast with Prunes

Yield: 4 servings

12 large dried prunes
1 cup beef bouillon
4 pounds boneless pork roast, cut into
    1-inch slices
½ teaspoon pepper

¼ teaspoon ground ginger
1½ teaspoons salt
2 large red apples
¾ cup water
1 tablespoon sugar
½ teaspoon lemon juice
Parsley, for garnish

Soak prunes in bouillon overnight. Remove and pit. Reserve bouillon and 4 prunes. Mix remaining prunes with pepper and ginger. Push them in between the slices of the roast. Place pork on a microwave oven roasting rack or on an inverted saucer in a glass baking dish to permit the fat to drain. Cook on the highest setting for 24 minutes. Turn roast over and rotate the dish one-quarter of a turn and cook for another 20 to 24 minutes on "roast" setting. Remove from oven and transfer roast to serving platter. Sprinkle with salt and cover with aluminum foil. Let the roast rest for 15 minutes before serving. The pork will continue cooking.

Pour off fat from roasting pan. Add reserved bouillon. Bring to boil on highest setting for 2 minutes. Stir and continue cooking to reduce juices.

Core apples. Slice each into 4 rings. Put water and sugar in a 1-quart glass dish. Heat for 1 minute to dissolve sugar; add lemon juice. Place apple rings in liquid and cook on highest setting for 3 minutes or until apples are soft but not mushy. Place apple rings around the roast and fill the center of each with a prune. Garnish with parsley.

Tagliatelle Bolognese

Yield: 4 to 6 servings

Meat Sauce
2 tablespoons butter
1 onion, finely chopped
1 carrot, diced
1 stalk celery, diced
1 clove garlic, optional, finely chopped
2 strips bacon, diced
½ pound ground beef
1 8-ounce can tomato sauce
1 bay leaf
½ cup beef bouillon
½ teaspoon salt
⅛ teaspoon pepper
1 teaspoon sugar
¾ pound Tagliatelle or other pasta
⅓ cup grated Parmesan cheese

Heat butter in a 3-quart glass casserole on the highest setting for 20 seconds. Add vegetables and diced bacon. Cook for 2 minutes. Add ground beef and cook on highest setting for 7 minutes; drain. Stir in tomato sauce, bay leaf, bouillon, salt, pepper, and sugar. Cover with a glass lid and cook on "reheat" setting for 7 minutes. Taste and add more seasoning if necessary. Remove the bay leaf.

In a 3-quart covered glass casserole, bring 6 cups of water, 1 tablespoon cooking oil, and 1 teaspoon salt to a full boil on highest setting. Stir in pasta and re-cover. Cook on "defrost" setting for 14 minutes or until tender. Drain and rinse thoroughly. Turn into a hot serving dish, pour cooked meat sauce into the center and sprinkle with Parmesan cheese.

Pot Roast

Yield: 6 servings

A 3-pound piece of beef is pot-roasted in 2½ hours the conventional way. With a microwave oven it takes 1½ hours.

1 3-pound boneless chuck steak, in one
    piece, or cross-cut shoulder of beef

Marinade

1½ cups young red wine such as
    Beaujolais or California Mountain
    red wine
2 tablespoons oil
1 onion, chopped
1 clove garlic, chopped
1 stalk celery, chopped
1 teaspoon salt
1 bay leaf
1 teaspoon thyme
3 sprigs parsley
10 peppercorns

Sauce for Pot Roast

2 tablespoons butter
2 tablespoons flour
1¼ cups cooking liquid from the
    casserole
½ cup tomato sauce
¼ cup mayonnaise
¼ teaspoon thyme

Tie the beef at ½-inch intervals so it will keep its shape. Combine the marinade ingredients in a 2½-quart glass casserole. Place the beef in the marinade. There should be enough liquid to cover the beef. If not, it will be necessary to turn the beef from time to time. Cover and refrigerate the beef for 12 hours or up to 3 days.

Place the beef, immersed in the marinade and covered, in the microwave oven. Cook on "simmer" setting for 45 minutes. Turn the beef over. Rotate the dish one-quarter of a turn after each 20 minutes. Allow to stand for 20 minutes before slicing.

Heat the butter in a 4-cup glass measuring cup for 30 seconds on the highest setting. Stir in the flour and cook for 20 seconds. Stir in all the remaining sauce ingredients with a wire whisk. Heat on "simmer" setting for 5 minutes.

Baked Ham with Cumberland Sauce

Yield: 6 servings

The ham may be served hot or cold—allow 10 minutes cooking time to the pound.

1 3-pound fully cooked ham

Glaze

1 jar (8 ounces) apricot preserves

Cumberland Sauce

Rind and juice of 1 orange
1 tablespoon lemon juice
3 scallions, finely chopped
½ cup port wine
½ cup red currant jelly
½ teaspoon powdered ginger
1 teaspoon dry mustard powder,
    dissolved in 1 tablespoon cold water

Remove the rind from the ham and score the fat with a sharp wet knife to form a diamond pattern. Place the ham in the oven on a roasting rack or on an inverted saucer set in a glass baking dish. Place the ham fat side down. Cook on "roast" setting for 15 minutes. Turn the ham over and remove from the oven

Remove the lid from the apricot preserves and heat in the jar on the highest setting for 5 minutes. Force the hot preserves through a strainer and brush the clear liquid over the ham. Rotate the dish one-quarter of a turn and continue cooking on "roast" setting for another 15 minutes. Allow the ham to stand for 15 minutes before slicing.

To make the sauce, peel the thin, colored part of the orange and cut into tiny julienne strips the length of a matchstick and half of the width. Squeeze the orange into a 4-cup glass measuring cup and add the orange rind to the orange juice. Add the lemon juice and scallions. Cook in the microwave oven on the highest setting for 3 minutes. Stir in the remaining ingredients. Cook uncovered in the microwave oven for 3 minutes, until the red currant jelly has dissolved.

Serve the sauce cold. It is traditionally a rather thin sauce.

Baked Ham with Mustard Crust

Yield: 10 servings

This beautiful-looking ham is very easy to prepare and is a good choice for a large buffet party. Allow 9 minutes to the pound for a ham weighing 5 to 10 pounds.

1 5-pound fully cooked ham
1 jar (8 ounces) apricot preserves
2 teaspoons dry English mustard powder
2 teaspoons Dijon mustard
1 tablespoon cornstarch
2 egg yolks
1½ cups freshly made bread crumbs
¼ cup parsley
¼ cup chopped chives
1 teaspoon marjoram
3 tablespoons butter, melted

Score the ham fat in a diamond pattern after removing the rind. Place the ham, fat side down, in a microwave oven roasting rack or set on 2 sauces inverted in a glass baking dish. Cook on "roast" setting for 25 minutes. Remove the ham from the oven.

Remove the lid from the apricot preserves and heat in the jar on the highest setting for 5 minutes. Force the hot preserves through a strainer and brush the clear liquid over the ham. Rotate the dish one-quarter of a turn and continue cooking on "roast" setting for 20 minutes. Remove from the oven and check the temperature with a meat thermometer. The reading should be 150°F. The temperature will rise 10 degrees as it stands. Leave the ham to rest for 15 minutes.

Preheat the conventional oven to 375°F. Combine the mustard powder, mustard, and cornstarch. Stir in the egg yolks. Spread the mixture over the surface of the ham.

Place the bread crumbs, parsley, chives, and marjoram in a blender and blend until the herbs are finely chopped. Press the bread crumbs lightly over the mustard covering. Place the ham on a roasting rack. Drizzle with melted butter. Cook in the preheated oven for 20 minutes until the crumbs are lightly browned.

Ham and Mushroom Pastry Slice

Yield: 4 servings

1 recipe double pie crust
2 tablespoons butter
¼ cup flour
¾ cup milk
¼ pound mushrooms, chopped
1½ cups cooked ham, diced
¼ teaspoon pepper
1 small egg, beaten

Prepare pastry. Melt butter in 2-quart glass or ceramic casserole for 20 seconds. Stir in flour with a wire whisk. Add milk gradually while continuing to stir. Cook for 3 minutes or until thickened to a sauce. During cooking, stir twice with whisk to ensure a smooth sauce. Stir mushrooms, ham, and pepper into the sauce.

Roll pastry into an oblong shape, 24 × 8 inches. Cut in half widthwise. Trim edges. Place one piece of pastry on a shallow rectangular glass casserole. Fold the other piece in half; cut out the center to leave a 1-inch border. Cut the center piece into strips.

Spoon sauce onto pastry base, spreading carefully to within 1 inch of the edges. Moisten edge of pastry and lay strips across the sauce. Place pastry border around the edge. Press to seal. Brush pastry with beaten egg. Cook in oven on highest setting for 8 minutes. Rotate casserole one-quarter of a turn after 4 minutes. Pie crust will not brown unless oven has a special unit. Place casserole in a conventional oven, preheated to 375°F for 10 to 15 minutes to brown crust.

Sugar-baked Ham

Yield: 6 servings

A covered dish is not required during the roasting of this ham, but, during the standing period, a cover is necessary to assure even heating and cooking.

3-pound boneless ready-to-eat ham
2 bay leaves
6 peppercorns
3 cups water
1 tablespoon corn oil
⅓ cup brown sugar
Watercress for garnish

Place ham in a large glass casserole. Add bay leaves and peppercorns. On highest setting, bring to a boil. Reduce heat to "simmer" setting and cook for 20 minutes. Remove from liquid and remove rind from ham. Brush ham with oil and sprinkle the surface of the ham with sugar. Cook on "roast" setting for 15 minutes. Cover and let stand for another 15 minutes before slicing. Garnish with watercress.

Sausage and Egg Roll

Yield: 4 servings

To keep sausage moist, cook in covered glass dish. Excess grease can be drained easily. Place smaller amounts on paper towels or napkins to absorb grease.

2 cups flour
Pinch of salt
¼ cup shortening
¼ cup butter
1 pound pork sausage meat
4 large eggs, hard-boiled
Milk, to brush

Sift flour and salt into a mixing bowl. Cut in shortening and butter, using a pastry blender or two knives. Stir in just enough water to give a firm dough. Roll out to a rectangle and trim to about 9 × 11 inches. Place in an ungreased glass baking dish.

Cook sausage meat in a covered glass dish on highest setting for 6 minutes. Pour off grease. Spread sausage meat in a rectangle 11 × 4 inches on center of pastry. Remove shell from eggs, slice, and place in a line down the center of sausage meat. Brush one long edge of pastry with water and fold over so edges meet. Seal and flute edges. Make a diagonal cut in the top pastry. Brush pastry top with milk. Cook on "roast" setting for 9 minutes. Cool.

Stuffed Sausages

Yield: 12 to 16 sausages

These may be prepared the day before.

1 pound fresh sausage links
4 tablespoons chutney
¼ cup butter
⅓ cup almonds, chopped

Preheat browning grill in oven on highest setting. Place sausages on grill and cook on highest setting for 8 minutes. Turn sausage over halfway through cooking. Drain off fat and cool. Chop any large pieces of chutney. Work chutney into butter. Cut a slit down the side of the sausage from end to end and open like a book. Spoon in a little chutney stuffing, partly close sausage, and dip the stuffed side into a saucer of almonds. Arrange on a dish and serve cold.

Frankfurters with Sauerkraut

Yield: 4 servings

Other meats, such as cooked pork chops, thickly sliced bacon, or a variety of sausages, including knockwurst, bratwurst, and pork sausages, can also be used to make this dish. Serve with mustard, potatoes baked in their jackets, and a mug of beer.

1 pound prepared sauerkraut
3 slices bacon
1 teaspoon caraway seeds
½ cup white wine
2 small boiled potatoes, grated
8 frankfurters
Freshly ground black pepper

Rinse the sauerkraut in cold water and squeeze dry. Place the bacon slices in a baking dish. Cook for 3 minutes on the highest setting, until crisp. Crumble the bacon and return it to the baking dish. Add all the remaining ingredients. Cover and cook 6 minutes. Rotate the dish a quarter of a turn after 3 minutes.

Butterfly Leg of Lamb

Yield: 6 servings

Ask the butcher to remove the bone from the lamb and "butterfly" it. You will then have a flattish piece of meat. The meat will be cooked in less than 20 minutes.

1 3-pound leg of lamb, weighed after the bone is removed
1 slice bread, broken into 6 pieces
½ cup parsley
1 teaspoon rosemary
3 tablespoons butter
2 cloves garlic, finely chopped
Salt and pepper

Place the lamb, fat side down, on a microwave oven roasting rack or on top of an inverted saucer set in a glass baking dish.

Place the bread, parsley, and rosemary in a blender and blend until finely chopped. Spread the mixture on the surface of the lamb.

Heat the butter and garlic in a custard cup on the highest setting for 40 seconds. Drizzle the garlic butter over the lamb.

Cook the lamb on the highest setting for 10 minutes. Rotate the dish one-quarter of a turn and cook on "roast" setting for 8 minutes. Season with salt and pepper and leave to rest for 10 minutes before slicing.

Lamb Chops Braised in Red Wine

Yield: 6 servings

6 thick loin lamb chops
2 tablespoons oil
1 onion, finely chopped

1 clove garlic, finely chopped
2 tomatoes, chopped
½ cup tomato purée
1 cup red wine
½ cup beef broth
1 teaspoon basil
1 bay leaf
Salt and pepper
1 tablespoon butter
2 tablespoons flour

Trim the lamb chops. Heat the microwave browning plate for 4 minutes on the highest setting. Add the oil and cook the chops, one at a time, for 1 minute on each side. Transfer the chops to a 2-quart glass or ceramic casserole and add all the remaining ingredients except the butter and flour. Cover and cook on "roast" setting for 30 minutes. Remove the chops. Arrange them on a hot serving plate and keep them warm while preparing the sauce.

Strain the liquid from the casserole. Heat the butter on the highest setting for 30 seconds. Stir in the flour and cook for 30 seconds. Stir in the strained cooking liquid with a wire whisk. Taste, add salt and pepper, and reheat if necessary. Serve the sauce over the lamb chops or separately.

Lamb Pilaf

Yield: 6 servings

2 tablespoons oil
1 onion, finely chopped
¼ teaspoon allspice
¼ teaspoon cinnamon
¼ teaspoon thyme
2 cups cooked lamb, cut into bite-size pieces
3 cups cooked rice
1 tomato, peeled, seeded, and chopped

1 cup cooked sliced zucchini or other
   green vegetable
⅓ cup slivered almonds
⅓ cup raisins, soaked in hot water for
   5 minutes and drained
½ cup beef broth

Heat the oil in a 1½-quart glass or ceramic casserole on the highest setting. Fry the onion in the oil for 1 minute. Stir in the spices and cook for 30 seconds. Stir in all the remaining ingredients and cook for 8 minutes. Rotate the dish one-quarter of a turn every 2 minutes.

Roast Lamb

Yield: 6 servings

For rare lamb cook for 8 minutes per pound. For medium lamb cook for 9 minutes per pound. For well-done lamb cook for 10 minutes per pound.

1 5-pound leg of lamb with the bone
3 cloves garlic
3 tablespoons butter, melted
1 teaspoon rosemary
Freshly ground pepper
Salt

Trim the excess fat from the lamb. Make a series of slits in the surface of the lamb with the point of a sharp knife. Cut the garlic into slivers and insert tiny pieces of garlic into the slits. Brush the lamb with melted butter. Press the rosemary onto the surface of the lamb and season with pepper.

Place the lamb fat side down on a rack or on an inverted saucer set in a glass or ceramic baking dish. Cook on the highest setting for 20 minutes. Turn the lamb on its other side and brush with butter. Cook on

"roast" setting or place a glass of hot water in the oven for 20 minutes longer (150°F) for rare lamb; 25 more minutes (160°F) for medium lamb; and 30 more minutes (170°F) for well-done lamb. Season with salt and cover with aluminum foil. Allow to stand for 15 minutes before carving. The temperature will continue to rise during this resting time.

Lamb Shanks

Yield: 4 servings

All stewed meats are spectacularly successful when they are cooked in the microwave oven, and the preparation time for this particular dish is reduced by one-third.

3 tablespoons oil
4 lamb shanks, weighing approximately
   12 ounces each
3 tablespoons flour
1½ cups beef broth
1 teaspoon rosemary
1 onion, finely chopped
2 cloves garlic, finely chopped
4 carrots, chopped into 1-inch pieces
1 8½-ounce package frozen peas

Heat the oil in a skillet and brown the lamb shanks on all sides. Transfer to a 2½-quart glass or ceramic casserole. Stir the flour into the oil. Add the beef broth gradually, stirring to form a smooth sauce. Add all the remaining ingredients except the peas, and pour over the lamb. Cover and cook on "roast" setting for 50 minutes. Add the peas and continue cooking for 10 minutes at the same setting.

Poultry

Belgian Chicken Casserole

Yield: 4 servings

In Belgium this casserole, made with chicken and vegetables, is served with chicken soup.

1 3-pound chicken, cut into
   serving pieces
Freshly ground black pepper
3 tablespoons butter
4 leeks, sliced, or 2 onions, finely
   chopped
2 stalks celery, sliced
2 carrots, sliced
2 cups chicken broth
2 egg yolks
2 tablespoons milk or cream
3 tablespoons finely chopped parsley
1 teaspoon salt

Season the chicken with pepper. Heat the butter in a 2½-quart glass or ceramic casserole on the highest setting for 40 seconds. Arrange layers of the vegetables in the casserole and place the chicken pieces on top of the vegetables. Add the chicken broth. Cover and cook on "roast" setting for 30 minutes.

Remove the chicken from the casserole. Discard the skin.

Stir the egg yolks and milk or cream together and add to the casserole. Add the chicken. Cook 2 minutes on the highest setting. Add the parsley and salt. Serve in shallow soup bowls.

Chicken Breasts with Lemon and White Vermouth

Yield: 4 servings

8 boneless chicken breasts with skin
   removed
4 tablespoons butter
4 scallions, finely chopped
Grated rind and juice of 1 lemon
½ teaspoon tarragon or marjoram
⅓ cup white vermouth
Salt and pepper

Sauce

½ cup whipping cream
1 tablespoon cornstarch dissolved in 2
   tablespoons cold water
Salt and pepper
2 tablespoons finely chopped parsley

Arrange the chicken breasts in a 10-inch glass baking dish. Dot with butter and add all the remaining ingredients except the salt and pepper. Cover the chicken with waxed paper. Cook on "roast" setting for 15 minutes. After 7 minutes rearrange the chicken, placing the center pieces at the edge of the dish. Rotate the dish one-quarter of a turn. Season with salt and pepper immediately after the chicken breasts are cooked.

Remove the chicken from the baking dish. Arrange on a bed of steaming hot rice and keep it hot while preparing the sauce.

Pour the cream into the baking dish and cook on the highest setting with the juices from the chicken breasts for 1 minute, until hot. Stir in the cornstarch dissolved in cold water and heat for 1 minute. Stir with a wire whisk. Season with salt and pepper and pour the sauce over the chicken breasts. Garnish with parsley.

Chicken Patties

Yield: 12 patties

Patties and filling may be made 1 or 2 days in advance. Flavors will blend and taste better.

1 package 2-crust pie crust mix
2 tablespoons butter
2 teaspoons flour
5 tablespoons milk
½ chicken bouillon cube
¾ cup cooked, diced chicken
2 or 3 tablespoons light cream

Mix pastry according to package directions. Roll out into a rectangle 7 × 10 inches. Cut 12 circles with a 2-inch biscuit cutter. Place on 2 flat-bottomed baking dishes. Mark the patties with a 1-inch biscuit cutter in the center. When baked, this will lift out to give a hollow. Cook one dish at a time on "roast" setting for 7 minutes or until brown spots start to appear on crust.

Melt butter on highest setting for 20 seconds, remove from heat, and stir in the flour. Stir in the milk. Cook for 2 minutes, stirring twice during cooking time. Crumble the bouillon cube into the sauce, and season to taste. Add the chicken and cream. Remove centers from patties, and spoon in filling. Replace small lid if desired.

Chicken Pie

Yield: 6 servings

To blend flavors, refrigerate this prior to serving.

3-pound chicken
1 teaspoon salt
¼ teaspoon pepper
1 bay leaf
2 cups water
¼ cup butter
3½ cups flour
5 tablespoons milk
10-ounce package frozen peas
3 tablespoons shortening
1 small egg, lightly beaten
Slices of cucumber for garnish

Wash chicken; pat dry. Place in a 3-quart casserole. Add salt, pepper, bay leaf, and 2 cups of water. Cover and cook on highest setting for 15 minutes. Turn chicken and cook on "simmer" setting for 40 minutes or until chicken is tender. Drain chicken, reserve stock, and cool.

Melt ¼ cup butter in a medium glass bowl on highest setting for 20 seconds. Add ½ cup flour and blend thoroughly. Cook for 2 minutes, stirring twice.

Use 2 cups of broth. Gradually stir into the flour mixture. Heat on highest setting for 2 to 3 minutes, until boiling.

Remove chicken meat from bones and cut up. Mix with sauce and stir in peas. Season with salt and pepper.

Sift rest of flour and a pinch of salt into a mixing bowl. Add remaining margarine and shortening. Cut with two knives or a pastry blender until mixture resembles cornmeal. Add just enough cold water to make a stiff dough. Roll out ⅔ of dough and line an 8-inch baking dish.

Spoon filling into dish. Roll out rest of dough to make a lid for the pie. Put in place. Trim and decorate edge. Reroll trimmings and cut out shapes to decorate top of pie. Brush with beaten egg and bake on "roast" setting for 9 minutes. Transfer to preheated conventional oven at 450°F and bake 10 to 15 minutes or until golden brown.

Roast Chicken

Yield: 4 servings

When roasting a chicken in the microwave oven, the cooking time remains the same whether or not it is stuffed. Poultry is best cooked on "roast" setting for half of the cooking time. If it is completely cooked on the highest setting, the meat shrinks from the bone. Allow 8 minutes cooking time per pound.

1 3½-pound chicken
2 tablespoons butter
Salt and pepper
1 jar (8 ounces) peach preserves
1 tablespoon soy sauce
1 teaspoon powdered ginger
1 teaspoon paprika

Place the butter, salt, and pepper in the chicken cavity. Truss the chicken and place it breast side down on a microwave oven roasting rack or on an inverted saucer set in a glass baking dish. Cook for 14 minutes on the highest setting. Remove from oven. Remove the lid from the jar of preserves and heat on the highest setting for 5 minutes. Force the preserves through a strainer and combine with soy sauce, ginger, and paprika.

Turn the chicken breast side up and brush with the soy sauce mixture. Rotate the chicken one-quarter of a turn. Cook on "roast" setting for 14 more minutes, basting frequently with the soy sauce mixture. Remove the chicken from the oven. The internal temperature should read 175°F. It will increase in temperature 20 degrees as it rests. Let the chicken rest 15 minutes before carving.

Roast Chicken Royal

Yield: 4 servings

2½ cups white bread crumbs
1¼ cups milk
1 large egg, beaten
2 medium-size mushrooms, cleaned and chopped
¼ pound ground veal
¼ pound ground pork
½ teaspoon salt
¼ teaspoon pepper
1 4½-pound chicken
2 strips bacon, uncooked
1 clove garlic, minced or crushed
1 tablespoon cooking oil
2 cups chicken broth or bouillon
1 tablespoon cornstarch
1 small jar artichoke hearts
1 8-ounce can mushrooms, drained
1 bunch watercress
1 large orange, cut into wedges

Put bread crumbs and milk in a bowl. Cover and let stand for 30 minutes. Add the beaten egg, chopped mushrooms, veal, and pork. Season well with salt and pepper. Mix to form a firm stuffing.

Dry the chicken skin on paper towels. Season inside with salt and pepper. Put bacon and garlic inside the chicken. Stuff. Truss the chicken and place it breast side down on a microwave oven roasting rack or on an inverted saucer set in a glass baking dish. Brush skin with oil. Cook for 16 minutes on the highest setting. Turn chicken breast side up and rotate pan one-quarter of a turn. Cook on "roast" setting for 16 more minutes, basting frequently with 1 tablespoon oil or drippings from the pan. Transfer chicken to a serving dish and let it rest for 15 minutes before carving.

Strain off all but 2 tablespoons of fat from the roasting pan. Add chicken stock. Stir the cornstarch with 2 tablespoons of cold water and stir into juices in baking dish. Bring to boil on highest setting and cook for 2 minutes or until thick. Stir once after one minute.

In separate glass bowls, heat mushrooms and artichoke hearts in juice from containers. Cook for 2 minutes or until warm. Drain.

Garnish chicken with artichoke hearts, mushrooms, watercress, and orange wedges.

Chicken with Mandarins

Yield: 4 to 6 servings

Poultry should be completely thawed before cooking. Use a microwave rack.

1 5-pound roasting chicken
2 cups orange juice
2 tablespoons orange rind
⅓ cup brown sugar
2 tablespoons butter, melted
1 tablespoon flour
Orange or mandarin segments for garnish

Combine orange juice, orange rind, sugar, and melted butter. Place chicken in glass baking dish. Sprinkle body cavity with salt and pepper. Truss the chicken with string. Place chicken, breast side down, on microwave roasting rack in a 2-quart glass baking dish. Pour juice mixture over the chicken. Cook on highest setting for 18 minutes. Baste every 15 minutes with pan juices. Turn breast side up and cook on "roast" setting for 18 minutes. Transfer chicken to a hot serving plate and cover with foil for 5 to 10 minutes before serving.

Mix flour with 2 tablespoons cold water and stir into pan drippings with a wire whisk. Bring to a boil on highest setting and cook for 2 minutes or until the sauce has thickened. Stir once after 1 minute. Garnish chicken with orange or mandarin segments and serve with rice or oven-fried potatoes. Serve the sauce separately.

Roast Turkey

Yield: 6 servings

It is quite difficult to cook a turkey perfectly in the conventional oven because more often than not it becomes dry and tasteless. In the microwave oven it remains moist and full of flavor.

1 10-pound turkey (there will be enough for sandwiches the next day)
3 tablespoons shortening
1 tablespoon paprika
10 strips bacon

Truss the turkey. Dry the skin with paper towels. Rub the shortening over the skin and sprinkle with paprika. Cover the skin with bacon strips, holding them in place with toothpicks. Cook the turkey, breast side down, uncovered, on a microwave oven roasting rack or on two inverted saucers set in a glass baking dish, for 30 minutes on "roast" setting.

Turn the turkey breast side up. Cover the leg and wing tips with lightweight aluminum foil to prevent them from overcooking. Rotate the turkey one-quarter of a turn and continue cooking for 30 minutes. The internal temperature should read 175°F. It will rise 20 degrees as it rests. Let the turkey rest for 15 minutes before carving.

Note: If you would like to serve stuffing with the turkey, see the recipe for Roast Duck Montmerency.

Curried Turkey

Yield: 6 servings

Brown the turkey well to seal the surface before adding the curry powder. Curry tends to mask the flavor of poultry.

3 turkey legs and thighs cut at joint into serving pieces
2 tablespoons seasoned flour (add ½ teaspoon salt and ⅛ teaspoon pepper)
2 onions, sliced
¼ cup butter
1 apple, peeled, cored, and chopped
2 tablespoons curry powder
2 cups chicken broth
1 tablespoon lemon juice
2 tablespoons chutney
4 tomatoes, chopped

Coat turkey pieces with seasoned flour. In a conventional oven, fry onions in hot butter until soft. Add turkey and fry until golden brown. Add chopped apple, curry powder, and any remaining flour. Stir well and cook 2 minutes. Add stock, lemon juice, chutney, and tomatoes and mix well. Transfer all ingredients to a large casserole or glass bowl. Cover and cook in microwave oven on "simmer" for about 30 minutes. Cooking time will vary according to the size of turkey pieces. Check for doneness frequently. Serve with rice.

Turkey and Cheese Cauliflower

Yield: 4 servings

It is much easier to remove cooked turkey from the bone while it is still warm—if tur-key has cooled, place in colander over hot water until the skin and turkey flesh have softened.

1 medium-size cauliflower, cut in large florets
Oil and vinegar dressing (mix ⅛ cup oil and ⅛ cup vinegar)
½ cup mayonnaise
¼ cup whipping cream
1 cup cooked turkey, chopped
Salt and pepper
¼ cup grated cheddar cheese

Cook cauliflower. Drain and sprinkle with oil and vinegar dressing. Mix mayonnaise with cream. Add salt and pepper to taste. Add turkey and cauliflower in glass or ceramic bowl; spoon over turkey sauce. Sprinkle with cheese.

Cook for 4 minutes on highest setting. Rotate dish one-quarter turn after 2 minutes. The cheese will not brown in the microwave oven unless you have one of the newer models with the browning element.

Spatchcock Turkey

Yield: 4 servings

2 turkey legs and thighs, cut at joint into serving pieces
2 teaspoons poultry seasoning
1 teaspoon salt
2 lemons, thinly sliced
¼ cup chutney
1 tablespoon catsup
1 lemon, juiced
¼ cup soft brown sugar
4 whole fresh tomatoes
4 baked or sautéed potatoes

Rub poultry seasoning and salt into tur-key. Cover each with lemon slices. In a small glass bowl or casserole combine chutney, catsup, lemon juice, and sugar. On "simmer" setting, heat 1 or 2 minutes, until bubbling. Spoon over turkey joints and cook uncovered on "roast" setting for 20 minutes. Serve with baked tomatoes and baked or sautéed potatoes. Tomato skins must be pierced in several places before cooking in microwave oven. Garnish with lemon slices and parsley.

Roast Duck Montmerency

Yield: 4 servings

In this recipe the cooking of the duck is completed in the conventional oven so that the skin will crisp and become almost black in color. The duck is served with black cherries.

1 5-pound duck

Stuffing

1 pound sausage meat
Liver from the duck
3 slices bread made into bread crumbs in the blender
½ cup chopped walnuts
1 small onion, finely chopped
3 tablespoons finely chopped parsley
1 cup apple sauce
1 teaspoon cinnamon
1 egg
Salt and pepper

Glaze

2 tablespoons honey
2 tablespoons butter, softened

Remove the giblets from the duck and discard excess fat from the duck cavity. The giblets will be used to make the foundation of the sauce for the duck.

Place the sausage meat on a ceramic plate and separate it into small pieces with a fork. Cook the sausage meat for 5 minutes on the highest setting. Chop the duck liver into small pieces and add to the sausage meat. Transfer these ingredients to a bowl. Stir in all the remaining stuffing ingredients and cook in the microwave oven for 3 minutes.

Place the stuffing in the duck cavity and truss the duck with string. Prick the duck skin in several places to allow the fat to drain. Place the duck on an inverted saucer in a 12-inch glass baking dish. Cook the duck on "roast" setting for 20 minutes, rotating the dish one-quarter of a turn after 10 minutes.

Combine the honey and butter and spread over the surface of the duck. Place the duck in a preheated moderate (350°F) oven for 20 minutes to complete the cooking.

Slice the duck meat or cut into quarters with poultry shears.

Black Cherry Garnish for Duck

Yield: 6 servings

This recipe can also be used for making cherries jubilee.

1 jar (1 pound) large black Bing cherries
1 tablespoon red currant jelly
1 tablespoon arrowroot or cornstarch dissolved in 2 tablespoons water

Drain the cherries and place in a 4-cup glass measuring cup with 1 cup of the juice. Add the red currant jelly and cook on the highest setting for 3 minutes. Stir in the arrowroot or cornstarch dissolved in cold water and cook for 1 minute until thickened. Stir and serve hot with the duck.

Sauce for the Duck

Yield: 6 servings

This sauce can be made in the microwave oven while the cooking of the duck is completed in a conventional oven.

1 tablespoon sugar
2 tablespoons red wine vinegar
Giblets from the duck, except the liver
½ small onion, finely chopped
1½ cups chicken broth
1 orange
2 tablespoons Grand Marnier
1 tablespoon Madeira or brandy
Salt and pepper
1 tablespoon cornstarch dissolved in 2 tablespoons cold water

Place the sugar and red wine vinegar in a custard cup. Cook on the highest setting for 2 minutes, until the sugar has caramelized. Place to one side.

Put the giblets, onion, and chicken broth in a 4-cup glass measuring cup and cook in the microwave oven for 15 minutes at "simmer" setting. Strain ¼ cup of the liquid into the container with the caramelized sugar and return to the measuring cup.

Cut the orange rind into tiny strips, half the length of a matchstick and as thin as possible. Squeeze the orange. Place the orange rind and juice in a custard cup in the microwave oven for 2 minutes on the highest setting. Add to the strained liquid. Add the Grand Marnier, and Madeira or brandy. Season the sauce with salt and pepper. Return to the oven for 2 minutes. Stir in the cornstarch dissolved in cold water and cook 1 minute, until the sauce is thick and bubbling hot.

Seafood

Striped Bass

Yield: 2 servings

1 pound striped bass, cleaned and boned
2 scallions, finely chopped
1 small tomato, peeled, seeded, and chopped
½ cup cucumber, diced
¼ teaspoon tarragon or 1 tablespoon chopped parsley
2 tablespoons butter
1 tablespoon lemon juice

Place the bass on a piece of waxed paper large enough to enclose it completely. Top the fish with all the remaining ingredients. Fold the long sides of the paper over the fish and tuck the edges beneath, forming a tidy package. Place on inverted plates and cook for 6 minutes on the highest setting. Rotate the fish one-quarter of a turn after 3 minutes.

Baked Cod

Yield: 4 servings

Other fish, such as haddock or rockfish, could be substituted for the cod in this recipe.

1 dressed fresh cod, about 2 pounds
4 tomatoes, sliced
3 lemons
1 pound mushrooms
½ teaspoon salt
⅛ teaspoon pepper

½ teaspoon marjoram
½ teaspoon thyme
1 bay leaf
1 large onion
3 tablespoons cooking oil

Wash fish, pat dry, and place in a medium glass baking dish. Sprinkle the juice of 1 lemon over the fish. Garnish with the tomatoes and remaining lemons cut into slices. Wash the mushrooms and place around the fish. Season with salt and pepper. Add marjoram, thyme, and bay leaf. Cut the onions into rings and add. Sprinkle with cooking oil. Cook covered on highest setting for 14 minutes. Let fish stand, covered, for 5 minutes.

Braised Halibut in Cream and White Wine

Yield: 6 servings

Other firm-textured fish, such as cod, salmon, bass, trout, or swordfish, can also be used for making this dish.

3 pounds halibut
4 scallions, finely chopped
2 carrots, thinly sliced
2 stalks celery, thinly sliced
½ teaspoon thyme
Grated rind of 1 lemon
2 tablespoons butter
½ cup cream
½ cup white wine
1½ tablespoons flour
Salt and pepper
2 tablespoons freshly chopped parsley

Place the fish in a 10-inch glass or ceramic baking dish. Arrange the vegetables around the sides of the dish. Sprinkle the fish with thyme and grated lemon rind. Dot with 1 tablespoon of the butter. Pour in the cream and wine. Cover with waxed paper and cook on "roast" setting for 12 minutes. Rotate the dish one-quarter of a turn after 6 minutes. Transfer the fish to a hot platter and season with salt and pepper. Allow to stand for 5 minutes. It should flake easily, indicating it is completely cooked.

Heat the remaining 1 tablespoon of butter in a 6-cup glass measuring cup on the highest setting for 20 seconds and then stir into the vegetables and liquid in the baking dish. Cook for 5 minutes on the same setting. Spoon the sauce over the fish and garnish with parsley.

Salmon in Pastry

Yield: 4 servings

1 tablespoon butter
2 tablespoons flour
¾ cup milk
1 small can salmon
½ teaspoon salt
¼ teaspoon white pepper
1 tablespoon chopped parsley
2 eggs, hard-boiled, shelled, and chopped
1 crust pie pastry, uncooked

Place butter, flour, and milk in a small pan. Bring to a boil on conventional burner, whisking constantly. Cook for 2 minutes.

Drain salmon; remove skin and bones. Stir salmon and remaining ingredients into sauce. Roll out pastry to a 10-inch square and place in a glass baking dish. Place filling in center. Brush pastry edges with water. Fold corners to center and pinch edges together so that the filling is completely enclosed. Brush with a little milk and cook on "roast" setting for 9 minutes or until crust has small brown spots.

Haddock with Tomato Sauce

Yield: 4 servings

2 pounds fresh haddock
2 tablespoons butter

Tomato Sauce

4 medium-size tomatoes, cut into
  wedges
1 onion, finely chopped
2 tablespoons white vermouth
1 tablespoon olive oil
1 teaspoon flour
2 teaspoons tomato paste
½ teaspoon thyme
½ teaspoon basil
Salt and pepper

Dot the haddock with butter. Wrap it in waxed paper. Place it in a 10-inch glass or ceramic baking dish and cook on the highest setting for 6 minutes. Rotate the dish one-quarter of a turn after 3 minutes.

To prepare the sauce, place all the ingredients in a glass or ceramic casserole. Cover and cook on the highest setting for 8 minutes. Purée the sauce in a blender and strain to remove the tomato skins and seeds. Reheat the sauce, uncovered, for 3 minutes and serve with the fish.

Baked Rockfish

Yield: 8 servings

1 dressed rockfish with head, approximately 4 pounds
2 tomatoes, cored, peeled, and seeded
1 pound mushrooms
6 scallions
1 small clove garlic, minced

½ teaspoon thyme
1 bay leaf
2 tablespoons finely chopped parsley
½ teaspoon salt
½ teaspoon pepper
2 cups dry white wine
6 tablespoons butter
½ lemon

Grease a large glass baking dish. Wash the fish, pat dry, and place in the dish. Slice tomatoes, mushrooms, and scallions, and place them around fish. Add garlic, thyme, bay leaf, parsley, salt, and pepper. Cover with wine and dot with 4 tablespoons of butter, cut into small pieces. Tuck waxed paper over dish to cover. Cook on highest setting for 18 minutes. Let stand, covered, for 5 minutes. Remove fish and place on a serving dish.

Soften (but do not melt) 2 tablespoons of butter. Strain and pour off juice from the baking dish and whip soft butter into it until the mixture is light. Add the cooked vegetables to the sauce. Taste and add additional seasoning if necessary. Add the juice of ½ lemon and serve with the fish.

Idea for vegetable: Cut 2 medium-size cucumbers into quarters, place in a cheese-cloth bag, and immerse in salted boiling water for 5 minutes. Immediately after boiling, butter the hot sections and sprinkle with chopped parsley. Arrange around the fish with section of lemon and sprigs of parsley. Serve immediately.

Fillets of Sole with Tomatoes

Yield: 8 servings

3 pounds fillets of sole
¼ pound butter
1 large onion, finely chopped

160

3 scallions
3 sprigs parsley
½ cup chopped watercress
2 large tomatoes, peeled, seeded, and
    chopped
½ teaspoon tarragon
½ teaspoon salt
⅛ teaspoon pepper
1 cup dry white wine
1 egg yolk, beaten
¾ cup heavy cream
1 tablespoon lemon juice

In a large glass baking dish add butter, onion, scallions, watercress, tomatoes, and tarragon. Add the sole to the dish. Add salt, pepper, and wine. Cover and cook on highest setting for 12 minutes. Let stand, covered, for 5 minutes. Remove the fillets and keep them warm. Continue to cook the sauce until the volume is reduced by one-third. Remove from microwave oven and rapidly stir in the egg yolk and the cream. Taste and adjust seasoning as desired. Add lemon juice. Return the fillets to the cooking dish and spoon the sauce over them. Broil in a conventional broiler on low heat for 5 minutes to brown.

Sole Fillets in White Wine

Yield: 4 servings

2 large sole fillets (ask for fish bones)
1 cup water
1 teaspoon salt
¼ teaspoon pepper
1 bay leaf
1 small carrot, sliced
½ small onion, sliced
5 tablespoons milk

½ cup flour
¼ cup butter
1 cup shelled shrimp, uncooked and
    chopped
Cayenne pepper, to taste
3 tablespoons grated Parmesan cheese
½ cup dry white wine
½ small green pepper, for garnish
1 small lemon, sliced, for garnish
Few sprigs of parsley, for garnish

Place the fish bones in a 2-quart glass bowl or casserole with water. Add salt, pepper, bay leaf, carrot, and onion. On highest setting, bring to a boil. Reduce heat to "simmer" setting and cook for 10 minutes. Strain stock and cool.

Combine milk and flour in a medium bowl and blend to a smooth paste. Stir in fish stock. Cook on "simmer" setting for 3 minutes, stirring twice. Remove from heat. Stir in 2 tablespoons butter and shrimp. Add a dash of cayenne pepper to taste. Stir in 2 tablespoons cheese. Roll fillets and stand them in a buttered baking dish. Ease open the middle of each fillet to make a 1-inch hole. Secure rolls with a toothpick. Fill the fillets with sauce. Cover and cook on highest setting for 8 to 9 minutes. Sprinkle the remaining cheese on fish, and re-cover. Let fish stand, covered, for 5 minutes to complete cooking.

Strain fish juices from baking dish into a medium glass bowl. Add 2 tablespoons butter and the white wine. Bring to a boil on highest setting and continue to boil until mixture is reduced by half. Pour into a sauce boat. Serve the fish on a bed of cooked rice mixed with sliced green pepper. Garnish with lemon twists and parsley.

Fillets of Sole with Vegetables

Yield: 2 servings

Fish is done when it is white and opaque. Separate the flakes near the center with a fork to test that it is fully cooked.

2 fillets of sole (about 1 pound)
¾ cup heavy cream
1 stalk celery, thinly sliced
1 scallion, thinly sliced
2 carrots, thinly sliced
½ teaspoon salt
1 tablespoon butter

Melt the 1 tablespoon of butter in a medium baking dish for 20 seconds on the highest setting. Add vegetable slices and salt. Cook for 2 minutes. While stirring rapidly, add the cream. Cook for 3 minutes. Add in the sole and cook 3 minutes. Remove fillets of sole and set on serving plate. Cook sauce 1 additional minute. Take out of oven. Pour sauce over slices of sole.

Swordfish with White Wine

Yield: 4 servings

2 pounds swordfish
½ cup dry white wine
1 tablespoon lemon juice
4 scallions, finely chopped
3 tablespoons finely chopped parsley
2 tablespoons butter
Salt and pepper

Remove the skin from the swordfish and place in a baking dish just large enough to accommodate it. Pour the wine and lemon juice over the fish. Sprinkle the surface with scallions and parsley. Dot with butter and season with pepper.

Cover with waxed paper and cook on "roast" setting for 12 minutes. Rotate the dish one-quarter of a turn every 3 minutes. Remove from the oven and season with salt. Let stand 5 minutes before serving.

Curried Shrimp

Yield: 4 servings

1½ pounds medium-size fresh shrimp
2 tablespoons oil
1 onion, finely chopped
½ green pepper, finely chopped
1 tablespoon curry powder
¼ teaspoon cumin
Dash cayenne pepper
2 tablespoons flour
1½ cups chicken broth
1 teaspoon lemon juice
1 tablespoon tomato paste

Peel and devein the shrimp and leave to one side.

Heat the oil in a 1½-quart glass or ceramic casserole on the highest setting for 30 seconds. Add the onion and green pepper and cook for 1 minute. Stir in the curry powder, cumin, and cayenne pepper. Cook for 20 seconds. Stir in the flour. Stir in the chicken broth, lemon juice, and tomato paste with a wire whisk. Cook for 3 minutes. Add the shrimp and cook 3 minutes.

Serve with rice and chutney. Sprinkle with toasted coconut.

To make toasted coconut, spread 1 cup grated coconut on a paper plate and cook, uncovered, on the highest setting for 2 minutes. Stir the coconut and cook for 1 minute more. Sprinkle part of the coconut over the shrimp and serve the remainder in a separate bowl.

Seafood Quiche Lorraine

Yield: 6 servings

Use the lowest setting for this custard-type dish.

Pastry

1¼ cups flour
6 tablespoons butter
3 tablespoons cold water
3 tablespoons light cream

Cheese Filling

3 eggs
1¼ cups grated Gruyère cheese
¼ cup grated Parmesan cheese
¾ cup milk
½ cup light cream
¼ teaspoon paprika or white pepper
⅛ teaspoon nutmeg
½ teaspoon salt
For shellfish choose among:
    4 ounces shrimp, crab, or lobster

Sift flour into a bowl. Cut in butter with a knife or pastry blender until mixture looks mealy. Make a hole in the center and pour the water and cream into it. Work the pastry with a spoon until it can be formed into a ball. Chill thoroughly. Roll out to fit an 8- or 9-inch glass pie plate. Flute edge; prick bottom and sides of crust with fork. Cook on "roast" setting for 7 minutes.

Beat the eggs. Add cheeses, milk, cream, seasonings, and spices. Arrange the shellfish, cleaned and shelled, in the pie shell. Pour the cream mixture into the pie shell and cook on "defrost" setting for 30 to 35 minutes or until a knife inserted in the center comes out clean. Let quiche stand 5 minutes before serving.

Seafood Rissoto

Yield: 4 servings

2 cups uncooked rice
1 small onion, chopped
¼ cup butter
½ pound medium shrimp
¼ pound mushrooms
1 stalk celery, chopped
1 red pepper, sliced
1 package frozen green peas
¼ teaspoon saffron
2 tablespoons finely chopped parsley
¼ cup grated Parmesan cheese
2 small onions, sliced
½ stalk celery
1 clove garlic
1 cup white wine
½ teaspoon salt
¼ teaspoon pepper

Peel and devein shrimp. Put stock ingredients plus shrimp peels and 2½ cups water in a 1½-quart glass or ceramic casserole. Cook at highest setting for 5 minutes. Strain.

Melt butter in a 2½-quart casserole for 20 seconds. Add onion and cook for 2 minutes, until transparent. Add rice and stir well. Pour in strained stock. Cook for 12 minutes. Rotate the dish one-quarter turn every 2 minutes. Add celery, red pepper, thawed peas, mushrooms, shrimp, and ground saffron. Cover casserole and cook 6 minutes on highest setting, until shrimp are pink. Stir mixture and rotate the dish one-quarter of a turn after 3 minutes. Before serving, sprinkle with parsley and grated Parmesan cheese.

Vegetables

Asparagus and Cottage Cheese Salad

Yield: 6 servings

This salad, made when the first tender asparagus appears in the springtime, can be served alone or with rolled slices of boiled Virginia ham.

1½ pounds thin asparagus spears
½ teaspoon salt
Freshly ground black pepper
2 tablespoons lemon juice
6 tablespoons olive oil
1 pound cottage cheese
1 cup sour cream
3 tablespoons chopped chives
Pimiento strips

Wash the asparagus in plenty of cold water to remove any sand. Cut the spears into uniform lengths. Peel the lower third of each spear with a potato peeler. Arrange in a 10-inch glass or ceramic flat baking dish with the tips in the center of the dish. Sprinkle with salt and add cold water to cover. Cook, covered, on the highest setting until the water reaches the boiling point. Rotate the dish one-quarter of a turn and cook for 3 more minutes. Taste a spear to be sure it is tender but slightly crisp. Drain and rinse immediately but briefly under cold running water. Return the asparagus to the baking dish.

Combine the salt, pepper, lemon juice, and oil, and pour over the warm asparagus. Let stand for 5 minutes and drain off the dressing.

Arrange the asparagus on a flat serving plate with the tips pointing to the edge of the plate. Combine the cottage cheese and sour cream and place in the center of the dish. Sprinkle with chopped chives and garnish with pimiento strips.

Asparagus with White Sauce

Yield: 6 servings

2 pounds uniform-size fresh asparagus spears
½ cup cold water
1 tablespoon lemon juice
1 teaspoon salt
1 tablespoon butter

White Sauce
2 tablespoons butter
2 tablespoons flour
¾ cup milk
¾ cup light cream
⅛ teaspoon nutmeg
Salt and pepper
2 hard-boiled eggs

Trim the asparagus (see recipe for Asparagus and Cottage Cheese Salad) and place in a baking dish. Add the water, lemon juice, and salt. Cover with waxed paper and cook on the highest setting for 6 minutes. Drain and immediately rinse under cold running water. Place on a serving dish, dot with butter, and keep the asparagus warm while preparing the sauce.

Heat the butter in a 4-cup glass measuring cup for 30 seconds on the highest setting. Stir in the flour, milk, cream, nutmeg, salt, and pepper, and cook for 3 minutes. Stir with a wire whisk twice to ensure a smooth sauce. Reserve 1 egg yolk. Chop the remaining yolk and whites and add to the hot sauce. Place the sauce in a sauce boat and sprinkle with the remaining chopped egg yolk. Reheat the asparagus for 1½ minutes just before serving with the sauce.

Green Beans with Parmesan Cheese

Yield: 4 servings

1½ pounds string beans
¼ cup water
1 teaspoon salt
¼ cup freshly grated Parmesan cheese
2 tablespoons butter
2 tablespoons finely chopped parsley
Freshly ground black pepper

Trim and wash the beans. Place in a shallow 10-inch glass dish and add water and salt. Cover with waxed paper and cook for 8 minutes on the highest setting. Drain and rinse immediately under cold running water. Return to the dish and sprinkle with cheese. Dot with butter. Cook uncovered for 2 minutes. Sprinkle with finely chopped parsley and season with pepper.

Stuffed Cabbage Leaves

Yield: 6 servings

Allow 2 stuffed cabbage leaves for each serving and then 1 or 2 extra.

1 medium-size cabbage
1 tablespoon oil
1 onion, finely chopped
1 pound ground chuck steak
1½ cups cooked rice
1 tablespoon tomato paste
¼ cup finely chopped parsley
¼ teaspoon allspice
½ teaspoon cinnamon
1 teaspoon salt
Freshly ground black pepper
½ cup beef broth
1 cup tomato sauce

Place the cabbage in a 3-quart glass or ceramic casserole. Add ½ cup cold water, cover, and cook 4 minutes on the highest setting, until the leaves can be loosened easily. Discard the tough outer leaves and select 12 or 14 large perfect leaves. Remove the heavy stems. (Use the remaining cabbage for another meal.)

Heat the oil in a 2-quart glass bowl in the microwave oven for 20 seconds. Add the onion and cook 1 minute on the highest setting. Add the ground beef and cook for 3 minutes. Break up the beef with a fork and rotate the dish one-quarter of a turn after 1½ minutes. Combine the onion and beef with the rice, tomato paste, parsley, allspice, cinnamon, salt, and pepper.

Place a little of the mixture in the center of each leaf. Fold the sides over and roll the leaves to form tidy packages. Place seam side down in a 12-inch glass baking dish. Add the beef broth and tomato sauce. Cover with waxed paper and cook for 8 minutes on the highest setting. Rotate the dish one-quarter of a turn after 3 minutes.

Braised Celery

Yield: 4 servings

1 bunch celery
½ teaspoon salt
¼ teaspoon pepper
2 tablespoons butter
1 chicken bouillon cube, dissolved in 1 cup boiling water
1 tablespoon finely chopped parsley

Cut off green leaves from celery and discard. Cut celery stalks in half. Wash well and place in a glass casserole. Season with salt and pepper. Dot with butter and pour chicken stock over celery.

Cover dish and cook on highest setting for 10 to 12 minutes. Sprinkle with finely chopped parsley.

Braised Endives

Yield: 2 servings

Braised endives are an extraordinarily fine accompaniment for fish and simple roast meats.

4 Belgian endives
1 tablespoon butter
1 teaspoon Dijon mustard
½ cup heavy cream
2 tablespoons grated Swiss cheese
1 tablespoon grated Parmesan cheese
Salt and pepper
1 tablespoon finely chopped parsley

Cut a V shape in the base of each endive to remove the bitter core. Remove the blemished outer leaves. Arrange the endives in a 9-inch glass or ceramic baking dish. Add the butter, mustard, cream, and cheeses. Cover with waxed paper and cook on the highest setting for 4 minutes. Season with salt and pepper and garnish with parsley.

Mushrooms with Cheese Sauce

Yield: 4 servings

8 large mushrooms
3 slices bacon
1 tablespoon butter
4 scallions, finely chopped
1 clove garlic, finely chopped
2 tablespoons flour
1¼ cups milk
¼ cup grated Swiss cheese
½ cup bread crumbs
¼ cup grated Parmesan cheese

Remove the stems from the mushrooms and chop them finely. Fry the bacon in an 8-inch glass baking dish on the highest setting for 3 minutes, until the fat is rendered. Remove and crumble the bacon. Add the butter to the bacon fat and brown the mushroom caps for 1½ minutes. Remove the mushroom caps and fry the chopped stems, scallions, and garlic for 1½ minutes. Stir in the flour and cook 30 seconds. Stir in the milk and cook 2 minutes. Stir in the grated Swiss cheese. Cook 50 seconds. Return the mushroom caps and crumbled bacon to the baking dish. Top with bread crumbs and grated Parmesan cheese. Place under a preheated broiler for 3 minutes. The crumbs will not brown in the microwave oven unless you have one of the newest models with the browning attachment.

Green Peas Bonne Femme

Yield: 6 servings

Frozen peas could be substituted for fresh peas in this recipe. Cooking time would be 12 minutes for a 20-ounce package of frozen peas.

¼ pound bacon, cut in 1-inch pieces
2 tablespoons butter
3 cups fresh green peas
6 small white onions
Inner leaves of a lettuce
½ cup water
½ teaspoon salt
¼ teaspoon pepper
1 tablespoon sugar
1 tablespoon finely chopped parsley

Fry bacon in a 1-quart glass casserole on the highest setting for 3 minutes. Add butter, peas, onions, lettuce, water, salt, and pepper. Cover and cook on highest setting for 10 minutes. Add sugar after 8 minutes. When peas are done, drain remaining liquid. Sprinkle with parsley before serving.

Pepper Salad

Yield: 6 servings

2 medium-size green peppers
3 large summer-ripe tomatoes, sliced
3 scallions, finely chopped
½ teaspoon salt
Freshly ground black pepper
½ teaspoon basil
2 tablespoons red wine vinegar
6 tablespoons olive oil
3 tablespoons chopped chives

Cut the green peppers into strips and cover with boiling water. Cook on the highest setting for 2 minutes. Drain and rinse immediately under cold running water.

Arrange the green pepper strips and tomato slices in a serving dish and sprinkle with scallions. Combine all the remaining ingredients and pour over the salad.

Spinach Tarts

Yield: 6 to 8 servings

Make pastry 3 or 4 days in advance and store in a plastic bag.

1½ cups flour
Pinch of salt
3 tablespoons butter
1 tablespoon shortening
4 or 5 tablespoons water
1 10-ounce package frozen chopped spinach
5 tablespoons sour cream
1 large egg
1 teaspoon grated nutmeg
Salt and pepper to taste

Sift flour and salt into a bowl. Cut in butter and shortening with 2 knives or a pastry blender until mixture resembles cornmeal. Add the water to make a firm pastry dough. Chill 1 hour before rolling out. Use 6 to 8 glass custard cups for tart pans. Line with pastry, and flute edges.

Cook spinach according to package directions. Drain and purée in a blender. Combine sour cream, egg, and spinach. Season to taste with nutmeg, salt, and paper. Spoon into pastry and cook 3 cups at a time on "defrost" or coolest setting for 12 minutes or until knife inserted near center comes out clean. Test every 2 minutes during end of cooking period. Tarts will not brown without special unit.

Potatoes Stuffed with Shrimp

Yield: 4 servings

With a tossed salad these potatoes can become a whole meal.

4 large baking potatoes
2 tablespoons butter
2 egg yolks
2 tablespoons whipping cream
Salt and pepper
Dash Tabasco sauce
1½ cups cooked small shrimp
2 tablespoons chopped chives
1 cup grated cheddar cheese
2 tablespoons chopped chives or
    parsley
Parsley for garnish

Pierce the potatoes with a fork or skewer in two places. Arrange the potatoes 1 inch apart on paper plates and cook for 12 minutes on the highest setting. Turn the potatoes over after 6 minutes and rotate the dish one-quarter of a turn. Leave the potatoes to stand for 5 minutes.

Cut a slice from the top of each potato and use a teaspoon to scoop out the inside. Take great care not to break the potato shells. Place the potato centers in a mixer and add the butter, egg yolks, and cream. Mix until smooth mashed potatoes are formed. Season with salt, pepper, and Tabasco sauce. Stir in the shrimp, chives, and half of the grated cheese. Place the mixture in the potato shells and sprinkle with the remaining cheese. Return the potatoes to the microwave oven and cook for 3 minutes on the highest setting. Rotate the potatoes one-quarter of a turn and cook for 2 more minutes.

Desserts

French Apple Flan

Yield: 6 servings

¼ cup butter
½ cup sugar
2 large eggs yolks
½ teaspoon vanilla extract or essence
1 cup flour
4 large cooking apples
3 tablespoons apricot jam, strained

Combine butter, ¼ cup sugar, and egg yolks and work together with fingers until smooth. Add vanilla extract and mix well. Work in flour and knead to form a smooth dough. Form into a ball and put into a plastic bag. Chill for 30 minutes and roll out to fit an 8- or 9-inch glass pie plate. Prick bottom and sides of crust with fork. Cook on "roast" setting for 6 minutes.

Meanwhile, wash, peel, core, and thinly slice cooking apples. Place one-third of the apple slices in the pastry shell; sprinkle on 2 tablespoons of remaining sugar. Repeat. Arrange the remaining apples in an attractive ring on top. Cook on high for 7 minutes or until apples are soft. Remove from oven.

Heat apricot jam in a small custard cup on highest setting for 1 minute. Brush jam over flan while hot.

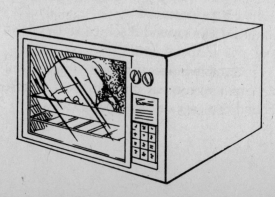

Banana Cake

Yield: 8 to 10 servings

1 cup butter
1 cup sugar
4 large eggs, beaten
4 medium-size ripe bananas
3 small lemons
3 cups self-rising flour, sifted
2 tablespoons cornstarch
¼ cup sugar
Yellow food coloring
1 cup heavy cream, whipped and
   sweetened
¼ cup milk
Candied lemon slices, optional

Line the base of 2 round glass baking dishes with waxed paper. Beat the butter with 1 cup sugar until light and fluffy. Gradually add the eggs, beating well.

Mash 2 bananas and beat into the mixture. Grate the rind from 2 lemons and add to the mixture. Fold in sifted flour. Spoon into prepared dishes. Bake one layer at a time. Cook on "simmer" setting for 7 minutes. Continue cooking on highest setting for 3 to 4 minutes or until toothpick inserted near center comes out clean. Repeat for second layer. Let cake stand for 5 minutes before turning out on serving plate.

Squeeze juice from lemons. Reserve 2 tablespoons. Add enough water to lemon juice to make 1¼ cups. Stir cornstarch into lemon juice and water in a small glass bowl. Add ¼ cup sugar and a few drops of food coloring. On highest setting, bring to boil and cook for 2 minutes. Stir once after 1 minute. Cover with lid or plastic wrap and cool.

Place ⅓ whipped cream in a decorating bag fitted with a star nozzle. Pipe 12 circles around the edges of one of the cakes.

Beat the lemon mixture and place a little in the center of each circle. Peel and slice the remaining bananas and brush with the reserved tablespoon of lemon juice. Arrange half of bananas in a circle on top of the cake. Place lemon candy in center. Spread the remaining lemon mixture, whipped cream, topping, and bananas between the layers. Serve within 2 hours.

Caramel Custard

Yield: 6 servings

¼ cup granulated sugar
3 eggs
2 egg yolks
⅓ cup sugar
2 cups milk
1 teaspoon vanilla extract

Place the sugar in a 1-quart glass or ceramic casserole. Cook in the microwave oven for 5 minutes on the highest setting. Swirl the sugar around the casserole after 2 minutes so that it will melt evenly to form caramel. The bowl will become hot, so use oven mitts. Rotate the casserole to coat the bottom and sides evenly with caramel.

Stir together the eggs, egg yolks, and sugar until just combined. Heat the milk in a 4-cup glass measuring cup for 2 minutes on the highest setting. Stir the hot milk into the eggs and sugar. Add the vanilla and pour into the caramel-lined casserole. Cook uncovered on "simmer" setting for 8 minutes. Stir the custard and rotate the dish one-quarter of a turn every 2 minutes. Cool.

Chill the custard for 4 hours and invert on a serving plate with a small rim. The caramel will form a sauce around the custard.

Chocolate and Molasses Cake

Yield: 6 to 8 servings

Line the bottoms of glass baking dishes with waxed paper. This method is more successful than greasing and flouring cake dishes.

> 1 tablespoon cocoa powder, regular, not instant
> ¼ cup butter
> ¼ cup sugar
> 1 large egg
> 1½ cups flour
> 2 teaspoons baking soda
> 2 tablespoons molasses
> ⅓ cup warm milk
> Candied cherries, optional

Blend cocoa powder with 3 tablespoons hot water and let cool. Beat butter with sugar until light and fluffy. Gradually add the egg, beating well. Mix in cocoa and butter.

Sift flour with baking soda. Mix molasses with warm milk. Fold flour and molasses alternately into the creamed mixture.

Line the bottom of a 9-inch round glass baking dish with waxed paper. Pour mixture into prepared dish. Cook on "simmer" setting for 7 minutes and then on highest setting for 3 to 4 minutes or until a toothpick inserted in the center comes out clean. Cool for 5 minutes before removing from dish.

Decorate with halves of candied cherries.

Chocolate and Orange Cake

Yield: 6 servings

> 1 cup butter
> 1 cup sugar
> 4 eggs, beaten
> 1 orange
> 2 cups self-rising flour
> ¾ cup whipping cream
> 1 small banana
> 1 pineapple ring (from can)
> ¼ cup chocolate frosting
> ½ cup confectioner's sugar
> Yellow food coloring

Line the bottoms of 2 round glass baking dishes with waxed paper. Beat butter and sugar together. Add eggs, one at a time, beating well, and grated orange rind. Reserve rest of orange. Sift flour and fold into mixture. Spoon into baking dishes and bake one at a time. Cook on "simmer" setting for 7 minutes. Continue cooking on highest setting for 3 to 4 minutes or until toothpick inserted near center comes out clean. Repeat for second layer. Let cake stand 5 minutes before turning out on serving plate.

Whip cream, sweetened to taste, and mix in sliced banana. Section orange and reserve 3 sections. Chop rest and fold into cream. Cut pineapple into pieces. Reserve 3 pieces of pineapple and fold remainder into cream. Spread over 1 layer.

Cut other cake into 6 wedges. Frost 3 wedges with chocolate icing. Top with pineapple.

Sift confectioner's sugar; add just enough water to make smooth icing. Add food coloring to color pale yellow and spread on 3 wedges. Decorate with orange. Assemble cake. Refrigerate and serve within a few hours.

Hazelnut Cookies

Yield: 16 cookies

Cookie dough may be made 4 or 5 days in advance and kept in a plastic bag in the refrigerator. Leave the dough at room temperature for 1 or 2 hours before making the cookies.

> ¾ cup shelled hazelnuts or walnuts
> ½ cup butter
> ¼ cup brown sugar
> 1¼ cups flour
> ¼ teaspoon salt

Set 16 nuts aside. Place remaining nuts on a baking tray and cook in a conventional oven, 350°F, until the skins loosen and the inner nut is turning golden. Rub in a towel to remove skins. Then grind nuts in a grater or coffee grinder.

Beat butter in a bowl and beat in the sugar. Add the nuts, sifted flour, and salt. Roll into 16 balls and pat out with a wet fork in 2 flat-bottomed greased baking dishes. Set a nut in the center of each. Cook 1 dish at a time on "simmer" setting for about 5 minutes. Cool before removing from dish. Dust with confectioner's sugar. Brown for a minute under a conventional broiler.

Victoria Lemon Cake

Yield: 10 to 12 slices

A Victoria Cake will keep moist for days if kept in an airtight container or plastic bag.

> 1 cup sweet butter
> Grated rind of ½ lemon
> 1 cup sugar
> 4 eggs
> 2 cups self-rising flour
> 1 to 1½ cups lemon pudding
> ¼ cup confectioner's sugar

Cream butter until soft. Add lemon rind. Gradually beat in sugar until the mixture is soft and pale. Beat eggs lightly and stir into the mixture a little at a time. Sift flour onto mixture and fold in with a spatula.

Line the bottoms of 2 round medium-size glass baking dishes with waxed paper. Divide mixture equally between the dishes. Cook one at a time on "simmer" setting for 7 minutes and then on highest setting for 3 to 4 minutes or until a toothpick comes out clean. Let cake stand 5 minutes to set. Spread lemon pudding on top of one layer and place second layer on top. Sprinkle with confectioner's sugar.

Oranges in Syrup

Yield: 6 servings

> 6 large, perfect eating oranges
> 1 cup sugar
> 1 cup water
> 2 tablespoons Grand Marnier

Peel the colored part of the orange rind very thinly, with a potato peeler. Cut the peel into strips the length of a matchstick and half the width. Remove all the white pith and cut each orange in half through the center, horizontally. Reassemble the oranges with toothpicks.

To prepare the syrup, put the sugar, water, and julienne strips of orange peel in a 2-quart glass bowl. Cook for 5 minutes on the highest setting. Add the Grand Marnier. Place the oranges in the hot syrup and allow to cool. Chill 4 hours before serving.

Lemon Meringue Pie

Yield: 8 servings

Though pastry does not brown in the microwave oven, it will become crisp and flaky and taste very good. The meringue topping is completed in the conventional oven.

1¼ cups flour
¼ teaspoon salt
3 tablespoons shortening
3 tablespoons butter, cut into small
     pieces
¼ cup water

Lemon Filling

⅔ cup cornstarch
1¼ cups sugar
2 cups water
4 egg yolks
Grated rind and juice of 2 lemons

Meringue

4 egg whites
⅛ teaspoon cream of tartar
¼ teaspoon salt
1 cup sugar

Place the flour, salt, and shortening in a bowl and blend with a pastry blender until the pieces are the size of small peas. Blend in the butter and stir in the water with a fork. Form the dough into a ball and roll on a floured board. Fit into a 9-inch pie plate. Prick the bottom and sides of the pastry with a fork. Cook on the highest setting for 8 minutes. Rotate the pie plate one-quarter of a turn after 4 minutes.

To prepare the filling, measure the cornstarch, sugar, and water into a 4-cup measuring cup. Cook for 2 minutes on the highest setting. Stir in the egg yolks and the grated rind and juice of the lemons. Spread the filling in an even layer in the baked pastry shell. Cook on "roast" setting for 4 minutes.

To prepare the meringue, preheat the oven to 250°F. Place the egg whites, cream of tartar, and salt in the mixer and beat until soft peaks are formed. Add the sugar gradually and beat until stiff and shiny. Spread the meringue on top of the lemon filling and cook in the conventional oven for 40 minutes, until the meringue is lightly browned.

Note: The meringue cannot be cooked in the microwave oven even in the models that have a browning unit. The meringue will completely disintegrate in the microwave oven.

Pear Pie with Red Wine

Yield: 6 servings

8- or 9-inch pie crust, frozen or
     homemade

Filling

6 large, fresh Anjou pears
⅓ cup sugar
2 teaspoons cinnamon
1 cup red wine

Line an 8- or 9-inch glass pie plate with pie crust. Flute edge; prick bottom and sides of crust with fork. Cook on "roast" setting for 7 minutes. Meanwhile cut pears in half, peel and remove cores. In a glass bowl, add pears, sugar, cinnamon, and wine. Cover bowl with a plate and cook on highest setting for 6 minutes. Fill the pie crust with the fruit and pour wine over pears. Cook on highest setting 6 to 8 minutes or until pears are tender. Serve warm.

Poached Pears in Wine Syrup

Yield: 4 servings

Fruits poached in the microwave oven retain their color and texture very well. This is an excellent dessert, quickly made. Serve it alone, with whipped cream, English custard sauce, or ice cream.

1 cup sugar
2 cups red wine
¼ teaspoon allspice
1 teaspoon candied ginger, chopped
1 cinnamon stick
4 Anjou pears, cut in half, core removed but peel left on

Place the sugar, wine, allspice, ginger, and cinnamon stick in a 10-inch round glass baking dish. Bring to the boiling point on the highest setting. It will take approximately 4 minutes. Cook on "simmer" setting for 10 minutes. Arrange the pears in the dish and cook on the highest setting for 5 minutes. Leave the pears to cool in the syrup. Chill for 4 hours before serving.

Molded Rice Pudding with Chocolate Sauce

Yield: 6 servings

A creamy rich dessert that makes a fine ending to a meal. The chocolate sauce is also good on ice cream.

1 cup long-grain rice
2 cups cold water
1½ cups milk
½ cup sugar
4 egg yolks
1 teaspoon vanilla extract
2 packages unflavored gelatin
2 tablespoons cold water
1 cup heavy cream, whipped

Chocolate Sauce

1 package (6 ounces) semisweet chocolate pieces
¼ cup water
2 tablespoons butter
1 cup heavy cream
1 teaspoon vanilla extract

Place the rice in a 1-quart glass casserole. Cover with cold water. Cover and cook for 10 minutes on the highest setting. Let stand for 10 minutes. Drain off any excess water. In the meantime, pour the milk into a 4-cup glass measuring cup. Add the sugar and cook for 1½ minutes. Stir in the egg yolks and vanilla extract. In a custard cup sprinkle the gelatin on the surface of the water. Cook in the microwave oven for 10 seconds, until the gelatin has dissolved.

Combine the rice, custard, gelatin, and whipped cream. Place in a 1½-quart oiled mold. Chill for 4 hours and unmold.

Place all the sauce ingredients in a 4-cup glass measuring cup. Cook 1 minute on the highest setting. Stir and cook 1 minute longer on "simmer" setting. Stir rapidly with a wire whisk to form a smooth sauce.

Pineapple Syrup Pudding

Yield: 6 servings

1 pound 14 ounce can pineapple slices
2 tablespoons butter
2 tablespoons corn syrup
5 maraschino cherries
¾ cup vegetable shortening
¾ cup light brown sugar
3 large eggs
3 cups self-rising flour
1 tablespoon baking powder

Drain pineapple rings; reserve juice. Spread butter inside a 2-quart glass bowl. Spread syrup over the butter. Place 1 pineapple ring in bottom of bowl and arrange 4 rings around the sides. Put a cherry in the center of each pineapple ring.

Chop the remaining pineapple rings. Place shortening, brown sugar, eggs, and pineapple in a mixing bowl. Sift flour and baking powder into the bowl. Beat mixture for several minutes. Add enough pineapple juice to give a soft consistency. Spoon into prepared bowl. Cover with glass lid or plastic wrap. Cook on "simmer" setting for 12 minutes. Cook on highest setting for 2 or 3 minutes or until a toothpick comes out clean. Remove lid; let stand 5 minutes, unmold. Serve hot or cold.

Pineapple Gateau

Yield: 6 servings

3 large eggs
¾ cup sugar
1 tablespoon cold water
¾ cup flour
¾ cup cornstarch
2 teaspoons baking powder
16-ounce can pineapple rings
1¼ cups heavy cream
3 tablespoons red currant jelly

Beat eggs, sugar, and water for 15 minutes or until very thick and creamy. Sift flour with cornstarch and baking powder. Fold into beaten egg mixture, lightly and carefully. Line the bottom of a 9-inch round baking dish with waxed paper. Pour mixture into the prepared dish. Cook on "simmer" setting for 7 minutes. Continue cooking on high for 3 or 4 minutes or until a toothpick comes out clean. Let cake stand 5 minutes to set. Turn out on serving plate to cool.

Drain the pineapple and chop finely. Whip cream and butter. Put half of cream in a pastry bag fitted with a medium star nozzle. Put the red currant jelly in a bag fitted with a fine plain nozzle. Cut cake in half. Spread half the remaining cream on 1 piece of cake. Spoon pineapple on top. Place other piece of cake on top and spoon remaining cream on top. Pipe on shell border of jelly around the top edge of cake. Pipe lines of red currant jelly in the center.

Pressure Cooker
Soups

Cream of Asparagus Soup

Yield: 4 to 6 servings

1 pound fresh asparagus, cut into
    1-inch pieces
1 slice lemon
2 cups chicken broth
1 tablespoon cornstarch
¼ cup water
1 cup milk and 1 cup cream, heated
1 teaspoon salt
¼ teaspoon pepper

Put asparagus, lemon, and chicken broth into cooker. Close cover and put pressure control in place. When pressure is reached, cook for 2 minutes. Cool at once under running water.

Blend cornstarch in water. Add to open cooker, stirring until slightly thickened. Add heated milk and cream, salt, and pepper. Simmer 1 minute.

Serve in soup bowls.

Green-Bean Soup

Yield: 4 to 6 servings

1 pound green beans, cut into 1-inch
    pieces
4 cups beef or chicken broth
1 tablespoon cornstarch
¼ cup cold water
½ teaspoon sugar
½ teaspoon salt
½ cup sour cream

Put beans and broth into cooker. Close cover and set pressure control in place. When pressure is reached, cook for 3 minutes. Cool cooker at once under running water. Return open cooker to a low flame.

Mix cornstarch and water; add to soup, stirring until thickened slightly. Season with sugar and salt; blend in sour cream.

Serve soup at once.

Beet Soup

Yield: 4 to 6 servings

2 large beets, diced
1 tablespoon vinegar
½ teaspoon salt
2 teaspoons sugar
4 cups beef broth
1 tablespoon flour
¼ cup water
1 small beet, grated
Sour cream for garnish

Put beets in cooker. Add vinegar, salt, sugar, and beef broth. Close cover and set pressure regulator in place. When pressure is reached, cook for 10 minutes. Cool at once under running water. Remove cooker cover.

Mix flour and water thoroughly; add to soup. Stir over a low flame until mixture thickens slightly. Sprinkle the grated beet on top of the soup.

Serve in soup bowls. Garnish with a spoonful of sour cream.

Cold Beet Soup

Yield: 4 to 6 servings

1 bunch young red beets with tops, sliced
1 tablespoon lemon juice
½ cup water
2 cups buttermilk
½ cup sour cream
½ cup liquid from cooked beets
½ teaspoon sugar
1 large cucumber, peeled and thinly sliced
2 hard-boiled eggs, sliced
2 teaspoons dill leaves
1 tablespoon chopped green onion

Place beets, lemon juice, and water in cooker. Close cover and set pressure regulator in place. When pressure is reached, cook for 5 minutes. Cool at once under running water. Drain beets; reserve the liquid. Chill.

Mix buttermilk, sour cream, and beet liquid. Add sugar. Put chilled beets, cucumber, eggs, dill, and green onion into buttermilk mixture. Blend. Serve soup very cold.

Corn Chowder

Yield: 4 to 6 servings

To vary the chowder, you might include celery, broccoli, or cauliflower in season.

3 tablespoons butter or margarine
1 large onion, chopped
1 10-ounce package frozen corn
2 cups canned tomatoes
1 large potato, diced
½ cup water
2 teaspoons salt
Dash of pepper

3 cups milk
2 tablespoons cornstarch
Liberal sprinkling of parsley

Melt butter in cooker; lightly tan the onion. Add vegetables, ¼ cup water, salt, and pepper. Close cooker and put pressure regulator in place. When pressure is reached, cook for 2 minutes. Cool cooker at once. Remove pressure control and top. Return cooker to low flame.

Add milk and bring just to a boil. Mix the cornstarch with ¼ cup water; add to cooker. Stir for 1 minute more to slightly thicken chowder.

Garnish with parsley; serve.

Leek Soup

Yield: 4 to 6 servings

4 leeks, washed, sliced lengthwise, and cut into 1-inch pieces
2 tablespoons butter or margarine
2 large onions, chopped
4 cups chicken or beef broth
½ teaspoon salt
1 cup milk
1 cup diced ham

Wash leeks and cut into 1-inch pieces.

Melt butter in cooker; sauté the leeks. Add the chopped onions. When leeks are soft, add broth and salt. Close cover of cooker and put pressure control in place. When pressure is reached, cook for 3 minutes. Cool cooker at once.

Return open cooker to a low flame. Add milk and ham; simmer for 3 minutes more. Serve.

Romaine-Lettuce Soup

Yield: 4 to 6 servings

1 small onion, minced
2 tablespoons shortening
4 cups chopped romaine lettuce
1 teaspoon salt
¼ teaspoon pepper
4 cups chicken broth
2 egg yolks
½ cup heavy cream

Tan onion in heated shortening. Add lettuce, salt, pepper, and broth. Close cover and put pressure control in place. When pressure is reached, remove from heat and cool cooker under running water. Return open cooker to low flame.

Beat together the egg yolks and heavy cream. Stir into the soup mixture. Do not boil. When soup begins to thicken, add extra salt if desired. Serve.

Fresh Okra Soup

Yield: 4 to 6 servings

1 pound fresh okra, chopped fine
1 medium onion, chopped
4 fresh tomatoes, diced
1 teaspoon salt
½ teaspoon pepper
1 bay leaf
4 cups beef broth

Put all ingredients into cooker in order given. Close cover and put pressure control in place. When pressure is reached, cook for 3 minutes. Cool cooker at once.

Since this is a Southern specialty, serve it with rice and corn bread.

Onion Soup

Yield: 4 to 6 servings

2 tablespoons shortening
2 cups thinly sliced onions
4 cups beef broth
Seasoned croutons
Parmesan cheese

Heat shortening in cooker; lightly tan onions. Add beef broth. Close cover and set pressure control in place. When pressure is reached, cook for 3 minutes. Cool at once under running water.

Serve soup in individual serving bowls, topped with croutons and Parmesan cheese.

Potato Soup

Yield: 4 to 6 servings

2 cups diced potatoes
2 scallions, chopped
4 cups chicken broth
1 cup milk
1 teaspoon Worcestershire Sauce
½ cup sour cream

Combine potatoes, scallions, and broth in cooker. Close cover and put pressure control in place. When pressure is reached, cook for 4 minutes. Cool cooker at once.

Spoon out the solid vegetables; put them through a sieve to mash fine. Return the vegetables to the broth; simmer. Gradually add milk, Worcestershire sauce, and sour cream.

Serve soup either hot or cold.

Potato and Cucumber Soup

Yield: 4 to 6 servings

6 medium potatoes, diced
1 medium cucumber, diced
1 small onion, grated
1 teaspoon salt
¼ teaspoon pepper
1 teaspoon dillweed
2 cups milk or cream

Put potatoes, cucumber, onion, salt, pepper, and dillweed into cooker. Close cover and set pressure control in place. When pressure is reached, cook for 5 minutes. Cool cooker at once.

Return open cooker to a low flame. Stir in the milk gradually, allowing all to blend and heat.

Serve in tureen or individual soup bowls.

Pumpkin Soup

Yield: 4 to 6 servings

2 cups fresh pumpkin, cut into 1-inch pieces
3 cups chicken broth
2 tablespoons brown sugar
½ teaspoon ginger
½ teaspoon cinnamon
½ cup finely chopped ham
1 cup light cream

Put pumpkin and chicken broth into cooker. Close cover and set pressure control in place. When pressure is reached, cook for 5 minutes. Cool at once under running water. Open cooker and return to low heat.

Add the rest of ingredients in order given. Simmer soup until hot; do not boil.

Serve soup at once.

Rice Broth with Parsley and Celery

Yield: 4 servings

1 cup uncooked rice
1 cup chopped celery
¼ cup minced parsley
1 teaspoon salt
4 cups beef or chicken stock

Place all ingredients in cooker in order listed. Close cover and set pressure regulator in place. When pressure is reached, remove cooker from heat. Allow to cool naturally.

Broth is ready to serve.

Sauerkraut Soup

Yield: 4 to 6 servings

1 pound sauerkraut (large can, well drained)
1 large onion, diced
1 tablespoon sugar
4 cups beef broth
1 tablespoon cornstarch
¼ cup water
Salt and pepper

Place sauerkraut, onion, sugar, and beef broth in cooker. Close cover securely and set pressure control in place. When pressure control jiggles, cook for 10 minutes. Cool at once under running water.

Mix cornstarch with water; add to soup, stirring constantly until slightly thickened. Season with salt and pepper to taste. Serve.

Spinach Soup

Yield: 4 servings

1 pound fresh spinach or 1 package
   frozen chopped spinach
1 quart chicken stock
1 tablespoon cornstarch
¼ cup water
1 teaspoon salt
Dash of ground pepper
¼ teaspoon nutmeg

Wash and chop spinach coarsely. If frozen spinach is used, thaw completely and drain.

Put chicken stock into cooker with chopped spinach. Close cover and set pressure control in place. When pressure is reached, cook for 1 minute. Reduce pressure instantly under running water.

Mix cornstarch with water; add to soup. Stir constantly until slightly thickened. Add salt, pepper, and nutmeg. Simmer for 1 minute more; serve.

Hot Tomato Soup

Yield: 4 to 6 servings

½ cup rice
1 medium onion, quartered
2 cups cut-up fresh tomatoes
2 to 3 hot red peppers
½ teaspoon salt
1 teaspoon sugar
4 cups water
Parsley for garnish

Put ingredients into cooker in order listed (except parsley). Close cover on cooker and put pressure regulator in place. When pressure is reached, cook for 1 minute. Remove cooker from heat and allow to cool naturally.

Serve in soup bowls, garnished with parsley.

Summer Vegetable Soup

Yield: 4 to 6 servings

1 cup diced carrots
1 cup fresh green peas
1 cup cauliflower florets
½ cup diced new potatoes
2 teaspoons salt
½ teaspoon pepper
3¼ cups water
1 tablespoon cornstarch
1 cup milk
1 egg yolk
¼ cup heavy cream
½ pound shrimp, cooked and cleaned
Chopped parsley or dill for garnish

Put carrots, peas, cauliflower, potatoes, salt, pepper, and 3 cups water into the cooker. Close cover and put pressure regulator in place. When pressure is reached, cook for 2 minutes. Cool at once under running water. Open cooker and return to a very low flame.

Mix cornstarch in ¼ cup water; add to the vegetable soup. Gradually add the milk.

Combine egg yolk and cream in a small bowl. Add 1 cup of the soup stock. Mix with a whisk. Add the mixture back into the soup, followed by the shrimp. Simmer for 3 minutes more. Add seasonings if necessary, such as more salt and pepper.

Pour into a soup tureen or serve in individual bowls, garnishing each portion with chopped parsley or dill.

Dutch Vegetable Soup

Yield: 4 to 6 servings

2 tablespoons shortening
½ pound beef cubes, cut small
¼ cup rice
1 cup diced carrots
A few Brussels sprouts
½ cup diced celery
1 leek
½ cup cauliflower florets
2 teaspoons salt
½ teaspoon pepper
Parsley for garnish

Melt shortening in cooker; brown beef. Add rest of ingredients (except parsley); close cover of cooker. Put pressure control in place. When pressure is reached and control jiggles gently, cook for 15 minutes. Cool cooker at once under running water.

Garnish soup with parsley, and serve.

Vegetable Chowder

Yield: 4 to 6 servings

1 large onion, chopped
3 tablespoons butter or margarine
1 package frozen corn (about 1 cup heavy)
1 package frozen baby lima beans
1 large potato, diced
1 cup water
2 teaspoons salt
Dash of pepper
3 cups milk
2 tablespoons cornstarch
Liberal sprinkling of parsley

Sauté the onion in butter in cooker. When onion is lightly tanned, add vegetables, ¾ cup water, salt, and pepper.

Close cover of cooker and put pressure control in place. When pressure is reached and control jiggles, cook for 2 minutes. Cool cooker at once under running water. Remove pressure control and top. Return to low flame.

Add milk to the vegetables; bring to a boil. Mix the cornstarch with ¼ cup water; add to the chowder. Stir continuously for 1 more minute.

Serve chowder with hot rolls and a salad. This will fill them up.

Peasant Soup

Yield: 4 to 6 servings

4 cups diced vegetables (any in season)
2 onions, diced
1 teaspoon salt
½ teaspoon pepper
4 cups water
½ cup sour cream

Put all vegetables into the cooker. Add salt, pepper, and water. Close cover on cooker. Set pressure regulator in place. When pressure is reached, cook for 5 minutes. Cool at once under running water.

Stir in the sour cream and simmer until hot.

Serve soup at once.

10-Minute Vichyssoise

Yield: 4 to 6 servings

2 cups diced potatoes
1 medium onion, chopped
2 cups chicken broth
1 teaspoon salt
2 cups milk or cream
1 tablespoon chopped chives

Put potatoes, onion, and chicken broth into cooker. Close cover and set pressure regulator in place. When regulator is rocking gently, cook for 5 minutes. Cool at once.

Mash the potatoes and liquid through a sieve into a large bowl. Add salt and milk; mix well to blend all the flavors. Chill well.

Garnish vichyssoise with chives when ready to serve.

Chilled Cherry Soup

Yield: 4 to 6 servings

½ cup raisins
6 thin orange slices
6 thin lemon slices
1 cup sliced fresh peaches
2 cups pitted cherries
½ cup sugar
½ teaspoon cinnamon
Dash of salt
1 cup water
1 tablespoon cornstarch
Whipped cream for garnish

Put fruit, sugar, cinnamon, salt, and water into cooker. Close cover and put pressure control in place. When pressure is reached, remove from heat and cool cooker at once under running water.

Remove ¼ cup liquid from fruit. Mix cornstarch with this; return to open cooker. Stir for 1 minute more as mixture thickens slightly. Put in a bowl and chill.

When served, garnish soup with whipped cream.

Fruit Soup

Yield: 4 to 6 servings

¼ pound pitted prunes
1 cup currants

1 cup fresh apples, quartered
1 quart water
½ cup cooked rice
3 tablespoons tapioca
¼ cup sugar
1 cinnamon stick
1 tablespoon lemon juice

Combine prunes, currants, apples, and water in cooker. Close cover and set pressure control in place. When pressure is reached, cook for 5 minutes. Allow cooker to cool normally for 5 minutes, then reduce pressure under running water.

Add cooked rice and tapioca to mixture; cook until clear. Add sugar, cinnamon stick, and lemon juice; cook for 2 minutes more, stirring gently.

Serve soup either hot or cold.

Almond Soup

Yield: 4 to 6 servings

2 cups water
½ teaspoon salt
1 cup white rice
2 teaspoons lemon juice
2 cups milk
¼ pound grated almonds
¼ cup sugar
1 teaspoon almond extract
¼ cup raisins

Combine water, salt, rice, and lemon juice in cooker. Close cover securely and set pressure control in place. When pressure is reached and control is jiggling gently, remove from heat. Allow to cool normally. Remove the cover.

Add milk, almonds, sugar, almond extract, and raisins to the rice. Stir until all ingredients are hot and blended.

Since this is a sweet soup, it is good served after the meat course.

Beef and Cabbage Soup

Yield: 4 to 6 servings

2 tablespoons shortening
½ pound ground beef
½ cup shredded cabbage
4 small potatoes, diced
1 carrot, diced
1 parsnip, diced
1 medium onion, chopped coarse
2 teaspoons salt
¼ teaspoon fresh ground pepper
4 cups beef broth

Melt shortening in cooker; brown ground beef thoroughly. Add the rest of the ingredients in order given. Close cover and set pressure regulator in place. When pressure is reached, cook for 15 minutes. Allow pressure to drop of its own accord. Serve.

Chicken and Broccoli Soup

Yield: 4 servings

1 package frozen chopped broccoli
½ cup chicken broth
½ teaspoon salt
¼ teaspoon pepper
1 10-ounce can cream of celery soup
1 cup heavy cream
1 cup diced, cooked chicken
Parsley for garnish, optional

Allow broccoli to thaw until it can be broken up.

Put broccoli, chicken broth, salt, and pepper into cooker. Close cover and set pressure control in place. When pressure is reached, cook for 2 minutes. Cool at once under running water.

Put cooked broccoli on a low flame. Add cream of celery soup, heavy cream, and chicken. Stir constantly but gently until soup is hot. Do not boil.

Garnish soup with parsley if desired. Serve.

Chicken and Corn Soup

Yield: 4 to 6 servings

2 whole chicken breasts, halved
2 cups fresh corn
1 onion, quartered
2 teaspoons salt
¼ teaspoon saffron
¼ teaspoon pepper
4 cups water
1 teaspoon chopped parsley
2 hard-cooked eggs, chopped

Put chicken, corn, onion, salt, saffron, pepper, and water into cooker. Close cover and set pressure control in place. When pressure is reached, cook for 15 minutes. Cool cooker at once under running water.

Remove chicken breasts and take meat from bones. Dice the cooked meat and return it to the soup. Simmer the soup for 2 to 3 minutes more.

Garnish soup with parsley and chopped eggs. Serve.

Maryland Crab Soup

Yield: 4 to 6 servings

1 large onion, chopped
1 stalk celery, diced
2 tablespoons shortening
2 cups crab meat, picked to remove shell
4 cups chicken broth

½ teaspoon salt
½ teaspoon pepper
½ cup heavy cream
2 tablespoons whiskey, optional
Parsley for garnish

Cook onion and celery in shortening until transparent. Add crab meat, broth, salt and pepper. Close cover and put pressure control in place. When pressure is reached and control jiggles, remove from heat. Cool cooker at once under running water.

Return open cooker to low flame. Add cream, stirring until hot; do not boil. Last, add whiskey.

Serve soup at once with parsley garnish.

Fish and Bacon Chowder

Yield: 4 to 6 servings

2 pounds fish fillets, cut into serving
  pieces
2 cups diced potatoes
1 large onion, quartered
1 teaspoon salt
Dash of pepper
1¼ cups water
1 tablespoon cornstarch
6 strips of cooked bacon in bits
1 cup milk or cream
Parsley for garnish

Place fish, potatoes, onion, salt, pepper, and 1 cup water into cooker. Close cover and put pressure regulator in place. When pressure is reached, cook for 4 minutes. Cool cooker at once under running water. Set cooker open on a low flame.

Mix ¼ cup water with cornstarch; add to open cooker. Stir; add the bacon bits as mixture thickens slightly. Last, add the milk; simmer for just 2 minutes more.

Serve in soup bowls, garnished with parsley, if desired.

Polish Fish Broth

Yield: 4 to 6 servings

1½ pounds fish, cut into 1-inch pieces
2 carrots, diced
2 celery stalks, diced
1 large onion, chopped
1 cup shredded cabbage
5 peppercorns
1 bay leaf
1 teaspoon salt
2 cups water
¼ teaspoon nutmeg

Put all ingredients (except nutmeg) into cooker. Close cover securely and set pressure control in place. When pressure is reached, cook for 3 minutes. Cool cooker at once under running water.

Add nutmeg; simmer for 1 minute more. Serve broth at once.

183

Meat

Beef Pot Roast

Yield: 4 to 6 servings

1 tablespoon shortening
4 pounds beef pot roast
Salt and pepper
1 onion, minced
1 bay leaf
1 cup water

Heat shortening in cooker and brown the roast on all sides. Add the seasonings and water in the order given. Cover the cooker and set pressure control in place. When the control is gently rocking, cook for 35 minutes. Allow the pressure to drop naturally.

Remove the roast and slice for serving. If gravy is wanted, thicken the essence left in the cooker.

Sweet-and-Sour Pot Roast

Yield: 6 servings

4 pounds beef pot roast, brisket or
　　chuck
1 teaspoon nutmeg
1 teaspoon cinnamon
½ teaspoon ginger
2 teaspoons salt
Dash of pepper
2 tablespoons shortening
2 onions, sliced
1 clove garlic, diced, optional
½ cup sugar
½ cup red wine
½ cup water

Rub the raw meat with a combination of nutmeg, cinnamon, ginger, salt, and pepper.

Place shortening in the cooker and allow to heat. Brown the meat well on all sides. Add the onions and garlic.

Dissolve the sugar in the wine and water and pour into cooker. Close cover securely, put on the pressure regulator and allow pressure to come up. When regulator is gently rocking, cook the meat for 40 minutes. Allow the pressure to drop of its own accord, about 10 minutes.

Slice and serve the roast.

Brisket with Wine

Yield: 4 to 6 servings

3- to 4-pound brisket
1 tablespoon shortening
Salt and pepper to taste
1 onion, minced
1 cup red wine

Brown the meat on all sides in the shortening. Add seasonings, onion, and red wine. Place cover on cooker and set pressure regulator in place. When the pressure is reached, cook for 35 minutes. Allow the pressure to drop naturally.

Slice and serve the brisket with gravy from the essence if desired.

Another variation of this is to use orange juice in place of the wine.

Beef Cubes in Sherry

Yield: 4 to 6 servings

2 tablespoons shortening
2 pounds lean stewing beef, cubed
1 package onion soup mix
1 cup sherry wine
1 can cream of mushroom soup
1 teaspoon garlic salt
¼ pound sliced mushrooms

Heat shortening in cooker. Brown the beef cubes on all sides. Add the remaining ingredients in order given. Close cover of cooker. Put pressure control in place. When pressure is reached, cook for 15 minutes. Allow cooker to cool normally.

Serve beef over broad noodles.

Stuffed Flank Steak

Yield: 4 servings

1 large 1-pound flank steak
Salt and pepper

Stuffing

¾ cup sausage meat
1 apple, peeled and sliced
1½ cups dried bread crumbs
1 tablespoon finely minced onion
¼ teaspoon salt
3 tablespoons shortening
¾ cup water

Trim edges of flank steak and sprinkle with salt and pepper. Set aside.

Brown the sausage in a fry pan and pour off excess fat. Add the apple, bread crumbs, onion, and salt. Mix together well. Spread this mixture over the flank steak and roll steak up loosely, tying it securely.

Put shortening in pressure cooker and brown the tied steak on all sides. Add water, cover securely, and set pressure control in place. After control jiggles, cook for 35 minutes. Cool cooker naturally for 5 minutes, then reduce pressure under running water.

If gravy is desired, thicken the essence that is in the cooker and pour over flank steak. Serve.

Short Ribs Hawaiian

Yield: 4 to 6 servings

1 onion, sliced into thin rings
2 tablespoons shortening
3 pounds beef short ribs
1 teaspoon ginger
2 teaspoons dry mustard
2 tablespoons sugar
1 teaspoon salt
¼ teaspoon pepper
1 teaspoon garlic salt
2 tablespoons chopped parsley
2 tablespoons soy sauce
2 tablespoons vinegar
½ cup water

Gently sauté onion rings in shortening. When onion rings are yellow and soft, remove from cooker.

Brown the ribs on all sides, adding extra shortening if needed.

Mix the remaining ingredients and pour over the ribs. Close cover and put regulator in place. When pressure is reached, cook for 25 minutes. Allow the ribs to cool naturally.

Serve the ribs with rice and a pineapple salad to complete the flavor of the islands.

Short Ribs in Teriyaki Sauce

Yield: 4 servings

2 pounds short ribs
Teriyaki sauce to cover the ribs
½ cup water

Marinate the short ribs in teriyaki sauce for at least 1 hour.

Place the ribs and marinade in cooker, adding the water. Close the cover of the cooker and place control on. When pressure is reached, cook for 25 minutes. Allow this to cool naturally. Serve.

Meat and Cabbage Balls

Yield: 6 servings

Boiling water
12 large cabbage leaves
1½ pounds ground beef
1 egg
1 medium onion, grated
¼ cup bread crumbs
Salt and pepper to taste
¾ cup water
3 or 4 pieces sour salt
½ cup brown sugar
1 8-ounce can tomato sauce

Pour boiling water over cabbage leaves and allow to sit 2 to 5 minutes, until leaves are soft and pliable.

Mix ground beef, egg, onion, bread crumbs, salt, and pepper; form into balls. Roll each ball into a cabbage leaf.

In the cooker, mix the ¾ cup water, sour salt, brown sugar, and tomato sauce. Place the cabbage balls in the liquid in the cooker, in layers if needed. Close the cooker and place regulator on top. Cook for 30 minutes after regulator rocks gently. Cool at once. Serve.

Chinese Meatballs

Yield: 4 servings

1 pound ground beef
1½ cups finely grated cabbage
1 large onion, finely grated
½ teaspoon ginger
2 tablespoons soy sauce
½ teaspoon salt
2 tablespoons shortening
½ cup water
1 teaspoon soy sauce

The night before you plan to serve them, mix ground beef, cabbage, onion, ginger, soy sauce, and salt in a large bowl. When thoroughly mixed, form into balls. Cover and set in the refrigerator. (While this can be done when preparing the meal, the flavors blend more fully under refrigeration.)

Heat shortening in cooker and brown the meatballs. Add water and soy sauce and close cover securely. Put pressure control in place. When pressure is reached, cook for 5 minutes. Cool at once under running water.

Serve meatballs with your favorite sweet-and-sour sauce or as is.

"Porcupine" Meatballs

Yield: 4 servings

1 pound ground beef
½ cup uncooked rice
1 medium onion, chopped fine
1 teaspoon salt
¼ teaspoon pepper

¾ cup water
1 10½-ounce can tomato soup

Mix together ground beef, rice, onion, salt, and pepper. Form into 8 meatballs.

In the cooker, mix water and tomato soup. Drop meatballs into the liquid mixture. Close the cooker and set pressure control in place. When pressure is reached, cook for 8 minutes. Cool cooker naturally for 5 minutes, then place under cold water. Serve.

Meatballs in Raisin Sauce

Yield: 4 servings

1 pound ground beef
1 onion, minced fine
¼ cup crushed corn flakes
1 egg
1½ teaspoons salt
¼ teaspoon pepper
⅛ teaspoon paprika
2 tablespoons shortening
½ cup water
1 tablespoon sugar
¼ cup raisins
2 tablespoons lemon juice

Combine beef, onion, corn flakes, egg, salt, pepper, and paprika. Shape this mixture into 8 meatballs.

Heat the shortening in the cooker and brown the meatballs. Add water, sugar raisins, and lemon juice. Close cover securely and put pressure control in place. When control is rocking gently, cook for 8 minutes. Cool the cooker at once under cold water. Serve.

Ham and Sweet Potatoes

Yield: 4 servings

Whole cloves
¾-inch-thick ham slices to make 4 serving pieces
1 tablespoon fat
2 tablespoons brown sugar
½ cup pineapple juice
½ cup water
2 sweet potatoes, peeled and halved
1 tablespoon cornstarch
2 tablespoons lemon juice

Press cloves into each piece of ham.

Heat fat in cooker and brown the ham. Add brown sugar, pineapple juice, water, and sweet potatoes. Close cover and set pressure control in place. When pressure is reached, cook for 9 minutes. Remove cooker from heat and allow to cool normally for 5 minutes, then place under running water. Set ham and potatoes on a warm platter.

Mix cornstarch and lemon juice and add to liquid in cooker. Stir until clear and slightly thickened.

Pour sauce over ham and sweet potatoes. Serve.

Lamb Stew

Yield: 4 to 6 servings

2 tablespoons shortening
2 pounds breast of lamb, cut in cubes
Salt and pepper to taste
1 green pepper, diced
4 onions, diced
1 tablespoon Worcestershire sauce
4 carrots, cut in half
½ cup hot water

Heat shortening in cooker. Brown the lamb thoroughly. Season with salt and pepper. Add green pepper, onions, Worcestershire sauce, carrots, and water. Cover cooker securely and put pressure control in place. When pressure is reached and control jiggling, cook for 15 minutes. Allow the pressure to drop naturally. Serve.

Note: If you want to add potatoes to this stew, add 1 cup diced potatoes with the other vegetables.

Moussaka

Yield: 4 servings

2 tablespoons shortening
1 pound ground lamb
1 medium onion, chopped
1 medium eggplant, pared and diced
3 tablespoons parsley
1 teaspoon salt
¼ teaspoon paprika
¼ teaspoon oregano
2 whole tomatoes, diced
¼ cup water
Grated cheese for garnish

Heat shortening in cooker. Brown the lamb and onion together. Add rest of ingredients in order given. Close cover and set pressure control in place. When pressure is reached, cook for 5 minutes. Cool cooker at once under running water.

Sprinkle moussaka with grated cheese; serve.

Breaded Pork Chops

Yield: 5 to 6 servings

5 to 6 pork chops, ¾ inch thick
Salt and pepper
1 teaspoon garlic salt
1 cup cornflake crumbs
1 egg, beaten
1 tablespoon milk
3 tablespoons shortening
½ cup orange juice

Season chops with salt, pepper, and garlic salt. Dredge in cornflakes and dip in combined egg and milk. Then dredge again in crumbs.

Heat shortening in cooker and brown each chop on both sides. Add orange juice; close cooker. Set pressure control in place and, when pressure is reached, cook for 14 minutes. Allow the pressure to drop naturally. Serve.

Pork Chops in Chili Sauce

Yield: 4 servings

2 teaspoons shortening
4 to 5 pork chops, ½ inch thick
4 to 5 lemon slices
1 onion, cut in rings
½ teaspoon salt
¼ teaspoon lemon pepper
½ cup chili sauce
½ cup water

Melt shortening in cooker. Brown the chops on both sides. When browned, place a lemon slice on top of each chop. Add onion and seasonings.

Blend chili sauce with water; pour over chops. Close cover of cooker; put pressure control in place. When pressure is reached, cook for 15 minutes. Cool cooker at once under running water.

Serve the chops in their own gravy.

Pork Chops in Cider

Yield: 4 to 6 servings

1 tablespoon shortening
4 to 6 pork chops, ½ inch thick
2 medium onions
2 apples, pared and diced
½ teaspoon salt
Dash of pepper
½ cup apple cider

Heat shortening in cooker. Brown each chop on both sides. Add onions, apples, salt, and pepper; pour apple cider over all. Close cover on cooker and set pressure regulator in place. When pressure is reached, cook for 15 minutes. Cool at once under running water. Serve.

Mashed potatoes and applesauce complete the meal.

Polynesian Pork

Yield: 4 servings

2 tablespoons shortening
1½ pounds pork, cut into bite-size cubes
1 medium onion, sliced
1 cup pineapple juice
¼ cup vinegar
¼ cup brown sugar
1 teaspoon salt
1 green pepper, diced
1 1-pound 4-ounce can pineapple chunks, drained
1 cut-up orange
1 tablespoon soy sauce
3 tablespoons cornstarch
¼ cup water

Heat shortening in cooker and brown the pork with the onion. Add pineapple juice, vinegar, brown sugar, and salt. Close cover of cooker and put pressure control in place. When pressure is reached, cook for 12 minutes. Reduce pressure under faucet. Open cooker. Add green pepper, pineapple chunks, orange, and soy sauce.

Mix cornstarch with water and pour into cooker. Stir constantly until slightly thickened.

Serve pork over rice or noodles.

189

Pork and Pears

Yield: 4 to 6 servings

2 tablespoons shortening
2 pounds boneless pork loin roast
3 large potatoes, diced
3 large ripe green pears, cut into
  eighths
1 teaspoon salt
¼ teaspoon pepper
¼ teaspoon dried marjoram
¼ teaspoon dillweed
1½ cups water

Heat shortening in cooker. Brown the meat on all sides. Add the rest of the ingredients in order given. Close cover and put pressure control in place. When pressure is reached, cook for 40 minutes. Allow pressure to drop normally.

Thicken gravy if desired. Serve.

Pork Chops with Pineapple

Yield: 4 servings

4 pork chops, ¾ inch thick
Salt and pepper
2 tablespoons shortening
4 whole pineapple slices
4 teaspoons brown sugar
½ cup pineapple juice
1 cup sour cream

Season the pork chops with salt and pepper.

Heat the shortening in cooker and brown the chops. On top of each chop lay 1 slice of pineapple, filling the center hole with 1 teaspoon of brown sugar. Add fruit juice. Close cover of cooker and put pressure regulator in place. When pressure is reached, cook for 12 minutes. Allow pressure to drop naturally.

Remove chops with fruit in place and set aside.

Add sour cream to the pan juices and serve over the chops.

Veal and Potatoes

Yield: 4 servings

3 tablespoons shortening
2 pounds veal, cut in cubes
1 teaspoon salt
Dash of pepper
1½ cups water
6 medium potatoes, peeled and diced

Heat shortening in cooker. Brown the veal cubes in the fat. Add salt, pepper, and water. Close cover securely and set pressure control in place. When pressure is reached and control jiggles, cook for 8 minutes. Allow cooker to cool for 5 minutes, then reduce the rest of pressure under running water.

Open cooker and add potatoes. Again, close cover and put control in place. When pressure is reached, cook for 8 minutes more. Reduce pressure at once under running water. Serve.

Veal Birds

Yield: 4 servings

1½ pounds veal steak, ½ inch thick
2 cups of your favorite bread stuffing
¼ pound bacon, sliced
Flour
Salt and pepper to taste
2 tablespoons shortening
½ cup water

Cut steak into serving pieces. Place a tablespoon of stuffing on the center of each portion. (Try some stuffed olives in that stuffing.) Roll up the veal and wrap with 1 slice of bacon. Tie with string or use a skewer. Roll the veal in flour seasoned with salt and pepper.

Heat shortening in cooker. Brown the veal birds on all sides. Add water. Close cover and set pressure regulator in place. When regulator rocks gently, cook for 10 minutes. Let pressure drop of its own accord. Serve.

Veal Fricassee

Yield: 4 servings

1½ pounds veal steak, ½ inch thick
1 teaspoon salt
Dash of pepper
3 tablespoons flour
2 tablespoons shortening
1 tablespoon chopped onion
1 teaspoon paprika
1 bouillon cube
¾ cup water
1 cup sour cream

Cut veal into serving pieces and season well with salt and pepper. Dredge in flour.

Put shortening in cooker. Brown the onion and veal steak in hot fat. Add paprika.

Dissolve the bouillon cube in water and pour over meat. Cover the cooker and set pressure control in place. When pressure is reached, cook for 15 minutes. Cool normally for 5 minutes, then place under running water. Remove cover. Add sour cream, stirring in until blended.

Serve fricassee with noodles or rice.

Poultry

Rolled Chicken Breasts

Yield: 6 servings

2 tablespoons melted butter or margarine
½ teaspoon salt
¼ cup bread crumbs
2 tablespoons finely chopped celery
1 tablespoon finely chopped onion
1 tablespoon parsley
3 whole chicken breasts, boned and halved
2 tablespoons cooking oil
1 cup water

In a fry pan mix melted butter, salt, bread crumbs, celery, onion, and parsley to make the stuffing.

Put chicken pieces skin-side-down. Put some of the stuffing mixture in the center of each piece. Roll the chicken over the stuffing and fasten together with skewers.

Heat cooking oil in pressure cooker. Brown each piece of chicken. Add water; close cover of cooker. Set pressure control in place. When pressure is reached, cook for 10 minutes. Cool at once under running water. Serve.

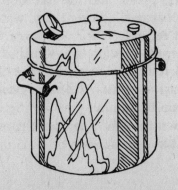

Chicken and Bananas

Yield: 4 to 6 servings

2- to 3-pound chicken, cut into serving
  pieces
Salt and pepper
2 tablespoons shortening
½ cup water
3 or 4 bananas, cut lengthwise and
  quartered

Season chicken with salt and pepper.

Heat shortening in cooker and brown the chicken. Add water and bananas. Close cover and put pressure control in place. When pressure is reached, cook for 15 minutes. Allow cooker to cool of its own accord.

Serve chicken and bananas with a fresh-fruit salad and homemade bread.

Battered Chicken

Yield: 4 to 6 servings

¼ cup flour
Salt and pepper
½ teaspoon paprika
2 to 3 pounds chicken, cut into serving
  pieces
2 tablespoons shortening
½ cup water

Mix flour, salt, pepper, and paprika together. Roll each piece of chicken in this.

Heat the cooker and add the shortening. Brown the battered chicken. Add water and close cover securely. Put regulator on vent pipe. When the pressure is reached and the regulator is rocking slowly, time the chicken. Cook 10 to 15 minutes. Allow to cool naturally, about 10 minutes.

If you want a gravy, thicken the essence to desired consistency. Serve.

Chicken Breasts in Wine

Yield: 4 to 6 servings

2 to 3 pounds chicken breasts
¼ cup flour
Salt and pepper to taste
½ teaspoon garlic salt
2 tablespoons shortening
½ cup red wine

Dredge the chicken in mixture of flour, salt, pepper, and garlic salt.

Heat the shortening in the cooker and brown the chicken in it. Add wine; close cover. Put valve on cooker. After pressure is reached and valve is slowly rocking, cook for 10 minutes. Allow the cooker to cool naturally. Serve.

Chicken Curry

Yield: 4 to 6 servings

2 tablespoons shortening
3 pounds chicken, cut into serving
  pieces
2 teaspoons curry powder
2 teaspoons salt
2 onions, chopped
1 teaspoon vinegar
1 cup water
2 tablespoons cornstarch
¼ cup orange juice

Heat shortening in cooker. Brown the chicken. Add curry powder, salt, onions, vinegar, and water. Close cover of cooker and set pressure regulator in place. When pressure is reached, cook for 10 minutes. Cool cooker at once under faucet. Set chicken aside to keep warm.

Combine cornstarch and orange juice; stir into remaining liquid in cooker.

When thickened, pour over the chicken and serve with boiled rice.

Chicken in Fruit Sauce

Yield: 4 to 6 servings

2- to 3-pound chicken, cut into serving
   pieces
Salt and pepper to taste
2 tablespoons shortening
1 cup orange juice
¼ cup honey
2 tablespoons lemon juice
½ teaspoon ground curry powder

Season the chicken pieces with salt and pepper.

Heat shortening in cooker. Brown the chicken on all sides. Add orange juice, honey, lemon juice, and curry powder. Close cover of cooker and set pressure regulator in place. When pressure is reached, cook for 15 minutes. Let pressure drop of its own accord.

Remove chicken from cooker and arrange in baking dish. Surround with your choice of fruit—peaches, pears, apricots, etc.

Pour sauce over the chicken and fruit and put under the broiler for 5 minutes or until fruit is hot. Serve.

Chicken Hawaiian

Yield: 4 to 6 servings

3 pounds chicken, cut into serving
   pieces
Flour to dredge chicken
2 tablespoons shortening
1 teaspoon salt
Dash of pepper

1 cup pineapple juice
¼ teaspoon ground cloves
¼ teaspoon nutmeg
½ cup pineapple tidbits
½ cup slivered almonds, optional

Dredge the chicken pieces in flour and set aside.

Place shortening in pressure cooker and add chicken. Brown each piece. Add salt, pepper, pineapple juice, cloves, and nutmeg. Close cover and set pressure control in place. When pressure is reached and control jiggles, cook for 10 minutes. Cool at once under running water.

Add pineapple tidbits and almonds and heat through.

Serve chicken on rice.

Chicken with Olives

Yield: 4 to 6 servings

2 tablespoons shortening
2- to 3-pound chicken, cut into serving
   pieces
1 medium onion, chopped
1 carrot, diced
1 or 2 tomatoes, peeled and quartered
2 tablespoons tomato puree
24 green olives, pitted and chopped
   fine
½ cup water

Heat shortening in cooker. Brown chicken pieces. Add the rest of the ingredients in order given. Close cover of cooker and put pressure control in place. When pressure is reached, cook for 10 minutes. Allow pressure to drop naturally. Serve.

Chicken Oriental

Yield: 4 to 6 servings

2 tablespoons shortening
3 chicken breasts, boned, halved, and
    skinned
Salt and pepper to taste
½ cup sliced water chestnuts
1 green pepper, chopped
1 tablespoon ginger
¼ cup sugar
1 tablespoon soy sauce
½ cup pineapple juice
½ cup wine vinegar
1 cup drained, crushed pineapple
2 tablespoons cornstarch
¼ cup water

Heat shortening in cooker.

Season chicken breasts with salt and pepper. Brown them in the cooker. Add water chestnuts, green pepper, and ginger.

Dissolve the sugar in soy sauce, juice, and vinegar. (Add extra sugar if preferred.) Add to the chicken. Last, put pineapple over chicken and close cooker. Set pressure control in place. When pressure is reached, cook for 10 minutes. Cool at once under running water. Return open cooker to low flame.

Dissolve the cornstarch in water. Add to the chicken, stirring until liquid is slightly thickened.

Serve chicken over rice or buttered noodles.

Chicken Paprika

Yield: 4 to 6 servings

2- to 3-pound chicken, cut into serving
    pieces
1 teaspoon salt
1 teaspoon garlic salt
Dash of pepper

1 teaspoon paprika
¼ cup flour
3 tablespoons shortening
1 cup water
1 cup sour cream

Dredge the chicken in a mixture of salt, garlic salt, pepper, paprika, and flour.

Heat shortening in cooker. Brown the chicken. Add water; close cover securely. Set pressure control in place. When pressure is reached, cook for 20 minutes. Cool cooker normally for 5 minutes, then reduce pressure under faucet.

Last, stir in the sour cream, heating thoroughly. Serve.

Chicken in Peanut Sauce

Yield: 4 to 6 servings

2 to 3 pounds chicken, cut into serving
    pieces
1 large onion, sliced
2 tablespoons shortening
3 tomatoes, chopped
¼ cup tomato paste
1 teaspoon salt
Dash of pepper
½ cup water
½ cup chunky peanut butter

In the cooker, brown chicken and onion in shortening. Add tomatoes, tomato paste, salt, pepper, and water. Close cover and put pressure regulator in place. When pressure is reached, cook for 15 minutes. Allow pressure to drop normally. Open cooker.

Remove some of the hot liquid from the chicken and mix with the chunky peanut butter. Pour this sauce over the chicken. Simmer and stir for 2 minutes. Serve.

Chicken Pilaf

Yield: 4 to 6 servings

1 cup rice
4 stalks celery, diced
1 large onion, quartered
1 large green pepper, chopped
3 tomatoes, chopped
1 cup chicken broth
2 cups diced cooked chicken
6 strips cooked bacon, broken into
    pieces

Place rice, celery, onion, green pepper, tomatoes, and chicken broth into cooker. Close cover and put pressure control in place. When pressure is reached and control jiggles gently, remove cooker from flame. Allow pressure to reduce normally.

Return open cooker to low flame. Add chicken and bacon. Simmer for 3 minutes, stirring to mix the flavors.

Serve chicken hot.

Chicken in the Pot

Yield: 4 to 6 servings

2- to 3-pound chicken, cut into serving
    pieces
¼ cup flour
2 tablespoons shortening
1 bay leaf
2 tablespoons minced onion
2 tablespoons salt
¼ teaspoon fresh ground pepper
½ teaspoon garlic salt
1 cup diced carrots
1 cup fresh peas
½ cup water

Dredge chicken pieces in flour.

Heat shortening in cooker and brown the chicken. Add seasonings, vegetables, and water. Close cover and set pressure regulator in place. When pressure is reached, cook for 10 minutes. Allow pressure to drop naturally.

Serve chicken with buttered noodles.

Spanish Chicken

Yield: 4 to 6 servings

2- to 3-pound chicken, cut into serv-
    ing pieces
Salt and pepper
2 tablespoons shortening
1 onion, sliced
1 garlic clove, minced
3 red or green peppers, diced
¼ pound ham, diced
3 tomatoes, chopped
½ cup water
12 green olives with pimientos, halved

Season chicken with salt and pepper; brown them in shortening. Add onion, garlic, peppers, ham, tomatoes, and water. Close cover of cooker and put pressure control in place. When pressure is reached, cook for 15 minutes. Allow pressure to drop normally.

Return open cooker to a low flame. Add the olives and simmer for 2 minutes.

Serve chicken with seasoned rice.

Chicken and Sausage

Yield: 4 to 6 servings

½ pound link sausage
2- to 3-pound chicken, cut into serving
    pieces
1 onion, minced
2 cups tomatoes, drained
½ cup water

Brown the sausage in cooker; pour off excess fat. Set sausage aside.

Brown the chicken in 2 tablespoons of sausage fat. Add onion, tomatoes, water, and sausage. Close cover securely and put pressure control in place. When pressure is reached, cook for 10 minutes. Allow the pressure to drop normally.

Enjoy the delicious combination of chicken and sausage.

Chicken Sub Gum

Yield: 4 to 6 servings

2 cups chicken, cooked and cut into
    pieces
2 cups shredded cabbage
1 cup diced green pepper
1 cup diced celery
1 cup chicken broth
1 tablespoon cornstarch
3 tablespoons soy sauce
2 tablespoons dark molasses
1 teaspoon salt
1 teaspoon vinegar
¼ cup water
2 tomatoes, cubed
½ cup blanched almonds

Combine chicken, cabbage, green pepper, celery, and chicken broth in cooker. Close cover and set pressure control in place.

When pressure is reached, cook for 2 minutes. Cool at once under running water.

Mix cornstarch, soy sauce, molasses, salt, and vinegar in water. Add to the chicken and vegetables, stirring gently. When mixture has thickened, add tomatoes and ¼ cup almonds. Cook for 1 minute more.

Sprinkle remaining almonds on top and serve with rice.

Stewed Chicken

Yield: 4 servings

3 pounds stewing chicken, cut into
    serving pieces
2 cups water
2 teaspoons salt
3 peppercorns
2 ribs celery with leaves
1 sliced carrot
1 medium-size onion, quartered

Place all ingredients in the pressure cooker in the order given. Close cover and set pressure regulator in place. When pressure is reached, cook for 25 minutes. Let pressure drop of its own accord.

If gravy is desired, remove chicken from the liquid and strain the liquid. Then thicken liquid to make gravy. Replace chicken to heat it thoroughly.

Serve chicken at once.

Easy Chicken Supreme

Yield: 4 to 6 servings

2 to 3 pounds chicken, cut into serving
    pieces
¼ cup flour
2 tablespoons shortening
1 package onion soup mix
½ cup water

Dredge chicken pieces in flour.

Heat shortening in cooker and brown the chicken. Add onion soup mix and water. Close cover of cooker and set pressure regulator in place. When pressure is reached and regulator jiggling gently, cook for 15 minutes. Allow pressure to drop of its own accord.

Thicken gravy, if desired, and you have a supremely good dish.

Tarragon Chicken

Yield: 4 to 6 servings

2 to 3 pounds chicken, cut into serving pieces
¼ cup fresh tarragon leaves or 2 tablespoons dried tarragon
4 green onions, minced
1 cup dry white wine
2 tablespoons shortening
1 tablespoon lemon juice
Parsley for garnish

Marinate the chicken in tarragon, onions, and wine for 1 hour. Remove chicken, reserving liquid.

Heat shortening in pressure cooker. Brown the chicken on all sides. Add marinade and lemon juice. Close cover and set pressure control in place. When pressure is reached, cook for 15 minutes. Let pressure drop of its own accord.

Garnish chicken with parsley and serve.

Chicken in Tomato Sauce

Yield: 4 to 6 servings

2- to 3-pound chicken, cut into serving pieces
Salt

2 tablespoons shortening
1 tablespoon dillweed
2 tablespoons chopped green onion
½ cup catsup
½ cup water

Rub the chicken pieces with salt.

Heat shortening in cooker and brown the chicken on all sides. Sprinkle with dillweed and onion; add catsup and water. Close cover of cooker and set pressure regulator in place. When pressure is reached, cook for 15 minutes. Allow cooker to cool of its own accord. Serve.

Sautéed Chicken Liver

Yield: 6 to 8 servings

2 slices bacon
2 pounds chicken liver, halved
¼ cup sliced onions
¼ cup sliced mushrooms
1 teaspoon salt
Dash of pepper
½ cup water

Crisp-fry the bacon in the pressure cooker. Remove the bacon and set aside.

Sauté chicken liver and onions in the bacon fat. Pour off any excess fat. Add the remaining ingredients. Close cover and set pressure regulator in place. When pressure is reached, cook for 5 minutes. Cool at once under running water.

Serve the chicken livers on a bed of rice and sprinkle with the crumbled bacon bits.

Stuffed Hens Hawaiian

Yield: 2 to 4 servings

2 tablespoons butter or margarine
¼ cup hot water
¼ cup packaged stuffing mix
1 egg, slightly beaten
¼ cup drained crushed pineapple
2 tablespoons finely chopped nuts
    (macadamia for the true Hawaiian)
2 Cornish hens
2 tablespoons shortening
½ teaspoon salt
Dash of pepper
1 cup pineapple juice

Melt butter in hot water. Stir in stuffing, egg, pineapple, and nuts. Stuff the hens with this mixture.

Heat shortening in cooker and brown the hens. Add salt, pepper, and pineapple juice. Close cover and set pressure control in place. When pressure is reached and control jiggles, cook for 8 minutes. Cool cooker at once under running water.

If desired, place hens under broiler until crisp. Serve.

Rock Cornish Hens

Yield: 2 to 4 servings

2 Rock Cornish hens
Salt and pepper
2 teaspoons crumbled tarragon leaves
3 tablespoons cooking oil
1 onion, diced
½ cup diced carrots
1 cup diced celery
1 tablespoon chopped parsley
1 bay leaf
4 tomatoes, peeled and quartered
½ cup white wine

Sprinkle the hens amply with salt and pepper. Put the tarragon leaves in the cavities, for flavor.

Heat the oil in the cooker and tan the onion lightly. Brown the hens and remove.

Combine carrots, celery, rest of seasonings, and tomatoes with the tanned onions. Put the hens back in cooker and pour wine over them. Close cover and set regulator in place. When pressure is reached, cook 8 minutes. Allow to cool normally.

Remove hens and put on a warming platter. Thicken gravy if desired. Serve hens with wild rice.

Cornish Hens in Sweet Sauce

Yield: 2 to 4 servings

2 Rock Cornish hens
Salt and pepper
2 tablespoons shortening
½ cup raisins
2 tablespoons lemon juice
½ teaspoon allspice
½ cup chicken broth
½ cup red currant jelly

Sprinkle the hens amply with salt and pepper.

Heat shortening in pressure cooker and brown the hens. Add raisins, lemon juice, allspice, and chicken broth. Close cover and set pressure regulator in place. When pressure is reached, cook for 8 minutes. Allow to cool normally.

Remove hens and blend jelly with the sauce in cooker, stirring constantly. Brush the sauce over the hens.

To crisp them, put hens under a broiler for 2 minutes. Serve.

Seafood

Seafood à la King

Yield: 4 to 6 servings

2 pounds fish fillets, cut into 1-inch
  pieces
1 cup chopped celery
1 cup peeled and diced eggplant
1 cup diced cucumber
1 teaspoon salt
Dash of pepper
½ cup water
1 can cream of mushroom soup

Put fish, celery, eggplant, cucumber, salt, pepper, and water in cooker. Close cover securely and put pressure control in place. When pressure is reached, cook 3 minutes. Reduce pressure at once under running water.

Return open cooker to low flame. Add undiluted can of soup, stirring gently to blend and heat.

Serve fish over toast, if desired.

Fish Creole

Yield: 4 to 6 servings

2 pounds fish fillets
1 No. 2½ can tomatoes
1 teaspoon salt
½ cup green pepper, chopped
6 green olives, chopped
1 tablespoon onion, minced
2 peppercorns

Wrap fillets in cheescloth to keep the fish from falling apart.

Put rest of ingredients into the cooker in order given. Place rack in cooker and place fish on rack. Close cover and set pressure regulator in place. When pressure is reached, cook for 7 minutes. Allow pressure to drop naturally. Remove fish and put on a warm platter.

Thicken sauce, if desired, and pour over fish. Serve at once.

Fish Fillets with Shrimp

Yield: 4 to 6 servings

2 pounds fillets (flounder is tasty)
Salt and pepper to taste
½ cup water
2 tablespoons butter or margarine
½ pound small cooked shrimp
Lemon wedges

Season the fillets with salt and pepper and wrap in cheesecloth.

Put water in cooker and set rack in place. Put fish on rack and close cover. Set pressure control in place. When pressure is reached, cook for 10 minutes. Cool at once under running water.

Melt the butter in a saucepan. Toss the shrimp in the butter so that each one becomes coated with butter.

Place the shrimp down the center of each fillet, pour browned butter over the fillets, and serve.

Fillet of Fish in Wine

Yield: 4 servings

2 tablespoons butter or margarine
1 pound of fish fillets (sole, halibut,
    pike, or haddock)
Salt and pepper to taste
¾ cup white wine
2 tablespoons lemon juice
2 tablespoons parsley

Melt butter in pressure cooker.

Sprinkle the fish fillets with salt and pepper, then put them into pressure cooker.

Combine remaining ingredients and pour over the fillets. Close cover and set pressure control in place. When pressure is reached, cook for 8 minutes. Cool at once under running water.

If sauce is desired, thicken the liquid left in cooker and pour it over the fillets. Serve.

Stuffed Fish

Yield: 6 servings

Stuffing
1½ cups bread crumbs
2 tablespoons melted butter or
    margarine
2 tablespoons chopped onion
¼ cup chopped celery
¼ cup diced green pepper
1 egg, beaten
Salt and pepper to taste
1 3-pound fish (your choice), cleaned,
    scaled, and eviscerated
½ cup white wine

Mix the stuffing ingredients together. Stuff the fish lightly. Wrap the fish in cheesecloth.

Put rack in cooker and set fish on rack. Pour white wine over the fish. Close cover. Set pressure control in place and, when pressure is reached, cook for 8 minutes. Cool pressure cooker at once under running water. Serve.

Carp in Red Wine

Yield: 6 servings

3 pounds carp, dressed
Salt and pepper to taste
1 medium onion, chopped
1 tablespoon parsley
1 teaspoon dillseed
3 whole peppercorns
½ cup red wine

Season the fish with salt and pepper, then wrap it in cheesecloth to prevent fish from falling apart when removed from cooker. Place the wrapped fish in pressure cooker. Add rest of ingredients. Close cover of cooker and set pressure control in place. When pressure is reached, cook for 8 minutes. Cool cooker at once under running water. Drain carp and remove cheesecloth.

Serve fish on a platter with lemon slices.

Scandinavian Cod

Yield: 6 to 8 servings

2 pounds codfish, cut into serving
    pieces
2 cups water
1 teaspoon salt
6 tablespoons butter or margarine
¼ cup flour
1 teaspoon salt
1 teaspoon dry mustard
2½ cups cream

Place fish, water, and salt in pressure cooker. Close cover and set pressure control in place. When control is rocking gently, cook for 1 minute. Reduce pressure at once under running water. Set aside fish to keep warm.

Melt butter and add flour, salt, and mustard. Stirring constantly, add cream until mixture is thickened. Place the fish in this sauce and be sure it is heated through.

Small, boiled potatoes complement this tasty dish.

Fresh Cod in Wine

Yield: 4 servings

4 cod fillets
2 tablespoons shortening
1 finely chopped onion
1 crushed clove garlic
¼ cup chopped parsley
3 tomatoes, peeled and quartered
½ cup dry white wine

Wrap fillets in cheesecloth if desired.

Heat shortening in cooker and tan the onion and garlic lightly. Put rack in cooker. Add rest of ingredients around the fish. Last, pour the wine over all. Close cover of cooker and put pressure control in place. When pressure is reached, cook for 4 minutes. Cool at once under running water.

Suggestion for serving: Arrange fish on a platter. Thicken the gravy, if desired, or dot the fish with butter and a shake of paprika. A slice of lemon has both eye- and taste-appeal.

Flounder with Blue-Cheese Sauce

Yield: 6 servings

2 pounds flounder fillets
1 tablespoon lemon juice
2 teaspoons minced onions
1 teaspoon minced parsley
¼ cup water
½ cup cream
⅓ cup blue cheese, crumbled fine

Lay flounder fillets in bottom of pressure cooker. Add lemon juice, onion, parsley, and water. Close cover and put pressure regulator in place. When regulator rocks gently, cook for 5 minutes. Cool cooker at once under running water.

When you have removed regulator and cover, stir in the cream and blue cheese over a very low flame. When this mixture is heated through, serve at once.

Perch

Yield: 4 servings

2 pounds perch
¼ cup flour
2 tablespoons shortening
Salt and pepper to taste
½ cup water

Thoroughly coat the fish in flour.

Add shortening to cooker and brown the fish on all sides. Remove from cooker.

Place rack in cooker and put perch on rack. Season with salt and pepper. Add water and close cooker. Put regulator in place and, when pressure is reached, cook for 10 minutes. Cool cooker at once. Serve.

Dill Perch

Yield: 4 to 6 servings

2 pounds perch fillets, cut into serving pieces
4 medium onions, sliced into rings
1 stalk celery, chopped
2 teaspoons salt
½ cup water
1 cup sour cream
2 dill pickles, chopped
4 teaspoons horseradish
1 teaspoon parsley flakes
Fresh chopped dill for garnish

Put perch, onions, celery, salt, and water in cooker. Close cover and set pressure control in place. When pressure is reached, cook for 3 minutes. Allow cooker to cool normally.

Return open cooker to a low flame. Add sour cream, pickles, horseradish, and parsley flakes. Stir until well-blended and hot.

Garnish perch with dillweed, and serve.

Finnan Haddie

Yield: 6 servings

Salt and pepper to taste
2 pounds haddock fillets
1 3-ounce can sliced mushrooms
¼ cup chopped onions
2 tablespoons butter or margarine
4 slices cooked bacon
½ cup water

With heavy-duty aluminum foil form a bowl to fit inside the pressure cooker.

Salt and pepper the fillets and layer them in the bowl.

Sauté the mushrooms and onions in butter and pour the mixture over the fish. Top with the crumbled bacon bits.

Set water, rack, and foil bowl in the cooker. Close cover securely and set pressure control in place. When pressure is reached, cook for 10 minutes. Cool at once under running water.

Garnish with lemon wedges and parsley, if desired.

Halibut Steaks

Yield: 4 or more servings

2 pounds halibut steaks, about 2 inches thick
1 teaspoon salt
3 peppercorns
1 cup tomato juice
½ teaspoon sugar
1 medium-size onion, quartered
½ cup heavy cream

Wrap steaks in cheesecloth.

Put salt, peppercorns, tomato juice, sugar, and onion into cooker. Add the wrapped steaks. Close cover and set pressure control in place. When pressure is reached, cook for 10 minutes. Cool at once under running water. Remove fish and set on a warming platter.

Add heavy cream to the remaining juice and heat thoroughly.

Pour sauce over the fish, and serve.

Pike in Horseradish Sauce

Yield: 4 to 6 servings

2 pounds pike
Salt and pepper to taste
½ cup white wine

Sauce

 1 can cream of celery soup
 3 tablespoons horseradish
 1 teaspoon sugar
 1 teaspoon dry mustard
 Lemon slices

Season fish with salt and pepper. Wrap in cheesecloth.

Put rack in cooker. Place fish on rack and pour wine over it. Close cover and put pressure control in place. When pressure is reached, cook for 4 minutes. Cool cooker at once under running water. Remove fish to a heated platter.

To the liquid left in cooker add cream soup (undiluted), horseradish, sugar, and mustard. Stir until all are heated. Pour over the fish.

Garnish fish with lemon slices. Serve.

Salmon Casserole

Yield: 4 to 6 servings

 1 16-ounce can salmon
 1½ cups soft bread crumbs
 2 stalks celery, diced fine
 2 tablespoons minced onion
 2 eggs, beaten
 1 can cream of mushroom soup
 ½ cup water
 Lemon slices for garnish

Remove skin and bones from salmon.

Mix salmon, bread crumbs, celery, onion, eggs, and soup in a bowl. Put mixture in a greased casserole dish that will fit into the cooker. (Make a dish out of foil if necessary.)

Put rack in cooker. Add water. Set salmon on rack. Close cover and put pressure regulator in place. When pressure is reached,

cook for 20 minutes. Let cool naturally.

If desired, dot the loaf with butter and put under the broiler for 2 minutes, or until butter melts. Garnish with lemon slices, and serve with fresh peas and a tossed salad.

Salmon Ring Mold

Yield: 4 servings

 2 cups cooked or canned salmon
 2 eggs, well-beaten
 1 cup milk
 Salt and pepper to taste
 1 teaspoon chopped parsley
 1 cup cracker crumbs

Remove dark skin and bones from the salmon and flake into bite-size pieces. In a mixing bowl add to the salmon the rest of ingredients in order given. Mix well. Grease a 3-cup ring mold. (Check to make sure the mold will set on the rack in your pressure cooker.) Pack the salmon mixture into the mold and cover with silver foil.

Put 2 cups water in the cooker and set rack in place. Put covered mold on the rack. Close cover and put pressure control in place. When pressure is reached, cook for 10 minutes. Cool cooker at once. Unmold salmon ring onto serving platter.

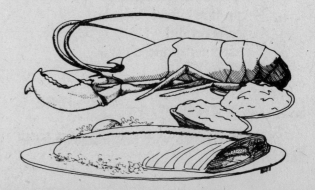

Salmon Steaks in Dill Sauce

Yield: 6 servings

1 tablespoon butter or margarine
2 teaspoons finely chopped onion
6 salmon steaks, ½ inch thick
3 tablespoons lemon juice
½ teaspoon dillseed
¼ cup water
½ cup sour cream

Heat butter in cooker and lightly brown the onion. Arrange the steaks in the cooker. Add the lemon juice, dillseed, and water. Close the cooker and set pressure regulator in place. When pressure is reached, cook for 10 minutes. Cool at once. Remove the salmon steaks from the cooker.

To the liquid left in the cooker, mix in the sour cream, stirring constantly. When this sauce has thickened slightly, pour it over the salmon steaks; serve at once.

Stuffed Red Snapper

Yield: 4 to 6 servings

1 3- to 4-pound red snapper, cleaned
Salt
4 tablespoons butter or margarine
½ small onion, minced
1 cup stale bread crumbs
½ cup fine cracker crumbs
½ teaspoon dill
2 teaspoons chopped parsley
¼ teaspoon salt
Pepper to taste
½ cup grapefruit juice

Sprinkle the fish with salt inside and out and set aside.

Combine in the cooker the butter, onion, bread and cracker crumbs, dill, parsley, salt, and pepper. When thoroughly mixed, use this stuffing to stuff the fish. Close with string and wrap the fish in cheesecloth.

Put the rack in the cooker. Place stuffed fish on the rack and pour grapefruit juice over it. Close cover and put pressure control in place. When pressure is reached, cook for 8 to 10 minutes. Cool cooker at once. Serve.

Clams Steamed in Beer

Yield: Depends on how many clams you steam

Soft-shell or little-neck clams
½ cup beer

This is the time to remember *not* to fill the pressure cooker over two-thirds full. Try 2 pounds of clams for starters. Wash clams thoroughly to remove all sand.

Put beer in cooker and set rack in place. Put clams on the rack. Close the cooker and set pressure regulator in place. When pressure is reached, cook for 3 minutes. Cool the cooker at once under faucet.

Reserve the clam liquid to serve with the clams, if desired. Serve.

Company King Crab

Yield: 10 servings

¼ cup butter or margarine
3 pounds king-crab meat, in bite-size chunks
½ cup chopped spring onions
Salt and pepper to taste
¼ cup water
1 cup cream

¼ cup buttered bread crumbs
¼ cup grated cheddar cheese

Melt butter in cooker. Add crab meat and onions, stirring until onions are lightly sautéed. Add salt, pepper, and water. Close cover of cooker and set pressure control in place. When pressure is reached, cook for 2 minutes. Cool cooker at once. Add cream to the hot mixture.

Turn crab mixture into well-greased baking dish. Top with bread crumbs and cheese mixed together. Place under the broiler until topping forms a crust. Serve.

Lobster Stew

Yield: 3 to 4 servings

2 to 3 pounds lobster
Boiling water
2 teaspoons salt
1 cup water
3 tablespoons butter
Enough cream to bring liquid to 4 cups
2 teaspoons onion juice
Salt and pepper to taste

Put live lobster in boiling water to cover. Remove lobster.

Put salt and water in cooker. Place lobster on rack in cooker. Close cover and set pressure control in place. When pressure is reached, cook for 5 minutes. Cool cooker at once under running water.

Drain lobster and reserve liquid. Pick out the lobster meat in bite-size pieces. Melt butter in open cooker. Coat lobster meat with butter. Add 4 cups liquid, and onion juice. Bring to a boil and simmer for 2 minutes. Add salt and pepper to taste, and serve.

Scallops

Yield: 4 servings

2 tablespoons shortening
1 clove garlic, split
1 pound scallops
1 teaspoon salt
Fresh ground pepper to taste
1 cup dry white wine

Heat shortening and garlic for 2 minutes. Remove garlic—the flavor will remain. Put rack in cooker. Add scallops and seasonings. Pour wine over scallops. Close cover and put pressure control in place. When pressure is reached, remove from heat. Cool cooker at once under running water.

Serve the scallops with tartar sauce and lemon wedges.

Scallops in Lemon Butter

Yield: 4 to 6 servings

4 cups scallops
1 cup white wine
½ teaspoon salt
1 tablespoon chopped parsley
4 tablespoons butter or margarine
2 teaspoons lemon juice

Place scallops in cooker with wine, salt, and parsley. Close cover and set pressure regulator in place. When pressure is reached and regulator jiggles gently, remove cooker from heat. Cool at once under running water.

Melt butter in a saucepan and add lemon juice. Pour over the drained scallops. Serve.

Scallops in Cream Sauce

Yield: 4 to 6 servings

2 tablespoons shortening
½ cup chopped onion
1 clove garlic, finely chopped
1 stalk celery, diced
¼ teaspoon powdered mustard
½ cup diced tart apple
1½ pounds sea scallops, cut in half
1 cup dry white wine or water
½ cup heavy cream

Heat shortening in cooker. Add onion, garlic, celery, mustard, and apple. Allow this to simmer for flavors to blend.

Put rack in cooker and place scallops on rack. Pour wine over all. Close cover and put pressure regulator in place. When pressure is reached and regulator jiggles, remove from heat and cool cooker under running water.

Return open cooker to a low heat. Remove the rack, lifting it out with a fork. Add heavy cream. Stir to heat; serve.

Scallops and Ham

Yield: 6 to 8 servings

4 cups scallops
1 cup white wine
½ teaspoon salt
4 tablespoons butter or margarine
4 spring onions, finely chopped
24 mushrooms, finely sliced
2 tablespoons minced parsley
2 tablespoons flour
4 tablespoons heavy cream
1 cup minced cooked ham

Place scallops in cooker with wine and salt. Close cover and set pressure control in place. When pressure is reached and regulator jiggles gently, remove cooker from heat. Cool at once under running water. Drain the scallops and reserve the liquid. Set both aside.

In the open cooker, melt the butter. Add spring onions, mushrooms, and parsley. Mix the flour in ¼ cup of the reserved liquid. Add this and the remaining liquid to the cooker. Put in heavy cream, stirring constantly. Do not boil. Last, add the scallops and ham to the hot sauce. Serve at once.

Steamed Shrimp

Yield: 4 servings

1½ pounds shrimp
1½ cups boiling water
1 tablespoon prepared seafood
    seasoning

Place rack in cooker. Put shrimp on rack and pour boiling water and seafood seasoning over it. Close cover securely and place pressure control on. Cook 3 minutes after control jiggles. Cool at once under running water.

Remove shrimp from cooker and cool in cold water. When shrimp are cool enough to handle, remove shells and black line. Prepare the cooked shrimp as desired.

Shrimp in Beer

Yield: 4 servings

1 pound shrimp, peeled and cleaned
½ stalk celery, diced
1 carrot, sliced
1 small onion, sliced
1 tablespoon lemon juice

1 teaspoon salt
1 teaspoon garlic salt
⅛ teaspoon pepper
1 cup beer

Put ingredients into cooker in order given. Close cover and put pressure control in place. When pressure is reached, cook 2 minutes. Cool cooker under running water at once. Stir and serve.

Shrimp Creole

Yield: 4 to 6 servings

2 tablespoons shortening
1 cup diced celery
1 medium onion, sliced in rings
1 teaspoon salt
1 teaspoon chili powder
1 cup tomato juice
2 teaspoons vinegar
½ teaspoon sugar
1 cup cooked shrimp
1½ cups cooked rice

Heat shortening in cooker. Tan the celery and onions in the fat. Add the rest of ingredients in order given; mix together well. Close cover securely and set pressure regulator in place. When the regulator rocks gently, cook for 3 minutes. Cool at once under running water; serve.

Shrimp Curry with Raisins

Yield: 4 servings

2 tablespoons shortening
¼ cup chopped onion
¼ cup sliced mushrooms
½ teaspoon curry powder
½ teaspoon salt

Dash of pepper
1 pound shrimp, peeled and cleaned
4 lemon slices
1 cup bouillon
½ cup raisins
3 tablespoons flour
1 cup milk

Heat shortening in cooker. Lightly sauté the onion and mushrooms. Add curry powder, salt, pepper, shrimp, lemon, bouillon, and raisins. Close cover and set pressure regulator in place. When regulator jiggles gently, cook for 2 minutes. Cool at once under running water.

Combine the flour and milk and add to the liquid in open pressure cooker. Over a low flame, stir constantly until the sauce thickens. This may be served over rice if desired.

Shrimp in Dill Sauce

Yield: 4 servings

1 tablespoon chopped onion
2 tablespoons shortening
1 pound shrimp, peeled and cleaned
1 cup white wine
2 tablespoons cornstarch
¼ cup milk
¾ cup milk or cream
1 teaspoon dillweed

Tan the onion in shortening. Add shrimp and wine. Close cover and put pressure control in place. When pressure is reached, cook for 2 minutes. Cool cooker at once. Return open cooker to a low flame.

Mix cornstarch with ¼ cup milk. Add to shrimp, and stir until thickened. Last, add remainder of milk and dillweed. Simmer for 5 minutes. Serve at once.

Shrimp Scampi

Yield: 4 to 6 servings

2 tablespoons shortening (olive oil, if
  you have it)
1 garlic clove, minced fine
1 pound shrimp, cooked, shelled, and
  deveined
1 can Italian tomatoes
⅓ cup canned tomato paste
1 tablespoon chopped parsley
¼ teaspoon oregano
⅔ cup water
Grated Parmesan cheese

Heat shortening in cooker. Brown the
garlic. Add shrimp, tomatoes, tomato paste,
parsley, oregano, and water. Close cover and
put pressure regulator in place. When pressure is reached, cook for 3 minutes. Cool
cooker at once.

Serve shrimp on a bed of spaghetti. Top
with Parmesan cheese.

Shrimp Teriyaki

Yield: 4 servings

1 pound shelled, deveined raw shrimp
½ pound Chinese pea pods
2 tablespoons soy sauce
3 tablespoons vinegar
¾ cup pineapple juice
3 tablespoons sugar
1 cup chicken broth

Put shrimp and pea pods in cooker.

Combine the rest of the ingredients, mixing well so that sugar dissolves. Pour the
liquid into the cooker and close cover. Set
pressure control in place. When pressure is
reached, cook for 2 minutes. Cool at once to
lower pressure under running water. Serve.

Vegetables

Italian-style Green Beans

Yield: 4 servings

1½ pounds green beans
½ cup water
¼ cup Italian salad dressing

Remove the ends of the beans and cut
into 1-inch pieces.

Place water and salad dressing in cooker
and add beans. Cover the cooker and place
pressure control on top. When control indicates pressure is reached, cook for 3 minutes.
Cool at once. Serve.

Green Beans with Sour Cream

Yield: 4 to 6 servings

1½ pounds fresh green beans, cut into
  1-inch pieces
1 teaspoon salt
½ cup water
1 cup water chestnuts
½ cup sour cream

Put beans, salt, and water in cooker.
Close cover and put pressure control in
place. When pressure is reached, cook for 3
minutes. Cool at once under running water.

Return cooker to low flame. Add water
chestnuts and sour cream. Stir until hot and
blended. Serve.

Sweet-and-Sour Beans

Yield: 4 to 6 servings

1 quart green beans, cut into 1-inch
  pieces
1 teaspoon salt
2 tablespoons sugar
2 tablespoons lemon juice or vinegar
½ cup water
2 tablespoons liquid from beans
1 tablespoon cornstarch

Place beans, salt, sugar, lemon juice, and water in cooker. Close cover securely and put pressure regulator in place. When regulator is rocking gently and pressure reached, cook for 3 minutes. Cool at once under running water. Open cooker.

Remove 2 tablespoons of the liquid and mix this with the cornstarch. Return liquid to beans and stir until slightly thickened. Add additional salt if needed. Serve.

Lima Beans in Tomato Sauce

Yield: 4 to 6 servings

2 packages frozen baby lima beans
2 or 3 tomatoes, diced
1 can tomato soup
2 tablespoons brown sugar
½ cup water

Defrost frozen lima beans for ½ hour or until the block can be separated. Put lima beans in cooker. Add rest of ingredients in order given. Close cover and put pressure control in place. When pressure is reached, cook for 2 minutes. Cool at once under running water.

Stir the vegetables gently. Serve.

Beets in Sour Cream

Yield: 4 servings

3 cups beets, diced or sliced
¾ cup water
½ cup sour cream
1 tablespoon horseradish
1 tablespoon chopped chives

Place beets in cooker with water. Close cover of cooker and set pressure regulator in place. When pressure, is reached, cook for 6 minutes. Cool at once. When pressure is reduced, drain the beets and allow to cool.

Mix sour cream, horseradish, and chives. Pour over the chilled beets; mix gently. Serve.

If you prefer hot beets in a hot sauce, warm the sour cream, horseradish, and chives over a double boiler. Pour over hot beets.

Broccoli in Cream Sauce

Yield: 4 to 6 servings

2 pounds broccoli (about 3 cups)
1 10-ounce can cream of celery soup
1 cup water
½ teaspoon salt

Wash broccoli. Cut stems in 1-inch pieces, leaving florets a little longer. Use all the broccoli. Put broccoli in cooker.

Mix undiluted soup with water and add salt. Pour over the broccoli. Close cover on cooker. Set pressure control in place. When pressure is reached, cook 3 minutes. Cool cooker at once under running water. Serve.

Brussels Sprouts and New Potatoes

Yield: 4 to 6 servings

1½ pounds Brussels sprouts
1 cup new potatoes, peeled and diced
½ cup beef or chicken broth
1½ tablespoons bread crumbs
1½ tablespoons butter

Wash and clean the vegetables. Put in cooker with liquid. Close cover of cooker and put pressure control in place. When pressure is reached, cook for 5 minutes. Cool at once under faucet.

Thoroughly mix the bread crumbs and melted butter. Spoon over the drained hot vegetables. Serve.

Cabbage in Meat Essence

Yield: 4 to 6 servings

1 medium head cabbage, shredded
1 teaspoon lemon-pepper seasoning
½ cup beef broth

Put shredded cabbage, seasoning, and beef broth into cooker. Close cover securely; put pressure control in place. When pressure is reached, cook for 3 minutes with control rocking gently. Cool at once under running water. Serve.

Chinese Cabbage with Mushrooms

Yield: 4 to 6 servings

1 medium head Chinese cabbage, washed and cut into 1½-inch pieces
½ pound fresh mushrooms, diced

1 teaspoon salt
½ cup water
4 tablespoons melted butter

Place cabbage, mushrooms, salt and water in cooker. Close cover and set pressure control in place. When pressure is reached and control jiggles gently, cook for 3 minutes. Cool cooker at once under running water.

Put vegetables in serving dish and pour melted butter on top.

Cabbage and Rice

Yield: 4 to 6 servings

½ cup finely chopped onion
3 tablespoons shortening
3 cups coarsely shredded cabbage
1 green pepper, diced
1 cup rice
2 cups canned tomatoes
½ cup beef broth

In cooker, brown onions lightly in shortening. Add cabbage, green pepper, rice, tomatoes, and beef broth. Close cover of cooker and set pressure control in place. When pressure control is rocking gently, cook for 1 minute. Allow pressure to drop naturally.

Be sure to mix vegetables well just before serving.

Carrots, Raisins and Pineapple

Yield: 4 to 6 servings

3 cups sliced carrots
1 cup pineapple juice
½ cup raisins
1 20-ounce can pineapple chunks, drained

1 tablespoon cornstarch
¼ teaspoon salt
¼ cup water
1 tablespoon butter or margarine

Put carrots, pineapple juice, and raisins in cooker. Close cover securely and set pressure regulator in place. When pressure is reached, cook for 2 to 3 minutes. Reduce pressure at once. With cooker open and over a very low flame, add pineapple chunks.

Mix cornstarch, salt, and water together and add to carrots. Stir until slightly thickened, being careful not to break up carrots. Add butter. Serve.

Celery and Almonds

Yield: 4 to 6 servings

2 or 3 cups celery, cut into 2-inch
  strips
1 small onion, chopped fine
1 teaspoon salt
½ cup chicken broth
½ cup slivered almonds

Put celery, onion, salt, and chicken broth in cooker. Close cover and put pressure control in place. When pressure is reached, cook 3 minutes. Cool cooker at once under running water.

Add almonds to celery; simmer together for 1 or 2 minutes more. Serve.

Scalloped Corn

Yield: 4 to 6 servings

2 cups uncooked corn, cut off the cob
1 cup diced green pepper
¼ cup chopped olives
½ cup water

Put corn, green pepper, and olives into cooker; pour water over them. (No salt in this one—the olives will supply that.) Close cover securely; put pressure control in place. When pressure is reached and control rocks gently, cook for 3 minutes. Reduce pressure at once under running water.

Stir to blend the vegetables. Serve at once.

Ratatouille

Yield: 4 to 6 servings

2 cups eggplant, diced and peeled
1 cup sliced onions
2 green peppers, cut into strips
2 cups diced zucchini
2 medium-size tomatoes, quartered
2 teaspoons salt
½ teaspoon oregano
2 tablespoons water

Place all of your prepared vegetables in the cooker. Sprinkle with salt and oregano. Add water. Close the cover and put the pressure control in place. When pressure is reached, allow to cook for 2 to 3 minutes. Cool at once under running water. Serve.

Dill Peas and Cucumbers

Yield: 4 servings

1 cup shelled peas
1 cup diced cucumber, with skin left on
½ cup water
1 teaspoon dillseed

Put shelled peas and cucumber into cooker. Add water and dillseed. Cover and set pressure control on. When pressure is reached, cook for 1 minute. Cool instantly under faucet.

Drain, and serve with melted butter, if desired.

Creamed Peas and Carrots

Yield: 4 to 6 servings

1½ cups diced carrots
2 cups shelled peas
1 10-ounce can cream of mushroom
   soup
½ cup water
½ teaspoon salt

Put peas and carrots together in the cooker.

Mix the soup and water. Pour over the vegetables. Add salt. Close cooker and set pressure regulator in place. When pressure is reached, cook for 2 minutes. Cool at once under running water. Serve.

Easy Creamed Onions

Yield: 4 to 6 servings

1 pound small onions, peeled
½ teaspoon salt
½ teaspoon cloves
1 teaspoon sugar
½ cup water
1 can cream of mushroom soup
1 cup seasoned croutons

Put onions, salt, cloves, sugar, and water into cooker. Close cover and put pressure control in place. When pressure is reached, cook for 5 minutes. Cool cooker at once. Open cooker and put on a low flame.

Add the cream of mushroom soup and stir to mix. Last, put in the croutons. Give one last stir, and serve.

Potatoes Supreme

Yield: 4 to 6 servings

These potatoes are delicious around a roast or with chops.

4 large potatoes, peeled and quartered
2 tablespoons shortening
1 medium onion, chopped fine
1 cup beef broth

Peel and quarter potatoes. Set aside in cold water so they do not darken.

Heat shortening in cooker; lightly tan the onion. Onion should be transparent, not browned. Add drained potatoes and beef broth. Close cover of cooker; put pressure control in place. When pressure is reached, cook for 4 minutes. Cool at once under running water.

Sliced Potatoes and Onions

Yield: 4 to 6 servings

4 large potatoes, peeled and sliced
2 tablespoons shortening
2 medium onions, cut in rings
1 teaspoon salt
½ cup water
Parmesan cheese

Peel and slice potatoes; set aside in cold water to keep from turning dark.

Heat shortening in cooker; tan the onions. Add potatoes, salt, and water. Close cover of cooker securely; put pressure control in place. When pressure is reached, cook for 3 minutes. Cool at once under running water.

Place potatoes in serving dish and sprinkle with Parmesan cheese. The heat of the potatoes will melt the cheese so that all flavors blend.

Sweet Potatoes and Apples

Yield: 4 to 6 servings

6 sweet potatoes, peeled and sliced
2 cups apples, peeled and sliced
1 cup thin maple syrup
2 tablespoons melted butter or
  margarine
2 teaspoons salt
½ cup water

Place sweet potatoes and apples in cooker in alternate layers, ending with sweet potatoes on top.

Combine the remaining ingredients and pour over potatoes and apples. Close cover of cooker and set pressure control in place. When pressure is reached, cook for 5 minutes. Cool at once under running water. Serve.

Sweet Potatoes and Pineapple

Yield: 4 to 6 servings

4 sweet potatoes, peeled and quartered
1 can pineapple chunks, drained
¼ cup brown sugar
1 teaspoon salt
1 cup pineapple juice
2 tablespoons butter or margarine

Place ingredients in the pressure cooker in order given. Close cover and set pressure control in place. When pressure is reached, cook for 8 minutes. Cool at once under running water.

If desired, remove potatoes and pineapple chunks to serving bowl, thicken syrup, and pour over the vegetables.

40-Minute Potato Salad

Yield: 6 to 8 servings

3 pounds potatoes
1 cup water
2 tablespoons salad oil
2½ tablespoons vinegar
1 tablespoon chopped parsley
1 small onion, chopped fine
¼ cup chopped green pepper
¾ cup diced celery
1 teaspoon salt
1 teaspoon dillseed
¾ cup mayonnaise

Wash and prepare the potatoes, cutting very large ones in half.

Place water in the cooker. Add the rack and then the potatoes. Close cover securely and place the pressure regulator on the cooker. When regulator rocks slowly, cook for 10 minutes.

While the potatoes are cooking, assemble and prepare the rest of the ingredients.

When cooking time is finished, cool the cooker at once under running water. Remove and dice the potatoes. Add the remaining ingredients to the diced potatoes in the order given, mixing carefully with a rubber spatula. Put the potato salad in a bowl and chill until time to eat.

Onions in Raisin Sauce

Yield: 4 servings

4 large onions, cut into ¼-inch rings
1 teaspoon shortening
1 tablespoon wine vinegar
1 teaspoon salt
1 teaspoon oregano, optional
¼ cup raisins
½ cup water

Place ingredients in cooker in order given. Close cover and put pressure control in place. When control indicates pressure is reached, cook for 4 minutes. Cool at once under running water. Serve.

Browned White Rice

Yield: 4 to 6 servings

2 medium onions, chopped fine
1 tablespoon shortening
1 green pepper, chopped
1 cup rice
2 cups beef broth

Tan onions lightly in shortening. Add green pepper, rice, and beef broth. Close cooker cover securely and put pressure control in place. When pressure is reached and control jiggles gently, remove cooker from heat. Allow to cook naturally.

Stir rice gently with a fork to fluff, and serve.

Fluffy White Rice

Yield: 4 to 6 servings

2 cups water
½ teaspoon salt
1 cup white rice
2 teaspoons lemon juice

Put water into cooker and bring to a rolling boil. Add salt, rice, and lemon juice. Close cover and set pressure regulator in place. When regulator is rocking gently, remove rice from heat and set aside to allow pressure to drop naturally.

Serve at once, fluffing rice with fork if necessary.

Rice with Chicken Broth

Yield: 4 to 6 servings

2 cups chicken broth
1 cup white rice
1 onion, finely minced
½ teaspoon saffron, optional
¼ cup butter

Place chicken broth in cooker and bring to a boil. Add the rice and onion. Close cover on cooker and place pressure control on it. When pressure is reached and control rocking gently, remove cooker from heat. Allow to cool naturally.

After opening cooker, add saffron and butter to rice. Serve at once.

Rice with Gruyère Cheese

Yield: 4 to 6 servings

2 tablespoons shortening
1 medium onion, chopped
1 cup rice
½ cup dry white wine
1½ cups chicken broth
½ cup grated Gruyère cheese

Heat shortening and lightly tan onion. Add rice, wine, and chicken broth. Close cover and put pressure regulator in place. When the regulator is rocking gently and pressure is reached, remove from heat. Allow cooker to cool normally. When pressure is fully reduced, open cooker.

Fold in the cheese until it has blended. It will melt very quickly. Serve at once.

Lemon Rice

Yield: 4 to 6 servings

2 tablespoons shortening
1 cup diced celery
1 cup green onions with tops
1 cup rice
1 tablespoon grated lemon rind, optional
1 teaspoon salt
¼ teaspoon pepper
1 cup water plus 2 tablespoons lemon juice

Heat shortening in cooker. Lightly tan celery and onions. Add rice, lemon rind, salt, pepper, and water mixture. Close cover of cooker and put pressure control in place. When pressure is reached, remove cooker from the flame. Allow to cool normally.

When cool, open cooker and stir rice with a fork to fluff. Serve.

Summer Rice

Yield: 4 to 6 servings

2 medium onions, cut in quarters
1 large zucchini, sliced in rings
1 cup yellow corn
1 green pepper, cut into 1-inch pieces
2 large tomatoes, quartered
8 radishes, cut in half
2 cups rice
1 teaspoon salt
¼ teaspoon pepper
1 teaspoon dillweed or fresh dill
½ cup water

Place vegetables in cooker in order given. Add seasonings and water and close cover securely. Put pressure control in place. When pressure is reached, cook for 3 minutes. Cool at once.

Stir vegetables, and serve.

Pineapple Sauerkraut

Yield: 4 to 6 servings

Delicious with any pork dish.

2 pounds sauerkraut, drained
2½ cups pineapple chunks
½ cup pineapple juice

Place ingredients in cooker in order given. Close cover and put pressure control in place. When pressure is reached, cook for 5 minutes. Cool at once, and serve.

Acorn Squash

Yield: 2 servings per whole squash

1 acorn squash
2 tablespoons honey
Dash of nutmeg
¾ cup water

Wash and halve squash. Remove seeds. Put 1 tablespoon honey in each half. Sprinkle each half with nutmeg.

Place water in cooker and put rack above it. Put squash on rack. Close cover; put pressure control in place. When pressure is reached and control jiggles gently, cook for 7 minutes. Cool at once under running water. Serve.

Summer Squash and Onions

Yield: 4 to 6 servings

3 cups diced summer squash
2 cups onion rings
1 teaspoon salt
½ teaspoon pepper
½ cup tomato juice

Prepare vegetables as directed; put them into pressure cooker. Add salt and pepper; stir gently to mix. Pour tomato juice over. Close cover of cooker; put pressure regulator in place. When pressure is reached and regulator rocking gently, cook for 3 minutes. Cool at once under running water.

Put vegetables into serving bowl; serve at once.

Green-Bean Succotash

Yield: 4 to 6 servings

2 cups uncooked corn off the cob
2 cups green beans, cut into 1-inch pieces
1 teaspoon salt
½ cup water

Combine all ingredients in cooker in order given. Close cover securely; place pressure control on air vent. When control jiggles gently and pressure is reached, cook for 3 minutes. Cool cooker at once.

Dot the succotash with butter, and serve it piping hot.

Summer Succotash

Yield: 4 to 6 servings

2 cups uncooked fresh corn off the cob
2 cups baby lima beans
½ cup pineapple juice
½ teaspoon salt

Put corn, lima beans, and pineapple juice in cooker together. Sprinkle with salt. Close cover securely; set pressure regulator in place. When pressure is reached, cook for 2 minutes. Cool cooker at once under running water.

Stir in vegetables gently, and put them into a serving dish. Dot with butter if you wish.

Tomatoes and Okra

Yield: 4 to 6 servings

2 tablespoons shortening
½ cup finely chopped onion
2 cups sliced okra

2 cups fresh tomatoes
1 teaspoon salt
½ teaspoon paprika
2 teaspoons brown sugar
¼ cup water

Heat shortening in cooker; tan the onion. Add okra and tomatoes.

Dissolve salt, paprika, and brown sugar in water; pour over vegetables. Close cover of cooker securely; put pressure regulator in place. When pressure is reached, cook for 3 minutes. Cool cooker at once under running water.

Stir the vegetables, and serve them hot.

Turnips in Tomato Sauce

Yield: 4 to 6 servings

4 to 6 medium turnips, peeled and diced
1 teaspoon salt
1 teaspoon sugar
½ cup water
1 can condensed tomato soup

Put turnips, salt, sugar, and water into cooker. Close cover and put pressure control in place. When pressure is reached, cook for 3 minutes. Cool cooker at once under running water. Open cooker and return to a low flame.

Add the condensed tomato soup and simmer for 3 minutes more or until the flavors are well-blended and the turnips are hot. Serve.

Zucchini, Corn and Tomatoes

Yield: 4 to 6 servings

2 pounds zucchini, diced or cut into wheels
2 or 3 tomatoes, quartered
1 cup corn off the cob
1 teaspoon salt
1 teaspoon sugar
½ cup water
2 tablespoons butter or margarine

Place ingredients into pressure cooker in order given. Close cover and set pressure control in place. When control jiggles gently, cook for 3 minutes. Cool cooker at once under running water.

Put in serving dish and dot with butter. Serve.

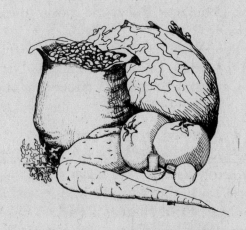

One-Pot Dinners

Apple Chicken and Rice

Yield: 4 to 6 servings

2 to 3 pounds chicken, cut into serving
  pieces
Salt and pepper
2 tablespoons shortening
1 large onion, chopped
1 apple, cored and quartered
1 cup rice
1½ cups apple juice
¼ cup heavy cream
Parsley for garnish

Season the chicken pieces liberally with
salt and pepper.

Heat the shortening in cooker. Brown
the onion and chicken. Add apple, rice, and
apple juice. Close cover. Put pressure regulator in place. When pressure is reached,
cook 15 minutes. Allow the cooker to cool
normally.

Return open cooker to a low heat and
add the cream. Stir gently to mix and heat.

Garnish with parsley, and serve at once.

Island Chicken Dinner

Yield: 4 to 6 servings

2 tablespoons shortening
1 onion, sliced
1 garlic clove, crushed
2½-pound chicken, cut into serving
  pieces
1 cup boneless ham or pork, cut into
  small cubes

2 tomatoes, chopped
1 cup diced sweet potatoes
2 carrots, diced
1 cup diced yellow squash
1 tablespoon parsley
1 bay leaf
½ teaspoon oregano
1 teaspoon salt
1 cup chicken broth

Heat shortening. Brown onion, garlic,
and then chicken pieces. Add rest of ingredients in order given. Close cover of
cooker and put pressure control in place.
When pressure is reached, cook for 10
minutes. Allow cooker to cool normally.

Stir and serve.

Brunswick Stew

Yield: 4 to 6 servings

2 to 3 pounds stewing chicken, cut
  into serving pieces
2 medium onions, sliced
1 cup corn
1 cup lima beans
1 green pepper, diced
2 tomatoes, quartered
1 tablespoon salt
Dash of Tabasco sauce
¼ teaspoon pepper
1 cup water
1 cup seasoned croutons, optional

Put ingredients into cooker in order
given. Close cover and put pressure regulator
in place. When pressure is reached, cook for
20 minutes. Cool cooker at once.

Optional but good—stir in 1 cup of
seasoned croutons, and serve.

Hamburger Vegetable Stew

Yield: 4 to 6 servings

2 tablespoons shortening
½ to 1 pound ground beef
1 cup canned tomatoes
½ cup diced carrots
½ cup diced celery
1 onion, chopped, or ½ cup spring
    onions
2 teaspoons salt
¼ cup rice
Dash of pepper
1½ cups water
1 cup diced potatoes

Heat shortening in cooker. Brown the meat. Add the tomatoes, carrots, celery, onion, salt, rice, pepper, and water. Last, add the potatoes. Close the cooker and place the pressure regulator in position. When pressure is reached and regulator is gently rocking, cook for 5 minutes. Allow to cool naturally. Serve.

Minced-Beef Stew

Yield: 4 to 6 servings

2 tablespoons shortening
1 pound beef, minced preferred, but
    ground twice will do
2 medium onions, sliced
1 tomato, diced
2 cups diced potatoes
1 teaspoon salt
¼ teaspoon pepper
½ cup beef broth
2 pears, peeled and sliced
2 peaches, peeled and sliced
4 plums, peeled and sliced
¼ cup seedless raisins

Heat shortening in cooker. Brown meat and onions together. Add tomato, potatoes, salt, pepper, and beef broth. Close cover securely and put pressure control in place. When pressure is reached, cook for 5 minutes. Cool cooker at once under running water.

Return open cooker to flame. Add the fruit in the order given. Stir and cook for 3 minutes more. Serve.

One-Pot Meat-Loaf Dinner

Yield: 4 servings

1 pound ground beef
1 teaspoon salt
Dash of pepper
1 egg, slightly beaten
1 medium onion, chopped
¼ cup corn-flake crumbs
1 tablespoon shortening
1 8-ounce can tomato sauce
½ cup water
4 whole potatoes, peeled
4 whole carrots

Mix together the ground beef, salt, pepper, beaten egg, onion, and corn-flake crumbs. Shape into a loaf and wrap in foil. Refrigerate for several hours (or overnight) to prevent loaf from falling apart.

Melt shortening in cooker and brown meat loaf on all sides. Remove.

Put tomato sauce and water into cooker. Add rack and arrange the meat loaf and vegetables on the rack. Close cover; put pressure control in place. When pressure is reached, cook for 12 to 15 minutes. Cool cooker normally for 5 minutes, then cool it under the faucet. Serve.

Petite Marmite

Yield: 6 servings

2 tablespoons shortening
2 pounds beef in 1 piece
1 pound chicken wings
1 onion stuck with 3 cloves
3 medium-size leeks, white parts only
3 small ribs celery
2 cups diced white turnips
2 carrots, diced
1 cup diced potatoes
1 bay leaf
1 teaspoon salt
6 peppercorns
4 cups beef broth

Heat shortening in cooker and brown meat on all sides. Put rest of ingredients in cooker in order given. Close cover and put pressure control in place. When pressure is reached and control jiggles, cook for 30 minutes. Allow cooker to cool naturally. When pressure is fully reduced, open cooker and remove meat and chicken wings.

Slice the meat and put a slice in each soup bowl, with vegetables and broth over it. Serve.

Sweet Meat Stew

Yield: 4 to 6 servings

1½ pounds lean ground beef
¾ cup bread crumbs
2 eggs
1 teaspoon oregano
1 teaspoon salt
¼ teaspoon pepper
2 tablespoons shortening
2 cups drained pineapple cubes
1 green pepper, chopped

2 cups chopped canned peaches
1 cup rice
1 cup water

Mix meat, bread crumbs, eggs, oregano, salt, and pepper in a bowl. Form mixture into meatballs.

Heat shortening in cooker. Brown meatballs. Add the rest of the ingredients. Close cover and put pressure control in place. When pressure is reached, cook for 8 minutes. Cool cooker at once, and serve.

Autumn Harvest (Beef and Eggplant)

Yield: 4 to 6 servings

This recipe calls for eggplant. Use any of your abundant garden produce in its place.

2 pounds beef, cut into 1-inch cubes
1 onion, chopped
1 garlic clove, crushed
2 tablespoons shortening
3 tomatoes, chopped
1 eggplant, peeled and cubed
1 teaspoon paprika
½ teaspoon oregano
1 teaspoon salt
Dash of pepper
Parsley for garnish

Brown meat, onion, and garlic in shortening. Add rest of ingredients (except parsley) in order given. Close cooker and put pressure control in place. When pressure is reached, cook for 12 minutes. Cool at once.

Garnish with parsley, if desired, and serve.

Stuffed Eggplant

Yield: 2 servings

1 medium eggplant
1 cup finely chopped leftover meat
½ cup cooked rice
1 medium onion, chopped
1 teaspoon dill leaves
1 egg
½ teaspoon salt
¼ teaspoon pepper
½ cup water

Sauce

1 tablespoon cornstarch
¼ cup beef broth
1 tablespoon tomato paste
½ teaspoon sugar
Parsley for garnish

Cut eggplant lengthwise and scoop out center seeds.

Mix meat, rice, onion, dill, egg, salt, and pepper in a bowl. Fill hollowed out eggplant with this stuffing.

Put water in cooker, add rack, and place stuffed eggplants on rack. Close cover and put pressure control in place. When pressure is reached, cook for 2 to 3 minutes. Cool cooker at once. Put eggplants on a baking dish.

Dissolve cornstarch in beef broth and put in a saucepan. Add tomato paste and sugar and blend until sauce is slightly thickened. Pour over the eggplant. Place under the broiler for 2 minutes more.

Sprinkle with parsley, and serve. A tossed salad completes the meal.

Wonderful Western Dinner

Yield: 4 to 6 servings

½ pound link pork sausage
2 to 3 pounds chicken, cut into serving pieces
1 onion, minced
2 cups canned tomatoes with juice
18 stuffed green olives
¼ cup olive juice
1 cup rice
1 cup water
1 package frozen peas (thawed)

Brown sausage in cooker and pour off most of excess fat. Leave about 2 tablespoons fat in cooker. Set sausage aside.

Brown the chicken. Add onion, tomatoes, olives and juice, rice, water, and sausage. Close cover and put pressure control in place. When pressure is reached, cook for 15 minutes. Allow pressure to drop naturally.

Return open cooker to low flame. Add peas and simmer for 3 minutes, stirring gently. Serve.

Hambolaya

Yield: 4 to 6 servings

1 cup rice
1 cup corn
1 cup green beans
1 medium onion, quartered
1 green pepper, diced
2 cups canned tomatoes (1-pound can)
1 teaspoon salt
½ cup beef broth
1 cup cooked ham, diced

Put all ingredients except the ham into the cooker in the order given. Close cover and put pressure control in place. When pressure is reached, cook for 3 minutes. Allow pressure to drop of its own accord.

Remove regulator and cover and return open cooker to a low light. Add diced ham and stir until all flavors blend and all is piping hot. Serve.

Pork Stew

Yield: 4 to 6 servings

2 pounds lean pork, cut into 3- by
    1-inch strips
2 tablespoons shortening
1 tablespoon paprika
1 large onion, chopped
2 whole carrots, cut in 3-inch strips
1 whole green pepper, cut in strips
2 medium tomatoes, chopped
1 cup sliced fresh mushrooms
1 teaspoon salt
¼ teaspoon pepper
¾ cup water
1 tablespoon cornstarch
1 cup sour cream

Brown pork strips in heated shortening. Add paprika and onion; mix well. Put in carrots, green pepper, tomatoes, mushrooms, salt, pepper, and ½ cup water. Close cover and put pressure control in place. When pressure is reached, cook for 10 minutes. Let pressure drop of its own accord.

Mix cornstarch with ¼ cup water and add to open cooker. Stir until slightly thickened. Keep stirring as you add the sour cream.

When all is hot, serve the stew with buttered noodles.

Pork and Pineapple Curry

Yield: 4 to 6 servings

1 tablespoon shortening
1 clove garlic, minced fine
1 medium onion, chopped
1 pound pork, cut into 1-inch pieces
1 cup rice
2 tablespoons soy sauce
1 teaspoon ground ginger
½ teaspoon saffron
2 ounces blanched almonds
2 cups drained pineapple chunks
1 cup pineapple juice

Heat shortening in cooker and brown garlic and onions, adding and mixing in the pork. Add rest of ingredients. Close cover and put pressure control in place. When pressure is reached, cook for 10 minutes. Cool cooker at once under running water. Serve.

Veal Stew

Yield: 4 servings

3 tablespoons shortening
2 pounds veal, cut into 2-inch cubes
1 teaspoon salt
Dash of pepper
1½ cups cooking wine
1 tablespoon sugar, optional
4 medium potatoes
4 medium whole carrots
4 medium onions

Heat cooker and add shortening. Brown veal cubes in hot fat. Add salt, pepper, wine, and sugar. Close cover securely and put pressure control in place. When pressure is reached and control jiggles, cook for 8 minutes.

While meat is cooking, scrub potatoes and carrots. Remove skin from onions.

After 8 minutes, allow cooker to cool for 5 minutes. Then place cooker under faucet to reduce all pressure. Open cooker and put vegetables on top of veal. Again, close cover and put control in place. When pressure is reached, cook for 8 minutes more. Reduce pressure at once under running water.

Add a salad and your meal is complete.

Veal and Spinach Delight

Yield: 6 servings

2 pounds veal, cut into 1-inch cubes
2 tablespoons shortening
1 large onion, sliced
½ cup minced green onions with tops
1 garlic clove, crushed fine
⅓ cup tomato paste
2 pounds fresh spinach, cleaned and cut up

1 teaspoon salt
Dash of pepper
½ cup water
1 cup plain yogurt
1 tablespoon dillweed

Brown veal in shortening. Add onion, green onions, garlic, tomato paste, spinach, salt, pepper, and water. Close cover and put pressure control in place. When pressure is reached, cook for 15 minutes. Cool at once under running water. Return open cooker to a low flame.

Add the yogurt and dill. Simmer until yogurt is hot and blended in.

Serve at once.

Lamb-Chop Ragout

Yield: 6 servings

6 lamb chops, shoulder cut
¼ cup flour
Salt and pepper to taste
2 tablespoons shortening
1 cup strong chicken broth
2 teaspoons steak or Worcestershire sauce
1 cup sliced onions
6 small whole carrots
6 medium potatoes, sliced

Dredge lamb chops in flour and salt and pepper.

Heat shortening in cooker and brown chops on both sides. Add rest of ingredients in order given. Close cover securely and set pressure control in place. When pressure is reached, cook for 8 minutes. Allow pressure to drop naturally.

Dish and serve ragout.

Seafood Stew

Yield: 4 to 6 servings

Use your imagination for the fish. Include some scallops or some shelled clams or shrimp. The mixed fish will add flavor to this stew.

2 tablespoons shortening
1 large onion, sliced
1 garlic clove, crushed
2 pounds mixed fish, cut into chunks
1 or 2 tomatoes, peeled and chopped
1 cup diced potatoes
¼ cup chopped parsley
1 teaspoon salt
Dash of pepper
1 cup dry white wine

Heat shortening. Brown onion and garlic. Add the rest of the ingredients in order given. Close cover and put pressure control in place. When pressure is reached, cook for 3 minutes. Cool cooker at once under running water. Serve.

Fish in Tureen

Yield: 6 to 8 servings

2 pounds haddock, cut into bite-size pieces
2 cups water
2 cups diced onions
2 cups diced potatoes
½ cup rice
1 large green pepper, diced
½ to 1 cup chopped celery
½ cup diced carrots
2 tablespoons salt
3 whole peppercorns
2 tablespoons minced parsley

Place ingredients in cooker in order listed. Close cover and set pressure control in place. When pressure is reached and control jiggles gently, cook for 5 minutes. Allow pressure to drop naturally.

Serve this in a large tureen, and complete the meal with a tossed salad.

Desserts

A Word about Desserts

Because it is an ideal steamer, the pressure cooker lends itself well to the making of many desserts. The heat attained is constant, which produces a uniform texture in the cooked foods.

The use of molds is required in the preparation of steamed puddings and custards. For this, individual custard cups of the standard size may be used. For a large pudding or bread recipe, a 1-quart aluminum or metal mold or an ovenproof bowl will serve well. If the recipe requires that the mold be covered, aluminum foil makes a good cover, as it shapes well to the mold.

Because a larger quantity of water is used in the steaming process, you may find water stains on the interior of the cooker. To avoid this, add 1 teaspoon of vinegar or ½ teaspoon of cream of tartar to the water required. This will help avoid water stains.

Do *not* cook applesauce, cranberries, or rhubarb in the pressure cooker. Such foods tend to foam or froth and may block the vent pipe.

Brown Bread

Yield: About 30 slices

2 eggs, beaten
2 tablespoons butter, melted
⅔ cup molasses
1 teaspoon baking soda
1 cup buttermilk
1 cup all-purpose flour
1 teaspoon baking powder
½ teaspoon salt
2 cups whole-wheat flour
1 cup seeded raisins
4 cups water

Prepare for this recipe by setting aside 3 tin cans (1-pound 4-ounce size). Grease the insides and bottoms of the empty cans well.

Stir eggs, butter, and molasses together. In a 2-cup measure, mix baking soda with buttermilk. Sift together white flour, baking powder, salt, and whole-wheat flour. Alternately add buttermilk mixture and flour to egg mixture. Last, add raisins; stir well. Fill the waiting tin cans half full; cover tightly with foil.

Put 4 cups water and the rack in cooker. Set the cans on rack; close cover securely. Do *not* put pressure control on. Allow a small stream of steam to escape from cooker for 1½ hours. Remove cooker from heat. Let stand 5 minutes more, then open. Your loaves are ready for butter or cream cheese.

Date and Nut Bread

Yield: 10 to 12 servings

1 egg
½ cup sugar
1 cup milk
2½ cups flour
2 teaspoons baking powder
½ teaspoon salt
½ cup chopped dates
½ cup chopped nuts
4 cups water

Beat egg and sugar together. Measure milk. Sift dry ingredients together. Alternate milk and dry ingredients to form the dough. Last, stir in dates and nuts.

Grease 1-quart mold; pour dough into it. Cover with aluminum foil. Put water and rack into cooker. Set mold on rack; close cover securely. Do *not* put pressure control on cooker. Allow a small stream of steam to flow from vent pipe for 1½ hours. Remove cooker from heat. Let stand 5 minutes, then open.

Custard

Yield: 4 servings

2 cups milk
2 eggs, beaten
⅓ cup sugar
¼ teaspoon salt
½ teaspoon vanilla
Dash of nutmeg
½ cup water

Scald the milk in a saucepan; allow to cool slightly. Combine eggs, sugar, and salt in a bowl. Add slightly cooled milk slowly, stirring constantly. Add vanilla. Pour mixture into individual custard cups; sprinkle each serving with some nutmeg. Cover each cup with aluminum foil.

Place water in cooker; put rack in place. Put custard cups on rack; close cover securely. Put pressure control in place. When pressure is reached, cook for 3 minutes. Cool at once. Chill the custards before serving.

Chocolate Custard

Yield: 4 to 6 servings

3 cups hot milk
1 square grated chocolate
3 eggs
3 tablespoons sugar
1½ teaspoons vanilla
¼ teaspoon salt
1 cup water

Melt grated chocolate in hot milk. Set aside to cool slightly. Mix eggs, sugar, vanilla, and salt. Gradually add chocolate milk, stirring constantly. Pour into 1-quart mold. Cover mold with foil.

Put water and rack into pressure cooker. Set mold on rack; close cover securely. Put pressure regulator in place. When pressure is reached, cook for 7 minutes. Remove cooker from heat; allow to cool normally. Chill the custard before serving.

Peppermint-Candy Custard

Yield: 4 servings

2 cups milk
2 eggs, beaten
½ cup ground peppermint-stick candy
¼ teaspoon salt
½ teaspoon vanilla
½ cup water

Scald the milk; set aside to cool slightly. Combine eggs, candy, and salt in a bowl. Gradually add milk and vanilla, stirring constantly. Pour mixture into individual custard cups. Cover each cup tightly with aluminum foil.

Place water in cooker; set rack in place. Put custard cups on rack; close cover securely. Put pressure control in place. When pressure is reached, cook for 3 minutes. Cool at once under running water. Chill the custards before serving.

Bread Pudding

Yield: 4 to 6 servings

3 slices stale bread, cubed
1 tablespoon melted butter or margarine
¼ teaspoon salt
½ cup brown sugar
1 teaspoon cinnamon
2 cups hot milk
2 eggs, slightly beaten
½ teaspoon vanilla
½ cup raisins
½ cup chopped nuts
4 cups water

Put bread in mixing bowl. Add all ingredients in order given. Mix well. Gently pour bread mixture into well-greased mold that will set loosely in your cooker. Cover mold with aluminum foil.

Put water and rack in cooker. Put mold on top of rack. Close cover securely. Do *not* put pressure control on yet. Allow cooker to steam for 5 minutes, then put pressure control in place. When pressure is reached, cook for 15 minutes. Allow pressure to drop of its own accord.

Steamed Chocolate Pudding

Yield: 10 to 12 servings

3 tablespoons butter
⅔ cup sugar
1 egg
2¼ cups all-purpose flour

4¼ teaspoons baking powder
¼ teaspoon salt
1 cup milk
2½ ounces baking chocolate, melted
4 cups water

Cream butter and sugar thoroughly. Add egg; mix well. Sift dry ingredients together; add to creamed mixture alternately with milk. Stir in melted chocolate. Grease 1-quart mold; pour mixture into it. Cover with aluminum foil.

Put water and rack into cooker. Add covered mold. Close cooker cover. Allow a small stream of steam to escape from vent for 1½ hours. Do *not* use pressure control. Remove cooker from heat. Let stand 5 minutes. Serve the pudding with your favorite hard sauce.

Date and Nut Rice Pudding

Yield: 4 to 6 servings

2 cups milk
2 eggs, slightly beaten
⅓ cup brown sugar
½ teaspoon salt
⅔ cup cooked rice
½ teaspoon vanilla
½ cup chopped dates
½ cup walnuts
½ cup water

Heat but do not boil milk. Allow to cool slightly. Combine eggs, sugar, and salt in a bowl. Add milk slowly, stirring constantly. Add rice, vanilla, dates, and walnuts. Pour mixture into custard cups. Cover each cup with aluminum foil.

Put water and rack in cooker; place custard cups on rack. Close cover; put pressure control in place. When pressure is reached, cook for 3 minutes. Cool cooker at once under running water. Uncover custard cups and stir slightly before chilling in refrigerator.

Fresh-Fruit Cocktail

Yield: 4 to 6 servings

½ pound peaches, diced
¼ pound pears, diced
¼ pound apricots, diced
2 sticks cinnamon
1 teaspoon lemon juice
1¼ cups water
Sugar to taste

Prepare fruit by coring, paring, and dicing into small pieces. Place rack in pressure cooker. Put fruit on rack. Add cinnamon sticks.

Mix lemon juice with water; pour over fruit. Close cover securely; put pressure control in place. When pressure is reached and regulator rocking gently, remove from heat. Cool at once under running water. Add sugar to taste while liquid is hot enough to dissolve it. Stir gently. Allow fruit to cool, and serve slightly chilled.

Dried-Fruit Compote

Yield: 4 to 6 servings

Do not fill cooker over two-thirds full. This allows for the expansion of the fruit.

½ pound dried apricots
½ pound dried peaches
½ pound dark raisins
3 cups water

Soak fruit in water 1 hour. Reserve this water to be used when cooking.

Place fruit in cooker and pour water in which it soaked over it, adding water, if needed, to make 3 cups. Close cover of cooker; put pressure control in place. When pressure is reached, cook for 3 to 5 minutes. Cool cooker at once under running water. Add sugar to taste, if desired.

Fresh Spiced Peaches

Yield: 4 to 6 servings

1 pound peaches, peeled, seeded, and halved
2 sticks cinnamon
1 teaspoon lemon juice
1¼ cups water
Sugar to taste

Put prepared fruit on rack in cooker. Add cinnamon sticks. Mix lemon juice in water; pour over fruit. Close cover of cooker; put pressure control in place. When pressure is reached, cook for 2 minutes. Cool at once under running water. Add sugar to taste.

Serve the peach halves chilled.

Mint Pears

Yield: 4 to 6 servings

1 pound pears, cored, pared, and quartered
½ cup sugar
1¼ cups water
3 tablespoons crème de menthe

Place pears on rack in cooker. Mix sugar in water until dissolved; pour over pears. Close cover securely; put pressure control in place. When pressure is reached, cook for 2 minutes. Cool at once under running water. Allow fruit to cool completely. When pears are cold, add creme de menthe.

Serve the pears with meat or as a dessert.

Spiced Pineapple

Yield: 4 to 6 servings

1 cup sugar
1 cup vinegar
½ cup water
2 sticks cinnamon
20 whole cloves
1 whole pineapple, peeled, cored, and sliced

Place sugar, vinegar, water, and spices in cooker. Boil together 5 minutes. Put pineapple slices into liquid. Close cover of cooker; put pressure control in place. When pressure is reached, cook for 5 minutes. Cool at once under running water.

Skillet
Appetizers

Party Drumsticks

Yield: 24 drumsticks

12 chicken wings
½ cup flour
1 teaspoon salt
¾ teaspoon ginger
¼ teaspoon cinnamon
¼ teaspoon pepper
Fat for deep frying

The trick to this recipe is in dividing the chicken wings. Separate each wing at the joints. This will give you 3 pieces. Reserve wing tips for soup later.

Mix flour, salt, and seasonings well. Coat each chicken piece thoroughly. Drop floured chicken into deep fat. Fry them quickly until crisp and golden brown. Drain.

Serve with your favorite sweet-and-sour sauce or by themselves. Party drumsticks can be made ahead, frozen, and reheated in a moderate oven.

Swedish Meatballs

Yield: 48 balls

1 pound ground beef
¼ pound ground veal
¼ pound ground pork
2 cups bread crumbs
½ cup milk
1 onion, diced fine
2 tablespoons butter

2½ teaspoons salt
¼ teaspoon pepper
2 teaspoons nutmeg
2 teaspoons paprika
1 teaspoon dry mustard
3 beaten eggs
4 teaspoons butter or margarine

Sauce

¼ teaspoon garlic
5 tablespoons butter
2 teaspoons tomato paste
1 teaspoon beef concentrate
2 cups bouillon or soup stock
1 teaspoon aromatic bitters, optional
1 cup sour cream

Have the meat ground together twice. Soak bread crumbs in milk. Add meat; mix.

Sauté onion in large skillet in 2 tablespoons butter. Mix together seasonings, eggs, onion, and meat in a bowl. Mix well; form into 48 small balls. Melt butter in skillet; brown meatballs on all sides. Remove and set aside to make the sauce.

Add garlic and 1 tablespoon butter to fat left in skillet. Blend in 4 more tablespoons butter, the tomato paste, beef concentrate, and stock. Add bitters here, if desired. Stir mixture over low heat until it thickens, then pour sauce into a lighted chafing dish. Stir in sour cream. Add meatballs to sauce, stirring once or twice to be sure all heats through.

The sauce may be poured into a casserole dish and heated in the oven, if preferred. This recipe improves if made one day ahead of time.

Teriyaki Steak Bits

Yield: 6 to 8 servings

½ cup soy sauce
1 clove garlic, chopped fine
1 teaspoon ground ginger
2 tablespoons sugar
2 tablespoons sherry wine
1½ pounds steak, cut into 1-inch
   cubes
2 or more tablespoons margarine

Combine soy sauce, spices, sugar, and wine to make a marinade. Marinate meat in this at least 1 hour. Drain meat, reserving liquid.

In a medium skillet, melt 2 tablespoons margarine. Brown meat cubes quickly on all sides. Place meat in a chafing dish; pour sauce over it. Stir occasionally. You won't have to stir much, as your guests will eat the steak on handy toothpicks very quickly. If you like, add some pineapple chunks to the chafing dish.

Party Liver Pâté

Yield: 10 to 16 servings

¼ pound butter or chicken fat
1 large onion, chopped fine
1 pound chicken livers
1 tablespoon Worcestershire sauce
Salt and pepper to taste

Melt butter or chicken fat in medium skillet; lightly tan chopped onion. Add chicken livers; cook until they are slightly pink at the center, about 5 minutes. Remove from heat.

Put entire mixture through a food mill so it is ground very smooth. If you use a colander instead of food mill, you may want to put the liver mixture through twice to ensure a smooth texture. Last, add Worcestershire sauce and salt and pepper. Mix together well with a spoon.

Shape pâté into a greased mold for a party. Turn out on a serving plate and surround with party crackers so that guests may help themselves.

Shrimp Fritters

Yield: About 12 fritters

½ cup water
2 tablespoons butter
½ cup flour
2 eggs, well-beaten
½ cup grated cheese (American or
   Gruyère)
1 cup diced cooked shrimp
Fat for deep frying

Bring water and butter to a boil in a saucepan. Add flour all at once, stirring vigorously with a wooden spoon. Stir until mixture pulls away from sides of pan. Remove from heat. Add eggs. The mixture will be smooth and thick. Stir in shrimp and cheese.

Heat fat for deep frying in skillet. Drop mixture by teaspoonfuls into fat. Cook until evenly browned and crisp.

Shrimp in Garlic Butter

Yield: 6 to 10 servings for a party

¼ pound butter or margarine
1 garlic clove, cut in half
48 jumbo shrimp, peeled and cleaned

3 tablespoons finely chopped parsley
½ cup sherry

Melt butter in skillet and heat garlic halves 2 minutes. Remove garlic. Add shrimp to butter and sauté for 5 minutes or until shrimp are pink. Remove to a hot platter or chafing dish. Add parsley and sherry to the butter in the skillet; stir until hot, about 30 seconds. Pour the sauce over the shrimp and watch them disappear.

Fish Balls for a Party

Yield: 24 to 36 balls

2 pounds frozen haddock fillets
1 cup cracker meal
2 teaspoons salt
Dash of white pepper
1½ cups light cream
Fat for deep frying
Parsley and paprika for garnish

Put haddock, partially thawed, through a food grinder twice. Place it in a large bowl. Add cracker meal, salt, pepper, and cream. Mix until smooth. Now, put your hands under cold water. With moist hands, shape fish mixture into 1-inch balls.

Heat fat in medium skillet; using a slotted spoon, drop fish balls into fat. Allow to simmer for 10 minutes. Remove cooked fish balls with slotted spoon; drain on paper towels. Cook rest of balls in same way.

Put fish balls on a heated platter and sprinkle with parsley and paprika. Keep toothpicks handy for picking up these delicacies.

Salmon Balls

Yield: 6 to 10 servings

These can be kept warm in an oven or on a hot plate for continual serving during a party evening.

1 15-ounce can salmon
1 egg, beaten
½ cup flour
½ cup freshly ground black pepper
1 heaping teaspoon baking powder
Fat for deep frying

Drain salmon and reserve liquid. Add egg to salmon, followed by flour and pepper. Mix baking powder in ¼ cup salmon liquid and add to salmon mixture. Heat fat in skillet. Drop salmon mixture by teaspoonfuls to form balls. Fry until golden brown and crusty. Drain on paper towels; serve salmon balls at once.

Cheese Cubes

Yield: About 2 dozen

1½ cups bread crumbs mixed with ½ teaspoon dillweed
2 eggs, beaten
1 pound Swiss cheese, cut into 1-inch cubes
Fat for deep frying

Take 2 tablespoons from bread crumbs and beat with eggs. Put rest of crumbs in a pie plate. Dip cheese cubes into egg mixture, then into dry crumbs. Coat all over.

Heat shortening in medium skillet and drop breaded cheese into it, a few cubes at a time. Cook for 1 minute, until golden, then lift out. Drain on paper towels. Keep cubes warm until all are cooked, then pass the platter.

To make these successfully, be sure cheese cubes are well battered in egg and crumbs, and work fast in the fryer.

Sweet-Potato Fingers

Yield: About 4 servings

4 to 6 cooked sweet potatoes
¼ cup flour
Fat for deep frying
½ cup brown sugar
1 teaspoon salt
½ teaspoon nutmeg

Cut sweet potatoes into strips or fingers. Dip each finger into flour so it is well-coated. Heat fat in medium skillet. Fry potato fingers until golden brown. Drain on paper towels. Sprinkle with a mixture of brown sugar, salt, and nutmeg.

Keep these tasty appetizers on a hot tray until party time.

Curried Nuts

Yield: 2 cups

¼ cup olive oil
1 tablespoon curry powder
1 tablespoon Worcestershire sauce
⅛ teaspoon cayenne
2 cups nuts, assorted are best

Combine olive oil and seasonings in medium-size skillet. When mixture is hot, add nuts, stirring constantly until nuts are completely coated.

Line a baking pan with brown paper. Spread out nuts. Bake at 300°F for 10 minutes. The nuts should be crisp and tasty.

Salted Almonds

Yield: 4 cups

2 tablespoons butter or margarine
1 pound blanched almonds

Generous sprinkling of salt, onion salt, or garlic salt

Melt the butter in a medium-size skillet. Do not let the butter brown. Stir in the blanched almonds; let them cook over low heat. Stir from time to time, or shake the skillet. When the almonds are lightly browned, sprinkle them generously with salt. Drain them on brown paper for 3 minutes. Then put the almonds on fresh brown paper to drain off remaining butter.

If you enjoy the taste of other salts, sprinkle the almonds with onion or garlic salt for a variety. Any way you season them, they are going to be a hit.

Biscuit Sticks

Yield: About 36 sticks

1 recipe of your favorite biscuit dough
   or 1 package prepared biscuits
Salt to taste
Fat for deep frying
1 garlic clove

Roll out the biscuit dough; cut into sticks ½ inch high by ½ inch wide by 3 inches long. Sprinkle the sticks with salt. Melt the fat in a medium size skillet; season it with the garlic clove. Leave the clove in until you smell it in the fat, then remove it. Drop the sticks, a few at a time, into the hot fat; brown them lightly.

These are best served and eaten warm.

Breakfast in the Skillet

Fried Bananas

Yield: 4 to 6 servings

¼ cup flour
1 teaspoon cinnamon
6 bananas, sliced lengthwise
2 or more tablespoons shortening

Mix flour and cinnamon together; thoroughly coat each piece of banana with mixture. If bananas are very long, you may prefer to quarter them.

Heat shortening in medium skillet. Brown the floured bananas, slowly turning them once. Remove bananas to a heated platter; sprinkle with sugar.

Skillet Bread

Yield: 4 to 6 servings; 1 loaf

This is simple to mix, tricky to turn in the skillet, and so good dripping with melted butter and jelly.

2 cups flour
4 teaspoons baking powder
2 teaspoons salt
1¼ cups milk
2 tablespoons butter or margarine

Mix dry ingredients in a bowl. Add milk; blend with a wooden spoon. This will make a biscuit-like, spongy texture.

Heat butter in medium-size skillet. Keep heat low. Spread butter around evenly. Pour in batter. Cook for 15 minutes or until underside is golden brown. Here's the tricky part. Lift with a large spatula and turn to cook the other side for 15 minutes more. Turn bread out onto a round plate; serve at once.

Basket Eggs

Yield: 6 servings

1½ pounds lean ground beef
1 small onion, chopped fine
2 tablespoons catsup
1 teaspoon salt
¼ teaspoon pepper
¼ cup milk
6 hard-cooked eggs, shelled
1 raw egg, beaten
⅔ cup cornflake crumbs
Fat for deep frying

Mix ground beef with onion, catsup, salt, pepper, and milk. When well-blended, form into 6 balls. Shape each ball of meat around a hard-cooked egg to completely cover the egg, forming an oval shape. Brush each meatball with beaten egg, then roll each in crumbs until covered all over.

Melt fat in medium skillet to make a 2-inch depth. Fry meatballs, 3 at a time, until crispy brown. (You will not have to turn them if you use deep fat.) Drain and keep them hot until all are done.

To serve, cut each meatball in half lengthwise. The eggs will then be in the basket.

233

Bacon and Egg Cake

Yield: 4 servings

½ pound bacon
6 eggs
1 tablespoon flour
½ teaspoon salt
½ cup milk or cream
3 tablespoons finely cut chives

Cut each bacon slice in half. Fry lightly but not too crisp in large skillet. Drain and set aside. Remove all but about 1 tablespoon of bacon fat from skillet.

Combine eggs, flour, and salt in a bowl. Gradually add milk. Over moderate heat, warm the fat in the skillet. Pour in egg mixture; turn heat down to low. Do not stir. Let eggs set firm. This will take about 20 minutes. When mixture is firm, remove from heat.

Arrange bacon slices and chives on top. Serve directly from the pan.

Danish Egg Cake with Sausage

Yield: 6 servings

3 medium boiled potatoes, sliced
1 8-ounce can cocktail sausages
2 tablespoons butter or margarine
4 eggs
¼ cup cream
Green pepper for garnish
1 or 2 tomatoes for garnish

Dice potatoes. Slice cocktail sausages into same bowl; set aside. Melt butter in medium skillet; brown potatoes and sausages together. Add well-beaten eggs mixed with cream. Cook over slow heat until mixture sets firm in the center.

Turn egg cake out onto a hot platter. Garnish with green pepper and tomato wedges.

Eggs Italian

Yield: 4 to 6 servings

2 tablespoons butter or margarine
1 tablespoon chopped onion
1 tablespoon diced green pepper
6 eggs
1 cup tomato soup
⅛ teaspoon salt

Melt the butter in a medium skillet. Add the onion and green pepper; cook over low heat for 3 minutes. Stir the eggs, tomato soup, and salt in a bowl until well blended. Pour into the skillet; cook until they are thick and creamy.

Eggs Scandinavian

Yield: 6 to 8 servings

6 eggs
3 tablespoons condensed milk
1 teaspoon salt
Dash of pepper
2 dill pickles, sliced or diced
2 tablespoons chives
2 tablespoons chopped dill
8 ounces Danish cheese, diced
3 tablespoons butter
2 tomatoes
1 extra tablespoon chives for garnish

In a bowl mix eggs with milk, salt, and pepper. Add pickles, chives, dill, and cheese. Heat butter in a large skillet. Add egg mixture; cover. Simmer on low heat 10 minutes.

234

While eggs are cooking, wash, peel, and quarter tomatoes. When egg mixture has set in the middle, place tomatoes on top for decoration. Sprinkle with chives. Serve at once.

Scrambled Eggs with Chicken

Yield: 4 to 6 servings

8 eggs
1 cup diced cooked chicken
1 cup cream or milk
½ teaspoon salt
Dash of pepper
2 tablespoons butter or margarine
2 teaspoons chopped parsley or finely cut chives

Beat eggs slightly. Add chicken, cream, salt, and pepper. Melt butter in medium skillet; add egg mixture. Stir lightly with a large spoon until eggs are firm and set.

Place eggs on a serving plate. Garnish with parsley or chives. Serve at once.

Scrambled Eggs with Sour Cream

Yield: 4 to 6 servings

The sour cream adds a richness that makes these far more than just "plain scrambled eggs."

2 tablespoons butter or margarine
8 to 10 eggs, beaten
½ cup sour cream
1 teaspoon salt
¼ teaspoon freshly ground pepper

Melt butter in large skillet. It should just bubble, not brown.

In a bowl beat eggs until frothy. Add sour cream, salt, and pepper. Blend all together. Pour this mixture into skillet. Scramble mixture until eggs reach desired firmness.

Scrambled Country Corn

Yield: 4 to 6 servings

6 slices lean bacon, diced
1 medium onion, chopped
1 green pepper, chopped
2 cups corn kernels, fresh preferred, but canned may be used
1 large tomato, chopped
6 eggs
1 teaspoon Worcestershire sauce
1 teaspoon salt
Dash of freshly ground pepper

In a deep skillet cook bacon until almost crisp. Pour off excess fat. Add onion, green pepper, corn, and tomato. Sauté until onion is transparent.

Beat eggs and seasonings in a bowl until light and frothy. Stir into the skillet vegetables. Continue to stir until eggs are set. Serve with your favorite pan of sweet rolls.

Scramburger for Brunch

Yield: 4 to 6 servings

1 tablespoon oil
½ pound lean ground beef
1 small onion, finely chopped
8 eggs
½ cup milk
1 teaspoon salt
¼ teaspoon freshly ground black
  pepper

Heat oil in large skillet; brown ground beef and onion together. In a bowl beat eggs, milk, salt, and pepper until light and frothy. Pour this over meat. Do not rush this. Cook it slowly and stir gently until eggs are firm.

Split and toast some bagels or English muffins to go with this.

Cottage-Cheese Scrambled Eggs

Yield: 4 to 6 servings

6 eggs, beaten
¾ cup cottage cheese
2 tablespoons milk
1 tablespoon chopped chives
1 teaspoon dill
½ teaspoon salt
Dash of freshly ground black pepper
2 tablespoons butter or margarine

In mixing bowl beat eggs with a wire whisk or fork. Add cottage cheese, milk, and seasonings. Heat butter in medium skillet, keeping heat low. Add egg mixture. As it cooks, lift edges with a spatula to allow liquid to flow off the top. Do not stir, but continue until eggs are set on top. Turn skillet over to bring eggs out of pan onto the serving plate.

Potato Omelet

Yield: 4 to 6 servings

2 large potatoes, peeled and chopped
  fine
1 medium onion, chopped fine
1 teaspoon salt
5 tablespoons oil
6 eggs, beaten
⅓ cup milk
Parsley for garnish

Cook potatoes and onion with salt in 3 tablespoons oil. Use a medium skillet. Cook about 5 minutes. Remove from heat. Combine eggs and milk in a bowl. Add potato mixture to this.

Heat 2 or more tablespoons oil in same skillet. Pour in egg mixture; reduce heat to low. Omelet will be nearly set in about 10 minutes. Turn and cook until the underside is firm. Garnish with parsley, if desired.

Strawberry Omelet

Yield: 4 to 6 servings

2 cups frozen whole strawberries
1 tablespoon sugar
4 eggs, separated
½ teaspoon salt
1 tablespoon lemon juice
1 tablespoon butter or margarine

Sprinkle strawberries with sugar; let stand for 2 hours to thaw.

Beat egg whites until stiff. Beat egg yolks with salt and lemon juice. Fold this into stiffly beaten egg whites until no yellow streaks remain.

Melt butter in medium skillet that can go into oven. Pour in egg mixture and tilt pan to coat sides. Cook over low heat just 5 minutes. When mixture is set on the bottom, bake at 350°F for 5 minutes more. Lift omelet onto a heated plate and spoon strawberry mixture over it. Cut in pie wedges to serve.

Cinnamon French Toast

Yield: 4 servings

3 eggs, beaten slightly
1 teaspoon sugar
1 teaspoon cinnamon (more, if you prefer)
1 teaspoon salt
1 cup milk
10 slices slightly stale white bread
1 tablespoon butter or margarine

Break eggs into a pie plate; stir in sugar, cinnamon, salt, and milk. Dip each bread slice into this mixture as you are ready to put it in the skillet. Be sure bread absorbs on both sides.

Heat butter in medium skillet. Put in 1 slice of soaked bread. When bottom side is golden, turn it. Remove cooked toast to a warming platter. Serve French toast with your favorite syrup or thick jam.

Hawaiian French Toast

Yield: 4 servings

2 eggs, beaten
1 cup pineapple juice
½ teaspoon salt
8 slices bacon, cooked and set aside
6 to 8 slices bread (day old is better)
Drained pineapple slices

Combine eggs, pineapple juice, and salt. This will be the liquid in which you soak each piece of bread.

Cook bacon crisp in medium skillet, drain it, and set aside, reserving fat.

Soak each piece of bread in the liquid. Fry it quickly on both sides in bacon drippings. Put it on a heated platter. Garnish with bacon strips and a slice of pineapple.

Apple Fritters

Yield: 4 to 6 servings

4 to 6 apples, peeled and cored
Wine to cover

Fritter Batter

2 egg yolks
⅔ cup milk
1 tablespoon lemon juice
1 tablespoon melted butter
1 cup flour
¼ teaspoon salt
2 tablespoons sugar
2 egg whites, beaten stiff

Deep fat for frying

Cut the apples crosswise into ½-inch slices. Each slice will have a hole in the center. Soak the slices in wine for 2 hours.

Combine the fritter batter ingredients in the order given by stirring them with a wooden spoon. Fold in the egg whites last.

Heat the fat in a large skillet. Drain the apple slices, then dip them singly in the fritter batter. Fry them until lightly browned all over. Drain on a paper towel. Serve the fritters piping hot.

Cheese Fritters

Yield: About 20 fritters

If you want these for appetizers, make them smaller. Drop by teaspoons into hot fat.

1 egg, beaten
½ cup milk
1 teaspoon Worcestershire sauce
1 small onion, minced fine
Dash of hot pepper, optional
2 cups biscuit mix
1½ cups diced American cheese
Fat for deep frying
Jelly or jam of your choice

In a bowl mix egg, milk, Worcestershire sauce, onion, pepper, and prepared biscuit mix. Blend well, then stir in the cheese.

Preheat fat in skillet. Drop mixture by tablespoons into hot fat. Fry until golden-brown fritters. Drain on paper towels. Serve with your favorite jelly or jam.

Corn Fritters

Yield: About 12 fritters

2 eggs, separated
2 cups corn cut off the cob
½ teaspoon salt
¼ teaspoon pepper
¼ cup flour
¼ cup or more shortening

Separate egg yolks from whites; beat whites stiff. Put corn in a mixing bowl. Add beaten yolks, salt, pepper, and flour. Mix well with a wooden spoon or rubber spatula. Gently fold in beaten egg whites.

Heat shortening. Drop fritters by spoon-fuls into hot fat. When browned on both sides, drain on paper towels, then put onto a heated platter.

Pineapple Fritters

Yield: 4 to 6 servings

Fritter Batter
2 egg yolks
⅔ cup milk
1 tablespoon lemon juice
1 tablespoon melted butter
1 cup flour
¼ teaspoon salt
2 egg whites, beaten stiff

Deep fat for frying
1 large can pineapple slices, drained
Confectioners' sugar

With a wooden spoon, stir the fritter batter ingredients in the order given. Fold in the egg whites last.

Heat the fat for deep frying in a large skillet. Dip each pineapple ring in the batter, coating it thoroughly. Fry until lightly browned all over. Drain fritters on a paper towel. Sprinkle fritters with confectioners' sugar, if desired. Serve.

Dollar Nut Pancakes

Yield: 16 to 24 pancakes

Make these pancakes small—about the size of a silver dollar. They're a little more trouble to make, but they do add to a brunch spread.

1½ cups flour
2 tablespoons sugar
1 tablespoon baking powder
½ teaspoon salt
1 egg, beaten
1½ cups milk
¼ cup chopped nuts
Fat for frying

Mix ingredients in order given, beating in nuts after all else is smooth. Drop by teaspoons onto hot skillet or griddle. When pancake top is covered with bubbles and edges are firm, turn to brown the other side. Store on a hot platter until ready to bring to the table.

Johnnycake

Yield: 12 4-inch cakes

1 cup yellow or white cornmeal
½ teaspoon salt
2 teaspoons sugar
1 cup water
2 tablespoons butter or margarine
¼ cup milk
Margarine and oil for frying

Put cornmeal, salt, and sugar into a mixing bowl. Heat water and 2 tablespoons butter in a saucepan. Bring to rolling boil. Slowly pour this hot liquid into cornmeal, stirring constantly. When all liquid has been absorbed, add milk. This will be a thick batter.

Heat margarine and oil in skillet— enough to cover entire cooking surface generously. Drop batter by tablespoons into skillet, to form 4-inch cakes. Cook until golden brown, then turn to brown the other side. Serve at once with maple syrup.

Rice Pancakes

Yield: About 6 servings

4 tablespoons butter, melted
3 whole eggs, beaten
2 cups cooked rice

2 teaspoons baking powder
1 teaspoon salt
1 cup flour
¼ cup milk or cream
Shortening for frying

Mix ingredients in order given, adding milk to batter last. Heat shortening in skillet. Drop by tablespoons into hot fat. When golden brown on one side, turn pancake. Add extra shortening if needed. Serve rice pancakes with apricot preserves.

Sourdough Pancakes

Yield: 4 servings

½ cup sourdough starter
1 cup evaporated milk
1 cup warm water
2 cups flour
2 eggs
2 tablespoons sugar
½ teaspoon salt
1 teaspoon soda
2 tablespoons oil

Mix sourdough starter, milk, water, and flour in a bowl. Blend; leave at room temperature overnight.

Next morning, add rest of ingredients (except oil); mix, but do not beat. Use a wooden spoon for this. Heat oil in skillet. Put in enough batter to make pancakes the size you prefer. Turn pancakes, and, when done, place on a warmed platter.

Fried Ham and Potato Cakes

Yield: 4 servings

1 cup mashed potatoes (instant will do)
1 cup finely diced cooked ham
1 tablespoon chopped parsley
½ teaspoon onion salt
¼ teaspoon pepper
Flour
3 tablespoons oil for frying

Mix potatoes, ham, parsley, and seasonings. This mixture will be able to be shaped into flat cakes. Dip each cake into flour, being sure to batter both sides.

Heat oil in skillet. Sauté cakes in oil, adding more oil if needed. When cakes are browned on both sides, set on a warm platter until ready to serve.

Ham and Cheese Divine

Yield: 4 to 6 servings

½ cup chopped cooked ham
2 tablespoons butter or margarine
1 small onion, chopped fine
1 green pepper, diced
1 teaspoon prepared mustard
1 10½-ounce can condensed cheddar-cheese soup
¼ cup beer or sherry (milk, if preferred)
1 cup grated Swiss cheese
Freshly buttered toast

In a medium skillet lightly sauté ham in butter. Add onion and pepper; cook until onion is transparent. Add mustard, soup, and liquid; stir. You will have to stay with this dish. When mixture is smooth and hot, add grated cheese.

Spoon blended mixture over buttered toast.

Rarebit for Brunch

Yield: 4 to 6 servings

2 tablespoons butter or margarine
2 tablespoons flour
¾ cup milk
⅛ teaspoon baking soda
1 1-pound can tomatoes, drained
1½ cups shredded Cheddar cheese
½ teaspoon dry mustard
½ teaspoon salt
6 buttered, toasted English muffins, split open

Melt butter in a medium-sized, heavy skillet. Stir in flour and remove from heat. Gradually add milk to make a smooth, thick paste. Return to low heat.

Mix baking soda with tomatoes; add to skillet. Gradually add remaining ingredients (except muffins), stirring over low heat until all cheese melts. Spoon this mixture over English muffins; serve.

Tomato Rarebit

Yield: 4 servings

1½ cups tomato puree
1 cup diced American cheese
1 beaten egg
½ teaspoon salt
2 teaspoons brown sugar

Use a heavy medium-size iron skillet for this and low heat all the way.

Heat the tomato puree and cheese together until the cheese is melted and mixed. Add the beaten egg; stir until slightly thickened. Last, add salt and brown sugar; stir to blend. Serve the rarebit over hot toast.

Meat

Beef Barbecue

Yield: 4 to 6 servings

1½ pounds lean ground beef
2 tablespoons shortening
1 onion, chopped
1 green pepper, diced
½ cup catsup plus ½ cup water
2 tablespoons brown sugar
1 tablespoon Worcestershire sauce
1 tablespoon prepared mustard
1 teaspoon salt

Sauté ground beef in shortening in medium skillet about 10 minutes or until brown. Remove from skillet. Put onion and green pepper in same shortening, cooking until onion is yellow and soft. Replace ground beef.

Mix together rest of ingredients; add to skillet. Stir to mix; simmer about 10 minutes. Serve over hamburger rolls.

Beef Burgundy

Yield: 4 to 6 servings

4 tablespoons oil
4 or 5 medium onions, sliced
2 pounds lean beef, cut into 1-inch
    cubes
1½ tablespoons flour
½ teaspoon marjoram or thyme (if you
    like both flavors, use ¼ teaspoon of
    each)
1 teaspoon salt
½ teaspoon pepper
½ cup bouillon

1 cup dry red wine
½ pound fresh mushrooms, sliced

Heat oil in large, heavy skillet. Cook onions until transparent. Remove onions; set aside. Sauté beef cubes until brown. Sprinkle browned meat with flour and seasonings. Add bouillon and wine; simmer slowly until meat is tender, about 1½ hours. Add more liquid if needed to keep beef covered (1 part bouillon to 2 parts wine).

When meat is tender, add onions and mushrooms; cook about 30 minutes more, stirring occasionally. The sauce will be thick and delicious.

Beef Chinese

Yield: 4 to 6 servings

1 7-ounce package frozen Chinese pea
    pods
3 tablespoons oil
1 pound beef tenderloin tips, sliced
    thin across grain
½ cup chopped onion
1 small garlic clove, minced fine
4 cups sliced raw cauliflower florets
1 cup beef broth
2 tablespoons cornstarch
¼ cup soy sauce
½ cup water

Separate pea pods by pouring boiling water over them. Drain at once.

Heat 2 tablespoons oil in skillet. Add half the beef; brown quickly. Remove cooked beef, allow skillet to heat again, and brown rest of meat. Remove from skillet. Add remaining tablespoon of oil; sauté onion and garlic 1 minute. Add cauliflower and beef broth. Cook just 3 minutes.

Mix cornstarch, soy sauce, and water; stir into skillet. Add beef and pea pods; stir until sauce thickens. Serve at once over rice.

Beef and Pepper Rice Skillet

Yield: 4 to 6 servings

1 pound ground beef
2 green peppers, chopped
1 cup sliced onion
1 cup uncooked rice
1 10½-ounce can beef broth
1 10½-can water
1 tablespoon soy sauce

Brown the beef in medium skillet. Stir in peppers, onion, rice, liquids, and soy sauce. Allow mixture to come to a boil. Reduce heat, stir once, and cover. Simmer about 25 minutes. Serve at once.

Beef Round Over Noodles

Yield: 4 to 6 servings

2 tablespoons shortening
1 teaspoon soy sauce
½ teaspoon sugar
2 teaspoons sherry
3 cups thinly sliced onions
2 teaspoons cornstarch
1 tablespoon soy sauce
1½ pounds beef round, cut into 1-inch pieces
1 tablespoon Worcestershire sauce
1 teaspoon garlic salt
1 can mushrooms, optional

Heat shortening in large skillet with 1 teaspoon soy sauce, sugar, and 1 teaspoon sherry. Sauté onions in this.

Mix cornstarch, 1 tablespoon soy sauce and 1 teaspoon sherry in a bowl. Dredge meat in this mixture, coating every piece. Put dredged meat in onion mixture; brown it. Stir in Worcestershire sauce and garlic salt. Cover skillet; let simmer for 1 hour. This meat draws its own gravy, but you may want to stir occasionally while it cooks.

Serve on a bed of noodles and enjoy.

Beef in Sour Cream

Yield: 4 to 6 servings

2 pounds beef round, cut into 1-inch pieces
2 tablespoons lemon juice
2 tablespoons flour
2 tablespoons butter or margarine
1 tablespoon oil
1 large onion, sliced thin
1 clove garlic, minced
1½ cups beef broth
1 teaspoon salt
Dash of pepper
1 package frozen peas, thawed
1 cup sour cream
2 tomatoes, diced

Sprinkle meat with lemon juice, then flour. Allow to stand for 10 minutes.

Heat butter and oil in large skillet; brown the meat. Add onion, garlic, beef broth, salt, and pepper; cover. Cook over low heat 1 hour or until meat is fork-tender. This may be done in the morning and reheated at mealtime.

Just before serving, add thawed peas, sour cream, and tomatoes. Allow this to get hot over low heat, then serve at once. Noodles go well with this.

Sweet-and-Sour Beef

Yield: 6 to 8 servings

1 tablespoon shortening
2 pounds cubed lean stewing beef
½ teaspoon salt
2 cups canned tomatoes
⅓ cup brown sugar
⅓ cup vinegar
½ cup finely chopped onion
½ bay leaf
1 green pepper, cut into thin strips

Melt shortening in large skillet; brown beef on all sides. Add salt, tomatoes, brown sugar, vinegar, onion, and bay leaf. Cover skillet; lower heat. Allow to simmer about 2 hours or until beef is tender.

Last, add pepper strips to beef; cook for 10 minutes more to blend all flavors. Serve over hot rice or with noodles.

Camper's Chili

Yield: 4 to 6 servings

Because this is a one-pot dish, it works well when camping out, and it tastes good, too.

1 tablespoon shortening
1 pound lean ground beef
1 large onion, chopped
1 green pepper, chopped
1 tablespoon chili powder
1 can tomato soup
2 cans red kidney beans, undrained

Heat shortening in medium skillet. Brown the ground beef with onion and green pepper. When all meat is browned, add chili powder, tomato soup, and kidney beans. Simmer for 10 to 15 minutes. stirring occasionally.

Serve on hamburger buns.

Hungarian Goulash

Yield: 4 to 6 servings

2 pounds lean stewing beef, cut into
    1-inch cubes
5 tablespoons flour
1 tablespoon fat or bacon drippings
2½ cups tomato juice
1 small onion, diced
1 tablespoon Worcestershire sauce
2 teaspoons salt
1 teaspoon paprika
¼ teaspoon pepper
½ cup sour cream

Dredge meat cubes generously with flour. Melt fat in large skillet. Brown meat on all sides. Add tomato juice, onion, and seasonings. Bring to a boil, then reduce heat. Cover skillet; simmer for 1 hour or until meat is tender.

When ready to serve, stir in sour cream; simmer just 2 minutes. Hot broad noodles go well with this goulash.

Gingersnap Meatballs

Yield: 4 to 6 servings

1 pound lean ground beef
¾ cup bread crumbs
1 medium onion, minced fine
2 teaspoons salt
¼ teaspoon black pepper
6 tablespoons lemon juice
2 tablespoons water
4 tablespoons margarine or shortening
2½ cups beef broth
½ cup brown sugar
¾ cup gingersnap crumbs

Mix ground meat, bread crumbs, onion, salt, pepper, 3 tablespoons lemon juice, and water in a bowl. Mix well; form into 1-inch balls. Heat shortening in medium skillet; brown the meatballs. Remove balls from pan.

Add beef broth and 3 tablespoons lemon juice to pan drippings. Bring to a boil, then add brown sugar and gingersnap crumbs. Add meatballs to this sauce and cook, covered, for 10 minutes. Stir once; allow to simmer uncovered 5 more minutes. This goes well with noodles.

Meatballs Special

Yield: 6 or more servings

1 pound veal
1 pound pork
¼ cup flour
1 tablespoon salt
½ teaspoon white pepper
4 eggs
½ cup light cream
1 cup milk
1 medium onion, chopped
1 tablespoon butter or shortening
Extra shortening if needed

Grind veal and pork together several times. Put in a large bowl. With your electric beater at low speed, add flour, salt, and pepper. Add eggs one at a time, still at low speed. Add cream and milk.

In large skillet brown onion in 1 tablespoon butter just 5 minutes. Add this mixture to meat. Mix enough so that meat can be easily handled. Shape meat into oval cakes; brown on both sides, adding extra shortening if needed. Cook over low heat 15 minutes. Because pork is included, these meatballs must be thoroughly cooked.

Meat Patties

Yield: 8 to 10 patties

½ pound boneless veal
½ pound boneless pork
1 medium onion, grated
3 tablespoons flour
1½ cups club soda
1 egg
1 teaspoon salt
¼ teaspoon pepper
6 tablespoons butter or vegetable oil

Have butcher grind meats together twice. Grate onion; mix with meat. Add flour; mix well. An electric beater can be used. Gradually add club soda; beat until meat is light. Last, add beaten egg, salt, and pepper. Cover bowl; refrigerate at least 1 hour, so that meat can be handled easily. Shape meat into 4-inch rectangles, 1 inch thick.

Melt butter in large skillet; add meat patties a few at a time. Cook each batch at least 6 to 8 minutes per side. Since pork is in the mixture, meat must be cooked all the way through. The finished patties will be brown on the outside with no tinge of pink in the center.

Pan-Fried Liver and Peppers

Yield: 4 servings

2 tablespoons butter or margarine
3 large green peppers, cut in ½-inch
  strips
4 slices calves' liver, ½ inch thick
2 tablespoons flour
1 teaspoon salt
1 teaspoon paprika
1 teaspoon lemon juice
Green pepper strips for garnish

Heat butter in large skillet. Cook pepper strips until tender, about 10 minutes. Remove peppers from skillet to platter to keep them warm.

Mix flour, salt, and paprika on waxed paper. Coat each liver slice with this mixture. Place floured liver slices in same skillet, adding more butter if needed. Cook until crisp and brown on the outside—2 to 4 minutes per side.

Sprinkle cooked liver with lemon juice. Serve surrounded by pepper strips.

Round Steak in Beer

Yield: 4 to 6 servings

1½ pounds round steak, cut in 1-inch
  cubes
4 tablespoons butter or margarine
½ cup minced chives or chopped
  onion
1 bay leaf
½ teaspoon thyme
1 teaspoon salt
Pepper to taste
2 cups beer

1 tablespoon cornstarch
¼ cup water

Brown steak cubes in heated butter in medium skillet. Add chives, spices, and beer. Cover; cook over medium heat 1 hour or until meat is tender. Add extra seasonings, if desired.

Mix cornstarch with water to form a paste; add to skillet. Stir until gravy thickens slightly, then serve.

Pepper Steak

Yield: 4 to 6 servings

1½ pounds boneless steak, cut into
  thin strips
½ cup chopped onions
3 tablespoons salad oil
2 cups beef bouillon
1 can water chestnuts, sliced
1 can mushrooms
2 green peppers, sliced
1 can pineapple tidbits, optional
2 tablespoons cornstarch
2 tablespoons soy sauce
½ cup water
Salt and pepper to taste

Brown the meat and onions in hot oil in large skillet. Gradually stir in bouillon; simmer until meat is tender. Add water chestnuts, mushrooms, and peppers. If using pineapple, drain and add it, too. Simmer for 5 minutes.

Blend cornstarch with soy sauce and water. Add to meat; stir constantly until slightly thickened. Season with salt and pepper. This is especially good served on a bed of hot rice.

Swiss Steak in Sour Cream

Yield: 4 servings

1½- to 2-pound round steak, 1 inch
thick
¼ cup flour
1 teaspoon salt
¼ teaspoon pepper
2 tablespoons oil
2 medium onions, sliced
½ cup water
½ cup sour cream
2 tablespoons grated cheese
Paprika to taste

Dredge round steak on both sides with flour seasoned with salt and pepper.

Heat oil in large skillet. Brown the steak well. Add remaining ingredients; cover skillet. Simmer for 1 hour or until meat is tender to the fork.

Apricot Veal Birds

Yield: 4 to 6 servings

½ cup chopped dried apricots
¼ cup chopped celery
½ cup soft bread crumbs
1 teaspoon sugar
12 thin veal scallops
¼ cup oil
2 teaspoons salt
Dash of pepper
1 cup water

Combine apricots, celery, crumbs, and sugar in a bowl. This is your stuffing for the veal. Place 1 tablespoon stuffing on each veal slice. Roll up each slice and secure it with a wooden toothpick.

Heat oil in large skillet. Sauté veal birds until well-browned on all sides. Season meat with salt and pepper. Add water; cover skillet. Simmer for 30 minutes, until tender to the fork. Remove skewers before serving.

Veal with Artichoke Hearts

Yield: 4 to 6 servings

2 cloves garlic
2 tablespoons oil
2 pounds veal round, pounded thin
and cut in bite-size pieces
Salt and pepper to taste
2 cups canned tomatoes
½ cup sherry or dry white wine
¼ teaspoon oregano
2 10-ounce packages frozen artichoke
hearts

Sauté garlic in oil in large skillet. Remove garlic.

Season veal generously with salt and pepper. Brown veal in oil. Add tomatoes, wine, and oregano, mixing well. Last, add artichoke hearts. Cover skillet; simmer for 1 hour. Meat should be tender when served.

Serve this veal with broad noodles and a tossed salad.

Veal and Noodles

Yield: 4 servings

1 tablespoon shortening or oil
1 pound ground veal
1 medium onion, chopped
1 green pepper, chopped
1 can tomato soup
1 cup water
1 cup noodles
2 tablespoons margarine

2 cups creamed corn
½ cup chopped ripe olives
1 cup grated cheese for garnish

Heat oil in medium skillet; brown together the veal, onion, and green pepper. Add soup, water, and noodles; simmer for 5 minutes. Add margarine, corn, and olives; cover. Simmer for 15 minutes or until noodles are tender.

Sprinkle cheese on top of individual servings. Complete the meal with your favorite salad and hot rolls.

Veal Cutlets with Zucchini

Yield: 6 servings

This is good for calorie-counters and those who watch their cholesterol.

6 veal cutlets
2 egg whites, slightly beaten
½ cup bread crumbs
4 tablespoons oil
2 cups canned tomatoes
1½ teaspoons salt
¼ teaspoon oregano
3 medium zucchini, sliced ½ inch thick

Dip cutlets first in egg whites, then in crumbs.

Brown cutlets in heated oil in large skillet. Pour off excess oil. Add tomatoes, salt, and oregano. Cover skillet; simmer for 30 minutes. Last, add zucchini slices; cook, covered, for 20 minutes more.

Sweet-and-Pungent Ham

Yield: 4 to 6 servings

1 green pepper, cut into 1-inch pieces
¼ cup vinegar
¼ cup brown sugar
1 cup water
1 tablespoon molasses
1 fresh tomato, diced
2 tablespoons cornstarch
1 teaspoon salt
¼ teaspoon pepper
1 cup canned pineapple cubes (use pineapple liquid in place of water, if desired)
2 to 3 cups diced cooked ham

Place green pepper, vinegar, sugar, ¾ cup water, and molasses into medium skillet. Stir until this boils. Add tomato pieces.

Mix cornstarch with remaining ¼ cup water; stir into sauce. Cook until mixture thickens. Add seasonings, pineapple cubes, and ham. Heat through, stirring very gently.

Hash in a Hurry

Yield: 4 to 6 servings

1 can condensed mushroom soup
¼ cup milk
1 cup cubed, cooked ham or other leftover meat
2 sliced hard-cooked eggs
Salt and pepper to taste
Triangles of toast

Mix soup and milk in a medium skillet, until well-blended. Add ham, egg slices, and seasonings. Heat this mixture over very low heat until all is blended.

Spoon the mixture over toast triangles. Serve.

Pork Chops with Apples

Yield: 4 servings

1 pound pork chops (cut from a roast)
Salt
Black pepper
2 tablespoons butter
2 onions
2 apples
Parsley

Salt the pork chops; spice them with pepper. Heat butter in a deep skillet; brown the meat. Add enough water so that meat does not stick to skillet. Cover and cook on low heat at least 1 hour.

Peel onions; cut them into rings. Core and peel apples; cut them into eighths. Add onions and apples 10 minutes before end of cooking period. Cook until all ingredients are golden brown.

Remove chops; put them on a serving platter. Pour stock, onions, and apples over meat; garnish with parsley.

Pork Chops in White Wine

Yield: 4 servings

4 lean pork chops, about 1 inch thick
Salt and pepper to taste
1 teaspoon bacon drippings
2 teaspoons flour
½ cup chicken broth
½ cup dry white wine
1 large onion, sliced

Season chops with salt and pepper. In medium skillet sear pork chops slowly on both sides in hot bacon fat. Remove chops from skillet.

Stirring constantly, blend flour into remaining fat in skillet. When very smooth, return chops to skillet with broth and wine. Spread sliced onion over chops. Cover skillet; simmer about 45 minutes.

Stuffed Pork Tenderloin

Yield: 6 servings

1 pork tenderloin
12 prunes, pitted
4 tablespoons butter
1 teaspoon salt
Dash of freshly ground black pepper
½ cup water

With a sharp knife cut a slit in the meat deep enough to insert the prunes. After prunes are inserted, close the opening with skewers, or wrap with twine.

Melt butter in large skillet and brown the meat on all sides. Sprinkle with salt and pepper. Add ½ cup water; cover, and cook slowly 2 hours or until meat is tender. Add more water if needed. Slice and serve.

Thicken juice in the pan slightly if gravy is desired.

Lamb in Grape Sauce

Yield: 4 servings

1½ pounds uncooked lamb, diced
2 tablespoons oil or margarine
½ cup grape jelly or jam
1 teaspoon dry mustard mixed with
    1 teaspoon water
1 teaspoon grated orange peel
1 can prepared beef gravy
1 tablespoon bourbon or brandy,
    optional

248

Sauté lamb in hot oil in medium skillet. Lower heat to simmer. Add grape jelly and mustard. When these are forming a sauce, add remaining ingredients, stirring constantly. Cover; cook over low heat 25 minutes more.

This is delicious served with rice and a salad.

Leftover Lamb Curry

Yield: 4 to 6 servings

1 small chopped onion
1 cup diced celery
1 tablespoon oil
1 tablespoon flour
1 teaspoon curry powder
2 cups beef broth
¼ cup catsup
½ teaspoon salt
2 cups diced cooked lamb
½ cup chopped apple with skin for color

In medium skillet brown onion and celery in oil 3 minutes. With these, mix flour and curry powder, blending until smooth. Add beef broth, catsup, and salt. Let simmer about 1 hour, stirring occasionally.

Last, add cooked lamb and chopped apple; continue to simmer for 20 minutes more. Serve the lamb curry over rice.

Sweet-and-Sour Lamb Chops

Yield: 4 servings

4 lean lamb chops, 1 inch thick (shoulder chops will do)
1 13-ounce can pineapple chunks
¼ cup soy sauce
¼ cup vinegar
½ teaspoon dry mustard
1 tablespoon oil
¼ cup brown sugar
1 teaspoon cornstarch

Put chops in the bowl for the marinade. Drain pineapple chunks; reserve liquid. Combine pineapple liquid with soy sauce, vinegar, and mustard. Pour over chops. Cover; refrigerate at least 4 hours.

Drain chops; reserve liquid. Heat oil in medium skillet; brown chops over medium heat. Add ¼ cup marinade to chops. Cover; simmer chops 30 to 45 minutes, until tender.

Mix sugar, cornstarch, and remaining marinade in a small saucepan. Heat to a boil, stirring constantly. Simmer for 5 minutes more. Add pineapple chunks; heat through. Spoon over chops; serve.

Pan-Fried Lamb Slices

Yield: 8 to 10 servings

1 leg of lamb
2 or 3 medium onions
Butter or vegetable shortening
Salt and pepper to taste

With a sharp knife cut lamb into ½-inch slices.

Peel and slice onions into rings; brown onions in butter in large skillet. Drain onions and set aside to keep warm. In same shortening, fry meat slices; season with salt and pepper.

To serve, arrange meat on a platter. Cover slices with drained onions. Serve with mashed potatoes and a salad.

Poultry

Chicken à la King

Yield: 6 to 8 servings

½ pound mushrooms, sliced
½ cup butter or shortening
½ cup flour
2 cups chicken broth
2 cups light cream
2 egg yolks, beaten
3 cups diced cooked chicken or turkey
½ cup pimiento, cut into strips
1 teaspoon salt
¼ teaspoon pepper

Sauté mushrooms in butter in medium-sized, heavy skillet.

Mix flour with chicken broth; add to skillet. Stir; add cream. Simmer this 5 minutes. Add beaten egg yolks, chicken, and pimiento. Stir until thoroughly hot, but do not let mixture boil. Add salt and pepper.

Spoon over toast or English muffins. Peas always seem to complement Chicken à al King.

Chicken with Almonds

Yield: 4 to 6 servings

3 tablespoons butter or margarine
3 tablespoons flour
1 cup milk
1 cup chicken broth
1 teaspoon salt
½ teaspoon freshly ground black pepper
Leftover sliced chicken (diced can be used)

2 tablespoons sherry
½ cup slivered almonds

Melt butter in medium skillet; blend in flour. Gradually stir in milk and chicken broth. Continue stirring until liquid thickens. Add salt, pepper, and chicken; simmer until hot. Blend in sherry; last, sprinkle with almonds. Save a few to garnish with.

Serve over hot toast squares.

Chow-Mein Chicken

Yield: 4 to 6 servings

The fixings for this take time to do, but the cooking goes quickly. Rice and/or noodles make a fine complement for this dish.

2 cups raw chicken breasts, thinly sliced or julienne
2 tablespoons oil
1 small onion, thinly sliced
1 cup finely diced celery
1 cup sliced water chestnuts
1 5-ounce can bamboo shoots (1 cup)
1 10-ounce package snow pea pods
2 cups chicken broth
2 tablespoons soy sauce
1 teaspoon sugar
2 tablespoons cornstarch
¼ cup cold water
1 teaspoon salt
Slivered almonds for garnish

In a large skillet sauté chicken in oil just 3 minutes, stirring. Add onion and celery; cook uncovered 5 minutes more. Add water chestnuts, bamboo shoots, pea pods, broth, and soy sauce. Cover; cook for 5 minutes.

Blend sugar, cornstarch, and cold water. Pour over chicken; stir until slightly thickened. Add salt. Serve, garnished with nuts if desired.

Chicken Cutlets

Yield: 6 servings

2 tablespoons flour
2 cups chicken stock
3 egg yolks
3 cups diced, cooked chicken
12 mushrooms, finely diced
Salt and pepper to taste
1 whole egg, beaten
Bread or cracker crumbs
1 cup or more of shortening for deep frying

Mix flour with ¼ cup chicken stock in a large skillet. Gradually add rest of heated stock. Stir until thickened. Add beaten egg yolks to sauce. Add chicken, mushrooms, and seasonings. Stir constantly while mixture cooks for 5 minutes. Cool, then chill mixture several hours, so it becomes stiff.

Shape mixture into cutlets. Dip each cutlet into beaten egg, then into crumbs. Chill battered mixture again. Fry cutlets in deep fat until thoroughly browned; serve.

Chicken Delight

Yield: 4 to 6 servings

1 2- to 3-pound frying chicken, cut into serving pieces
Flour seasoned with salt, pepper, and garlic salt
2 tablespoons margarine
2 tablespoons oil

1 small can mandarin oranges with juice
4 tablespoons lemon juice
½ cup orange juice
2 tablespoons honey
2 teaspoons soy sauce
½ teaspoon ginger

Put seasoned flour in a brown paper bag. Shake chicken pieces in the bag to coat with flour mixture. Heat margarine and oil in skillet; brown the chicken pieces.

Drain mandarin oranges, reserving juice. Mix mandarin juice with lemon juice, orange juice, honey, soy sauce, and ginger. Pour this sauce over chicken in skillet. Cover; allow to simmer for 30 minutes. When chicken is tender to the fork, add mandarin oranges; simmer just 5 minutes more.

Honey-Glazed Chicken

Yield: 4 to 6 servings

1 2- to 3-pound chicken, cut into pieces
¼ cup flour
1 teaspoon salt
¼ teaspoon pepper
Fat for frying chicken
1 cup orange juice
1 tablespoon honey
4 tablespoons soy sauce
1 clove garlic, peeled and halved

Dredge chicken in mixture of flour, salt, and pepper. Fry in medium skillet; set aside to keep warm. Remove all but 1 tablespoon of fat from skillet.

Mix orange juice with other ingredients in same skillet. Bring to a boil; let bubble gently until reduced to a glaze, about 20 minutes. Remove garlic pieces. Dip chicken into glaze, coating thoroughly, and serve.

Chicken Hungarian

Yield: 4 to 6 servings

1 2½- to 3-pound frying chicken, cut
    into pieces
5 tablespoons butter or margarine
1 medium onion, sliced in rings
1 tablespoon paprika
½ teaspoon celery salt
½ teaspoon garlic salt
½ cup hot water
1 tablespoon cornstarch
2 tablespoons cold water
½ pint sour cream

Brown the chicken pieces in butter. Add
onion, seasonings, and hot water. Cover;
simmer until chicken is tender, 30 to 45
minutes. Remove chicken pieces; keep them
warm.

Mix cornstarch and water to form a
paste. Stir into liquid left in skillet. Allow to
thicken slightly. Slowly stir in sour cream
until all is piping hot. Return chicken to
pan; serve.

Chicken and Meatballs

Yield: 6 to 8 servings

1 cup chopped celery
2 medium onions, chopped
1 green pepper, chopped
2 tablespoons margarine
1 pound ground beef or veal
1 onion, minced
Salt and pepper to taste
1 frying chicken, cut into serving
    pieces
Salt, pepper, and garlic salt to taste
2 cups water

Sauté celery, 2 chopped onions, and
green pepper in margarine in a large skillet.
Set aside.

Mix ground meat with minced onion and
seasonings to taste. Form into meatballs.
Season chicken pieces liberally.

Place meatballs on vegetables in skillet.
Place chicken on top of meatballs. Add
enough water to cover meatballs only. The
chicken will steam. Cover skillet; cook at
least 1 hour. You may want to simmer this
longer. When chicken is tender, the dish is
done. This can all be prepared in the morning and reheated at mealtime.

Chicken and Shrimp

Yield: 4 to 6 servings

4 ounces dried mushrooms
1 cup water
1 3-pound frying chicken, cut into
    serving pieces
3 tablespoons flour
3 teaspoons salt
½ teaspoon freshly ground black
    pepper
4 tablespoons shortening
⅓ cup port wine
¼ cup chili sauce
½ teaspoon rosemary
½ pound tiny cooked shrimp

Soak mushrooms in water overnight.

Place chicken in paper bag with flour,
salt, and pepper.

Heat shortening in skillet; brown the
chicken pieces. Add wine, chili sauce, rosemary, and mushrooms plus their liquid.
Cover; simmer until chicken is tender, about
1 hour. This can be done ahead.

When ready to serve, reheat chicken,
and add the shrimp. When all is hot, the
dish is ready.

Walnut Chicken

Yield: 4 to 6 servings

¼ cup soy sauce
1 tablespoon dry sherry
½ teaspoon ground ginger
1 pound boneless chicken breasts, cut into 1-inch pieces
4 tablespoons vegetable oil
½ cup sliced green onions
1 clove garlic, cut in half
1 cup coarsely chopped walnuts

Make a marinade of the soy sauce, sherry, and ginger. Add chicken pieces; let stand for ½ hour.

Heat large skillet (wok can be used). Add 2 tablespoons oil. Sauté onions, garlic, and walnuts 2 to 3 minutes. Remove garlic halves. Set aside onion and walnut mixture in a bowl. Heat remaining oil; add chicken pieces with the liquid. Stir this about 5 minutes, then add walnuts and onions; stir together 2 minutes more.

Spoon the chicken mixture over hot rice.

Chicken Breasts in White Wine

Yield: 4 to 6 servings

1½ tablespoons flour
½ teaspoon salt
Dash of pepper
4 chicken breasts, boned and halved
4 tablespoons butter
½ pound mushrooms, thinly sliced
¼ cup chopped onion
¼ cup chopped parsley
1 cup white wine

Combine flour, salt, and pepper. Coat chicken in this mixture. Shake off excess flour; save it. Melt 2 tablespoons butter in large skillet. Brown the chicken; remove it from skillet.

Add remaining butter to skillet; add mushrooms, onion, and parsley. Cook until onion is transparent. Remove from heat. Stir in remaining flour; blend in wine. When all is smooth, return to heat; bring liquid to a boil. Add chicken. Cook 30 minutes more, until chicken is tender. Garnish with extra parsley.

Breast of Chicken and Ham

Yield: 4 to 6 servings

This dish can be made ahead and re-heated in a slow oven before serving.

3 whole raw chicken breasts, boned, skinned, and halved
¼ cup flour
1 teaspoon salt
¼ teaspoon white pepper
3 tablespoons olive oil
3 tablespoons butter or margarine
½ teaspoon dried sage
6 slices ham
½ cup dry white wine

Put chicken between 2 pieces of waxed paper and pound very thin. Dip in mixture of flour, salt, and pepper.

Heat oil and butter in large skillet. Sauté chicken breasts until browned on underside. Turn and sprinkle each breast with sage. Lay a slice of ham on top of each chicken piece. Cook on low heat 5 minutes. Add wine; simmer for 2 minutes more. Serve chicken with pan juices poured over it.

Fried Chicken with Cream Gravy

Yield: 4 to 6 servings

Salt, pepper, and garlic salt
1 cup flour
1 2½- to 3-pound frying chicken, cut
  into serving pieces
Fat for deep frying

Cream Gravy

2 tablespoons cornstarch
¾ cup hot chicken broth
½ cup milk at room temperature
1 teaspoon salt
¼ teaspoon pepper

Mix seasonings with flour; coat each piece of chicken with this.

Heat fat in skillet; fry chicken, a few pieces at a time. Cook about 25 minutes per batch of chicken, so that pieces are crisp and crusty. Drain on paper towels; set on a warmed platter.

Pour off most of fat in skillet, leaving about 2 tablespoons.

Mix cornstarch with chicken broth. Add to hot fat, stirring constantly. Gradually add milk, salt, and pepper. When slightly thickened, gravy is ready.

Put gravy in gravy boat and serve with chicken.

Mock Fried Chicken

Yield: 4 to 6 servings

1 2½-to 3-pound frying chicken, cut
  into serving pieces
1 teaspoon salt
¼ teaspoon pepper
2 large onions, sliced into rings
½ cup water

Put chicken pieces skin-side-down into a large, heavy skillet. Sprinkle chicken with salt and pepper; put onion slices on top. Cover skillet; cook chicken over low heat 30 minutes.

Tilt lid of skillet slightly to allow liquid to evaporate as it continues to cook slowly another 20 minutes. Chicken will be tender and golden. Remove chicken to a heated platter.

Put onions back in open skillet with the water. Stir together for several minutes, until onions darken and absorb the liquid. Spoon this over chicken; serve.

Mustard Fried Chicken

Yield: 4 to 6 servings

This recipe gives a delicious, different taste to fried chicken.

2 or more tablespoons dry mustard
¼ cup water
1 2½- to 3-pound frying chicken, cut
  into serving pieces
Flour seasoned with salt and pepper
Fat or oil for frying
1 can condensed cream of celery soup
1 cup plus 2 tablespoons milk
1 can condensed tomato soup

Mix dry mustard with water to form a thick paste. Spread paste liberally over chicken pieces. Dredge chicken with flour. Heat fat in large skillet; cook chicken on all sides until golden brown. Remove from skillet.

Reduce fat in skillet to about 3 tablespoons. Add celery soup, milk, and tomato soup to skillet; mix well. Replace chicken in this gravy; cover skillet. Simmer for 30 minutes, until chicken is tender.

Groundnut Stew

Yield: 8 to 10 servings

This is an African dish that goes well with rice or mashed yams.

1 2- to 3-pound frying chicken, cut into small pieces
Salt and pepper to taste
1 pound beef cubes, 1-inch size
2 tablespoons oil (peanut oil is good)
1 teaspoon salt
1 cup chopped onions
1 green pepper, chopped
2 large tomatoes, peeled and diced
1½ teaspoons cayenne
2 cups water
1½ cups peanut butter

Season chicken with salt and pepper; set aside.

Brown the beef cubes in hot oil in large skillet. Add salt, ½ of the onions, ½ of the pepper and tomatoes, cayenne, and water. Simmer this gently 30 minutes.

Mix 1 cup cooking liquid with peanut butter to make a smooth paste. Add to skillet; cook for 15 minutes more. Add chicken pieces and remainder of vegetables. Simmer for 30 minutes more, until all is tender.

Chicken Livers with Beer

Yield: 4 to 6 servings

¼ pound butter or margarine
1 medium onion, chopped fine
¼ teaspoon garlic powder
1½ pounds chicken livers
1 tablespoon flour
½ cup beer
3 cups cooked rice

Melt butter in medium skillet; cook onion until transparent. Add garlic powder and chicken livers; cook until livers are browned on all sides.

Mix flour with 1 tablespoon beer; add to livers. Stirring constantly, add rest of beer until sauce thickens and livers are done through, about 5 minutes.

Put hot cooked rice in center of platter and mound the chicken livers around it.

Chicken Livers with Sage

Yield: 4 to 6 servings

1 pound chicken livers, halved
1 teaspoon salt
¼ teaspoon pepper
1 tablespoon dried sage
4 tablespoons butter or margarine
2 slices raw bacon, diced fine
¼ cup dry white wine

Season chicken livers with salt, pepper, and sage. Heat butter and bacon together in medium skillet. Add chicken livers; cook for 5 minutes, until browned. Stir in the wine; allow to simmer 2 minutes more.

Spoon chicken livers and sauce over spaghetti.

Chicken Livers on Toast

Yield: 4 servings

1 can mushroom gravy
2 tablespoons sherry
½ cup flour
½ teaspoon dried dillweed
1 pound chicken livers
1 egg, beaten
4 or more tablespoons butter or
    margarine

Mix mushroom gravy and sherry in a saucepan; bring to a boil. Lower heat; simmer for 5 minutes.

Combine flour and dillweed for batter. Put each chicken liver first into beaten egg, then into flour. Be sure to coat all sides of livers well.

Melt butter in medium skillet. Add chicken livers; cook over moderate heat 10 minutes or until livers are golden brown. Serve on toast squares with hot gravy.

Turkey Sukiyaki

Yield: 4 to 6 servings

3 tablespoons oil
1 cup diced green pepper
1 cup celery, sliced on the diagonal
1 cup green onions, diced with tops
2 cups cooked, diced turkey
¼ cup soy sauce

Heat oil in medium skillet; add vegetables. Cook, stirring, over medium heat 5 minutes or until vegetables are tender but not mushy. Add turkey and soy sauce; stir until mixed and heated through.

Serve over piping-hot rice.

Twice-Turkey Treat

Yield: 4 to 6 servings

This is a quick-and-easy way to use leftover turkey after any holiday. Delicious served over rice, open hamburger rolls, or toast.

3 cups cooked diced turkey
½ pound mushrooms, sliced
½ cup chopped onion
1 tablespoon oil or margarine
3 tablespoons cornstarch
1 cup chicken stock
½ teaspoon salt
1½ teaspoons curry powder
1 cup finely chopped apple
¼ cup chopped parsley
¾ cup skim milk

In medium skillet gently sauté turkey, mushrooms, and onion in oil until onion is transparent.

Mix cornstarch with chicken stock; add to skillet. Add salt, curry powder, chopped apple, and parsley. Add skim milk last. (If diet is no problem, use whole milk or cream.) Stir as you simmer for 3 minutes. The apples will be crisp and tender.

Seafood

Fish Cakes

Yield: 4 to 6 servings

1 egg
1 tablespoon lemon juice
1 onion, minced fine
2 tablespoons prepared mustard

½ teaspoon salt
¼ teaspoon pepper
1 teaspoon parsley flakes
1 pound cooked fish, boned and flaked
¼ cup cornflake crumbs (at least)
Fat for deep frying

Mix egg, lemon juice, onion, and seasonings in a bowl. Toss with flaked fish. Add enough cornflake crumbs to allow you to shape fish cakes easily. Roll each cake in extra crumbs to coat the outside.

Heat fat in medium skillet; fry cakes until crisp and brown on the outside. Drain on paper towels, then place on a heated platter.

Fillets in Creole Sauce

Yield: 4 to 6 servings

1 medium onion, chopped
½ cup celery, chopped
1 tablespoon butter or margarine
1 8-ounce can tomato sauce
½ teaspoon salt
½ teaspoon curry powder
Dash of freshly ground black pepper
1 cup chopped green pepper
2 pounds frozen fish fillets of your
    choice

Sauté onion and celery in butter in a large skillet. Add rest of ingredients except fish. Simmer mixture while you cut fish blocks in thirds, giving you 6 pieces. Put fish blocks in skillet side by side. Do not pile them on each other. Bring to a boil, then reduce to a simmer. Cook about 15 minutes or until fish flakes easily.

Florida Fish Fillets

Yield: 4 servings

¼ cup flour
1 teaspoon dillweed
1 teaspoon salt
4 small fish fillets, skinned
4 tablespoons butter or margarine
Grapefruit and/or orange rings

Mix flour and seasonings; use to batter fillets. Heat butter in medium skillet; sauté fillets until golden brown on both sides. Remove from skillet to a hot platter.

Put grapefruit slices or orange rings on top of each fillet. Pour pan gravy over all. Serve at once.

Fillets of Sole

Yield: 4 to 6 servings

2 pounds fish fillets
½ cup or more milk
¼ cup or more flour
1 teaspoon salt
3 teaspoons dillweed
8 tablespoons butter
Blanched toasted almonds for garnish
Lemon slices

Dip the fillets in milk, then dust them with flour. Sprinkle them generously with salt and dillweed. Melt 4 tablespoons butter in a medium-size skillet. Sauté the fillets, turning them once. When done, remove to a serving platter.

Add the remaining butter to the skillet; allow it to brown. Pour this over the fillets; sprinkle the almonds on top. Use lemon slices for garnish around the platter.

Fish Fillets India

Yield: 4 servings

½ cup flour
2 teaspoons curry powder
¼ teaspoon salt
1 pound fresh or frozen fillets (your
 choice of favorite fish)
½ cup margarine
½ cup chopped blanched almonds
Chutney

Mix flour, curry powder, and salt well. Thoroughly coat each piece of fish with this mixture. Heat margarine in a large skillet. Brown the fish over moderate heat, about 4 minutes per side. When fish flakes easily, it is done through. Remove fillets; put them on a heated serving dish.

Add almonds to shortening left in skillet; stir until nuts are browned. Pour over fish. Serve the chutney as a relish.

Butterfish in Sour Cream

Yield: 4 to 6 servings

2 pounds butterfish
Salt and pepper to taste
½ teaspoon salt
¾ cup flour
1 egg, beaten
½ cup milk
1 tablespoon melted butter or
 margarine
Fat for deep frying
1 cup sour cream
1 tablespoon chopped parsley
1 tablespoon minced green onion
1 tablespoon lemon juice

Season fish with salt and pepper. In a bowl mix ½ teaspoon salt, flour, egg, milk,

and melted butter to form a batter. Dip fish in this to coat it thoroughly. In large skillet fry fish in hot, deep fat until golden brown all over. Drain fish and set on hot platter.

In a saucepan combine sour cream, parsley, onion, and lemon juice until just hot. Serve over the fried fish.

Coddies

Yield: 4 to 6 servings

Coddies are popular served on saltine crackers with plenty of mustard.

3 medium potatoes, cooked and
 mashed
¼ pound butter or margarine
3 eggs, beaten
1 medium onion, chopped fine
1 teaspoon salt
¼ teaspoon pepper
1 tablespoon chopped parsley
3 15-ounce cans codfish
Fat for deep frying

Mash potatoes smooth; add butter while potatoes are still hot. Add beaten eggs, onion, salt, pepper, parsley, and codfish. Mix well; let stand at least 1 hour.

Shape coddies into 2-inch cakes. Heat fat in medium-size skillet. Fry coddies until brown and crisp. Drain on paper towels.

Flounder with Shrimp

Yield: 4 servings

Salt
4 fillets of flounder
Flour
2 eggs
2 tablespoons water

Bread crumbs
8 tablespoons butter
½ pound small cooked shrimp
Lemon wedges

Salt fillets lightly; dip in flour, being sure to shake off excess. Beat eggs together with water. Put bread crumbs on wax paper. Batter fish by dipping each fillet first in egg mixture, then in bread crumbs, coating each side thoroughly. Set aside battered fish at least 10 minutes.

Heat 4 tablespoons butter in a medium skillet. Sauté fillets 3 to 4 minutes. Keep them warm while preparing shrimp.

Melt 4 tablespoons butter in a separate skillet. Toss shrimp in butter so that each shrimp becomes coated with butter. Place shrimp down the center of each fillet; pour browned butter over fillets. Garnish with lemon wedges; serve.

Sherry Delight

Yield: 4 servings

1½ pounds haddock fish fillets
¼ cup flour
¼ cup oil
½ teaspoon ginger
¼ teaspoon garlic powder
1 tablespoon soy sauce
1 tablespoon sherry
Water
½ teaspoon freshly ground black
    pepper
¼ cup chives or ends of spring onions
1 tablespoon parsley
2 medium-size tomatoes, chopped
1 teaspoon cornstarch
Salt to taste
½ cup water or sherry

Coat fillets with flour. Heat oil in skillet; brown fish on both sides.

Combine sugar, ginger, garlic, soy sauce, sherry, and water to make 1 cup. Pour over fish. Cover skillet; simmer for 10 minutes. Add black pepper, chives, parsley, and tomatoes. Cook uncovered for 5 minutes.

Mix together cornstarch, salt, and ½ cup water or sherry. Blend well; add to fish. Simmer uncovered 5 minutes more. Sauce will thicken slightly and smell heavenly.

Haddock Potato Cakes

Yield: 4 to 6 servings

4 medium potatoes, cooked and
    mashed
1 pound haddock fillets, cooked and
    flaked
1 egg, beaten
2 tablespoons minced onion
1 teaspoon seafood seasoning
¼ cup flour
Fat for deep frying

Mix together potatoes, fish, egg, onion, and seafood seasoning. Form into flat cakes; batter each one in flour. Heat fat in skillet; drop cakes into fat. When fish cakes are browned on both sides, drain on paper towels.

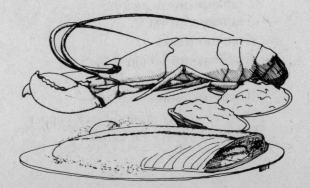

Salmon Croquettes

Yield: About 12 croquettes

2 cups canned salmon, drained
2 cups mashed potatoes
1½ teaspoons salt
⅛ teaspoon pepper
1 beaten egg
1 tablespoon chopped parsley
1 teaspoon lemon juice
Flour
Seasoned bread crumbs
Fat for deep frying

Mix together in a large bowl the salmon, potatoes, salt, pepper, beaten egg, parsley, and lemon juice. This should be a fairly dry mixture that can be easily shaped into croquettes. (Refrigerate it for an hour before shaping.)

When croquettes are ready to be fried, roll them first in flour, then in seasoned bread crumbs. Heat fat in skillet. Put in a few croquettes, so they will have room to brown evenly on all sides. Cook about 3 minutes each. Drain on paper towels; keep them warm on a heated platter until finished cooking all.

Salmon Steaks with Dill

Yield: 4 servings

2 tablespoons margarine
2 tablespoons oil
4 salmon steaks
4 tablespoons lemon juice
1 tablespoon dillweed
1 teaspoon salt
Dash of freshly ground black pepper
Chopped parsley for garnish

Heat margarine and oil in skillet. Put salmon steaks into hot fat.

Mix lemon juice, dillweed, salt, and pepper. Sprinkle half the liquid over steaks. Cover skillet; cook for 5 minutes. Turn salmon steaks; sprinkle with remaining liquid. Cover again; cook for 5 minutes more. Remove steaks to warm platter.

Add parsley to juices in skillet; pour over steaks. Serve at once.

Fried Smelts

Yield: 4 to 6 servings

Smelts are special because they are small fish with a very sweet flavor.

2 pounds smelts, heads off, cleaned, and washed
2 eggs, beaten
2 tablespoons milk
1 teaspoon salt
¼ teaspoon pepper
½ cup flour
½ cup dried bread crumbs or cracker crumbs
Fat for frying

Drain smelts as dry as possible on paper towels. Mix eggs, milk, and seasonings in a bowl. Mix flour and bread crumbs together on a large piece of wax paper. Dip each smelt in the liquid and then in crumbs.

Heat fat in skillet. Add smelts, cooking them until crisp and brown. If deep fat is used, cook about 10 minutes. If you prefer less fat, cook about 5 minutes per side. Drain on paper towels and serve.

Fisherman's Trout

Yield: 4 servings

4 (approximately 8-inch) brook trout
Flour seasoned with lemon pepper
¼ cup butter or margarine
3 tablespoons more butter or margarine
Lemon wedges

Clean and wash the trout, cutting off the fins. Leave head and tail on or not, as desired. Dip the cleaned trout in seasoned flour. Melt ¼ cup of butter in a large skillet; sauté the trout until they are tender and browned on both sides. Remove to a hot platter.

Add the remaining 3 tablespoons of butter to the skillet; allow it to brown. Pour this over the fish. Serve the fish with lemon wedges.

Mandarin Tuna

Yield: 4 to 6 servings

4 tablespoons oil
1 large clove garlic, minced
1 cup celery strips, cut on the diagonal
1 large onion, diced coarsely
1 green pepper, cut in strips
2 tablespoons cornstarch
1 cup water
1 tablespoon soy sauce
1 teaspoon salt
1 13-ounce can tuna, drained and flaked
½ cup sautéed almonds, optional

Heat oil in medium skillet; add garlic, celery, onion, and green pepper. Stir until slightly tender but still crisp.

Blend cornstarch with 2 tablespoons water. Add remaining water and soy sauce to skillet. Stir in cornstarch mixture. Add salt and tuna, continuing to stir gently until sauce thickens slightly. Serve with rice garnished with almonds.

Seafood Scampi

Yield: 6 to 8 servings

12 tablespoons margarine
6 cloves garlic, crushed
1 teaspoon salt
1½ pounds shrimp, cleaned and deveined
1½ pounds raw fish, your choice, cut in chunks
4 spring onions, chopped
½ cup chopped parsley

Melt margarine in large skillet. Add garlic and salt, then add seafood; cook for 5 minutes, stirring constantly. When shrimp is pink and fish flakes tender, add spring onions and parsley. Cook for 3 minutes more.

Add a Chinese touch to the scampi by serving over Chinese noodles.

Seafood Linguine

Yield: 4 to 6 servings

¼ pound butter or margarine
2 cans minced clams, drained
1 clove garlic, minced fine
1 teaspoon salt
¼ teaspoon pepper
½ pound shrimp, cooked and deveined
2 teaspoons lemon juice
1 pound linguine, cooked

Melt butter in medium skillet. Add all ingredients (except linguine) in order given. Cook on low heat 15 minutes, stirring occasionally. Pour over linguine; serve.

Seafood Newburg

Yield: 6 to 8 servings

4 tablespoons butter or margarine
4 cups fresh or frozen uncooked seafood
  (lobster, shrimp, crab meat, or
  fish fillets, all in 1-inch pieces)
3 tablespoons lemon juice
1 tablespoon flour
1 teaspoon salt
½ teaspoon paprika
⅛ teaspoon cayenne pepper
2 cups light cream
3 egg yolks
2 tablespoons sherry
6 cups hot cooked rice
Parsley for garnish

Melt butter in large skillet. Sauté seafood about 5 minutes, stirring constantly. Sprinkle with lemon juice. Mix flour, salt, paprika, and pepper; add to seafood. Remove from heat. Gradually stir in 1½ cups of cream. Return to heat until sauce comes to simmer.

Combine egg yolks with remaining ½ cup cream; blend ¼ cup hot liquid mixture with this. Return this to skillet: stir until slightly thickened. Add sherry last, and liberally if you prefer.

Serve over rice, garnished with parsley.

Clam Cakes

Yield: 4 servings

3 medium potatoes, cooked and
  mashed
1 8-ounce can minced clams
1 medium onion, chopped
1 teaspoon chopped parsley
1 egg, beaten
½ cup flour
1 teaspoon salt
Dash of pepper
Oil for deep frying

To the dry mashed potatoes add clams with their juice, onion, and parsley. Mix together, then add egg, flour, and seasonings. This will be a fairly liquid mixture.

Heat oil for deep frying in skillet. If preferred, use half liquid shortening and half butter or margarine. Drop potato and clam mixture by spoonfuls into hot fat. Fry until crisp and brown on all sides. Drain on paper towels.

Serve with your favorite slaw.

Clam Sauce Supreme

Yield: 4 to 6 servings

2 tablespoons butter or margarine
1 tablespoon flour
1 teaspoon garlic salt
2 8-ounce cans minced clams with
  liquid
1 teaspoon parsley
1 teaspoon salt
½ teaspoon pepper
Cooked thin spaghetti

In medium skillet melt butter on low heat. Stir in flour and garlic salt, using a wire whisk. Add juice from canned clams; continue to stir. Add seasonings and, last, the clams. Simmer this 10 minutes. Pour over cooked thin spaghetti.

Crab Bisque

Yield: 4 to 6 servings

1 medium onion, diced
½ green pepper, diced
2 tablespoons butter or margarine

¼ pound mushrooms, sliced
2 tomatoes, diced
1 pound crab meat
1 teaspoon salt
Dash of cayenne
1½ cups cream
1 tablespoon minced parsley

In medium skillet sauté onion and green pepper in melted butter until onion is transparent. Add mushrooms; cook for 3 minutes more. Stir in tomatoes; cook again 3 minutes. Add remaining ingredients; heat mixture to a boil, but do not boil.

Add more parsley for garnish if desired. Serve over rice.

Crab Cakes

Yield: 4 to 6 servings

1 pound crab meat
1 egg yolk
1½ teaspoons salt
Healthy dash of black pepper
1 teaspoon dry mustard
2 teaspoons Worcestershire sauce
1 tablespoon mayonnaise
1 tablespoon chopped parsley
½ teaspoon paprika
1 tablespoon melted butter
Bread crumbs for coating cakes
Liquid shortening for frying

Lightly toss crab meat and all ingredients (except bread crumbs) in order listed. When well-blended, shape into cakes. Roll each cake in bread crumbs until coated on all sides. Heat shortening in skillet. Fry crab cakes quickly in hot fat until golden brown.

Fisherman's Crab Meat

Yield: 4 to 6 servings

½ cup vinegar
6 tablespoons melted butter
1 tablespoon chopped chives
2 teaspoons Worcestershire sauce
1 pound fresh lump crab meat

Heat vinegar, butter, chives, and Worcestershire sauce in medium skillet. Add crab meat; simmer until hot, stirring gently to blend flavors.

Soft-Shelled Crabs

Yield: 4 to 6 servings

4 tablespoons butter or margarine
2 tablespoons lemon juice
6 to 8 soft-shelled crabs, cleaned
1 tablespoon cornstarch or flour
¼ cup water

Heat butter and lemon juice in medium skillet. On medium heat, cook crabs until browned, 5 minutes per side. Remove crabs to a heated platter.

Mix cornstarch and water. Add to pan juices; stir until slightly thickened. Pour sauce over crabs. Serve at once.

Oysters Baltimore

Yield: 4 to 6 servings

4 slices bacon
18 oysters
3 tablespoons chili sauce
1 tablespoon Worcestershire sauce
6 tablespoons heavy cream
½ teaspoon tarragon
2 tablespoons lemon juice
1 teaspoon salt
¼ teaspoon pepper

In medium-size skillet fry bacon until crisp. Set bacon aside to drain, then crumble into bits for garnish. Pour off all but 1 tablespoon fat from skillet. Add oysters with their liquid. Cook uncovered over medium heat until most of pan juices are absorbed.

Mix remaining ingredients; add to oysters. Simmer no more than 5 minutes to blend all flavors. Add extra seasonings if desired.

These oysters are delicious served over hot buttered toast. Garnish with crumbled bacon.

Fried Scallops with Dill

Yield: 4 to 6 servings

1 pound scallops
1 egg with 2 tablespoons water
2 teaspoons dillweed
Seasoned bread crumbs
Deep fat for frying

Wash scallops quickly; dry them between paper towels. Beat the egg, water, and dillweed together. Dip each scallop in the egg mixture, then in bread crumbs. Repeat this process once, then let scallops stand for 30 minutes.

Heat fat for frying in a medium-size skillet. Fry each scallop for 3 or 4 minutes. Drain and serve.

Dill Scallops in Lemon Butter

Yield: 4 to 6 servings

1½ pounds scallops
½ cup dry bread crumbs
8 tablespoons butter or margarine
¼ teaspoon salt
Dash of pepper
Dash of paprika
1 tablespoon chopped parsley
2 teaspoons dillweed
3 tablespoons lemon juice

Batter scallops in bread crumbs until well-coated.

Melt 4 tablespoons butter in skillet; add salt, pepper, and paprika. Sauté scallops slowly until evenly browned, about 8 minutes. Remove scallops to a heated platter. Add remaining butter to skillet with parsley, dill, and lemon juice. Stir until hot, then pour over scallops. Serve at once.

Butterfly Shrimp

Yield: 4 to 6 servings

1½ pounds large shrimp, cleaned and deveined, leaving tails on
¾ cup flour
1 teaspoon baking powder
½ teaspoon salt
¾ cup milk
1 egg, beaten
Fat for frying

Cut almost through shrimp lengthwise; spread out to form the butterfly. This is a trick of the knife that gets easier as you go along.

Mix flour, baking powder, and salt with milk and beaten egg. Stir until very smooth. Heat fat in skillet. Batter each shrimp; put into hot fat. Fry until golden brown, about 7 minutes. Drain cooked shrimp on paper towels.

Serve as is or with your favorite sauce.

Skillet Shrimp Gumbo

Yield: 6 servings

⅓ cup oil
2 cups sliced fresh okra or 1 package
   frozen okra, sliced
1 pound shrimp, peeled and deveined
½ cup chopped green onions and tops
3 cloves garlic, minced fine
1½ teaspoons salt
½ teaspoon freshly ground pepper
2 cups water
1 cup canned tomatoes, drained
2 whole bay leaves
6 drops Tabasco sauce
1½ cups cooked rice

Heat oil in a large skillet. Cook okra 10 minutes, stirring occasionally. Add shrimp, onions, garlic, salt, and pepper. Simmer for 5 minutes. Add water, tomatoes, and bay leaves. Cover; simmer for 20 minutes. Remove bay leaves; stir in Tabasco.

Place a liberal scoop of rice in each soup bowl. Fill to the top with gumbo. Serve.

Shrimp Marinara

Yield: 4 to 6 servings

This marinara is equally good using fish, crab, or lobster as its base.

2 pounds shrimp, shelled and deveined
2 tablespoons olive oil
1 medium onion, chopped
2 garlic cloves, crushed fine
1 teaspoon salt
1 tablespoon soft bread crumbs
1 small tomato, chopped
¼ teaspoon oregano
½ cup dry sherry wine
½ cup water

In large skillet sauté shrimp in oil on moderate heat. When lightly browned, add onion, garlic, salt, and bread crumbs. Cook for 2 minutes, stirring to blend. Add tomato and oregano. Simmer for 3 minutes. Last, add sherry and water; simmer for 3 minutes more. Serve hot.

Shrimp in Wine Sauce

Yield: 4 to 6 servings

Serve this over hot rice and mop up the sauce with some good French bread.

2 tablespoons butter or margarine
1 pound cooked shrimp, shelled and
   deveined
1 tablespoon cornstarch
½ teaspoon seafood seasoning
¼ cup dry sherry
2 tablespoons water

Melt butter in medium skillet; sauté shrimp 2 minutes.

Mix cornstarch and seafood seasoning with sherry and water until very smooth. Add to shrimp; stir until sauce is thickened, about 5 minutes.

Sweet-and-Sour Shrimp

Yield: 4 to 6 servings

¼ cup brown sugar
1½ tablespoons cornstarch
½ teaspoon salt
¼ cup vinegar
1 tablespoon soy sauce
½ teaspoon ground ginger
1 20-ounce can pineapple chunks
1 green pepper, diced
1 medium onion, sliced in rings
1 pound shrimp, cleaned, shelled, and
    cooked
4 cups hot cooked rice

Into large skillet put sugar, cornstarch, salt, vinegar, soy sauce, ginger, and liquid from canned pineapple. Stir as you cook liquid until it thickens. Add pineapple, pepper, and onion; cook for 3 minutes. Last, add cooked shrimp. Continue to stir until all is hot.

Serve on a bed of rice.

Vegetables

Dressed-up Green Beans

Yield: 4 to 6 servings

1 cup chicken stock
2 tablespoons chopped onions
¼ cup chopped green pepper
½ teaspoon dillseed
2 9-ounce packages frozen cut green
    beans

Heat chicken stock in medium skillet. Add onions, green pepper, and dillseed.

Cook for 3 minutes to release flavors, then add green beans. Cover; simmer for 10 minutes or just until beans are tender.

Mint Lima Beans

Yield: 4 servings

1 10-ounce package frozen lima beans
¼ cup chopped onion
1 clove garlic, crushed
2 tablespoons margarine
1 cup canned tomatoes
½ teaspoon dried mint leaves

Cook frozen lima beans according to directions on package. Drain; set aside.

In a medium skillet sauté onion and garlic in margarine until tender. Stir in lima beans, tomatoes, and mint leaves. Heat through until piping hot, then serve.

Cabbage with Bacon and Dill

Yield: 4 or more servings

1 small head cabbage
6 slices bacon
1 small onion
½ teaspoon salt
¼ teaspoon pepper
1 teaspoon dillweed

Wash, core, and slice cabbage. Set it aside to drain.

Fry bacon slices until crisp in large skillet; set aside.

Slice onion fine; brown it in bacon fat. Add salt, pepper, and dillweed. Last, gradually add drained cabbage, stirring to blend flavors. Cover skillet; simmer on low heat.

Cook until cabbage is tender, no more than 1 hour. Add water if needed during the cooking.

When cabbage is tender, remove it from pan to serving dish. Garnish with bacon slices.

French-fried Cabbage

Yield: 4 to 6 servings

A bit of trouble for the cook, but sure to be a favorite with the family.

1 medium head cabbage, shredded into about ¼-inch strips
½ cup or more milk
¼ cup or more flour seasoned with lemon pepper and salt
Deep fat for frying

Crisp the cabbage in cold water, then drain and dry it well. Dip it in milk, then in seasoned flour. Heat fat for deep frying in a medium-size skillet. Cook the cabbage in small amounts until lightly browned. Drain it on paper towels.

Red Cabbage and Apples

Yield: 6 to 8 servings

1 medium head red cabbage
4 tablespoons butter or margarine
2 medium onions, chopped
½ teaspoon nutmeg
2 teaspoons salt
½ teaspoon ground black pepper
2 cups water
2 tablespoons cider vinegar
4 firm apples, peeled, cored, and sliced
3 tablespoons fresh lemon juice

Quarter the cabbage, remove hard core, and shred it.

Melt butter in large skillet. Add onions, nutmeg, salt, and pepper. Cook until onions are just golden. Add water and vinegar; gradually add cabbage, stirring as you do. Cover; cook over medium heat for 30 minutes.

Add sliced apples; continue cooking, covered, for no more than 30 minutes. Add extra water if needed. Stir in lemon juice just before serving.

Glazed Carrots

Yield: 4 to 6 servings

10 to 12 small young carrots, washed and trimmed
2 tablespoons margarine
1 tablespoon brown sugar
2 tablespoons honey
2 tablespoons fresh mint or parsley

Cook prepared carrots in small amount of boiling salted water 10 minutes. When tender, drain and set aside.

Melt margarine in medium skillet. Add sugar and honey; when blended, put in carrots. Cook 3 or 4 minutes over low heat, stirring so that each carrot is glazed. Sprinkle with fresh mint; serve.

Sautéed Grated Carrots

Yield: 4 to 6 servings

4 tablespoons melted margarine
3 to 4 cups grated carrots
1 tablespoon lemon juice
1 tablespoon honey or thick corn syrup
½ teaspoon salt
1 tablespoon chopped chives
2 tablespoons white wine, optional

To the melted margarine add grated carrots and rest of ingredients in order given. Stir several times to mix thoroughly. Simmer mixture in covered skillet 10 to 15 minutes.

Carrots and Raisins

Yield: 4 to 6 servings

2 tablespoons butter or margarine
1½ pounds young carrots, scraped and
    cut into ¼-inch slices
⅓ cup water or dry white wine
½ teaspoon ground nutmeg
⅔ cup white raisins
3 teaspoons light brown sugar

Melt butter in medium skillet. Add carrots, water, and nutmeg. Cover; cook over low heat 15 minutes. Stir in raisins and sugar; cook for 5 minutes more or until raisins are plump and carrots are glazed.

Cauliflower Sautéed

Yield: 4 to 6 servings

This makes a party dish out of a common vegetable. The cauliflower should be steamed a day ahead.

2 tablespoons butter or margarine
2 tablespoons salad oil

1 teaspoon garlic salt
1 head cauliflower, broken into florets
1 teaspoon salt
½ teaspoon nutmeg
Chopped chives for garnish

Melt the butter and salad oil in a medium-size skillet. Mix in the garlic salt; sauté the florets for 3 minutes, stirring gently. Season with salt and nutmeg.

Put the cauliflower into a serving bowl; garnish it with chopped chives.

Deep-fried Corn Fritters

Yield: 4 to 6 servings

1 1-pound can whole-kernel corn,
    drained
1 egg
½ teaspoon salt
¼ cup milk
1 cup flour
2 teaspoons baking powder
2 teaspoons melted butter or margarine
½ teaspoon sugar
Deep fat for frying

While allowing corn to drain, mix egg, salt, milk, flour, baking powder, melted butter, and sugar. Stir with a wooden spoon—you don't need a mixer for this. Add drained corn. After corn is mixed in allow to sit for 5 minutes.

Drop mixture by teaspoonfuls into hot fat. Cook until puffy and golden brown, drain on paper, and transfer to a warmed platter.

French-fried Fennel

Yield: 4 servings

1 large head fennel
½ cup flour
1 egg, beaten
½ cup milk
Salt and pepper to taste
Fat for deep frying

Slice white part of fennel into ¼-inch rings. Wash and pat dry. Save some green leaves to garnish the platter.

Mix flour, egg, milk, and seasonings in a bowl. This will be a smooth batter.

Heat oil in medium skillet. While oil is heating, dip pieces of fennel into batter. Then deep fry them just 2 minutes, until crusty and brown. After draining, put them on a heated platter and garnish with green fennel leaves.

Hominy Deluxe

Yield: 4 to 6 servings

½ pound pork sausage
3 cups canned hominy, drained
3 tablespoons chopped onion
1 cup canned tomato soup
½ teaspoon salt
½ cup seasoned bread or cracker
    crumbs

In a medium-size skillet cook the pork sausage until the fat begins to come off it. Add the hominy and onion; cook until all are browned and blended. Add the tomato soup and salt; stir until hot.

To serve this, top the hot hominy with the seasoned bread crumbs. It looks hefty and tastes good, too.

Skillet Lettuce

Yield: 4 servings

1 head lettuce, cored and cut into
    quarters
½ cup beef stock
Salt to taste
Melted butter to pour over the
    finished vegetable

Use a medium-size skillet with a top for this. Put the lettuce and beef stock into the skillet. Cover the skillet; cook lettuce over low heat 6 to 8 minutes. Most of the stock will be absorbed into the lettuce. Salt to taste, then pour melted butter over the lettuce. Serve it hot.

Beer Fried Onion Rings

Yield: 4 to 6 servings

1½ cups flour
1½ cups beer
4 very large onions
Shortening for deep frying

Combine flour and beer in a large bowl, blending thoroughly with a wooden spoon. Cover bowl; keep at room temperature at least 3 hours.

Peel and slice onions into ¼-inch rounds. Divide into individual rings.

In large skillet heat enough shortening to drop in the onion rings. Dip a few onion rings at a time into prepared batter, then into hot oil. Fry until golden brown.

Place fried rings on a cookie sheet lined with paper towels. Keep warm in preheated 200°F oven.

These onion rings can be frozen and reheated in 400°F oven if desired.

Onions and Green Peppers

Yield: 4 servings

3 tablespoons butter or margarine
6 medium-size onions, peeled and
   sliced thin
3 whole green peppers, diced
2 tablespoons beef broth
Salt and pepper to taste

Melt butter in medium skillet; sauté onions about 10 minutes. Add peppers; cook for 5 minutes more. Add beef broth and seasonings; cover. Simmer for 8 minutes more. Serve at once.

A variation of this is to add 2 whole diced tomatoes just before you cover the vegetables.

Caesar's Vegetables

Yield: 4 to 6 servings

Serve this with your favorite steak.

3 to 4 onions, sliced in rings
3 to 4 medium potatoes, diced small
   into ¼-inch squares
¼ cup prepared Caesar's dressing

Prepare vegetables as indicated. Heat the Caesar's dressing in a medium skillet. Add onions and potatoes. Stir over low heat several minutes. When onions are transparent, the dish is done. The potatoes will be crisp and all will have the well-seasoned flavor of the salad dressing.

Potato Balls

Yield: 4 to 6 servings

2 cups mashed potatoes
1 egg with 2 tablespoons water

Crushed cornflakes
Fat for deep frying

Shape the mashed potatoes into ice-cream-scoop balls. Roll each ball in the egg mixture, then in the crushed cornflakes. Heat fat in a medium-size skillet. Fry the balls in the deep fat until nicely browned all over. Put them on a warming platter until all are cooked.

Garlic Potatoes

Yield: 4 to 6 servings

1 medium onion, chopped
1 small garlic clove, crushed
2 tablespoons olive oil
¾ cup chopped parsley
¼ cup chopped pimiento
1 teaspoon salt
Dash of pepper
1 cup chicken soup stock
4 to 6 medium potatoes, pared and
   sliced thin

In medium skillet place chopped onion and crushed garlic in heated olive oil, stirring until soft. Add parsley, pimiento, salt, pepper, and stock. When stock has come to a boil but not boiled, remove from heat.

Put potato slices into broth in layers. Return skillet to heat; bring to a boil. Cover; simmer potatoes 20 minutes or until tender to a fork.

Potato Pancakes with Chives

Yield: 4 servings

2 tablespoons chopped chives
4 medium baked potatoes, grated

2 teaspoons salt
Several twists of freshly ground black
   pepper
1 tablespoon flour
2 tablespoons butter or margarine
2 tablespoons vegetable oil

Chop chives first; set aside.

Peel and grate potatoes coarsely into a large mixing bowl. Potatoes will accumulate potato water. Do not drain. Mix in chopped chives, salt, and pepper. Work as quickly as you can, so that potatoes do not turn brown. Add flour, mixing well.

Melt shortening in a large skillet. Drop potato mixture by spoonfuls into hot fat. The 3-inch pancakes will take about 3 minutes a side to become crisp and golden. Serve piping hot.

Party Sweet Potatoes

Yield: 4 to 6 servings

About 2 cups mashed sweet potatoes
2 tablespoons melted butter
½ teaspoon salt
¼ teaspoon nutmeg
½ teaspoon cinnamon
¼ teaspoon ginger
1 cup chopped nuts
Flour
Fat for deep frying

Beat the sweet potatoes until they are light and fluffy. Add the butter and seasonings; mix well. Last, fold in the nuts. Shape this mixture into round balls about 2 inches in diameter. Roll each ball in flour.

Melt fat in a medium-size skillet. Drop the floured balls into the fat; cook them until light brown. Put the balls that are finished first on a warming platter until all are cooked and ready.

Sour-Creamy Sauerkraut

Yield: 4 to 6 servings

3 tablespoons butter, margarine, or oil
1 onion, chopped
1 pound sauerkraut, undrained
½ teaspoon freshly ground black
   pepper
Salt to taste
4 tablespoons sour cream

Melt shortening in medium skillet and lightly brown onion. Add sauerkraut, stirring to mix; cover skillet. Simmer for 1 hour. Uncover pan. Drain off excess liquid. Add pepper and salt if needed. Just before serving, stir in sour cream.

Skillet Spinach

Yield: 4 to 6 servings

Skillet spinach is good because the vegetable is not overcooked.

2 tablespoons oil
1 pound loose fresh spinach, washed
   and drained
½ teaspoon salt
½ teaspoon garlic salt
¼ teaspoon sugar

Heat oil in large skillet. Add spinach, stirring with a wooden spoon until leaves are oil-coated. Cover; cook just 1 minute. Uncover skillet; sprinkle spinach with seasonings. Stir; cook for 30 seconds more, until spinach leaves are just wilted.

Mexican Rice

Yield: 4 to 6 servings

4 tablespoons oil
1 small can mushrooms, drained
1 medium onion, chopped
1 green pepper, chopped
2 cups canned tomatoes, drained
½ cup water or beef stock
1 cup uncooked rice
2 tablespoons chopped parsley
1½ teaspoons salt
Dash of pepper
½ teaspoon oregano

Heat oil in large skillet. Add mushrooms, onion, and green pepper; cook until onions are lightly tanned. Add tomatoes and water. When mixture has come to a boil, but not boiled, add rice and seasonings. Cover; simmer for 30 minutes, until rice is tender and most of the liquid has been absorbed.

Thanksgiving Rice

Yield: 2 large casseroles

This holiday treat can be used in two ways—as a vegetable addition to the meal or as an unusual stuffing for the turkey. It can be made ahead, frozen, and reheated in the oven if desired.

3 cups uncooked rice
1 pound country sausage
1 cup chopped celery
2 medium onions, chopped
1 green pepper, diced
1 egg, beaten
Salt and pepper to taste

Boil rice first; set it aside in a colander. Use a large skillet for this. Cook country sausage thoroughly. It will draw enough fat

to sauté the celery, onions, and green pepper. When vegetables are tanned, not brown, add rice to mixture; stir well about 3 minutes. Remove to your largest bowl. Add beaten egg and seasonings; mix well.

Put rice in well-greased casseroles for serving or freezing. Reheat in oven just enough so that rice is hot.

Skillet Summer Squash

Yield: 4 to 6 servings

4 tablespoons oil
1 large onion, chopped
1½ pounds summer squash, cubed
1 tomato, cut in wedges, optional
1 teaspoon salt
¼ teaspoon ground pepper
¼ teaspoon dillweed or fresh dill

Heat oil in medium skillet; cook onion until soft. Add squash, tomato, and seasonings. Cover skillet; cook for 10 minutes. Do not allow squash to get mushy. Overcooking will spoil the dish.

Fried Green Tomatoes

Yield: 4 to 6 servings

This is an excellent way to use a bumper crop of tomatoes that has not ripened fast enough. Green tomatoes go well with corn on the cob—a true summer delight.

4 medium green tomatoes, sliced
    ½ inch thick
1 teaspoon salt
½ teaspoon pepper
1 teaspoon dillweed
1 cup cornmeal
Fat for frying

Wash and prepare tomatoes—and these must be green.

Mix seasonings with cornmeal in a pie plate. Batter each tomato slice, being sure both sides are coated. Heat fat in medium skillet; cook tomatoes until brown on both sides. Drain on paper towels.

Fried Zucchini

Yield: 4 to 6 servings

3 to 4 large zucchini, sliced into
   rounds
1 egg
1 tablespoon milk
3 tablespoons flour
1 teaspoon salt
1 teaspoon garlic salt
Deep fat for frying

Wash and slice zucchini into rounds about ¼ inch thick. Set aside.

Combine egg, milk, flour, salt, and garlic salt in a bowl. Mix well to form batter. Dip each zucchini round into batter; fry in deep fat. Batter zucchini as you are ready to fry it, so each piece is coated. Fry until crisp and golden brown. Drain on paper towels. Serve hot.

Zucchini Italian

Yield: 4 servings

2 tablespoons butter or shortening
1 onion, sliced into rings
1 pound zucchini, sliced (2 to 3 cups)
1 cup diced fresh tomatoes
1 teaspoon salt
Dash of pepper
1 teaspoon dillweed

Heat butter in medium skillet. Use skillet with its own top. Cook onion rings in butter until yellow. Add zucchini, tomatoes, salt, pepper, and dillweed. Cover; lower heat to simmer. Cook for 10 to 15 minutes, until vegetables are tender.

If you want this for company and want to make it ahead, put the cooked vegetables in a casserole dish and sprinkle with grated cheese. Just before serving, put into moderate oven for 5 minutes or until cheese has browned.

Dinner in the Skillet

Fast Fish Dinner

Yield: 4 servings

2 cups canned tomatoes, drained
   (1-pound can)
2 tablespoons butter or margarine
1½ cups diced celery
2 medium onions, sliced
1 pound frozen fish fillets, cut into
   bite-size pieces
1 teaspoon salt
¼ teaspoon black pepper
2 cups canned potatoes, drained and
   sliced
Parsley for garnish

Put drained tomatoes and butter in medium skillet; bring to a boil. Add celery and onions; simmer until onions are soft, 3 to 5 minutes. Add fish, salt, pepper, and potatoes, stirring once. Cover skillet; simmer this 10 minutes.

Garnish with parsley, and serve.

Chicken-in-a-Pot Dinner

Yield: 4 to 6 servings

3 tablespoons butter or margarine
1 2½- to 3-pound frying chicken, cut
    into serving pieces
Salt and pepper to taste
¾ cup chicken broth
6 to 8 mushrooms, sliced, optional
1 1-pound can whole potatoes, drained
1 medium onion, sliced into rings
1 teaspoon salt
½ teaspoon paprika
1 10-ounce package frozen peas,
    thawed
4 tomatoes, quartered

Heat butter in a large skillet; brown the chicken pieces. Add salt and pepper while cooking. Add chicken broth, cover skillet, and simmer for 30 minutes. Add mushrooms, potatoes, onion rings, salt, and paprika; cook for 5 minutes more, adding ¼ cup chicken broth if needed. Last, add peas and tomatoes; cook for a few minutes more, until chicken and vegetables are heated through.

Serve with your favorite hot bread.

Chicken Dinner with Asparagus

Yield: 3 servings

3 whole chicken breasts, boned,
    skinned, and cut into strips
    1½ inches long
6 tablespoons vegetable oil
8 to 10 stalks fresh asparagus, cleaned
    and cut into 1½ inch lengths
1 cup chopped green onions
1 3- or 4-ounce can sliced mushrooms
    with liquid

1 can condensed chicken broth
1½ teaspoons ground ginger
1 teaspoon salt
1 teaspoon sugar
½ teaspoon garlic salt
2 tablespoons cornstarch
⅓ cup dry sherry
3 tablespoons soy sauce
4 cups cooked rice

In large skillet sauté chicken strips in 4 tablespoons oil until meat turns white. Remove from skillet; keep chicken warm.

Heat remaining oil in skillet; add asparagus and onions. Stir for 2 minutes. Add chicken, mushrooms, broth, and seasonings. Stir, cover, and simmer for 3 minutes.

Mix cornstarch with sherry and soy sauce to make a smooth paste. (Water may be used instead of wine if preferred.) Add to skillet; stir until mixture thickens slightly. Serve over hot rice.

Veal and Rice Skillet Dinner

Yield: 4 to 6 servings

1 pound ground veal
2 green peppers, chopped
1 cup sliced onion
1 cup uncooked rice
1 can beef broth plus 1 cup water
    (totaling 2½ cups liquid)
1 tablespoon soy sauce

Brown the veal in medium skillet until all pink disappears. Add remaining ingredients. Allow to come to a boil, but do not boil. Reduce heat; cover. Cook for 25 minutes.

Busy-Day Rice Ragout

Yield: 4 to 6 servings

This fast put-together makes hearty eating.

1 small onion, chopped
1 green pepper, chopped
1 tablespoon oil
1 pound lean ground beef or veal
1 teaspoon salt
Dash of black pepper
1 tablespoon prepared mustard
2 tablespoons catsup
1 tablespoon Worcestershire sauce
3 cups cooked rice
3 cups canned tomatoes

Use a medium to large skillet. Stir onion and green pepper in oil until soft. Add ground meat, salt, and pepper; stir until meat loses its pink color. Add remaining ingredients; stir until well-blended. Reduce heat; cover skillet. Simmer just 15 minutes.

Macaroni and Beef Dinner

Yield: 4 to 6 servings

1 cup elbow macaroni
1 pound lean ground beef
2 medium onions, diced
1 clove garlic, mashed fine
2 tablespoons oil
1 8-ounce can tomato sauce
1 teaspoon salt
¼ teaspoon black pepper
1 cup catsup
1 can mushrooms, optional
2 tablespoons Worcestershire sauce
½ teaspoon oregano

Cook macaroni according to package directions; drain.

In medium skillet sauté meat, onions, and garlic in oil. Add rest of ingredients in order given. Bring to a boil, then simmer for a few minutes. Add cooked macaroni; simmer for 5 minutes more. Serve at once.

Spinach and Beef Dinner

Yield: 4 to 6 servings

1 medium onion, chopped
6 mushrooms, sliced
1 pound ground beef
2 tablespoons shortening
1 10-ounce package frozen chopped
    spinach
1 cup sour cream
2 cups creamed cottage cheese
½ teaspoon oregano
1 teaspoon dillweed
1 teaspoon salt
1 teaspoon garlic salt
½ teaspoon freshly ground black
    pepper

Brown onion, mushrooms, and beef in shortening in a medium-sized, deep skillet. Stir until meat loses its pink color. Add frozen spinach as is. Cook uncovered on medium heat until spinach has thawed and some of the liquid is absorbed. Stir in sour cream and cottage cheese, mixing until all is heated but not boiling. Add seasonings; mix well. Let skillet stand until ready to serve.

Return skillet to heat for 2 or 3 minutes just before dinner is ready. Serve with French bread and a salad.

Tomato Ground Beef

Yield: 4 to 6 servings

1 tablespoon shortening
1 large onion, diced
1 green pepper, diced
1½ pounds ground beef
1 carrot, diced
1 can tomato soup
1 teaspoon salt
1 teaspoon garlic salt
¼ teaspoon freshly ground black
   pepper

Heat shortening in medium skillet; tan the onion and green pepper. Add beef and diced carrot. Sauté for 1 minute. Add can of soup without diluting; add seasonings. Simmer about 5 minutes to blend flavors.

To make this a complete meal, add 1 cup of cooked rice, or serve over cooked noodles or spaghetti. This is another quick-and-easy meal.

Sausage and Apple Casserole

Yield: 4 to 6 servings

8 cups cubed white bread (about 15
   slices)
1 pound country sausage
1 large onion, diced
1 green pepper, diced
½ cup water
2 large apples, pared, cored, and
   chopped
1 teaspoon salt

Use stale white bread for cubes, or stale them by putting in 250°F oven for 10 minutes. Brown the country sausage in a large skillet. Cook until there is no trace of pink in meat. Add onion and green pepper; cook for 2 minutes more. Stir in bread cubes, water, apples, and salt. Mix together until all is evenly moist.

Turn out cooked mixture into a well-greased casserole. Cook in 350°F oven 30 minutes or until the top crusts.

Sausage, Cabbage and Rice

Yield: 4 to 6 servings

1 pound country sausage
1 small head cabbage, shredded
½ cup uncooked rice
2 teaspoons dillweed
1 cup chicken broth
1 teaspoon salt
¼ teaspoon pepper

Brown the country sausage in large skillet. It will render enough fat to cook remaining ingredients. Add shredded cabbage; stir until cabbage is thoroughly coated with fat. Add rest of ingredients in order given. Cover skillet; cook on low heat 25 minutes or until rice is done.

Complete the dinner with a big plate of raw vegetables.

Desserts

Apple Rings

Yield: 12 or more rings

3 or 4 large apples
2 eggs, separated
2 teaspoons sugar

¼ teaspoon salt
¼ teaspoon ground cardamom
2 tablespoons butter, melted
¾ cup milk
1 cup flour
Shortening for deep frying

Peel, core, and slice apples ½ inch thick.

Beat egg whites stiff; set aside. Beat egg yolks; add sugar, salt, and cardamom. Add melted butter, milk, and flour. Beat thoroughly. Fold in stiffened egg whites.

Dip a slice of apple into batter; drop at once into hot deep fat. Fry until lightly browned. Drain apples, put them on serving platter, and sprinkle with sugar. Serve them warm.

Bananas Flambé

Yield: 4 servings

4 tablespoons butter or margarine
2 tablespoons brown sugar
1 teaspoon cinnamon
6 peeled ripe bananas, cut in half lengthwise
¼ cup rum

Melt butter in medium skillet.

Mix brown sugar and cinnamon; sprinkle some of this over cut bananas.

Put bananas in butter on a moderate to low heat; cook until lightly browned. Turn once and sprinkle with remaining sugar mixture. Last, add rum.

You can ignite this for a glamorous dessert. Serve bananas by themselves or over vanilla ice cream.

Brown Betty with Hard Sauce

Yield: 4 to 6 servings

4 cups cinnamon-raisin bread cubes
4 tablespoons butter or margarine
½ cup brown sugar
1 jar or can applesauce (2 cups)
½ teaspoon cinnamon
½ teaspoon salt

Hard Sauce

2 tablespoons soft butter or margarine
½ cup confectioners' sugar
½ teaspoon lemon or orange rind

In medium skillet sauté bread cubes in melted butter. When lightly browned, add sugar, applesauce, cinnamon, and salt. Stir until hot.

Serve warm with a dollop of hard sauce on top. To make the sauce, mix ingredients together in order given in a bowl until hard sauce is very smooth. It will melt into the warm Brown Betty.

Easy Chocolate Crepes

Yield: 18 to 24 crepes

2 eggs
½ cup flour
2 tablespoons cocoa
¼ cup sugar
1 cup milk plus 2 tablespoons cream
1 teaspoon vanilla
1 tablespoon butter, melted and cooled

Place eggs in a bowl. Add remaining ingredients in order given and beat well, by twos—mix flour and cocoa; beat; sugar and milk; beat; vanilla and cooled butter; beat. Set batter aside for at least 1 hour.

Heat a small skillet or crepe pan. Brush very lightly with butter. Place 1 tablespoon crepe batter into pan. Pick up pan by its handle and swirl batter so it covers the edges. This is fun. Cook just 1 minute, then turn. These cook quickly. (One recipe suggests you turn crepes with fingers, not with a lift. It works, too.) When done, remove to paper towels.

These can be stored in freezer for the future.

Dessert Pancakes with Fruit

Yield: 4 to 6 servings

1 cup prepared pancake mix
1 4-ounce package butterscotch
  pudding mix
1 cup milk
2 eggs, beaten
2 tablespoons oil
Oil for lightly greased skillet
½ cup sour cream
2 packages frozen fruit, thawed

Combine pancake mix, pudding, milk, eggs, and oil in a bowl. Beat with rotary beater or spoon until batter is even. Heat a lightly greased medium skillet. Drop in batter 1 tablespoon at a time. When golden on the bottom, turn with a spatula; allow to cook until both sides are golden. Keep cooked pancakes warm.

When ready to serve, arrange several pancakes per plate. Top with a spoonful of sour cream and spoon over the thawed fruit.

Christmas Crullers

Yield: About 36 crullers

These crullers can be made well ahead of when needed and stored in a tin.

3 eggs
⅓ cup sugar
⅔ cup butter or margarine, melted
¼ teaspoon ground cardamom
Grated rind of 1 lemon
3 tablespoons cream
4 cups flour
Shortening for deep frying
Powdered sugar for topping

Beat eggs and sugar together until very light. Stir in melted butter, cardamom, and lemon rind. Add cream and flour. The dough will be quite buttery and easy to handle.

Roll out dough about ¼ inch thick. Cut with pastry cutter or knife into oblongs 1 inch wide. Cut a slit into the middle of each oblong and pull one corner through to make a knot. If you prefer, just twist the oblong to make a ribbon effect.

Heat fat in skillet. Fry crullers until lightly browned; drain on paper. Store in a tightly covered container. When ready to serve, sprinkle with powdered sugar.

Grandmother Cookies

Yield: 3 dozen plus

½ cup margarine
½ cup sugar
2 eggs
2 cups flour
2 teaspoons baking powder
1 teaspoon salt
1½ teaspoons cinnamon
½ cup raisins, optional

Cream together margarine, sugar, and eggs until smooth.

Combine dry ingredients; add to egg mixture. Last, add raisins if desired. Batter will be stiff and buttery.

Take a teaspoonful, roll it between your palms, and flatten it to the size of a 2-inch circle. Put into lightly greased skillet. When cookie puffs up, turn it once and brown the other side.

Hartshorns

Yield: 36 hartshorns

This is a two-part recipe, but is worth the trouble, since hartshorns store well and can be made ahead.

¼ pound butter or margarine
4 eggs
1 cup sugar
½ lemon rind, grated
½ teaspoon ground cardamom
2 teaspoons baking soda
4½ cups flour
Fat for deep frying

Melt butter and allow to cool. Beat eggs and sugar together. Add butter, lemon rind, cardamom, baking soda, and flour. Mix well; place in refrigerator to chill overnight.

Roll small lumps of dough into strips 6 inches long and as thick as your little finger. Form each strip into a ring. Cook rings in deep fat until golden brown. Drain well on paper towels; store in a sealed tin.

Peaches in Wine Sauce

Yield: 8 servings

This can be made in a saucepan, but a heavy skillet with a lid preserves all the syrup.

8 ripe peaches
¾ cup sugar
⅓ cup water
⅓ cup white wine

Scald and peel skins off peaches, leaving fruit whole. Combine sugar and water in medium skillet; cook for 5 minutes. Add peaches; simmer for 5 minutes more. Add wine; simmer again for 5 minutes. Five minutes cooking time is usually enough to make fruit tender and syrup slightly thickened. Baste 3 times while cooking.

Transfer cooked peaches to a bowl; cover with a syrup. Refrigerate; serve when chilled.

Rum Rice Dessert

Yield: 4 to 6 servings

¼ cup raisins
¼ cup rum
1 cup uncooked rice
1 teaspoon salt
1 cup sugar
3 cups milk
2 tablespoons chopped nuts
1 teaspoon lemon juice
1 egg, beaten
¼ pound butter or margarine
Cinnamon and sugar mixed together

The night before, or at least several hours ahead, soak raisins in rum.

In top part of double boiler or in very heavy saucepan, cook rice, salt, sugar, and milk 30 minutes. Rice will be tender and the liquid absorbed. To this add raisins, nuts, lemon juice, and beaten egg.

Melt butter in a medium skillet. Do not let butter brown. Add rice mixture; cook until it is crusty on edges. Then turn rice so that other side browns, too.

When ready to serve, sprinkle with cinnamon-sugar.

Snowballs

Yield: A large, full cookie tin

This old family recipe makes a delicious cookie confection that melts in the mouth. It takes a bit of time but is worth it for the taste. These store well.

2 eggs
1 eggshell of water (about
 3 tablespoons)
1 teaspoon salt
2 cups sifted flour

Fat for deep frying
Confectioners' sugar

In a large bowl beat eggs, water, and salt with a fork. Add flour gradually until dough is sticky. Knead gently on a floured board until dough can be easily handled. Divide dough into 4 round balls; let stand 1 hour. Roll out dough as thin as you can. Let stand rolled out 30 minutes or until dry.

Cut dough into 3-inch squares or triangles (or some of each).

Heat fat in deep skillet; drop snowballs into hot fat. They cook quickly. When golden brown, remove from fat; drain on paper towels. Sprinkle them liberally with confectioners' sugar.

Sour-Cream Doughnuts

Yield: 2½ to 3 dozen

3 eggs, slightly beaten
1¼ cups sugar
1 cup sour cream
4 plus cups flour
2 teaspoons baking powder
1 teaspoon nutmeg
½ teaspoon salt
Fat for deep frying
Sugar mixed with cinnamon

Beat eggs and sugar in a large bowl. Add sour cream. Sift together dry ingredients; gradually add to egg mixture. When mixture has formed a dough, allow to rest 15 minutes.

Roll out dough on a well-floured board. Cut with floured doughnut cutter, the hole too; set aside. The cut doughnuts will rest 15 minutes more.

Drop doughnuts into preheated deep fat; cook until evenly browned.

Roll the hot cooked doughnuts in sugar mixed with cinnamon.

Toaster Oven
Appetizers

Anchovy Appetizers

Yield: Approximately 24

¼ cup butter
1½ ounces cream cheese
½ cup flour
Anchovy paste

Blend butter with cream cheese. Mix in flour. Chill for 1 hour. Roll dough very thin; cut with 2-inch cookie cutter. Spread each round with anchovy paste; fold over. Bake in 375°F toaster oven 8 to 10 minutes.

Clams Casino

Yield: 12 appetizers

12 cherrystone clams in shell
2 drops Worcestershire sauce
2 drops hot sauce
3 strips partially cooked bacon, cut into quarters
Seasoned bread crumbs

Open shells, letting each clam remain in one half. Discard other half of shell. Place clams in shallow baking pan. On each clam put Worcestershire sauce, hot sauce, a piece of bacon, and bread crumbs. Place in toaster oven; top brown until edges of clams curl and bacon is done, about 2 to 3 minutes.

Crab Hors d'Oeuvres

Yield: 2 cups

1 cup crab meat
1 8-ounce package cream cheese, softened
1 tablespoon milk
1 tablespoon instant minced onion
½ teaspoon horseradish
Salt to taste
Freshly ground pepper to taste

Remove cartilage from crab meat; set aside.

Blend together cream cheese, milk, onion, and horseradish. Gently mix in crab meat. Add salt and pepper. Put into 1-quart baking dish. Bake at 350°F in toaster oven until lightly browned on top, about 15 to 20 minutes. Serve on crackers or as a dip.

Crab-stuffed Mushrooms

Yield: 12 stuffed mushrooms

12 large fresh mushrooms
½ cup crab meat
1 tablespoon butter
¼ cup finely chopped celery
2 tablespoons mayonnaise
1 teaspoon lemon juice
Dash of salt
2 tablespoons buttered fine bread crumbs

Wash mushrooms. Trim tips of stems. Remove caps; set aside. Finely chop stems.

Cut or chop crab meat into small pieces.

Melt butter in skillet; cook chopped mushroom stems until just tender. Add crab, celery, mayonnaise, lemon juice, and salt. Stuff mushroom caps; sprinkle with crumbs. Broil about 7 minutes. Serve hot.

Lobster Appetizers

Yield: 12 appetizers

12 2-ounce frozen rock-lobster tails
6 tablespoons butter
6 tablespoons flour
1½ cups half-and-half
1 teaspoon grated lemon rind
½ teaspoon paprika
2 egg yolks, beaten
Salt to taste
Freshly ground pepper to taste
½ cup grated Parmesan cheese
2 stiffly beaten egg whites

Drop frozen lobster tails into boiling, salted water; bring to boil again. Drain lobster tails; plunge them into cold water. Remove the underside membrane; pull out lobster meat, reserving shells. Dice lobster meat.

Melt butter in top of double boiler over boiling water. Stir in flour, stirring until smooth. Add cream slowly, stirring constantly. Cook until mixture is thickened. Add lemon rind and paprika. Stir small amount of sauce into egg yolks, then stir mixture back into sauce. Cook for 2 minutes, stirring constantly. Season with salt and pepper.

Combine lobster meat and half the sauce, blending thoroughly. Spoon lobster mixture into reserved shells. Place shells on oven tray.

Heat remaining sauce; add cheese. Stir until cheese is melted. Let cool a little; fold in beaten egg whites. Spoon egg mixture over mixture in shells. Bake in preheated toaster oven at 350°F for 20 to 25 minutes or until lightly browned.

Oysters Casino

Yield: Approximately 30 appetizers

3 slices bacon, chopped
1 small stalk celery, chopped
1 small onion, chopped
1 teaspoon lemon juice
½ teaspoon salt
¼ teaspoon freshly ground pepper
5 drops Worcestershire sauce
4 drops hot sauce
¼ teaspoon seafood seasoning
1 pint shucked oysters, drained

Fry bacon until partially cooked. Add celery and onion; cook until tender. Add lemon juice, salt, pepper, Worcestershire sauce, hot sauce, and seafood seasoning.

Arrange oysters in single layer in baking pan. Spread bacon mixture over oysters. Bake in toaster oven at 375°F until edges of oysters begin to curl, about 10 minutes.

Miniature Steak Kabobs

Yield: Approximately 15 pieces

1 pound 1-inch-thick sirloin steak
1⅔ cups pineapple tidbits
¼ cup soy sauce
2 tablespoons sugar
1 tablespoon sherry
¼ teaspoon ground ginger
1 clove garlic, minced

Slice meat into strips 3 to 4 inches long, about ⅛ inch thick. Drain pineapple, reserving ¼ cup liquid. In bowl combine pineapple juice with soy sauce, sugar, sherry, ginger, and garlic. Mix thoroughly. Add meat; stir. Let stand 1 hour at room temperature, stirring occasionally.

Thread meat loosely on small skewers, threading pineapple on as you weave in and out. Broil to desired doneness, browning on all sides.

Two-Bite Pizzas

Yield: About 30

1 loaf party rye bread
Tomato paste
Thin slice salami
Slice mozzarella cheese
Oregano

Spread each bread slice with tomato paste. Place salami slice on top, then a slice of cheese; sprinkle with oregano. Top brown in toaster oven until cheese is melted and just turning brown.

Cheese Puffs

Yield: About 12 to 15 balls

3 ounces cheddar cheese
½ cup minus 1 tablespoon flour
1 tablespoon butter, softened

Combine all ingredients. Roll dough into small balls. Bake about 6 minutes in toaster oven at 450°F.

Cheese Yums

Yield: 4 appetizers

4 saltine crackers
1 slice American cheese, cut into quarters
1 thick slice salami, cut into quarters
Garlic powder to taste
Pepper to taste

On each cracker place 1 quarter piece of cheese, then a quarter piece of salami. Sprinkle with garlic powder and pepper to taste. Place on oven tray in toaster oven at 350°F. Bake until cheese bubbles. Watch while baking—cheese will burn.

Olive-stuffed Cheese Balls

Yield: Approximately 36 pieces

¼ pound sharp cheddar cheese, shredded
¼ cup soft butter
¾ cup sifted flour
⅛ teaspoon salt
½ teaspoon paprika
36 stuffed green olives, small size

Blend cheese with butter, flour, salt, and paprika. Mix thoroughly. Shape 1 teaspoon of dough around each olive. Place on ungreased oven tray. Bake at 375°F in toaster oven 10 to 12 minutes.

Mushroom Appetizers

Yield: About 25 large stuffed mushrooms

1 pound fresh mushrooms, washed and stems removed
½ pound ground steak
Salt
Pepper
Butter or margarine

Wash mushrooms; remove stems carefully.

Season meat with salt and pepper. Fill each mushroom cap with meat mixture. Dot with butter or margarine; place on broiling pan in toaster oven. Broil until meat is browned. Serve immediately.

Spinach-stuffed Mushrooms

Yield: 12 appetizers

12 large mushrooms
1 small onion, chopped
2 tablespoons butter
1 package frozen chopped spinach
1 beaten egg
Salt to taste
Pepper to taste
½ cup seasoned bread crumbs

Remove stems from mushrooms; chop finely. Sauté with onion in melted butter.

Cook spinach according to package directions; drain well. Add sautéed mushroom stems, onion, and egg; stir. Season with salt and pepper. Stuff mushroom caps. Place into casserole; sprinkle crumbs on top. Place into toaster oven; top brown until bubbly.

Bread & Toast

Broccoli Toast

Yield: 2 to 4 servings

½ pound fresh broccoli
1½ cups beef broth (made from cubes, or instant)
4 slices white bread, toasted
1 tablespoon butter or margarine
1 tablespoon flour
1 cup milk
White pepper
Salt
Nutmeg
2 hard-boiled eggs
Pimiento strips for garnish
Parsley sprigs for garnish

Clean and wash broccoli; cut into bite-size pieces. Bring beef broth to a boil, add broccoli, and cook for 20 minutes. Drain thoroughly. Top toasted bread with broccoli.

Meanwhile, prepare sauce by melting butter, stirring in flour, and gradually adding milk. Cook until thickened, stirring constantly. Season to taste with white pepper, salt, and nutmeg.

Chop 1 egg; stir into sauce. Pour sauce over broccoli toast. Place on oven tray; top brown until nicely browned, approximately 3 minutes. Garnish with hard-boiled egg slices, pimiento strips, and parsley sprigs.

Garlic Bread

Yield: 2 to 4 servings

4 slices French bread
Softened butter
1 clove garlic, cut

Place slices of bread on baking sheet. Heat toaster oven to 400°F. Cream butter in bowl that has been rubbed with garlic. Spread bread generously with garlic butter. Heat about 10 minutes or until hot.

Hawaiian Toast

Yield: 4 servings

You may want to cover the surface of oven tray with aluminum foil for easy cleaning.

4 slices white bread
2 tablespoons butter
4 slices boiled ham
4 slices canned pineapple, drained
4 slices cheddar cheese

Garnish

- 4 large lettuce leaves
- 4 maraschino cherries

Toast and butter bread slices. Cover with slice of ham, then pineapple slice, and, finally, with cheddar-cheese slice. Place on oven tray; bake in preheated 450°F toaster oven about 5 minutes. Serve on large leaf of lettuce, garnished with a maraschino cherry.

Holland Toast

Yield: 4 servings

- 4 slices white bread
- 2 tablespoons butter
- 4 slices boiled ham
- 2 ounces whole cranberry sauce
- 4 slices Gouda cheese

Garnish

- 1 tomato
- Boston lettuce leaves (¼ of head)
- Parsley sprigs
- Paprika

Toast bread; spread with butter. On each toast slice place a slice of ham. Spread with ½ tablespoon cranberry sauce; top with slice of Gouda cheese. Cover oven tray with aluminum foil. Place toast slices on sheet; bake in preheated 400°F toaster oven about 8 minutes.

Prepare garnish. Peel and quarter tomato. Wash and trim lettuce leaves; pat them dry. Wash parsley. Arrange lettuce leaves on 4 plates, top with toast, and garnish with tomato quarters and parsley sprigs. Sprinkle toast with paprika.

Pear Toast with Camembert

Yield: 4 servings

- 4 pear halves, canned
- 4 slices white bread, toasted
- 1 tablespoon butter, softened
- 2 boxes Camembert cheese
- 2 teaspoons sliced almonds
- 1 tablespoon butter
- 2 teaspoons whole cranberry sauce

Drain pear halves thoroughly. Toast bread; spread with softened butter. Place pears on top of toast.

Slice cheese; arrange around pears, slices overlapping. Sprinkle with almonds. Dot pears with butter. Broil in preheated toaster oven until cheese melts. Remove, garnish each slice with ½ teaspoon cranberry sauce, and serve immediately.

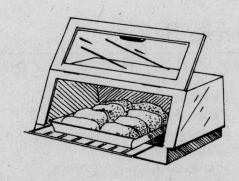

Cheese & Eggs

Breakfast Casserole

Yield: Approximately 3 to 4 servings

6 hard-boiled eggs
4 ounces canned shrimp
4 ounces salami
1 red pepper
2 tablespoons butter
4 tablespoons heavy cream
1 teaspoon mustard
Salt to taste
White pepper to taste
2½ tablespoons grated Swiss cheese
2 tablespoons chopped parsley

Peel eggs; cut into slices. Drain shrimp. Cut salami into thin slices. Cube red pepper. Melt 1 tablespoon butter in ovenproof dish. Arrange egg slices, shrimp, salami slices, and pepper cubes attractively in dish.

Blend cream with mustard; season to taste with salt and pepper. Pour over egg mixture. Sprinkle with grated cheese and chopped parsley. Dot with remaining butter. Bake in preheated 400°F toaster oven 10 to 15 minutes. Serve immediately.

Cheese Bake

Yield: 5 to 6 servings

2 cups cooked rice
2 cups shredded carrots
2 cups grated American cheese
½ cup whole milk
2 eggs, beaten
2 tablespoons minced onion

1 teaspoon salt
¼ teaspoon freshly ground black pepper

In bowl combine rice, carrots, 1½ cups cheese, milk, eggs, onion, salt, and pepper. Pour into greased 1½-quart baking dish. Sprinkle with remaining cheese. Bake in 350°F toaster oven 45 minutes.

Cheese Pudding

Yield: 4 servings

6 slices toasted bread
Soft butter
3 cups shredded American cheese
3 eggs, slightly beaten
2½ cups milk
½ teaspoon salt
¼ teaspoon dry mustard

Toast bread in toaster oven; butter and quarter each slice. In 1½-quart baking dish arrange alternate layers of toast and cheese, ending with cheese.

Combine eggs, milk, salt, and mustard. Pour over toast and cheese in baking dish. Bake in 325°F toaster oven 20 to 30 minutes or until inserted knife comes out clean.

Mushroom Macaroni and Cheese

Yield: 4 servings

8 ounces macaroni
1 can cream of mushroom soup
2 eggs, beaten
2 slices American cheese, grated
1 tablespoon butter
½ teaspoon salt
Freshly ground black pepper to taste

Cook macaroni according to package directions; drain. Combine with rest of ingredients; place in greased casserole dish. Bake in 300°F toaster oven approximately 45 minutes, or until bubbly and lightly browned.

Welsh Rarebit

Yield: 6 servings

¼ cup butter
¼ cup flour
1 teaspoon dry mustard
¾ cup beer
1¼ cups milk
1¼ cups grated sharp cheddar cheese
½ tablespoon wine vinegar
½ tablespoon Worcestershire sauce
Salt to taste
White pepper to taste
6 slices bread
Parsley for garnish

Melt butter in saucepan over low heat. When melted, increase heat to medium. Add flour and mustard; stir until smooth. Add beer; bring to boil, stirring constantly. Add milk alternately with cheese, stirring after each addition, until smooth. Add vinegar, Worcestershire sauce, salt, and pepper; mix thoroughly.

Spread each bread slice with generous amount of butter. Place in toaster oven; toast.

Remove bread from toaster oven. Place on ovenproof plate. Spoon cheese sauce over each slice. Place small amount of butter on top of each slice. Place in toaster oven; top brown until bubbly and golden. Garnish with parsley sprigs.

Egg and Mushroom Casserole

Yield: 2 to 3 servings

2 tablespoons bacon drippings
1 medium onion, chopped
8 ounces canned sliced mushrooms (or stems and pieces), drained
¾ pound tomatoes, peeled, seeded, and cubed
Salt to taste
Pepper to taste
Paprika to taste
2 tablespoons chopped parsley
Butter or margarine to grease casserole dish
4 eggs
Pinch of salt
2 ounces grated Emmentaler or Swiss cheese

Garnish

2 tablespoons chopped chives
1 small tomato, cut into wedges

Heat bacon drippings in medium saucepan. Add onion; cook until golden. Add mushrooms. Carefully stir in tomatoes. Season to taste with salt, pepper and paprika. Stir in parsley.

Grease baking dish with butter or margarine. Spoon in mushroom and tomato mixture. Break eggs; carefully slide them on top of mixture. Sprinkle egg whites with a little salt. Top with grated cheese. Bake in 375°F toaster oven approximately 25 minutes or until top is golden. Remove; garnish with chopped chives and tomato wedges.

Eggs with Vegetables

Yield: 2 servings

1 small onion, chopped
1 tablespoon butter
1 medium cooked potato, peeled and
   diced
1 clove garlic, pressed
1 red pepper, chopped
½ cup diced ham
1 large tomato, skinned
Salt to taste
Freshly ground pepper to taste
2 eggs
Parsley for garnish

Sauté onion in butter until tender. Stir in potato, garlic, pepper, ham, and tomato. Cook over medium heat, stirring constantly, until heated through. Add salt and pepper; blend thoroughly.

Turn mixture into 2 small ovenproof bowls. Make indentation in center of each. Place an egg in each indentation. Cover bowls lightly with aluminum foil. Bake in preheated 350°F toaster oven 8 minutes or until eggs are set but not overcooked. Garnish with parsley.

Creamed Eggs

Yield: 4 servings

4 rusks, buttered (or English muffins)
2 tablespoons prepared mustard
1 4½-ounce can deviled ham
4 hard-cooked eggs
1 can condensed cream of mushroom
   soup
¼ cup milk
2½ tablespoons finely chopped onion
Dash of Worcestershire sauce

Spread rusks with mustard, then with ham. Place in toaster oven at 300°F about 8 minutes or until warmed through.

Meanwhile, chop 2 eggs; combine with remaining ingredients in saucepan. Heat through.

To serve, place each rusk on a plate; spoon sauce over. Slice remaining 2 eggs; arrange on rusks. Sprinkle with paprika, if desired.

Creamed Eggs in Patty Shells

Yield: 4 servings

A good brunch dish.

4 frozen patty shells, baked according
   to package directions
1 can cream of mushroom soup
½ cup milk
4 hard-cooked eggs, sliced

Bake patty shells in toaster oven.

Blend soup and milk in saucepan. Heat through. Gently stir in eggs. Spoon into patty shells.

Noodles & Rice

Noodle Pudding

Yield: 3 to 4 servings

2 eggs
2 tablespoons sugar
1 tablespoon cinnamon
½ cup crushed pineapple, drained

2 cups cooked noodles, drained
¼ cup white raisins
½ cup cottage cheese
½ cup sour cream
2 tablespoons melted butter

Beat eggs and sugar until fluffy. Add remaining ingredients; mix thoroughly. Put into greased 1-quart casserole; bake in preheated 375°F toaster oven approximately 35 to 40 minutes or until browned.

Baked Noodles Swiss Style

Yield: 2 to 3 servings

1½ quarts water, salted
½ pound egg noodles
1 tablespoon butter or margarine
1 tablespoon flour
½ cup hot water
¼ pound grated Gruyère cheese
2 egg yolks
¼ pound cooked ham, cubed
2 egg whites
Butter or margarine to grease baking dish
1 tablespoon butter

Bring salted water to boil. Add noodles; boil for 10 minutes.

Melt 1 tablespoon butter in large saucepan. Add flour; blend well. Pour in hot water; cook for 5 minutes, stirring constantly. Add cheese; blend until melted. Remove sauce from heat; cool. Stir in egg yolks.

Drain noodles. Add noodles and ham to sauce. Beat egg whites until stiff. Fold into noodles.

Grease baking dish. Spoon in noodles; dot with butter. Bake in preheated 400°F toaster oven 20 minutes. Serve with a tossed green salad.

Rice Casserole

Yield: 5 to 6 servings

2 cups grated carrots
2 cups cooked rice
2 eggs, beaten
1 teaspoon salt
¼ teaspoon pepper
4 tablespoons grated onion
½ cup light cream
2 cups grated American cheese
Butter to grease casserole

Combine carrots, rice, eggs, salt, pepper, onion, cream, and 1 cup cheese. Pour into greased 1½-quart casserole. Sprinkle with remaining cheese. Bake in 350°F toaster oven 40 minutes.

Rice and Mushroom Casserole

Yield: 5 to 6 servings

1 cup rice
½ pound fresh mushrooms
1 medium-large onion
Butter
Salt to taste
Pepper to taste

Boil 1 cup rice, following directions on box.

Chop mushrooms and onion; sauté in generous amount of butter.

When rice is cooked, mix with mushroom and onion mixture. Add salt and pepper to taste; add more butter. Mix thoroughly. Place into 1½-quart casserole. Bake in 350°F toaster oven about 35 to 40 minutes.

Curried Rice

Yield: 3 to 4 servings

1 tablespoon minced onion
2 tablespoons butter
3 cups cooked rice
¼ teaspoon salt
¼ teaspoon pepper
1 teaspoon curry pepper

Cook onion in butter until yellow. Gently stir in remaining ingredients; mix gently but thoroughly. Put into casserole. Dot with a little more butter. Bake in 350°F toaster oven 15 minutes.

Spanish Rice

Yield: 4 servings

⅛ cup oil
1 clove garlic, crushed
¼ cup chopped celery
1½ cups long-grain rice
1¼ cups canned tomatoes
⅓ cup tomato paste
1 teaspoon salt
½ bay leaf
Dash cayenne pepper
1 cup hot water
½ pound ground beef
⅔ cup chopped green pepper
½ teaspoon chili powder
½ teaspoon sugar
5 ounces beef bouillon

Heat oil in heavy skillet. Add garlic and celery; brown, stirring constantly.

In bowl mix rice, tomatoes, tomato paste, salt, bay leaf, cayenne pepper, and hot water. Add to garlic and celery in skillet. Stir well; cover. Bring to a boil, reduce heat, and simmer over low heat 10 minutes.

Brown the beef and green pepper in separate skillet. Remove from heat. Stir in chili powder, sugar, and bouillon. Combine rice and meat mixtures in 1½-quart baking dish. Bake in 350°F toaster oven 25 minutes. If necessary, add a little more water.

Meat

Meat and Vegetable Pie

Yield: 4 servings

This is a terrific way to use leftover roast and make a completely different meal from it.

Filling

2 tablespoons butter or margarine
1½ tablespoons flour
1½ cups hot beef broth
Salt to taste
Pepper to taste
1 pound cooked leftover roast
2 medium onions, diced
2 stalks celery, sliced
4 carrots, sliced
1 medium potato, cut into cubes
Pinch of marjoram

Pie Crust

6 ounces flour
½ teaspoon salt
3½ tablespoons shortening or bacon
   drippings
3 tablespoons water

Heat butter or margarine in saucepan. Stir in 1½ tablespoons flour; gradually pour in beef broth, stirring constantly. Add salt and pepper to taste. Cook over low heat 7 minutes.

Cube leftover roast.

Dice onions; slice celery and carrots; cube potato. Add to sauce; simmer over low heat 5 minutes. Season with marjoram. Let cool slightly. Pour into ovenproof dish; set aside.

Put flour into mixing bowl. Sprinkle with salt; stir in. Add shortening or bacon drippings; cut into flour. Using a fork, stir in the water. Use your hands to knead mixture until it forms a dough.

Sprinkle board with flour. Place dough on board; roll out into a round approximately 1 inch larger than baking dish. Place dough round over filling in dish, tuck dough under, and prick in a few places with sharp knife. Bake in preheated 450°F toaster oven 10 minutes, then turn temperature down to 350°F and bake for another 30 minutes.

Dinner Pie

Yield: 3 to 4 servings

3 medium potatoes, cooked
1 onion, sliced and fried
1 egg
1 pound ground beef
Salt to taste
Freshly ground black pepper to taste
Garlic powder to taste, optional
Paprika

Mash potatoes with fried onion and egg. Spread half of mixture in bottom of greased 8-inch pie plate.

Mix ground beef with salt, pepper, and garlic powder. Spread mixture on top of potatoes. Cover with remaining potatoes. Sprinkle with paprika. Bake in preheated 350°F toaster oven 40 minutes.

Beef Casserole

Yield: 4 to 5 servings

2 medium onions, sliced
2 tablespoons shortening
2 cups leftover diced cooked beef
1 tablespoon flour
16 ounces stewed tomatoes
¾ cup Burgundy wine
¼ cup water
½ teaspoon salt
¼ teaspoon oregano
¼ teaspoon pepper
3 cups cooked macaroni, drained
1 cup shredded cheddar cheese, optional

In skillet cook onions in shortening until golden. Stir in beef; brown quickly over high heat, turning often. Stir in flour; add tomatoes, wine, water, salt, oregano, and pepper. Simmer over low heat until slightly thickened.

Place a layer of macaroni in bottom of 1½-quart casserole. Then place a layer of meat mixture, then a layer of cheese. Repeat, ending with cheese. Bake in 375°F toaster oven 20 minutes or until hot.

Stuffed Onions

Yield: 6 servings

6 large Spanish onions, peeled
Salted water
½ pound lean ground beef
½ teaspoon thyme
¼ cup tomato paste
1 egg yolk, beaten
Salt to taste
Freshly ground pepper to taste
Oil
Your favorite meat-sauce recipe
Sprigs of resemary for garnish

Put onions into boiling, salted water until covered; simmer for 30 minutes or until tender. Remove with slotted spoon; let drain and cool. Hollow out onions, being careful to leave shells intact. Put aside. Chop onion centers.

Sauté ground beef until just browned. Remove from pan with slotted spoon; put into mixing bowl. Add chopped onion, thyme, tomato paste, egg yolk, salt, and pepper; mix well. Spoon beef mixture into onion shells; place in baking dish. Brush onions lightly with oil; cover with aluminum foil. Bake in preheated 350°F toaster oven 10 to 12 minutes or until heated through.

Heat meat sauce; pour into serving dish. Place onions in sauce. Garnish with sprigs of rosemary.

Stuffed Tomatoes

Yield: 2 servings

4 tomatoes
Salt
Pepper

Stuffing

1 hard roll
1 cup water
¼ pound lean ground beef
1 slice bacon, diced
1 small onion, chopped
1 egg
Salt to taste
Pepper to taste
Margarine to grease baking dish
1 tablespoon grated Swiss cheese
Parsley for garnish

Cut "lids" from tops of tomatoes. Carefully scoop out tomatoes; lightly salt and pepper the insides. Set aside.

Soak roll in 1 cup water. In mixing bowl combine ground beef, bacon, onion, egg, salt, and pepper. Squeeze as much water as possible from roll, tear into small pieces, and add to meat mixture. Blend all ingredients thoroughly; stuff tomatoes with mixture.

Grease baking dish. Place stuffed tomatoes in dish. Sprinkle with grated cheese and put "lids" back on tomatoes, arranging them slightly slanted so that stuffing is exposed. Bake in preheated 350°F toaster oven 20 minutes.

Ground Beef and Macaroni Casserole

Yield: 3 to 4 servings

1 pound lean ground beef
¼ cup diced onion
Small amount shortening
2 cups cooked macaroni, drained
Catsup to taste
Salt to taste
Freshly ground pepper to taste
Garlic powder to taste
Sprinkle of sugar

Sauté beef and onion in shortening. Add macaroni, catsup, salt, pepper, garlic powder, and sugar. Blend thoroughly. Transfer to casserole. Bake in 325°F toaster oven 20 minutes.

Eggplant and Ground Beef Casserole

Yield: 4 servings

1 large onion, diced
¼ to ½ cup oil or margarine
1 pound ground beef
½ cup tomato sauce
½ cup water
1 teaspoon salt
¼ teaspoon pepper
1 medium eggplant

Sauté onion in 2 tablespoons oil or margarine until tender. Add ground beef; cook until brown. Combine tomato sauce, water, salt, and pepper; pour over meat mixture. Bring to boil; simmer for 5 minutes. Using perforated spoon, remove meat from pan; set aside.

Slice eggplant into ¼-inch slices. Brown lightly in remaining oil or margarine. Place a layer of eggplant in bottom of 1½-quart casserole. Spread a layer of ground beef on top. Place another layer of eggplant next; end with a layer of ground beef. Pour the sauce over all. Bake in 325°F toaster oven 20 to 25 minutes or until eggplant is done.

Beef Tamale Pie

Yield: Approximately 4 servings

1 pound ground beef
¾ cup chopped onion
2 tablespoons shortening

2 cups canned tomatoes
2 teaspoons chili powder
2 teaspoons salt
¾ cup cornmeal
2 cups boiling water

Brown beef and onion in shortening. Add tomatoes, chili powder, and 1 teaspoon salt. Simmer for 30 minutes. Remove from heat.

Add cornmeal to boiling water and 1 teaspoon salt. Cook until thickened, stirring constantly. Spread half of cornmeal mixture in bottom of greased 1½-quart casserole. Add meat mixture; top with remaining cornmeal mixture. Bake in 350°F toaster oven 40 minutes.

Chili Casserole

Yield: 5 to 6 servings

1 pound ground beef
Small amount hot fat
¼ cup chopped celery
1 cup chopped onion
1 15-ounce can chili con carne with beans
Pepper to taste
2 cups corn chips, slightly crushed
1 cup shredded, sharp process cheese

Brown meat in small amount of hot fat. Add celery and ¾ cup onion. Cook until just tender. Drain off excess fat. Add chili and pepper; heat through.

Place layer of chips in 1½-quart casserole. Alternate layers of chili mixture, chips, and cheese, reserving ½ cup chips and ¼ cup cheese for trim. Sprinkle center with remaining cheese and ¼ cup onion. Cover; bake in toaster oven at 325°F for 15 minutes or until hot. Just before serving, garnish with corn chips and cheese.

Baked Steak and Mushrooms

Yield: 2 servings

2 tablespoons butter or margarine
1 pound minute steaks
Butter to grease casserole
½ cup chopped onion
½ cup dry white wine
½ teaspoon Worcestershire sauce
1 can (3½ ounces) chopped
   mushrooms with liquid
½ teaspoon salt
Freshly ground pepper to taste

Heat butter in skillet; brown meat quickly on both sides. Transfer to greased casserole.

Add onion to remaining butter in skillet; sauté until tender, but do not overcook. Add wine, Worcestershire sauce, mushrooms, salt, and pepper. Heat and stir, scraping crust in skillet. Pour over steak in casserole. Bake in 375°F toaster oven 30 to 35 minutes or until steaks are tender.

Broiled Steak with Garlic Sauce

Yield: 2 servings

2 steaks

Garlic Sauce

¼ cup butter
1 tablespoon Worcestershire sauce
1 teaspoon garlic powder
1 teaspoon salt
Dash of pepper

Place steaks on toaster oven broiler pan. Prepare sauce. Melt butter; stir in

Worcestershire sauce, garlic powder, salt, and pepper. Mix well. Brush sauce on steaks before broiling, brush more on during broiling, and again just before removing from broiling pan.

Breaded Veal Cutlets

Yield: 2 servings

This is delicious with spaghetti.

2 eggs, beaten
1 cup cornflake crumbs
Salt to taste
Freshly ground black pepper to taste
Oil
2 small onions, sliced
2 veal cutlets
1 small can tomato sauce

Beat eggs in bowl. Mix together cornflake crumbs, salt, and pepper on plate.

Heat oil in frying pan. Sauté onions until soft. Remove from pan and set aside.

Dip both sides of veal cutlets into beaten eggs, then into seasoned cornflake crumbs. Fry on low heat about 10 minutes on each side or until golden brown.

Pour half of tomato sauce into baking dish. Add veal cutlets, onion, and remainder of tomato sauce. Cover; bake in 350°F toaster oven 30 minutes.

Veal Parmesan

Yield: 4 servings

4 veal chops or cutlets
Salt to taste
White pepper to taste
1 egg
1 tablespoon evaporated milk

1½ tablespoons grated Parmesan
   cheese
3 tablespoons packaged bread crumbs
2 tablespoons flour
4 tablespoons oil
2 tablespoons tomato catsup
4 slices mozzarella cheese

Rub chops with salt and pepper. On a plate blend egg and milk. On another plate mix Parmesan cheese and bread crumbs. Spoon flour onto a third plate. Now coat veal chops by first dipping into flour, then into egg mixture, and finally into cheese and breadcrumb mixture.

Heat oil in large skillet, add chops, and fry for 1 minute on each side. Remove chops; arrange in baking dish. Spread catsup over chops; top each with slice of mozzarella cheese. Bake in preheated 400°F toaster oven 10 to 12 minutes. Serve with mashed potatoes and tiny peas.

Veal with Wine and Mushrooms

Yield: 3 servings

1¼ pounds veal for scallopini
2½ tablespoons flour
½ teaspoon salt
⅛ teaspoon freshly ground pepper
4 tablespoons olive oil
Butter or margarine to grease casserole
2 cloves garlic, minced
¼ cup finely chopped onion
1 cup fresh mushrooms, sliced
1 cup beef bouillon
1 cup dry white wine
1 tablespoon chopped parsley

Pound veal until very thin. Mix together flour, salt, and pepper. Dredge veal in flour mixture.

Heat olive oil in skillet; brown veal on both sides. As meat browns, transfer it to greased casserole. When all veal is browned, add garlic, onion, and mushrooms to skillet; brown. Spoon over veal in casserole.

Add bouillon and wine to skillet. Heat and scrape crust. Pour mixture over veal. Cover; bake in 350°F toaster oven 30 to 35 minutes. Remove cover, sprinkle with parsley, and bake for another 10 minutes.

Lamb Chop Casserole

Yield: 2 servings

2 shoulder lamb chops, with fat
   trimmed
1 cup flour
Oil for browning
¾ cup cubed raw potatoes
½ cup sliced raw carrots
½ cup frozen peas (canned may be
   substituted)
¼ cup diced celery
2 tablespoons chopped onion
Salt and pepper to taste
¼ cup hot water
1 tablespoon minced parsley

Dip chops in flour; brown in hot oil in skillet.

Place potatoes, carrots, peas, celery, and onion into casserole dish. Sprinkle with salt and pepper. Add hot water. Place chops on top; sprinkle with parsley. Sprinkle with additional salt and pepper, if desired. Cover; bake in 350°F toaster oven 1 hour.

Lamb and Broccoli Casserole

Yield: 4 servings

2 tablespoons butter
2 tablespoons flour
1 cup milk
1 cup shredded cheddar cheese
¼ teaspoon salt
⅛ teaspoon freshly ground pepper
¼ teaspoon dry mustard
¼ teaspoon celery seed
¼ teaspoon Worcestershire sauce
About 1 pound cooked lamb, sliced
1 package frozen broccoli, cooked and
   well drained
1 tomato, peeled and thinly sliced
¼ cup shredded American cheese

Cook butter and flour until bubbly. Slowly stir in milk; cook until mixture boils and is thickened, stirring constantly. Remove from heat. Add cheddar cheese, salt, pepper, mustard, celery seed, and Worcestershire sauce. Stir until cheese is melted.

Arrange layers of lamb, broccoli, and tomato slices in 1½-quart casserole. Pour sauce over top. Bake in 350°F toaster oven 15 minutes. Sprinkle with American cheese; bake for an additional 5 minutes.

Baked Lamb Chops with Feta Cheese

Yield: 4 servings

8 small lamb chops
1 clove garlic
½ teaspoon salt
Pepper
3 tablespoons oil

1 tablespoon butter or margarine
1 large onion, sliced
4 to 5 ounces feta cheese, sliced

Pat chops dry with paper towels. Crush garlic clove with salt; rub chops with mixture. Sprinkle with pepper. Baste with oil. Place chops in a dish, cover, and let stand 24 hours.

Remove chops; drain oil into skillet. Heat oil, add chops, and brown quickly ½ minute on each side. Continue cooking, 3 minutes on each side.

Melt butter in second skillet. Add onion; cook for 5 minutes.

Arrange chops in ovenproof dish. Spread onion over chops. Top with cheese. Bake in preheated 400°F toaster oven 10 minutes.

Zucchini and Lamb

Yield: 2 to 3 servings

3 medium zucchini
Butter or margarine to grease casserole
Salt to taste
Freshly ground pepper to taste
1 tablespoon olive oil
½ cup chopped onion
1 clove garlic, minced
¾ pound ground lamb
¼ cup cooked rice
½ teaspoon salt
½ teaspoon grated lemon rind
1 tablespoon chopped fresh mint
½ cup chicken broth
½ cup buttered crumbs

Wash zucchini; cut into thin slices crosswise. Put half the slices into greased casserole; season with salt and pepper.

Heat olive oil; sauté onion, garlic, lamb, and rice until lamb is partially cooked but not browned. Add ½ teaspoon salt, pepper, lemon rind, and mint. Spoon over zucchini; top with remaining zucchini. Pour broth over zucchini and lamb. Sprinkle with crumbs. Bake in 350°F toaster oven 20 to 25 minutes.

Barbecued Frankfurters

Yield: 2 servings

This is very tasty served open-face on a toasted hot-dog bun.

4 frankfurters
¼ cup chopped onion
1 tablespoon oil
2 teaspoons sugar
¼ teaspoon salt
1 teaspoon prepared mustard
½ teaspoon paprika
¼ teaspoon freshly ground black
   pepper
2 tablespoons vinegar
⅓ cup catsup
½ cup water
Dash of garlic powder

Split frankfurters in half lengthwise; place, cut-side-down, in baking dish.

Cook onion in oil until tender. Add remaining ingredients. Simmer, stirring occasionally, for 10 minutes. Pour over frankfurters. Bake in 325°F toaster oven 15 minutes.

Easy Beans and Franks

Yield: 2 servings

1 14-ounce can vegetarian baked beans
   in tomato sauce
2 frankfurters cut into bite-size pieces
1 small onion, minced
1 teaspoon mustard, optional

Place beans in 1-quart baking dish. Add frankfurters and onion. Carefully mix. If desired, mix in mustard. Bake, covered, in 350°F toaster oven 25 minutes or until heated through.

Hot Dog Casserole

Yield: 3 to 4 servings

Children enjoy this casserole.

6 hot dogs, sliced
¼ cup brown sugar
1 medium onion, sliced thin
1 bottle chili sauce

Place half of hot dogs in 1½-quart casserole or in loaf pan. Sprinkle with half the brown sugar. Cover with half the onion slices; pour half the bottle of chili sauce over all. Repeat for second layer. Cover casserole. Bake in 325°F toaster oven 1 hour and 15 minutes.

Quick Spaghetti

Yield: 4 servings

12 small onions
¼ cup grated American cheese
½ pound link sausages
2 cups canned spaghetti in tomato
   sauce

Precook onions until tender. Arrange around edge of shallow baking dish. Sprinkle with cheese.

Cut link sausages in half crosswise, then fry. Combine with spaghetti. Spoon into center of onions. Bake in 325°F toaster oven 15 minutes.

Short Ribs

Yield: 2 to 3 servings

2 pounds short ribs
Fat for browning
Salt and pepper to taste
½ cup hot water
Onions, optional
Carrots, optional

Brown short ribs in hot fat. Season with salt and pepper. Place in baking dish. Add hot water; cover tightly. Bake in 300°F toaster oven 2 to 2½ hours, adding more water as necessary. If desired, add onions and carrots last 40 minutes of cooking.

Ham Rolls

Yield: 8 servings

Good with mashed potatoes and a tossed green salad.

½ pound fresh mushrooms
Juice of half a lemon
1½ tablespoons butter or margarine
2 small onions, chopped
Salt to taste
2 tablespoons chopped parsley
Freshly ground black pepper to taste
8 slices boiled ham
2 strips bacon
½ cup sour cream
½ pound sliced Edam cheese
1 tablespoon packaged bread crumbs

Clean and slice mushrooms. Sprinkle with a little of the lemon juice to prevent mushrooms from turning brown.

Heat butter in saucepan. Add onions; cook for 3 minutes. Add mushrooms; season lightly with salt. Cover; simmer for 10 minutes. Stir in parsley; season with rest of lemon juice and freshly ground pepper to taste. Spread mushroom mixture on ham slices; roll up jelly-roll fashion.

Dice bacon. Cook in ovenproof dish 3 minutes. Arrange ham rolls on top of cooked bacon, setting them close together. Spread half of sour cream over rolls, top with cheese slices, and spread rest of sour cream over cheese. Sprinkle with bread crumbs. Bake in preheated 400°F toaster oven 20 minutes.

Poultry

Baked Chicken

Yield: Approximately 2 servings

1¼ pounds chicken parts
1 teaspoon poultry seasoning
1 teaspoon garlic powder
¼ teaspoon pepper
½ teaspoon salt
1 cup cornflake or cracker crumbs

Sprinkle chicken parts with seasonings. Coat with crumbs. Place in foil-lined baking dish. Bake in preheated 350°F toaster oven approximately 1 hour or until juices running from chicken when pricked with fork are no longer pink.

Baked Chicken and Broccoli

Yield: 2 to 3 servings

1 package frozen broccoli, cooked
    according to package directions
1 cup cooked chicken, sliced
3 tablespoons butter
3 tablespoons flour
1½ cups chicken stock
¼ cup heavy cream
¼ teaspoon Worcestershire sauce
2 teaspoons prepared mustard
1 tablespoon minced onion
1 tablespoon dry sherry
½ cup shredded Parmesan cheese
Salt to taste
Pepper to taste

Place drained broccoli in bottom of
1½-quart casserole. Place chicken on top of
broccoli.

Melt butter in saucepan. Blend in flour.
Add chicken stock gradually; cook, stirring
constantly, until thick. Add remaining ingredients to sauce. Stir until cheese is melted
and mixture is well-blended. Pour sauce over
broccoli and chicken. Bake in 375°F toaster
oven 25 minutes.

Baked Chicken and Spinach Casserole

Yield: 3 servings

1 package frozen chopped spinach,
    cooked according to package
    directions, and drained well
4 tablespoons butter
1 clove garlic, crushed
Dash of marjoram

Dash of basil
4 tablespoons flour
⅓ cup heavy cream
Meat from 2- to 2½-pound chicken,
    cooked
¾ cup heavy cream
¾ cup chicken stock
Salt to taste
Pepper to taste
1 cup grated Parmesan cheese

Cook and drain spinach.

Melt 1 tablespoon butter in saucepan.
Add garlic, marjoram, and basil; cook and
stir constantly. Add 1 tablespoon flour; mix
well. Add ⅓ cup cream and spinach; blend
thoroughly. Place mixture in bottom of
1½-quart casserole. Cover with chicken.

Melt 3 tablespoons butter in saucepan. Add
3 tablespoons flour; blend well. Stir in ¾
cup cream, chicken stock, salt, and pepper.
Cook until thickened. Pour over chicken.
Cover with grated cheese. Bake in 375°F
toaster oven for 20 minutes or until cheese is
bubbly.

Chicken Breasts Baked in Cream

Yield: 4 servings

2 whole chicken breasts
4 tablespoons fat
½ cup chopped onion
1 garlic clove, minced
¾ cup chicken broth
¾ cup cream
1 teaspoon salt
¼ teaspoon pepper
2 teaspoons Worcestershire sauce

Heat toaster oven to 300°F.

Cut chicken breasts in two, making 4 pieces. Brown breasts in fat until golden brown. Heat remaining ingredients in saucepan. Place chicken breasts into 1½-quart casserole dish; pour sauce over them. Cover; bake for 2 hours. Remove cover; bake for another 15 minutes.

Chicken and Noodles

Yield: 4 servings

2 tablespoons butter
2 tablespoons flour
½ teaspoon salt
1 cup chicken stock
1 cup milk
1 4-ounce can sliced mushrooms
⅛ cup sherry
¼ teaspoon marjoram
1 tablespoon chopped chives
4 ounces noodles, cooked according to package directions and well-drained
2½ cups diced cooked chicken
Butter to grease casserole
¼ cup grated Parmesan cheese

Melt butter in saucepan. Add flour and salt; cook until bubbly. Gradually stir in chicken stock, milk, and liquid from mushrooms. Cook and stir until mixture boils and is thickened. Add sherry, marjoram, and chives. Mix with noodles, chicken, and mushrooms. Spoon into buttered 1½-quart casserole. Sprinkle with cheese. Bake in 350°F toaster oven 20 to 25 minutes.

Simple Chicken Chow Mein

Yield: 4 servings

2 cups cooked chicken, diced (turkey may be substituted)
1 cup celery, sliced
2 tablespoons chopped green onions
1 can condensed cream of mushroom soup
1 cup pineapple tidbits or chunks
1 tablespoon soy sauce
2 cup chow mein noodles

Combine all ingredients except noodles; mix well. Gently fold in 1 cup noodles. Spoon mixture into 8-inch-square baking dish. Sprinkle with remaining noodles. Bake in 350°F toaster oven approximately 40 minutes or until casserole is hot. Serve with additional soy sauce if desired.

Chicken Florentine

Yield: 4 servings

1 small chicken, about 2 to 2½ pounds
Salt
2 tablespoons olive oil
1 medium onion

2 cloves garlic
4 small tomatoes
4 stuffed green olives
⅛ teaspoon thyme
½ teaspoon dried basil
1 teaspoon oregano
Pinch of celery salt
Freshly ground black pepper to taste
4 bay leaves

Cut chicken into 4 pieces. Rub with salt. Place each piece on large piece of aluminum foil that has been brushed with olive oil. Sprinkle any leftover olive oil over chicken pieces.

Dice onion. Mince garlic. Peel and seed tomatoes; cut into cubes. Chop olives. Mix these ingredients; season with thyme, basil, oregano, celery salt, and pepper. Divide mixture evenly; spread over 4 chicken pieces. Top each with a bay leaf. Close aluminum foil loosely over chicken. Place on oven tray; place in preheated 450°F toaster oven. Bake for 35 minutes. Open aluminum foil; bake for another 15 minutes at 400°F (or bake until chicken is done). Remove bay leaves before serving.

Chicken and Oyster Royal

Yield: 5 to 6 servings

3 cups cooked chicken, coarsely diced
½ pint raw oysters, drained
2 hard-boiled eggs, peeled and sliced
Butter to grease casserole
½ cup chopped celery
3 tablespoons butter
3 tablespoons flour

2 cups chicken broth
¼ teaspoon sage
Salt to taste
Freshly ground pepper to taste

Layer chicken, oysters, and eggs in buttered 1½-quart casserole.

Cook celery in butter until tender. Blend in flour; cook until bubbly. Gradually stir in chicken broth; cook and stir until mixture boils and is thickened. Add sage, salt and pepper. Pour over layers in casserole. Cover; bake in 400°F toaster oven 25 minutes.

Super Supper Casserole

Yield: 3 to 4 servings

This is delicious served over noodles and accompanied by a salad.

2 cups diced leftover chicken
1 16-ounce can sliced carrots, drained
1 can (10¾ ounces) cream of mushroom soup, undiluted
Freshly ground black pepper to taste
2 teaspoons chopped parsley

Blend together chicken, carrots, mushroom soup, and pepper. Pour into 1½-quart casserole. Sprinkle with parsley. Bake in 325°F toaster oven 25 to 30 minutes.

Cornish Hen with Orange Sauce

Yield: 2 servings

1 Cornish hen, approximately 1 to 1½ pounds
Margarine
Garlic powder to taste
Pepper to taste
Onion powder to taste
Paprika
Orange marmalade (amount to suit your taste)
Small amount water

Place Cornish hen in baking dish; dot with margarine. Sprinkle with garlic powder, pepper, onion powder, and small amount paprika. Place in toaster oven; bake at 325°F for 45 minutes, basting occasionally.

Heat orange marmalade in saucepan with small amount of water until boiling. Simmer on low, stirring frequently, 2 to 3 minutes. Pour over chicken; bake for another 20 minutes or until nicely browned and desired doneness is reached.

Turkey Casserole

Yield: 2 servings

½ cup sliced onion
½ cup chopped green pepper
2 tablespoons butter or margarine
20-ounce can pineapple tidbits or chunks, drained, reserving liquid
1¼ cups turkey broth (chicken broth can be substituted)
2 tablespoons cornstarch
1½ teaspoons salt
1 teaspoon curry powder
3 cups toasted bread cubes (about ½ inch size)
2 cups chopped turkey
¼ cup slivered almonds
Butter or margarine to grease casserole

Cook onion and green pepper in butter until tender.

Drain pineapple tidbits; add turkey broth to juice to make 2 cups. Dissolve cornstarch, salt, and curry powder in liquid; add to cooked onion and pepper. Cook and stir until sauce boils and is thickened.

Arrange half of bread cubes, turkey, pineapple, and almonds in layers in buttered 1½-quart casserole, ending with bread cubes. Pour half of sauce over. Repeat. Bake in 350°F toaster oven 30 minutes.

Seafood

Barbecue Baked Fish

Yield: 3 servings

1 pound fish fillets
1½ tablespoons butter or margarine
1½ tablespoons lemon juice
⅓ cup barbecue sauce
½ teaspoon Worcestershire sauce
Salt to taste
Pepper to taste

Wash and dry fish.

Melt butter in small pan. Mix in lemon juice, barbecue sauce, and Worcestershire sauce. Pour ½ of sauce into shallow baking pan.

Sprinkle fish with salt and pepper; place in single layer in pan. Pour remaining sauce over fish. Bake in 350°F toaster oven until fish flakes easily when tested with a fork, about 20 to 25 minutes.

Fish and Pineapple

Yield: 2 servings

1 large halibut fillet, or another fish of your choice
Butter or margarine to grease baking pan
1¼ cups crushed pineapple, drained, reserving juice
½ cup cooked rice
½ cup bread crumbs
1 small onion, chopped fine
⅛ teaspoon pepper
½ teaspoon paprika
½ teaspoon salt
½ teaspoon poultry seasoning
½ cup pineapple juice

Place fish fillet in greased baking pan.
Mix together pineapple, rice, bread crumbs, onion, pepper, paprika, salt, and poultry seasoning. Spread over fish. Pour pineapple juice over this. Bake in 350°F toaster oven until fish is tender, about 30 minutes.

Fish Steaks

Yield: 3 to 4 servings

Salt
2 pounds white fish, sliced (or use fillets of your favorite fish)
1 carrot, diced
1 stalk celery, sliced
1 green pepper, diced

2 medium onions, diced
1 clove garlic, minced
Oil
1 small can tomato sauce

Salt fish and place in greased baking dish; set aside.
Sauté vegetables in oil in skillet 10 minutes. Add tomato sauce, mix well, and sauté for another 3 minutes. Spoon vegetables over fish, spreading evenly. Bake in 350°F toaster oven 30 minutes.

Flounder Stuffed with Salmon

Yield: 2 servings

1 7-ounce can salmon
1 egg
¼ cup fine cracker crumbs
2 teaspoons catsup
1 pound flounder fillets
1 large onion, sliced
Butter
1 small can tomato sauce

Mix salmon, egg, cracker crumbs, and catsup. Spread each fillet with salmon mixture, roll up, and secure with toothpicks.
Grease baking dish; line bottom with onion slices. Place fillet rolls on top. Dot fish with butter. Pour tomato sauce over all. Bake in 350°F toaster oven 25 minutes.

Baked Halibut

Yield: 2 servings

2 halibut steaks
1 beaten egg
½ can cream of mushroom soup
¼ cup milk
¼ cup grated cheese
3 teaspoons dry bread crumbs
1 tablespoon melted butter

Place halibut in small baking dish.

In saucepan combine egg, soup, milk, and half of cheese. Stir over low heat until cheese is melted and mixture is hot. Pour sauce over fish.

Combine bread crumbs with melted butter and remaining cheese. Sprinkle on top of fish. Bake in 350°F toaster oven approximately 20 minutes or until fish flakes.

Halibut with Vegetables

Yield: 2 to 3 servings

1 large onion, sliced
Halibut steak, approximately 2 pounds
2 carrots, sliced
2 stalks celery, sliced
1 green pepper, sliced
Salt to taste
Pepper to taste
2 tablespoons butter
1 15-ounce can tomatoes

Line bottom of baking dish with onion. Place fish on onion slices. Put carrots, celery, and green pepper on fish. Sprinkle with salt and pepper; dot with butter. Pour tomatoes on top. Bake in preheated 350°F toaster oven about 50 minutes.

Baked Salmon

Yield: 2 servings

2 fresh salmon steaks
Salt and pepper to taste
2 tablespoons butter
½ pint sour cream
Paprika

Place salmon steaks in buttered 8-inch glass pie plate. Sprinkle with salt and pepper to taste.

Cut butter into small pieces; add to salmon. Bake in preheated 325°F toaster oven 10 minutes. Turn fish; spoon sour cream over fish. Sprinkle with paprika. Bake for 20 minutes more.

Salmon Loaf

Yield: Approximately 6 servings

1-pound can salmon, drained, reserving liquid
⅓ cup salmon liquid
1 cup bread crumbs
¾ cup milk
2 eggs, beaten
¼ teaspoon salt
⅛ teaspoon pepper
2 tablespoons melted butter
¼ cup chopped celery
¼ cup chopped onion
1 teaspoon lemon juice

Flake salmon. Add salmon liquid and remaining ingredients. Spoon into greased loaf pan. Bake in 350°F toaster oven approximately 40 minutes.

Creamed Salmon in Patty Shells

Yield: 4 servings

4 frozen patty shells, baked according to package directions
¼ cup chopped onion
2 tablespoons butter
1 can cream of celery soup
⅓ cup milk
1 can (8 ounces) salmon, drained and flaked

Bake patty shells in toaster oven.

In saucepan cook onion in butter until tender. Blend in soup, milk, and salmon. Heat, stirring occasionally. Spoon into patty shells.

Tuna Loaf

Yield: 4 to 6 servings

2 cans tuna (6½ or 7 ounces, or one 13-ounce can)
1 tablespoon lemon juice
1 cup white sauce
½ cup half-and-half or milk (not skimmed)
1 beaten egg
¼ cup chopped celery
1 cup bread crumbs
½ teaspoon salt

Drain and flake tuna. Add remaining ingredients in order given. Mix well. Put into greased baking dish in 350°F toaster oven about 25 minutes or until browned.

Tuna-Cashew Casserole

Yield: About 4 servings

1 small can chow mein noodles (reserve some for top)
1 can cream of mushroom soup
¼ cup water
1 can (1 cup) chunk-style tuna
¼ pound cashew nuts
¼ cup diced celery
¼ cup diced onions
Salt and pepper to taste

Set aside ½ of noodles. In 1½-quart casserole combine rest of noodles with remaining ingredients. If nuts are unsalted, add a little extra salt. Sprinkle reserved noodles over top. Bake in 350°F toaster oven 30 minutes.

One-Dish Seafood Dinner

Yield: Approximately 3 servings

1 can pea soup
1 can tomato soup
¼ cup dry sherry
1 cup light cream
½ teaspoon curry powder (more or less, to suit your taste)
¼ teaspoon cayenne
1 pound crab meat

Mix all ingredients together; place in casserole. Bake in 350°F toaster oven 20 minutes. Serve on toast.

Crab Casserole

Yield: 2 servings

½ pound fresh mushrooms, sliced
4 tablespoons butter
2½ tablespoons flour
5 ounces chicken broth
¾ cup light cream
Salt to taste
Pepper to taste
½ pound crab meat
Buttered crumbs
Grated American cheese

Sauté mushrooms in 1 tablespoon butter for 3 minutes; set aside.

In saucepan melt 3 tablespoons butter. Blend in flour. Add chicken broth, cream, salt, and pepper; cook until thickened.

In 1-quart casserole arrange alternate layers of mushrooms, sauce, and crab meat. Sprinkle with buttered crumbs and cheese. Place in 350°F toaster oven; bake about 25 minutes.

Crab Imperial

Yield: 4 servings

4 tablespoons butter
1 tablespoon chopped green pepper
¼ teaspoon dry mustard
¼ teaspoon paprika
¼ teaspoon salt
4 tablespoons flour
1 cup milk
½ teaspoon Worcestershire sauce
1 pound crab meat, cartilage removed
1 egg yolk
6 tablespoons mayonnaise
Butter to grease casserole

Heat butter; sauté green pepper 2 minutes. Add mustard, paprika, salt, and flour; let bubble. Stir in milk; cook, stirring constantly, until mixture boils and is thickened. Blend in Worcestershire sauce.

Mix crab meat with egg yolk and mayonnaise; add to sauce. Spoon into buttered casserole. Bake in 375°F toaster oven 20 minutes or until hot.

Deviled Crabs

Yield: 6 servings

2 cups crab meat
¼ cup sherry
1 teaspoon Worcestershire sauce
3 egg yolks, beaten
3 tablespoons butter
2 tablespoons flour
½ teaspoon salt
1 teaspoon dry mustard
White pepper to taste
2 cups milk
6 crab shells
½ cup buttered bread crumbs

Mix crab meat with sherry, Worcestershire sauce, and egg yolks.

Melt butter in saucepan. Stir in flour, salt, mustard, and pepper. Add milk slowly, stirring until thickened. Add crab meat; blend well. Fill crab shells with mixture; sprinkle with buttered crumbs. Bake in 350°F toaster oven about 10 minutes or until browned.

Deviled Shrimp

Yield: 4 servings

2 tablespoons butter
2 tablespoons chopped onion

2 tablespoons flour
⅔ cup milk
1 teaspoon Worcestershire sauce
2 teaspoons prepared mustard
Freshly ground pepper to taste
1 cup cooked, cleaned shrimp (or
   1 7-ounce can)
2 hamburger buns, split and toasted
¾ cup grated American cheese

Melt butter in saucepan. Add onion; cook for 1 minute. Slowly blend in flour. Gradually add milk; cook until thick, stirring constantly. Add Worcestershire sauce, mustard, pepper, and shrimp. Heat through.

Toast hamburger buns in toaster oven; spoon mixture on buns. Sprinkle with cheese. Place in toaster oven; top brown until bubbly.

Shrimp Casserole

Yield: 6 servings

2 pounds raw shrimp
1 cup bread crumbs
½ cup butter, melted
2 cloves garlic, minced
½ cup chopped green onions
2 tablespoons chopped parsley
½ teaspoon thyme
1 teaspoon tarragon vinegar
½ cup sherry
1 teaspoon salt
Freshly ground pepper to taste
Butter to grease casserole

Topping

2 tablespoons butter melted
¼ cup bread crumbs

Peel, devein, and wash shrimp. Pat dry with paper towels.

Combine 1 cup crumbs with ½ cup butter, garlic, onion, parsley, thyme, vinegar, sherry, salt, and pepper.

Place layer of shrimp in buttered 1½-quart casserole. Place layer of crumb mixture next. Repeat. Top with mixture of 2 tablespoons melted butter combined with ¼ cup bread crumbs. Bake in 350°F toaster oven about 50 minutes or until browned.

Patty Shells with Shrimp Filling

Yield: 6 servings

6 patty shells (can be purchased frozen)
1 tablespoon butter
1 tablespoon flour
1 cup hot beef broth
6 ounces frozen shrimp, thawed
4 ounces canned whole mushrooms
8 ounces canned white asparagus
   (green may be substituted), cut up
Salt to taste
Pepper to taste
3 tablespoons heavy cream
½ teaspoon dried dillweed
4 teaspoons lemon juice
6 sprigs parsley

Bake patty shells in toaster oven, following directions on package. Melt butter in saucepan; stir in flour; gradually add beef broth, stirring constantly. Add shrimp, mushrooms, and asparagus. Heat for 10 minutes. Season to taste with salt and pepper. Remove from heat. Stir in cream, dillweed, and lemon juice. Remove patty shells from oven, fill with stuffing, and garnish with any leftover shrimp and/or mushrooms and parsley sprigs. Serve immediately.

Curried Lobster in Patty Shells

Yield: 4 servings

This makes a nice luncheon dish or late supper.

4 frozen patty shells, baked according
    to package directions
1 can frozen cream of shrimp soup
½ cup milk
1 cup flaked cooked lobster
½ teaspoon curry powder

Bake patty shells in toaster oven.
Combine soup, milk, lobster, and curry powder in saucepan. Heat, stirring occasionally. Serve in patty shells.

Oyster Casserole

Yield: 6 servings

⅔ cup melted butter
3 cups coarse soda-cracker crumbs
2 pints shucked oysters in liquor
Salt to taste
Pepper to taste
¼ cup oyster liquor
½ cup heavy cream

Mix together butter and cracker crumbs. In bottom of 1½-quart baking dish place ⅓ of cracker crumbs. Arrange 1 pint of oysters on top of crumbs. Place another layer of crumbs on oysters, another layer of oysters, then end with a layer of crumbs. Sprinkle with salt and pepper.

Mix together oyster liquor and cream; pour over crumbs. Bake in 350°F toaster oven 30 minutes.

Scallops in White Wine

Yield: 3 servings

¾ pound scallops
2 tablespoons butter
¼ pound fresh mushrooms, sliced
¼ cup finely chopped onion
1 tablespoon flour
½ cup dry white wine
1 teaspoon lemon juice
½ teaspoon salt
Freshly ground pepper to taste
1 tablespoon chopped parsley
½ cup buttered crumbs
Paprika

Wash and dry scallops; cut in two if large.

Heat butter in skillet; sauté mushrooms and onion until tender but not overcooked. Stir in flour; cook several minutes. Stir in wine, lemon juice, salt, pepper, and parsley; bring to a boil. Add scallops. Spoon into casserole; sprinkle with buttered crumbs and paprika. Bake in 375°F toaster oven 25 minutes.

Vegetables

Baked Acorn Squash

Yield: 2 servings

1 acorn squash
Salt to taste
Butter

Cut squash in half lengthwise; scoop out seeds and fibers. Place on oven tray, cut-side-down. Bake in 375°F toaster oven 25 minutes. Turn squash over; bake for another 20 to 25 minutes or until soft. Sprinkle with salt; serve immediately with butter.

Vegetable Casserole

Yield: 6 servings

1½ cups sliced carrots
1 medium onion, sliced
1 10-ounce package frozen leaf spinach
3 tablespoons butter
3 tablespoons flour
1½ cups milk
1 cup shredded process cheese
¼ teaspoon salt
Pepper to taste
½ cup soft bread crumbs
Butter

Cook carrots and onion covered in small amount of boiling salted water about 6 minutes or until almost tender. Drain; set aside.

Cook spinach according to package directions. Drain.

Prepare sauce. Melt 3 tablespoons butter in saucepan. Blend in flour. Gradually stir in milk. Cool and stir until thick. Remove from heat. Add cheese, salt, and pepper. Stir until cheese melts.

Place half of spinach in 1-quart casserole. Cover with half the carrots and onions. Top with half the cheese sauce. Repeat for another layer. Top with crumbs; dot with butter. Bake in 325°F toaster oven 20 minutes.

Broccoli Casserole

Yield: 4 servings

1 package frozen broccoli
1¼ cups milk
3 eggs, lightly beaten
½ teaspoon salt
½ teaspoon nutmeg
½ cup grated cheese

Cook broccoli in small amount of boiling water for 3 minutes. Drain.

Pour milk into small saucepan; bring to boil. Cool until lukewarm.

Mix eggs with salt and nutmeg. Add milk and cheese, beating constantly. Pour into greased baking dish; add broccoli. Bake in 350°F toaster oven 25 to 30 minutes or until a knife inserted in center comes out clean. Serve immediately.

Baked Eggplant

Yield: 3 to 4 servings

1 medium eggplant
Butter or margarine to grease baking
   dish
Salt to taste
Pepper to taste
2 egg yolks, beaten
1 cup grated cheese (American, or
   kind of your choice)

Peel eggplant; cut lengthwise into 1-inch slices. Place in bowl of cold salted water for 1 hour. Drain; pat dry with paper towels. Place eggplant in greased baking dish. Sprinkle with salt and pepper; brush with egg yolks. Sprinkle cheese over top. Bake in 350°F toaster oven for 20 to 25 minutes.

Cauliflower Casserole

Yield: 4 servings

1 medium cauliflower, separated into
   florets
2 tablespoons butter
2 tablespoons flour
1½ cups milk
Salt to taste
Pepper to taste
1½ cups grated cheese (American or
   cheddar)
Bread crumbs
Butter

Cook cauliflower in salted water until tender but not mushy.

Blend butter and flour in medium saucepan. Add milk and salt and pepper to taste. Cook over low heat, stirring constantly, until it comes to a boil. Add cheese; mix through. Drain cauliflower; place in baking dish. Pour sauce over cauliflower; sprinkle bread crumbs over sauce. Dot with butter. Bake in 350°F toaster oven until golden brown.

Carrot Squares

Yield: 12 to 16 squares

¼ cup margarine
¾ cup light brown sugar, lightly
   packed
1 egg
1 cup flour
1 teaspoon baking powder
¼ teaspoon salt
1 cup finely grated carrots
¼ cup chopped walnuts

Melt margarine in saucepan. Add sugar; blend well. Remove from heat; let cool. Beat in egg, then flour, baking powder, salt, and

carrots. Pour into greased 8-inch-square pan. Sprinkle with nuts. Bake for 20 to 25 minutes in 350°F toaster oven preheated for 2 minutes.

Corn Casserole

Yield: 4 servings

2 cups canned corn, drained
2 eggs, beaten
1 tablespoon butter
⅛ teaspoon chili powder
⅛ teaspoon anise seed
1 teaspoon flour
¼ pound thinly sliced Swiss cheese

Combine corn and eggs; set aside.

Heat butter in small skillet. Add chili powder, anise seed, and flour. Cook 1 minute. Combine with corn mixture. Pour half of mixture into well-greased 1-quart casserole. Cover with slices of cheese. Cover with remaining corn mixture. Bake in 350°F toaster oven 40 minutes.

Green Bean Casserole

Yield: 2 servings

1 large can whole string beans, drained
½ can cream of mushroom soup
Grated American cheese

Grease small casserole dish. Place layer of beans on bottom. Follow with layer of soup and layer of cheese. Repeat. Bake in 325°F toaster oven approximately 30 minutes.

Egyptian Okra Casserole

Yield: 2 to 3 servings

¾ pound okra
1½ tablespoons butter

½ small onion, chopped
½ pound ground beef
1 clove garlic, minced
3 tablespoons tomato paste
¾ cup hot beef broth
Pepper to taste
Salt to taste
½ cup yogurt
Butter or margarine to grease baking
  dish
1 lemon, cut into wedges
Parsley

Thoroughly wash okra. Remove stems; cut okra in half lengthwise.

Heat ¾ tablespoon butter in skillet. Add okra; cook for 5 minutes, stirring constantly. Remove with slotted spoon; drain in colander.

In another skillet add rest of butter (¾ tablespoon). Heat; stir in onion. Cook until golden. Add ground beef; cook for 10 minutes. Stir in garlic, tomato paste, and ½ cup hot beef broth. Season to taste with pepper and salt. Cook, uncovered for 10 minutes or until almost all liquid has evaporated. Remove skillet from heat; stir in yogurt.

Grease baking dish. Spoon in half of meat mixture, top with okra, then rest of meat. Pour ¼ cup hot beef broth over it. Place in preheated 375°F toaster oven; bake for 50 minutes. Garnish with lemon wedges and parsley before serving.

Green Peppers Stuffed with Vegetables

Yield: 4 servings

4 green peppers (medium size)
1 cup canned corn
¾ cup diced tomatoes

¼ cup finely chopped celery
1 tablespoon finely chopped onion
2 slightly beaten eggs (if eggs are
  jumbo, use 1 egg)
½ cup soft bread crumbs
2 tablespoons melted butter
Salt to taste
Freshly ground pepper to taste

Remove top and seeds from peppers. Parboil 5 minutes. Drain well.

Combine remaining ingredients; mix thoroughly. Stuff peppers. Place upright in greased baking dish. Add 3 tablespoons water. Place in 325°F toaster oven; bake about 1 hour.

Onion Casserole

Yield: 5 to 6 servings

3 cups small white onions, peeled
Boiling salted water
½ cup catsup
⅓ cup honey
2 tablespoons butter

Parboil onions in boiling salted water about 5 minutes. Drain; place in 1-quart casserole. Cover with catsup and honey. Dot with butter. Cover; bake in 350°F toaster oven about 40 minutes or until tender. Uncover casserole last 10 minutes of baking.

Pea Pod Casserole

Yield: 4 servings

1 package frozen pea pods, boiled
1 can water chestnuts, sliced
1 can bean sprouts, or fresh bean
   sprouts
1 can cream of mushroom soup
1 can onion rings, optional

Boil pea pods 2 minutes. Drain; place in casserole dish. Place sliced water chestnuts on top of pea pods. Next place layer of bean sprouts. If canned bean sprouts are used, drain. If fresh are used, first blanch, then rinse with cold water; drain well. Cover with cream of mushroom soup. Bake for 15 minutes in 350°F toaster oven. Place onion rings on top; heat again about 2 or 3 minutes.

Fluffy Potato Casserole

Yield: 4 to 5 servings

5 medium potatoes, peeled and cut
   into pieces
Salt to taste
Pepper to taste
Hot milk
½ cup heavy cream, whipped
⅓ cup shredded sharp cheese

Cook potatoes in boiling, salted water until soft, about 30 minutes. Drain and mash. Season with salt and pepper, and add enough hot milk to whip light. Pile into 1-quart casserole. Whip cream and fold cheese into cream. Spread mixture over potatoes in casserole. Bake in toaster oven at 350°F for 15 minutes or until lightly browned.

Potato and Bacon Casserole

Yield: 4 servings

2½ pounds potatoes
Salt
½ pound bacon
1 medium onion, chopped
Butter or margarine to grease casserole
2 tablespoons flour
2 cups sour cream
1 egg
Salt to taste
1 tablespoon packaged bread crumbs
2 ounces grated Swiss cheese
1½ tablespoons butter

Clean potatoes under cold running water. Place in large pot; cover with salted water; cook, covered, for 25 minutes. Drain, rinse quickly under cold running water. Peel, let cool slightly, and slice. Dice bacon. Chop onion.

Grease baking dish. Fill with half the potato slices. Mix bacon and onion; spread over potato slices. Cover with rest of potato slices.

In small bowl blend flour and 3 tablespoons sour cream until smooth. Stir in rest of sour cream and egg. Season to taste with salt; pour over potatoes. Sprinkle with bread crumbs and grated cheese. Dot with butter. Bake in preheated 400°F toaster oven 40 minutes. Serve with a tossed green salad.

Potato Scallop

Yield: 4 servings

3 cups sliced cooked potatoes
Butter to grease casserole
1 cup sour cream
2 eggs, slightly beaten
¼ cup milk
¼ cup chopped chives
½ teaspoon salt
⅛ teaspoon freshly ground pepper
1 cup shredded American cheese

Arrange potatoes in buttered 1½-quart casserole.

Mix sour cream with eggs, milk, chives, salt, and pepper. Pour over potatoes. Cover with cheese. Bake in 350°F toaster oven 30 minutes or until lightly browned.

Swedish Parmesan Potatoes

Yield: 3 to 4 servings

6 small potatoes
Butter or margarine to grease baking
   dish
Salt
2 tablespoons butter
1 tablespoon grated Parmesan cheese
   (more if desired)

Peel and wash potatoes. Pat dry with paper towels. Cut potatoes into ¼-inch slices, but do not cut through completely. Potato should still be in one piece on bottom. A good way to do this is to put the po-tato on a soup spoon and cut into it. Place potatoes close together in a greased baking dish, sliced-side-up. Sprinkle with salt; dot with butter. Place in preheated 350°F toaster oven; bake about 1 hour. Baste occasionally with pan drippings. Five minutes before end of cooking time, sprinkle with Parmesan cheese. Serve immediately.

Twice-Baked Potatoes

Yield: 4 servings

2 baking potatoes, prepared for baking
Butter
Milk
Salt
Pepper
Paprika
Grated cheese, optional

Place potatoes on toaster oven baking pan. Preheat oven to 400°F. Bake approximately 35 to 45 minutes, depending on size of potato. When potato feels soft to the touch, remove from oven. Cut in half lengthwise. Scoop out potato, reserving skins. Whip potato until fluffy with butter, enough milk to make it smooth, and salt and pepper. Spoon back into shells. Sprinkle with paprika and cheese, if desired. Heat in toaster oven until golden brown.

Sweet Potato Bake

Yield: 4 servings

1 18-ounce can sweet potatoes, drained
  and mashed
½ cup mandarin oranges, drained
  (reserve ¼ cup liquid)
¼ cup firmly packed brown sugar
2 tablespoons butter or margarine
24 miniature marshmallows

Preheat toaster oven at 400°F for 2 minutes.

Mix together sweet potatoes and oranges. Divide into 4 custard cups. Pour some of reserved liquid into each cup. Sprinkle with brown sugar; dot with butter. Place dishes on oven tray; set tray on toaster rack. Bake 10 minutes at 400°F. Remove from toaster oven; place marshmallows on top of mixture. Bake for another 8 minutes. Serve immediately.

Yam and Pecan Casserole

Yield: 4 servings

4 medium yams, cooked, peeled, and
  mashed
1 tablespoon lemon juice
3 teaspoons grated lemon rind
½ cup chopped pecans
2 tablespoons butter
¼ teaspoon salt
½ cup firmly packed brown sugar
Butter to grease casserole
2 tablespoons brown sugar
2 tablespoons chopped pecans

Combine yams, lemon juice, 2 teaspoons lemon rind, ½ cup pecans, butter, salt, and ½ cup brown sugar. Mix well; put into buttered 1½-quart casserole.

Combine 2 tablespoons brown sugar, 2 tablespoons pecans, and 1 teaspoon grated lemon rind. Sprinkle over yam mixture. Bake in 350°F toaster oven 20 minutes.

Spinach Casserole

Yield: 4 servings

2 packages frozen spinach, cooked and
  well drained
Butter to grease casserole
2 cups cooked noodles, well drained
1 cup shredded American cheese
1 can condensed cream of mushroom
  soup
⅓ cup milk
⅛ teaspoon ground nutmeg

Place layer of spinach in greased 1½-quart casserole. Place layer of noodles on top; sprinkle with half of the cheese.

Mix soup with milk and nutmeg; pour over cheese layer in casserole. Top with remaining cheese. Bake in 350°F toaster oven about 40 minutes.

Tomatoes Royale

Yield: 4 to 5 servings

4 slices toast, cut into cubes
2 cups canned tomatoes
2 teaspoons grated onion
Salt to taste
Freshly ground pepper to taste
¼ cup melted butter

Toast bread in toaster oven; cube.

Alternate layers of tomatoes and toast cubes in greased 1-quart casserole, ending with layer of toast cubes. Sprinkle with onion, salt, and pepper. Pour butter over all; place in toaster oven. Bake at 350°F for 20 minutes or until heated through.

Snacks

Cheese Roll-overs

Yield: Varies

Bread slices, crusts removed
Soft butter
Grated cheese

Remove crust from bread slices. Spread slices with butter. Sprinkle with grated cheese. Fasten opposite corners together with toothpicks. Bake in 400°F toaster oven 10 minutes.

Crab Burgers

Yield: 4 servings

½ pound crab meat, cartilage removed
1 tablespoon finely chopped green
  pepper
⅓ cup finely chopped celery
1 tablespoon minced onion
½ cup mayonnaise
Few sprinkles Worcestershire sauce
Few sprinkles hot sauce
Salt to taste
Lemon and pepper seasoning to taste
4 hamburger buns, split
Grated Parmesan cheese for topping

Mix crab meat, green pepper, celery, onion, and mayonnaise in bowl. Add Worcestershire sauce, hot sauce, salt, and lemon and pepper seasoning.

Place hamburger buns on toaster oven broiler tray; lightly brown. Remove from toaster oven; spread crab meat mixture on buns. Sprinkle cheese over top. Broil until lightly browned.

Baked Orange

Yield: 4 servings

2 oranges, cut in half
4 tablespoons honey
1 tablespoon butter
Juice of ½ lemon

Place oranges in casserole. Drizzle honey over each half; dot with butter. Sprinkle with lemon juice. Bake in 350°F toaster oven 45 minutes.

Quick Pizza

Yield: 6 individual pizzas

3 English muffins. split
1 8-ounce can tomato sauce
Oregano
6 slices mozarella cheese

Place 6 English muffin halves on oven tray. Toast, using top brown cycle. Spread tomato sauce on each muffin half, sprinkle with oregano, and place 1 slice cheese on each muffin half. Return to toaster oven; top brown until cheese is bubbly. Serve immediately.

Snack Puffs

Yield: 16 pieces

16 slices cocktail rye bread
½ cup mayonnaise
¼ cup finely chopped onion
2 tablespoons chopped parsley
8 slices Swiss cheese

Toast bread on both sides.

Combine mayonnaise, onion, and parsley. Spread on toast. Cut out rounds of cheese to fit toast. Place a cheese round on top of each piece of toast, covering mayonnaise mixture. Top brown until golden and cheese is puffy, approximately 2 minutes.

Rye-Cheese Melts

Yield: 4 servings

This is good with a bowl of cream of tomato soup for a light or late supper.

4 slices thin rye bread
Butter
4 slices red onion
4 slices Swiss cheese
Freshly ground pepper to taste

Butter each slice of rye bread. Place slice of onion on each; top with slice of cheese. Place on oven tray; put in toaster oven. Top brown until cheese is bubbly.

Tuna Surprise

Yield: 4 sandwiches

1 small can tuna (6½ or 7 ounces), drained and flaked
2 tablespoons chopped onion
2 tablespoons sweet pickle relish

¼ cup mayonnaise
4 hamburger buns, split and toasted
Butter
4 slices sharp processed cheese

Combine tuna, onion, pickle relish, and mayonnaise.

Split and toast hamburger buns; butter bottom halves; spread with tuna mixture. Top each with slice of sharp processed cheese. Top brown until cheese melts. Add tops of buns.

Desserts

Apple Crisp Delight

Yield: 4 to 6 servings

1 22-ounce can apple pie filling
1 cup quick-cooking oats
½ cup firmly packed brown sugar
½ cup butter or margarine, softened
¼ cup flour
1 teaspoon cinnamon
½ teaspoon (scant) nutmeg

Preheat toaster oven at 325°F for 2 minutes.

Spread apple filling in 8-inch-square pan.

Combine remaining ingredients in bowl; mix thoroughly. Spread over apple filling. Bake for 25 minutes at 325°F. Serve with vanilla ice cream or whipped cream.

Apple Kuchen

Yield: 6 servings

A delicious kuchen—especially good with vanilla ice cream.

1 cup flour
1 tablespoon sugar
½ cup butter
1 egg yolk
Dash of salt
4 or 5 apples, peeled, cored, and cut into eighths
Sugar and cinnamon (be generous)

Custard

2 eggs, well-beaten
½ cup sugar
2 tablespoons cream
1 teaspoon vanilla

Mix flour with sugar. Cut in butter. Add egg yolk and salt; mix well. Pat into 8-inch-pie plate. Refrigerate for 1 hour.

Prepare apples; place in even rows in prepared pie plate. Sprinkle with sugar and cinnamon.

Mix together all custard ingredients well; pour over apples. Bake in preheated 375°F toaster oven 20 minutes. Reduce heat to 300°F; bake for another 25 minutes or until crust is browned.

Apples Flambé

Yield: 4 servings

4 apples
2 tablespoons chopped walnuts
2 tablespoons chopped dates
Confectioner's sugar
Butter
1 cup white wine

2 jiggers rum
1 cup heavy cream, whipped and slightly sweetened

Wash and core apples. Scoop out centers to get holes about 1½ inches in diameter.

Mix nuts and dates with a little confectioners' sugar. Fill apples.

Grease baking dish with butter. Place apples in dish; surround with any leftover filling. Pour in wine. Bake for 10 minutes in 325°F toaster oven. (Apples should still be crunchy, not too soft.)

Heat rum. Remove apples from oven. Pour hot rum over apples; ignite. Decorate with whipped cream; serve immediately.

Chocolate Applesauce Cake

Yield: Approximately 10 to 12 pieces

½ cup shortening
2 eggs
1 cup sugar
½ cup applesauce
2 squares unsweetened chocolate, melted
1 cup flour
¼ teaspoon baking soda
½ teaspoon baking powder
½ teaspoon salt
1 teaspoon vanilla
½ cup chopped walnuts
1 cup chopped raisins

Cream shortening. Add eggs and sugar; mix well. Add applesauce and melted chocolate; mix well. Blend in dry ingredients, vanilla, nuts, and raisins. Pour into greased and floured loaf pan or 8-inch-square pan. Bake in 350°F toaster oven 45 minutes or until done.

Apricot-Almond Cookies

Yield: About 2 dozen cookies

¼ pound butter
1½ tablespoons sugar
1 egg yolk
½ cup almond paste
2 tablespoons lemon juice
1 tablespoon grated lemon rind
Pinch of salt
8 ounces flour
Butter or margarine to grease oven tray
1 egg white
1 teaspoon water
Apricot jam
3 tablespoons chopped almonds

Beat butter and sugar until creamy. Gradually add egg yolk and almond paste. Now add and thoroughly stir in lemon juice and rind, salt, and flour. With cold hands, knead dough until smooth. Shape into a ball, wrap in aluminum foil, and place in refrigerator for 30 minutes.

Meanwhile, grease oven tray. Preheat toaster oven to 400°F.

Dust working surface with flour. Roll out dough and cut out cookies with cookie cutter 2-inches in diameter. Place on oven tray.

Beat egg white with water; brush cookies with mixture. Place in oven; bake for 8 to 10 minutes. Remove; spread generously with apricot jam. Sprinkle with almonds.

Baked Bananas with Honey Glaze

Yield: 4 servings

4 bananas
Juice of 1 lemon
Butter or margarine to grease baking dish
2 tablespoons honey
2 to 3 ounces blanched chopped almonds
3 tablespoons packaged bread crumbs
2 tablespoons butter

Peel bananas; sprinkle with lemon juice. Grease baking dish; arrange bananas in dish. Pour honey over bananas.

Mix chopped almonds and bread crumbs; sprinkle over crumbs. Dot with butter. Bake in preheated 400°F toaster oven 12 to 15 minutes. Remove; serve while still hot.

Blueberry Cake

Yield: Approximately 12 pieces

2 tablespoons soft butter
1 cup sugar
2 egg yolks, beaten
1½ cups flour
1¼ teaspoons baking powder
½ teaspoon salt
⅓ cup milk
1 teaspoon vanilla
2 egg whites, stiffly beaten
1½ cups fresh blueberries, drained and lightly floured

Cream butter and sugar. Add beaten egg yolks; mix well. Blend in flour, baking powder, and salt. Add milk and vanilla; mix thoroughly. Fold in stiffly beaten egg whites. Pour half of the batter into greased and floured 8-inch-square pan. Cover with floured blueberries, then add remaining batter. Bake in 350°F toaster oven 25 to 30 minutes or until done.

Blueberry Pudding

Yield: 6 servings

This is delicious served with whipped cream or vanilla ice cream.

    4 cups fresh blueberries
    ⅓ cup sugar
    2 teaspoons lemon juice
    4 tablespoons butter or margarine
    ⅓ cup light brown sugar, firmly
        packed
    ⅓ cup sifted all-purpose flour
    ¾ cup quick-cooking oats

Place blueberries in 1½-quart baking dish. Sprinkle with sugar and lemon juice.

Cream butter or margarine. Gradually add brown sugar. Blend in flour and oats with a fork, mixing until just blended. Spread topping over blueberries. Bake in 350°F toaster oven 35 to 40 minutes or until lightly browned.

Brownies

Yield: 16 squares

    2 squares unsweetened chocolate
    ½ cup butter or margarine
    1 cup sugar
    2 eggs
    ¾ cup flour
    ½ teaspoon salt
    ½ teaspoon baking powder
    ½ cup broken nuts, optional

Heat toaster oven to 350°F. Grease an 8-inch-square pan.

Melt chocolate and butter or margarine together over hot water. Beat in sugar and eggs.

Sift together flour, salt, and baking powder. Stir into chocolate mixture, mixing thoroughly. Mix in nuts. Spread evenly in pan. Bake 30 minutes or until a slight crust has formed on top.

Baked Custard Supreme

Yield: 3 servings

These can be unmolded and served with thawed frozen strawberries or raspberries. They make a very tasty and pretty dessert.

    1 egg
    ¼ cup sugar
    ⅛ teaspoon salt
    1 cup scalded milk
    ¼ teaspoon vanilla
    Nutmeg

Heat toaster oven to 350°F.

Beat egg. Add sugar and salt; mix well. Stir in milk and vanilla. Pour into 3 custard cups; set in pan of hot water (about 1 inch deep). Sprinkle with nutmeg. Bake about 45 minutes or until silver knife inserted 1 inch from edge comes out clean. Cool, then refrigerate.

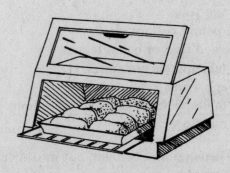

Egg White Cookies

Yield: About 4 dozen

3 egg whites
1 cup sugar
½ teaspoon lemon juice
½ cup slivered almonds

Beat egg whites until stiff. Add sugar gradually, continuing to beat. Add lemon juice. Fold in almonds.

Line toaster oven tray with aluminum foil. Drop meringue mixture by teaspoons onto foil. Bake in 350°F toaster oven about 8 to 9 minutes or until lightly browned.

Fruit and Cottage Cheese Casserole

Yield: 4 servings

This is a nice dessert after a simple dinner.

2 bananas
2 oranges
8- to 10-ounce can pitted cherries
Butter or margarine to grease baking dish
1 tablespoon chopped walnuts
5 tablespoons sugar
2 tablespoons butter or margarine
2 egg yolks
½ pound cottage cheese
Grated rind of half a lemon
5 tablespoons cornstarch
2 egg whites
1 tablespoon packaged bread crumbs
1 tablespoon butter

Peel bananas and oranges; cut into slices. Drain cherries.

In well-greased baking dish first arrange banana slices, then orange slices, and, on top of that, cherries. Sprinkle with chopped nuts and 1 tablespoon sugar.

Beat 2 tablespoons butter, 4 tablespoons sugar, and egg yolks together until smooth and creamy.

Put cottage cheese in blender; blend until smooth. Add grated lemon rind, cottage cheese, and cornstarch to egg-yolk mixture; mix thoroughly.

Beat egg whites until stiff; fold in. Spread cheese mixture over fruit. Sprinkle with bread crumbs; dot with butter. Bake in preheated 400°F toaster oven 30 to 35 minutes.

Fudge Bars

Yield: Approximately 12 to 16 pieces

⅓ cup shortening
6 ounces chocolate chips
½ teaspoon vanilla
½ cup sugar
2 eggs
½ cup flour
¼ teaspoon salt
1 cup chopped walnuts

Heat shortening and chocolate chips in top of double boiler until melted. Remove from heat, stir, and let cool. Add vanilla, sugar, and eggs, mixing well. Stir in flour, salt, and walnuts. Spread into 8-inch-square pan. Bake in 325°F toaster oven 20 to 25 minutes. Cut into bars (or squares) while still warm.

Gingerbread

Yield: 12 pieces

½ cup shortening
½ cup sugar
1 egg
½ cup light molasses
1½ cups sifted flour
¾ teaspoon salt
¾ teaspoon baking soda
½ teaspoon ginger
½ teaspoon cinnamon
½ cup boiling water

Cream shortening and sugar until light and fluffy. Add eggs and molasses; beat thoroughly.

Sift together dry ingredients. Add to molasses mixture alternately with boiling water, beating well after each addition. Bake in greased 8-inch-square pan in 350°F toaster oven approximately 30 to 35 minutes or until cake tests done.

Loaf Cake

Yield: About 12 slices

½ cup butter
1 cup sugar
2 eggs, separated
1½ cups flour
2 teaspoons baking powder
¼ teaspoon salt
⅔ cup milk
Juice of ½ orange
Juice of ½ lemon

Cream butter. Add sugar and egg yolks; beat until light and fluffy.

Sift dry ingredients together twice. Add flour mixture and milk alternately to first mixture. Add orange and lemon juice. Fold in beaten egg whites. Bake in greased loaf pan in 350°F toaster oven 20 minutes.

Nut and Date Bread

Yield: Approximately 12 slices

¾ cup chopped nuts
1 cup chopped dates
½ teaspoon salt
1½ teaspoons baking soda
¼ cup shortening
¾ cup boiling water
2 eggs
½ teaspoon vanilla
1½ cups sifted flour
1 cup sugar

Combine nuts, dates, salt, and baking soda in mixing bowl. Add shortening and boiling water. Let mixture stand 20 minutes. Stir to blend.

Beat eggs slightly; add vanilla.

Stir flour and sugar together. Add to date mixture. Mix until just blended. Place in greased loaf pan. Bake in 350°F toaster oven 1 hour or until bread tests done.

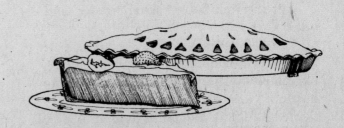

1-2-3 Cake

Yield: Approximately 16 pieces

This is a simple and delicious cake.

¼ pound butter, softened
1 cup sugar
2 eggs
2 cups sifted cake flour
1 teaspoon baking powder
1 teaspoon baking soda
½ pint sour cream
½ teaspoon vanilla

Blend all ingredients together. Pour batter into 8-inch-square pan. Bake in 350°F toaster oven about 40 minutes or until cake tests done.

Pineapple Cake

Yield: About 16 pieces

½ cup shortening
1 cup sugar
2 eggs
½ teaspoon rum flavoring
1 teaspoon vanilla extract
1¾ cups flour
1½ teaspoons baking powder
¼ teaspoon salt
¼ teaspoon baking soda
1 cup crushed pineapple, undrained

Cream shortening and sugar. Add eggs; beat until fluffy. Blend in rum flavoring and vanilla extract.

Sift together flour, baking powder, and salt.

Stir baking soda into crushed pineapple. Add flour mixture and pineapple mixture alternately to shortening and sugar mixture; beat until smooth. Bake in greased and floured 8-inch pan in 350°F toaster oven 40 minutes.

Peach Cobbler

Yield: 6 servings

3 cups sliced fresh peaches
Butter or margarine to grease baking
  pan
1 cup sugar
1 tablespoon lemon juice
1 teaspoon grated lemon rind
¼ teaspoon almond extract
1½ cups sifted flour
3 teaspoons baking powder
½ teaspoon salt
3 tablespoons sugar
⅓ cup shortening
½ cup milk
1 egg, well-beaten

Place peaches in greased 8-inch baking pan.

Mix together 1 cup sugar, lemon juice and rind, and almond extract. Put over peaches. Place pan in warm oven while preparing shortcake.

Sift together flour, baking powder, salt, and 1 tablespoon sugar. Cut in shortening until mixture is crumbly. Add milk and egg. Mix until flour is just moistened. Spread over hot peaches. Sprinkle with 2 tablespoons sugar. Bake in 400°F toaster oven 30 to 35 minutes.

Pear Casserole

Yield: 4 to 5 servings

6 fresh pears
½ cup chopped seedless raisins
¼ cup brown sugar
1 teaspoon grated lemon rind
Butter to grease casserole
¾ cup Sauterne wine
¼ cup brandy
½ cup macaroon crumbs

Peel and core pears; slice into thin slices.

Mix together raisins, sugar, and lemon rind; arrange alternately with pear slices in buttered 1-quart casserole. Pour wine and brandy over pears. Cover; bake in 350°F toaster oven 25 minutes. Uncover, sprinkle macaroon crumbs on top, and continue baking for another 7 minutes or until crumbs are browned.

Pumpkin Bread

Yield: About 12 slices

1¼ cups sugar
⅓ cup shortening
2 eggs, beaten
8 ounces pumpkin
⅓ cup water
1½ cups plus 1 tablespoon flour
¼ teaspoon baking powder
1 teaspoon baking soda
1 teaspoon salt
¼ teaspoon cloves
½ teaspoon cinnamon
⅓ cup chopped dates
⅓ cup chopped walnuts

Cream sugar and shortening until light and fluffy. Stir in eggs, pumpkin, and water.

Sift together flour, baking powder, baking soda, salt, cloves, and cinnamon. Gradually stir dry ingredients into pumpkin mixture. Add dates and nuts; blend thoroughly. Spoon batter into greased loaf pan. Bake in 350°F toaster oven about 1 hour and 5 minutes or until bread tests done.

Sugar-and-Cinnamon-Topped Coffee Cake

Yield: About 12 pieces

1¼ cups flour
¼ teaspoon salt
1 teaspoon cream of tartar
½ teaspoon baking soda
4 tablespoons butter
1 cup sugar
1 egg
½ cup milk
Butter to grease pan
⅓ cup brown sugar
2 tablespoons cinnamon

Sift together flour, salt, cream of tartar, and baking soda.

Cream the butter; gradually add sugar. Beat until fluffy. Add egg. Add flour mixture, alternating with milk. Pour into greased 8-inch-square pan. Sprinkle with mixture of brown sugar and cinnamon. Bake in preheated 350°F toaster oven 25 to 30 minutes.

Crunchy Rice Pudding

Yield: 4 to 5 servings

1 cup rice
¼ cup butter or margarine
⅞ cup sugar
½ teaspoon cinnamon
Rind of 1 lemon
3 eggs, well beaten
½ cup raisins
¼ cup chopped nuts

Cook rice according to package directions. Cool.

Cream butter or margarine and sugar. Add cinnamon, lemon rind, and eggs; mix well. Stir in raisins, nuts, and rice. Bake uncovered in greased 1-quart baking dish in 350°F toaster oven 45 minutes.

Walnut Squares

Yield: 12 to 16 squares

1 egg
1 cup light brown sugar, firmly packed
1 teaspoon vanilla
½ cup flour
¼ teaspoon salt
¼ teaspoon baking soda
1 cup coarsely chopped walnuts

Stir together egg, brown sugar, and vanilla. Add flour, salt, baking soda, and nuts. Spread into well-greased 8-inch-square pan. Bake in 350°F toaster oven 15 minutes. These will be soft when removed from pan. Cut into squares when cool.

Wok
Hors D'Oeuvres

Oriental Cocktail Kabobs

Yield: 40 to 50

1 15¼-ounce can pineapple chunks, drained
1-pound package brown-and-serve sausages, cooked according to the package directions, and cut into thirds
1 8-ounce can water chestnuts, halved
2 green peppers, cut into ¾-inch squares
¼ pound small mushrooms, stemmed
Reserved syrup from drained pineapple
4 tablespoons soy sauce
3 slices fresh ginger root
3 tablespoons brown sugar
2 tablespoons dry sherry

Alternate pieces of pineapple, sausage, water chestnuts, green pepper, and mushrooms on toothpicks. Combine the reserved pineapple syrup, soy sauce, ginger root, brown sugar, and sherry and heat in a wok. Add the kabobs, cover, and simmer 10 minutes. Remove from wok and serve warm.

Shrimp Puffs

Yield: About 16

1 pound shrimps, cleaned, deveined, chopped very fine
8 to 9 water chestnuts, minced
1 egg, beaten

1 teaspoon salt
½ teaspoon sugar
1 teaspoon cornstarch
2 teaspoons dry sherry
1 teaspoon soy sauce
2 cups oil for frying
Lemon wedges and soy sauce for dipping

Combine the shrimps, water chestnuts, egg, salt, sugar, cornstarch, sherry, and soy sauce. Heat oil in the wok to 375°F. Shape the shrimp mixture into balls the size of small walnuts and drop from a spoon into the hot oil. Fry until the balls float and turn pink and golden. Drain on paper towels. Serve hot with lemon wedges and a bowl of soy sauce for dipping.

Marinated Radishes and Celery

Yield: 6 servings

4 tablespoons soy sauce
6 tablespoons vinegar
1 tablespoon sesame oil
6-ounce bag radishes, cleaned
2 stalks celery, sliced diagonally into 1-inch pieces

Mix soy sauce, vinegar, and sesame oil in small bowl. Add radishes and celery. Cover and refrigerate 1 hour—no longer.

Hong Kong Meatballs

Yield: 6 servings

1½ pounds ground beef
½ cup celery, very finely chopped
1 teaspoon seasoned salt
1 teaspoon soy sauce
1 tablespoon vegetable oil
¼ cup bamboo shoots, sliced thin
1 1-pound can mixed Chinese
    vegetables or bean sprouts, drained,
    with liquid reserved
1 green pepper, seeded and cut in
    julienne strips
1 carrot, peeled and shredded
1 5-ounce can water chestnuts, drained
    and sliced thin
1½ tablespoons cornstarch
2 teaspoons (additional) soy sauce
2 teaspoons sherry
¼ cup blanched, slivered almonds

Mix ground beef with celery, seasoned salt, and soy sauce. Mix thoroughly to blend all ingredients, then shape into 1-inch-diameter meatballs.

Heat the vegetable oil in a large skillet or wok, and sauté the meatballs over high heat until browned on all sides. Stir in the bamboo shoots; cover, and simmer 5 minutes, stirring occasionally. At the end of the cooking time, pour off any accumulated fat.

Add the drained Chinese vegetables, green pepper strips, shredded carrot, and water chestnuts. Stir well. In a 2-cup measure, mix the cornstarch, soy sauce, and sherry until a thin paste is formed. Add the liquid from the Chinese vegetables and enough water to make 2 cups in all. Add to the meatballs and cook uncovered for 5 to 10 minutes, stirring occasionally, until sauce is thickened. Sprinkle on the almonds before serving.

Soups

Peking Egg Drop Soup

Yield: 4 to 6 servings

¼ pound lean pork shoulder, cut into
    fine strips
2 ounces bamboo shoots, finely sliced
4 or 5 dried black Chinese mushrooms,
    soaked 30 minutes in warm water
    and cut into small pieces
2 tablespoons vinegar
2 teaspoons soy sauce
¼ teaspoon (or less) ground pepper
1 quart chicken broth
½ teaspoon salt (or salt to taste)
1½ tablespoons cornstarch in 2
    tablespoons water
1 egg, beaten

Brown the strips of pork well in the wok or in a large saucepan. Add bamboo shoots, mushrooms, vinegar, soy sauce, pepper, chicken broth, salt, and cornstarch mixture. Bring mixture to a full boil, stirring constantly. Reduce heat. Add egg, a small amount at a time, stirring with a fork to separate it into shreds as it coagulates. Remove from heat and serve at once.

Chicken Egg Drop Soup

Yield: 4 servings

6 cups chicken broth
2 tablespoons cornstarch in 2
    tablespoons water
1 tablespoon soy sauce

½ teaspoon sugar
2 eggs, lightly beaten
Salt and pepper
2 scallions. sliced (green tops included)

Bring the chicken broth to a boil. Combine the cornstarch mixture with the soy sauce and sugar. Slowly stir into the broth. Heat and continue stirring until the soup is thickened and clear. Remove from the heat. Gradually add eggs, stirring with a fork until eggs separate into shreds. Season to taste with salt and pepper. Serve immediately garnished with sliced scallions.

Clam Soup

Yield: 3 or 4 servings

1 dozen large, fresh clams
5 cups water
1 teaspoon salt
1 teaspoon soy sauce
2 tablespoons dry sherry
1 scallion, sliced

Scrub the clams with a stiff brush to remove all sand and debris. Drop the clams into boiling water and boil just until the shells have opened. Remove from heat and discard the shells. Add the salt, soy sauce, and dry sherry to the broth. Place 3 or 4 clams in each bowl. Add the broth, and garnish with scallion slices.

Hot-and-Sour Soup

Yield: 4 to 6 servings

3 cups chicken broth
⅓ pound lean pork, shredded into
   matchstick-size pieces

4 Chinese dried black mushrooms,
   soaked for 20 to 30 minutes in
   warm water, and sliced
2 ounces bean curd, cut into
   matchstick-size pieces
2 tablespoons soy sauce
2 tablespoons dry sherry
1 teaspoon salt
½ teaspoon pepper
2 tablespoons vinegar
1 tablespoon cornstarch in 2
   tablespoons cold water

Bring the broth to a boil in the wok and add the pork, mushrooms, and bean curd. Simmer for 8 minutes, until the pork is done. Add the soy sauce, sherry, salt, pepper, vinegar, and the cornstarch mixture. Continue to heat until the soup has thickened. Serve hot.

Corn and Chicken Soup

Yield: 4 to 6 servings

6 ounces raw chicken meat, minced
1 tablespoon dry sherry
1 teaspoon salt
2 egg whites
1 quart chicken broth
1 10-ounce can cream-style corn
2 tablespoons cornstarch in ¼ cup
   cold water
Thin strips of ham

Combine the chicken with the sherry, salt, and egg whites. Bring the chicken broth to a full, rolling boil. Add minced-chicken mixture and corn. Simmer 2 minutes. Add cornstarch mixture and simmer an additional 2 minutes, stirring continuously. Add more salt, if needed. Pour into serving bowls and garnish with thin strips of ham.

327

Bird's Nest Soup

Yield: 8 servings

1½ cups bird's nest soaked overnight
in 1 quart of water, feathers and
debris removed
1½ pounds chicken (including bones)
6 cups cold water
4 teaspoons salt
5 dried red dates, if desired
½ cup cooked ham, chopped fine

Cook the bird's nest and water slowly for
1 hour in a wok and drain off the water.
Cold water may be added to cool the bird's
nest. Take a small portion of the bird's nest
in the hand and squeeze out the excess
water; remove and discard the black and
brown particles. Look over the entire quantity in this manner.

Place the chicken in 6 cups cold water,
add the salt, and skim off the substance that
rises to the top as the liquid comes to the
boiling point. Cook slowly for 1½ hours.
Add the dates and cleaned bird's nest and
continue simmering for 3 to 4 hours. Remove the chicken, separate the meat from
the bones, and chop the meat fine. Add 1
cup chopped chicken and ½ cup chopped
ham to the soup.

Mix slightly and serve hot. This soup is
usually served as the first course of a banquet
or elaborate dinner.

Chinese Soup

Yield: 4 to 6 servings

1 quart chicken broth
½ teaspoon salt (or salt to taste)
¼ teaspoon pepper (or less)
2 teaspoons soy sauce
2 ounces whole, cooked shrimps

2 ounces cooked ham, cut into thin
strips
2 ounces cooked chicken, cut into
thin strips

Bring the chicken broth to a boil and add
all the remaining ingredients. Simmer 3 to 4
minutes and serve immediately.

Chicken Soup Oriental

Yield: 4 to 6 servings

2 5-ounce cans boned chicken
5 cups chicken broth (use the liquid
from the boned chicken as part of
this liquid)
1 4-ounce can mushroom stems and
pieces, drained and liquid reserved
2 teaspoons soy sauce
2 cups fine egg noodles
4 thin slices lemon with rind

Add the chicken to the broth in the
wok. Cover and bring slowly to a boil. Add
the mushrooms, soy sauce, and noodles. Stir
and cook until the noodles are done. Garnish with lemon rind.

Celery Cabbage and Shrimp Soup

Yield: 6 servings

1 small head celery cabbage
5 water chestnuts
½ cup large dried or 1 cup canned
shrimps
1 cup water
1 tablespoon vegetable oil
3½ cups boiling water

1 teaspoon salt
4 green onions (with tops), finely
   chopped

Wash and cut the cabbage crosswise into 1-inch strips. Wash, peel, and cut the water chestnuts crosswise into ¼-inch slices. Soak the dried shrimps in 1 cup water for ½ hour. Drain the shrimps, but save the liquid. Heat the oil until it is very hot, add the shrimps, and fry for 2 to 3 minutes. Add the shrimp liquid, water chestnuts, 3½ cups boiling water, and salt. Bring the liquid to the boiling point and simmer for ½ hour. Add the cabbage and boil for 5 to 10 minutes, until the cabbage is tender but has not lost all its crispness. Add the finely chopped green onions and serve hot.

If wet-packed shrimps are used, substitute ⅔ cup liquid from the canned shrimps for ⅔ cup water. Clean the shrimps by removing the black vein along the back.

Celery Cabbage and Pork Soup

Yield: 6 servings

1 small head celery cabbage
5 water chestnuts
4 green onions (with tops), very finely
   chopped
½ cup ground pork
1 egg yolk
¾ teaspoon salt
4 cups boiling water

Wash and cut the cabbage crosswise into 1½-inch strips. Wash, peel, and cut the water chestnuts in cross sections ¼ inch thick. Chop the onions very fine and mix with the pork. Add the egg yolk. Combine

the salt, boiling water, and water chestnuts; cook for 15 minutes. Add the cabbage and cook until it is nearly tender. Drop the pork mixture, a teaspoonful at a time, into the soup. Boil for 5 minutes and serve hot.

Spinach Soup with Pork

Yield: 6 servings

1½ bunches spinach (1½ pounds)
1 tablespoon soy sauce
2¼ teaspoons salt
½ cup sliced lean pork, sliced
   1½ × ½ × ¼ inches
1 tablespoon vegetable oil
1 clove garlic, mashed
6 cups boiling water

Remove the tough stems from the spinach and wash the leafy portions thoroughly. Add the soy sauce and ¼ teaspoon salt to the pork. Heat the oil in a wok, add the mashed garlic and pork, and fry them for 3 minutes. Remove the garlic if desired. Add the boiling water, 2 teaspoons salt, and simmer for 10 minutes. Add the spinach and simmer for 5 minutes. Serve hot.

One-fourth cup dried shrimp may be substituted for the pork and the salt reduced to 1½ teaspoons. Wash and soak the shrimp for 15 minutes. Drain, but keep the liquid. Fry the shrimp, add the liquid, and simmer for 10 minutes, then add the spinach.

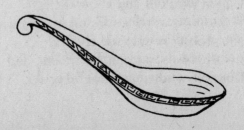

Pork and Watercress Soup

Yield: 4 to 6 servings

½ pound lean pork, shredded
6 cups chicken broth
1 small onion, sliced thin
1 celery stalk, sliced thin
1 teaspoon salt
¼ teaspoon pepper
1 cup firmly packed washed watercress,
  cut into 1-inch pieces

Simmer the pork in the chicken broth for 10 minutes. Add the onion, celery, salt, and pepper and simmer for 10 minutes longer. Add the watercress and heat briefly.

Cucumber Soup

Yield: 6 servings

¾ tablespoon salt
¼ teaspoon cornstarch
1 teaspoon soy sauce
½ cup pork, sliced in pieces
  ½ × ¼ × ¾ inch
1 tablespoon vegetable oil
4 cups water
10 medium-size mushrooms, cut into
  ½-inch strips
5 red dates, if desired
¾ cup bamboo shoots, sliced in pieces
  ½ × ¼ × ¾ inch
3 cucumbers
Fish balls, optional

Add ¼ teaspoon salt, cornstarch, and soy sauce to the pork and allow them to stand for 5 minutes. Heat the oil and brown the pork for 3 minutes. Add the water, mushrooms, red dates, bamboo shoots, and remaining salt, and simmer for 30 to 45 minutes. Discard the red dates. Peel the cucumbers and cut them into cross sections. Add the cucumber pieces to the soup and boil it for 3 minutes. Serve immediately.

Fish balls may be added. Drop them into the boiling soup and boil for 3 minutes after they come to the surface. Then add the cucumber pieces and boil the soup for 3 minutes.

Noodle Soup

Yield: 8 servings

1 box Canton or egg noodles
  (14 ounces)
2 eggs
½ tablespoon vegetable oil
5 medium dried mushrooms or ½ cup
  canned mushrooms
½ roll salted mustard cabbage root, if
  desired
5 cups meat, abalone, or chicken stock
1 tablespoon salt
3 tablespoons soy sauce
2 green onions, chopped fine
2 large pieces canned abalone
½ pound roast pork
Soy sauce and oil

Sauce

1 tablespoon peanut or vegetable oil
¼ cup soy sauce

Cook the noodles in salted boiling water for 15 minutes. Drain, and set them aside. Beat the eggs slightly. Heat the oil in a wok. Fry the eggs in one thin layer for 1 to 2 minutes or until firm. Turn over once. Fry for 1 minute. Remove from the wok and allow to cool.

Soak the dried mushrooms in water for 20 to 30 minutes. Drain mushrooms, remove, and discard the stems. Wash the salted cabbage root 3 or 4 times with cold water. Add the cabbage root and mushrooms to the stock and boil slowly for 45 minutes. Add the salt, soy sauce, and onions. Simmer for 2 to 3 minutes and remove the mushrooms.

Cut mushrooms, abalone, roast pork, and fried eggs into narrow strips about 1½ inches long and ⅛ inch wide. Place the noodles in a serving bowl. Spread the abalone over the noodles, then add the mushrooms, roast pork, and eggs. When ready to eat, pour the hot soup over this. Season at the table with the sauce mixture.

Combine the peanut oil and soy sauce and heat in a saucepan.

Meats

Beef with Chow Mein Noodles

Yield: 4 servings

1 pound beef (top of the round), cut
    into ¼-inch strips
2 tablespoons soy sauce
1 tablespoon cornstarch
2 tablespoons vegetable oil
1 slice of ginger root
2 green peppers, cut into ¼-inch strips
1 onion, sliced
Chow mein noodles

Combine the beef strips, soy sauce, and cornstarch. Allow to stand for 20 minutes. Heat oil in the wok and brown the slice of ginger. Remove and discard the ginger.

Stir-fry the green peppers and onion 2 to 3 minutes. Push aside. Stir-fry the beef 3 to 4 minutes. Return vegetables to the beef in the wok and reheat. Serve at once garnished with chow mein noodles.

Deep-fried Beef with Scallions

Yield: 4 servings

1 pound beef (flank or round) cut into
    ¼- x 3-inch strips

Frying Batter

1 large egg
1 cup sifted all-purpose flour
¾ cup water
2 cups oil for frying

8 scallions, sliced into ½-inch slices
1 clove garlic, minced
1 teaspoon grated ginger root
2 tablespoons vegetable oil
½ teaspoon salt
¼ cup dry white wine
1 to 2 tablespoons soy sauce
2 tablespoons black bean sauce

Combine batter ingredients. Let stand for 1 hour. Dip beef strips, a few at a time, into the batter and deep fry in oil at 400°F. Drain on paper towels and keep warm.

Combine remaining ingredients and simmer, covered, for 20 minutes. Place scallion mixture on a serving platter and top with deep-fried beef. Serve with boiled rice.

Beef Stroganoff

Yield: 4 servings

2 tablespoons vegetable oil
1 medium onion, sliced
¼ pound mushrooms, sliced into "T" shapes
1 pound beef, cut into ¼-inch strips
1 tablespoon flour
¼ teaspoon salt
½ cup sour cream
½ tablespoon tomato paste
2 cups canned, fried potato sticks

Heat oil in wok and add the onion. Stir-fry slowly until transparent. Push aside and stir-fry the mushrooms 1 to 3 minutes. Push aside and add more oil to wok if necessary. Dredge meat in the combined flour and salt. Brown well in the oil. Return the mushrooms and onions to the beef in the wok. Add sour cream and potato paste. Stir and heat just until heated through. Serve at once with potato sticks.

Sweet-and-Sour Pork

Yield: 4 servings

1 pound pork (shoulder or butt) cut into small, bite-size pieces

Batter

1 large egg
¾ cup water
1 cup sifted all-purpose flour
½ teaspoon salt
2 cups oil for frying

Vegetables

1 large onion, cut into 8 wedges and separated into layers
1 carrot, sliced diagonally into ⅛-inch slices
2 green peppers, cut into 1-inch squares

Sweet-and-Sour Sauce

2 tablespoons sugar
2 tablespoons soy sauce
2 tablespoons dry sherry
2 tablespoons vinegar
1 tablespoon cornstarch in 2 tablespoons cold water
1 cup cubed canned pineapple, well-drained

Prepare the batter for pork by combining egg with water. Beat in flour and salt until batter is smooth. Allow to stand about 1 hour. (Flour particles will take up some of the water.) Heat oil in the wok to 400°F. Dip the pork into the batter a few pieces at a time and place into the deep fat. Cook for 5 minutes, until cooked through and golden brown. Drain on paper towels, leave uncovered, and keep warm.

Combine onion, carrot slices, and green peppers. Stir-fry in a small amount of oil for 2 to 3 minutes. Combine the ingredients for the sweet-and-sour sauce and stir until cornstarch is well-distributed. Add all at once to the vegetables. Add pineapple chunks and heat until sauce boils and is thickened. Pour over pork and serve at once while batter on pork is still crisp.

Green Pepper Steak

Yield: 4 servings

1 pound flank steak, thinly sliced
    diagonally across grain with knife
    tilted at a 45° angle to the cutting
    board
3 tablespoons soy sauce
¼ teaspoon sugar
2 tablespoons vegetable oil
1 or 2 green peppers, cut into ¼-inch
    strips
2 tablespoons cornstarch in 2
    tablespoons cold water
1 cup chicken broth or water
2 or 3 firm tomatoes, cut into wedges
    (peeled, if desired)

Marinate the steak in the soy sauce and
sugar for 20 to 30 minutes. Heat oil in the
wok and stir-fry the green peppers 1 to 2
minutes or until their green color brightens.
Push aside. Stir-fry steak 3 to 4 minutes. Return the green peppers to the steak in the
wok. Add the cornstarch mixture and broth
to the steak and peppers. Add the tomato
wedges and heat, stirring gently, until the
sauce is thickened and clear and the tomatoes are heated through. Serve at once
with rice.

Chinese Beef

Yield: 4 to 6 servings

½ cup dried Chinese mushrooms
1½ pounds flank steak
2 small tomatoes, peeled*
1 green pepper
2 tablespoons olive oil
1 clove garlic, crushed
1 teaspoon salt
Dash pepper
¼ teaspoon ginger
3 tablespoons soy sauce
2 tablespoons sherry
½ teaspoon sugar
1 1-pound can bean sprouts, drained
1 tablespoon cornstarch
3 tablespoons water

Soak Chinese mushrooms in water to
cover for 20 minutes. Drain and halve large
mushrooms. Cut flank steaks in strips across
grain (about 2 × 1 × ¼ inches). Cut tomatoes in eighths. Cut green pepper in 1-inch
cubes.

Heat the oil in a large skillet or wok.
Add the flank steak strips, garlic, salt, pepper, and ginger. Sauté over high heat until
the meat is evenly browned on all sides. Add
the soy sauce, sherry, sugar, tomatoes, green
pepper, mushrooms, and bean sprouts. Stir
until well mixed, cover, and cook over medium heat for 5 minutes.

Make a paste of the cornstarch and water
and add to the beef mixture. Cook, uncovered, stirring occasionally, until sauce
thickens.

*Tomatoes can be peeled easily by dipping in boiling
water for a few seconds or by holding directly over a
flame for a few seconds. (If the second method is
used, be sure fork used to hold tomato has a wooden
handle.)

Beef Fuji

Yield: 4 servings

2 tablespoons vegetable oil
1 pound beef steak (round, chuck
  blade, or flank steak), 1 to 1½
  inches thick, cut into thin strips
½ pound fresh mushrooms, sliced into
  "T" shapes
1 small onion, sliced
½ cup chicken or beef broth
¼ cup soy sauce
1 tablespoon cornstarch in 2 tablespoons cold water
1 8-ounce can bamboo shoots, sliced
1 8-ounce can water chestnuts, sliced
3 scallions, cut into 1-inch lengths
1 6-ounce package frozen, defrosted
  pea pods
1 1-pound can sliced peaches, drained

Heat oil in the wok and stir-fry beef,
mushrooms, and onion for 4 to 5 minutes.
Add broth, soy sauce, and cornstarch mixture. Cook, stirring constantly, until sauce
thickens. Add vegetables and peaches. Continue heating until the vegetables are heated
through. Serve at once with rice.

Szechuan Beef

Yield: 4 servings

2 tablespoons vegetable oil
1 or 2 green peppers, cut into ⅛-inch
  strips
1 or 2 carrots, finely shredded into
  ⅛-inch, matchstick-size strips
  (sliced lengthwise, stack slices,
  slice lengthwise through stack)
1 scallion, quartered lengthwise, then
  into 3-inch-long strips

1 pound beef (round or chuck), cut
  into fine slivers or strips, ⅛ inch
  by 2 to 3 inches long
2 tablespoons dry sherry
2 tablespoons hoisin sauce
1 tablespoon black bean sauce
1 tablespoon vinegar
1 teaspoon sugar
¼ to ½ teaspoon chili paste (very
  hot!)

Heat oil in the wok and stir-fry the green
peppers, carrots, and scallion for 1 to 2 minutes. Push aside. Stir-fry the slivers of beef
for 1 to 2 minutes and recombine with the
vegetables. Add the remaining ingredients.
Stir and heat thoroughly. Serve at once with
boiled rice.

Beef with Asparagus and Hoisin Sauce

Yield: 4 servings

1 tablespoon soy sauce
1 tablespoon dry sherry
1 teaspoon cornstarch
1 teaspoon grated garlic
1 pound flank steak, thinly sliced with
  the knife held at 45° angle
  to the board
2 tablespoons vegetable oil
2 scallions, cut into ¼-inch diagonal
  slices
1 pound asparagus, cut diagonally into
  ¼-inch slices
3 tablespoons hoisin sauce
½ cup roasted peanuts

Combine the soy sauce, dry sherry, cornstarch, and grated garlic. Add the beef and marinate it for 20 to 30 minutes. Heat the oil in the wok and stir-fry the scallions for 1 to 2 minutes. Push aside. Stir-fry the asparagus for 2 to 3 minutes. Push aside. Stir-fry the beef 3 to 4 minutes, until done. Return the vegetables to the beef. Stir in the hoisin sauce and peanuts and serve at once.

Beef with Snow Pea Pods and Cashews

Yield: 4 servings

1 pound beef (top of the round steak), sliced into ¼-inch strips
2 tablespoons black bean sauce
2 tablespoons soy sauce
1 clove garlic, grated
2 tablespoons vegetable oil
12 to 16 snow pea pods, strings removed
1 tablespoon cornstarch in ½ cup cold broth or water
½ cup cashews
1 cup bean sprouts, optional

Marinate the beef in a combined mixture of bean sauce, soy sauce, and grated garlic in a small bowl for 20 to 30 minutes. Heat oil in the wok and stir-fry the snow pea pods 1 to 2 minutes, until their green color brightens. Push aside. Stir-fry the beef 2 to 3 minutes. Return the snow pea pods to the beef in the wok and stir in the cornstarch and broth mixture. Heat until sauce boils and is clear. Add cashews and serve at once. (Bean sprouts may be added just before the cornstarch mixture is added, if desired.)

Beef with Snow Pea Pods and Mushrooms

Yield: 4 servings

2 tablespoons vegetable oil
1 teaspoon fresh ginger root, grated
1 clove garlic, grated
½ pound mushrooms, sliced into "T" shapes
14 to 16 snow pea pods, strings removed
1 pound flank steak, cut into thin slices
½ cup chicken broth or water
1 tablespoon cornstarch in 2 tablespoons water
3 tablespoons soy sauce
¼ cup cashews or peanuts

Heat oil in the wok and stir-fry the ginger, garlic, and mushrooms 1 to 2 minutes. Push aside. Stir-fry the pea pods 1 to 2 minutes or until they become bright green. Push aside. Stir-fry the beef 2 to 3 minutes. Return the vegetables to the meat. Add the broth, cornstarch mixture, and soy sauce and heat until sauce boils and is thickened and beef and vegetables are heated through. Add nuts and serve at once with rice.

Shredded Beef with Vegetables

Yield: 4 servings

1 pound beef (round or flank steak), sliced very thin and cut into strips 2 inches long
1 teaspoon sugar
1 tablespoon soy sauce
¼ teaspoon salt
2 tablespoons vegetable oil
1 carrot, cut into very fine 2-inch shreds
1 onion, sliced into ¼-inch slices
1 cup bean sprouts
1 tablespoon cornstarch in ½ cup chicken stock or water
1 tablespoon dry sherry

Marinate beef strips for 10 to 20 minutes in the combined sugar, soy sauce, and salt. Heat oil in wok and stir-fry the carrot shreds and onion rings 2 to 3 minutes. Push aside. Stir-fry the bean sprouts 1 to 2 minutes. Push aside. Stir-fry strips of beef 2 to 3 minutes. Return vegetables to the beef in the wok. Combine the cornstarch mixture and dry sherry. Add to the beef and vegetables and heat and stir until sauce is thickened. Serve at once with fried rice.

Beef with Bamboo Shoots and Peppers

Yield: 4 servings

1 pound beef (round or flank), cut into thin strips
2 tablespoons soy sauce
2 tablespoons dry sherry
1 tablespoon cornstarch

½ teaspoon sugar
1 clove garlic, halved
2 tablespoons vegetable oil
1 green pepper, cut into ½-inch strips
1 red pepper (a green one that has vine-ripened), if available, cut into ½-inch slices
2 scallions, cut into ½-inch slices
1 8-ounce can bamboo shoots, sliced
½ cup chicken or beef broth

Marinate the beef strips in the combined soy sauce, sherry, cornstarch, and sugar for 20 to 30 minutes. Brown the garlic in the vegetable oil. Remove and discard the garlic. Stir-fry the pepper strips 2 to 3 minutes. Push up the sides. Stir-fry the scallions and bamboo shoots 1 to 2 minutes. Push up the sides. Stir-fry the beef 3 to 4 minutes. Return the vegetables to the beef in the wok and add the broth. Stir and heat until the sauce boils. Serve at once with rice.

Beef with Bean Sprouts and Mushrooms

Yield: 4 servings

2 tablespoons vegetable oil
¼ pound mushrooms, cut into "T" shapes
1 teaspoon fresh ginger root, grated
1 pound beef (round, chuck, flank), finely sliced
2 tablespoons soy sauce
2 tablespoons dry sherry
½ cup chicken broth or water
1 tablespoon cornstarch in 2 tablespoons water
1 or 2 cups bean sprouts
2 stalks celery, cut into small cubes

Heat the oil in the wok and stir-fry mushrooms and grated ginger for 1 to 2 minutes. Push aside. Stir-fry the beef for 3 to 4 minutes. Return the mushrooms to the beef in the wok. Combine the soy sauce, sherry, broth, and cornstarch mixture. Stir and add to the beef and mushrooms. Heat until sauce thickens. Add the bean sprouts and continue heating just until they are heated through. Garnish with cubed celery and serve at once with rice.

Beef with Celery and Celery Cabbage

Yield: 4 servings

1 pound beef (chuck or round), cut into 1-inch cubes
3 tablespoons soy sauce
1 tablespoon dry sherry
1 teaspoon sugar
2 tablespoons vegetable oil
1 cup celery cabbage (or bok choy), sliced diagonally across the stalks into ¼-inch slices
1 cup celery, sliced diagonally across the stalks into ¼-inch slices (leaves may be left on)
¼ pound mushrooms, sliced into "T" shapes
1 tablespoon cornstarch in 2 tablespoons water
1 cup chicken broth or water

Marinate the beef for 20 to 30 minutes in the combined soy sauce, sherry, and sugar. Heat oil in the wok and stir-fry the celery cabbage and celery for 1 to 2 minutes or until the light-green color intensifies. Push aside. Stir-fry the mushrooms for 1 to 2 minutes. Push aside. Stir-fry the beef 3 to 4 minutes. Return the vegetables to the beef in the wok. Add the cornstarch mixture and broth to the beef and vegetables. Heat and stir until sauce is thickened and clear. Serve at once with rice.

Beef with Oyster Sauce

Yield: 4 servings

2 tablespoons soy sauce
1 tablespoon dry sherry
1 tablespoon cornstarch
1 teaspoon sugar
1 pound beef (chuck or round), cut into ¼-inch strips
2 tablespoons vegetable oil
1 green pepper, cut into ¼-inch strips
8 canned water chestnuts, sliced
2½ tablespoons bottled oyster sauce

Combine the soy sauce, dry sherry, cornstarch, and sugar in a small bowl. Add beef and marinate 20 to 30 minutes. Heat oil in the wok and stir-fry the green pepper strips and water chestnuts 1 to 2 minutes. Push aside and stir-fry the beef 2 to 3 minutes. Return the green pepper and water chestnuts to the beef in the wok. Gently stir in the oyster sauce. Heat through and serve at once garnished with nuts, if desired.

Sweet-and-Sour Chinese Meatballs

Yield: 4 servings

1 pound extra-lean ground beef
¾ teaspoon salt
½ teaspoon pepper
½ teaspoon fresh ginger root, grated
2 tablespoons vegetable oil
1 green pepper, cut into ¼-inch cubes
1 onion, chopped
1 carrot, grated
2 tablespoons vinegar
2 tablespoons brown sugar
1 teaspoon soy sauce
1 teaspoon dry sherry
1 tablespoon cornstarch, stirred into
   ½ cup cold chicken or beef broth

Blend together the ground beef, salt, pepper, and ginger. Shape into 1-inch meatballs. Heat oil in the wok and brown the meatballs on all sides for about 2 minutes. Add all remaining ingredients. Cook over moderate heat, stirring constantly, until mixture thickens. Cook an additional 5 minutes. Serve at once with rice.

Ground Beef Oriental

Yield: 3 to 4 servings

1 tablespoon vegetable oil
1 pound ground chuck or ground round
1 small onion or 2 scallions, chopped
1 clove garlic, crushed
½ teaspoon salt
¼ teaspoon pepper
¾ cup beef bouillon
½ green pepper, cut in thin strips

1 fresh tomato, cut in eighths
¼ cup bamboo shoots, thinly sliced
1½ tablespoons soy sauce
½ teaspoon cornstarch

Heat vegetable oil in a wok. When hot, add the ground beef, onion, garlic, salt, and pepper. Stir with a fork, breaking up beef into small pieces, and sauté until beef is browned and onion soft. Pour off any fat that accumulates.

Pour in bouillon and add green pepper, tomato, and bamboo shoots. Bring mixture to a boil. Mix soy sauce and cornstarch together and add. Cook over low heat, stirring occasionally, until sauce thickens.

Calves Liver with Bean Sprouts

Yield: 4 servings

3 tablespoons dry sherry
1 teaspoon ginger root, grated
1 pound calves liver, cubed into bite-
   size pieces
2 tablespoons vegetable oil
¼ cup blanched, whole almonds
2 medium onions, finely chopped
¼ pound mushrooms, cut into cubes
1 cup fresh or frozen, defrosted peas
½ cup chicken or beef broth
2 tablespoons soy sauce
1 cup bean sprouts
1 tablespoon cornstarch in 2 tablespoons cold water

Combine the sherry and grated ginger in small bowl and add the cubed liver. Marinate for 20 to 30 minutes. Heat the oil in the wok and stir-fry the almonds for 2 to 3 minutes, until browned. Remove from pan.

Stir-fry the onions with the mushrooms 2 to 3 minutes. More oil may be necessary. Push aside. Stir-fry the peas 1 to 3 minutes. Push aside. Stir-fry the liver 2 to 3 minutes. Return the vegetables and almonds to the wok. Add the broth, soy sauce, and bean sprouts. Stir in the cornstarch mixture and heat until sauce becomes thick and clear and bean sprouts are heated through. Serve at once with rice.

Chinese-style Lamb

Yield: About 4 servings

2-pound boneless leg of lamb
Salt and pepper
2 tablespoons vegetable oil
1 small, sliced onion
2 large carrots, sliced
1 tablespoon corn syrup
3 tablespoons tomato catsup
1 tablespoon soy sauce or Worcestershire sauce
1 tablespoon juice from pineapple rings
8-ounce can pineapple rings
1 bunch spring onions

Remove and discard excess fat from the meat. Cut the meat into 1-inch cubes. Season well with salt and pepper.

Heat the oil in a wok. Gently fry the lamb, onion, and sliced carrots until golden. Add the syrup, catsup, soy or Worcestershire sauce, and 1 tablespoon of juice from the pineapple rings.

Drain the pineapple rings and cut them in half. Wash the spring onions and cut off some of the green part.

Cover pan with tightly fitting lid and simmer very gently for 45 minutes or until the lamb is very tender. Add the pineapple and spring onions about 5 minutes before the end of cooking time. Serve with boiled rice, mixed with peas and, if you like, bean sprouts.

Spicy Chunking Pork

Yield: 4 servings

1 slice ginger root
2 tablespoons vegetable oil
1 pound pork, boiled 1 hour and sliced very thin
1 8-ounce can bamboo shoots, sliced thin
10 to 12 water chestnuts, sliced
6 to 8 Chinese black mushrooms, soaked 30 minutes in water and sliced thin
3 tablespoons dry sherry
3 tablespoons hoisin sauce
1 cup sliced almonds or whole cashews

Brown the ginger slice in the hot oil. Remove and discard the slice. Add pork and stir-fry 2 minutes. Add bamboo shoots, water chestnuts, and mushrooms. Stir-fry 2 minutes. Add sherry and hoisin sauce. Stir and heat well. Add nuts. Serve at once with rice.

Javanese Spiced Pork

Yield: Approximately 6 servings

1½ pounds boneless pork
2 large yellow onions
1 teaspoon coriander
1 teaspoon curry
1 teaspoon salt
½ teaspoon freshly ground
   black pepper
2 medium cloves garlic, pressed
1 tablespoon soy sauce
¾ cup shelled and deveined shrimp
3 eggs

Sauce

4 tablespoons peanut butter
3 tablespoons milk
2 tablespoons soy sauce
½ to 1½ teaspoons Tabasco sauce
1 teaspoon corn syrup

Cut the pork into very thin slices. Peel and finely chop the onions. Brown the pork and onion in some oil in the wok, cover, and continue to fry on very low heat for 10 minutes. Add the coriander, curry, salt, black pepper, garlic, and soy sauce. Mix thoroughly. Let fry slowly for another 10 minutes. Add the shrimp and let them get warm. Meanwhile, beat the eggs and stir them into the wok. Let simmer for 1 minute and remove from the heat. Serve with boiled rice and the special sauce.

Sauce: Beat the peanut butter rapidly with the milk and soy sauce. Keep these ingredients cold. Add the Tabasco sauce and the corn syrup. Beer makes an excellent companion beverage.

Oriental Pork Stew

Yield: 4 servings

1 pound cooked pork, cut into bite-size
   pieces
1 leek or 2 scallions, sliced
1 small head of cabbage, sliced into
   ¼-inch slices

Marinade

2 tablespoons vegetable oil
2 tablespoons soy sauce
1 teaspoon ginger, grated
½ teaspoon garlic salt
8- to 10-ounce can pineapple slices (4
   or 5 slices), cut into pieces
Syrup from drained pineapple slices

Combine the ingredients for the marinade in a small bowl. Add pork, cover, and marinate a few hours in the refrigerator. Pour the meat and marinade into the wok or saucepan. Add the scallions and cabbage. Simmer for 30 minutes. Serve with boiled rice.

Oriental Pork Loin

Yield: About 4 servings

2 pounds pork loin
1 red and 1 green pepper
½ teaspoon curry powder
½ teaspoon paprika powder
3 tablespoons vegetable oil
3 tablespoons flour
1 cup bouillon
½ cup milk
½ cup cream
1 small can of vegetable juice

Salt
Garlic powder
1 tablespoon mango chutney
2 tablespoons dry white wine (if
   desired)

Cut the meat into strips and the peppers into small pieces. Brown the curry and paprika in the vegetable oil until pungent. Add, while stirring in the wok, the flour, bouillon, milk, and cream. Add the juice, meat, and the diced peppers. Simmer for about 5 minutes. Add water, if needed, spices, mango, and wine. Serve with almonds and rice.

Pork with Peppers and Cashews

Yield: 4 servings

1 pound pork, cut into ¾-inch cubes
1 tablespoon soy sauce
½ teaspoon sugar
2 tablespoons vegetable oil
1 small onion, cut into ¾-inch cubes
1 large green pepper, cut into ¾-inch
   cubes
1 large red (vine-ripened green)
   pepper, cut into ¾-inch cubes
1 tablespoon soy sauce
1 tablespoon cornstarch in ½ cup cold
   water or chicken broth
4 ounces cashews

Combine pork, soy sauce, and sugar; let sit while vegetables are prepared. Heat oil in wok; stir-fry pork mixture 4 to 5 minutes, until pork is well done. Push aside. Stir-fry onion 1 to 2 minutes, add green peppers, and continue to stir-fry for 2 to 3 minutes. Return the pork and add the combined soy sauce and cornstarch mixture. Heat and stir gently until sauce is thickened and clear. Add cashews and allow them to heat through. Serve at once with rice.

Deep-Fried Pork with Sweet-and-Sour Sauce

Yield: 4 servings

1 pound pork, cut into ¼-inch strips
2 tablespoons vegetable oil
3 tablespoons soy sauce

Frying Batter

1 egg
¾ cup milk
1 cup sifted all-purpose flour
2 teaspoons baking powder
½ teaspoon salt
2 cups oil for frying

Sweet-and-Sour Sauce

½ cup brown sugar
½ cup vinegar
½ cup pineapple juice
½ cup water or chicken broth
1½ tablespoons soy sauce

Stir-fry pork in oil 3 to 4 minutes or until well-done. Allow to marinate in soy sauce for 20 to 30 minutes.

Combine ingredients for the frying batter and beat until smooth. Allow to stand for 1 hour. (Flour absorbs some of the liquid.)

Dip pork strips in batter and deep-fry in oil at 400°F a few strips at a time until light, golden brown. Remove pork with a slotted spoon and drain on paper towels. Keep warm.

In a small saucepan, combine the ingredients for the sweet-and-sour sauce. Bring to a boil over moderate heat, stirring continuously. Arrange pork in a serving bowl and pour sauce over immediately before serving.

Mandarin Combination

Yield: 4 servings

2 tablespoons oil
1 medium onion, chopped
2 cloves garlic, minced
1 green pepper, cut into ¼ × 1-inch
  strips
¼ pound cooked pork or chicken,
  shredded
2 cups cold, boiled rice
1½ tablespoons soy sauce
¼ pound whole shrimp, cooked
1 cucumber, sliced lengthwise,
  unpeeled
2-egg omelette, cut into ½-inch strips

Heat the oil in the wok and add onion, garlic, and green pepper. Stir-fry 1 to 2 minutes. Add cooked meat and stir-fry 1 to 2 minutes. Add rice, soy sauce, and shrimp. Continue to stir-fry until all ingredients are thoroughly heated. Cut the lengthwise cucumber slices crosswise every ¼-inch but not all the way through. They will hang together like a comb. Insert them here and there in the dish. Garnish with strips of egg omelette.

Pork and Spring Onions

Yield: 2 servings

2 tablespoons vegetable oil
½ pound pork (butt or shoulder),
  trimmed and cut into thin strips
  across the grain
½ cup chicken broth
2 tablespoons tomato paste
1 teaspoon sugar
1 teaspoon chili sauce
8 scallions, cut in quarters lengthwise,
  then into 4-inch lengths

Heat oil in wok and stir-fry pork strips 5 to 10 minutes, until crisp and golden. Combine remaining ingredients and add to pork. Simmer for 1 to 2 minutes. Serve at once.

Twice-Cooked Szechuan Pork

Yield: 4 servings

1 pound lean pork
2 tablespoons vegetable oil
1 large green pepper, cut into ¼-inch
  strips
1 scallion, sliced
1 teaspoon ginger root, grated
1 clove garlic, grated
1 tablespoon black bean sauce
2 tablespoons water
2 tablespoons hoisin sauce
1 tablespoon dry sherry
¼ to ½ teaspoon chili paste (hot!)
1 teaspoon sugar
½ teaspoon salt

Cover pork with water and simmer, covered, for 1 hour, until done. Cool and slice into ¼-inch slices. Heat oil in wok and stir-fry green pepper for 1 minute. Add pork and scallion and continue to stir-fry for 1 minute. Combine remaining ingredients and add to pork-and-green pepper mixture. Heat thoroughly and serve at once with boiled or fried rice.

Curried Pork with Shrimp

Yield: 4 servings

½ pound pork (shoulder or butt),
  shredded into thin strips
2 tablespoons soy sauce

2 tablespoons vegetable oil
2 tablespoons curry powder
1 small onion, minced
3 celery stalks, cut into ¼-inch slices
2 scallions, cut into ⅛-inch slices
½ tablespoon cornstarch in ½ cup
   water or chicken broth
½ pound whole cooked shrimp

Marinate pork in soy sauce for 20 minutes. Heat oil in wok and brown curry powder and onion until the aroma becomes strong. Stir-fry the pork for about 4 minutes or until well-done. Push aside. Combine celery and scallions and stir-fry 1 to 2 minutes. Return pork and add cornstarch mixture. Heat until sauce is clear and thickened and shrimp are heated through. Serve with noodles.

Northern-style Pork Dumplings

Yield: About 48 dumplings

½ pound bok choy (or Chinese celery
   cabbage)
1 pound lean boneless pork, finely
   ground
1 teaspoon fresh ginger root, grated
1 tablespoon Chinese rice wine or
   pale dry sherry
1 tablespoon soy sauce
1 teaspoon salt
1 tablespoon sesame seed oil
2 tablespoons peanut or vegetable oil
1 cup chicken broth, fresh or canned
¼ cup soy sauce combined with 2
   tablespoons white vinegar (to be
   used as a dip or sauce)

With a cleaver or heavy, sharp knife, trim the wilted leaves and root ends from the bok choy and separate the cabbage into stalks. Wash the stalks under cold running water, drain, and chop finely. Squeeze the chopped cabbage in a kitchen towel or double layer of cheesecloth to extract as much of its moisture as possible.

Combine the ground pork, chopped ginger root, wine, soy sauce, salt, and sesame seed oil, and then add the chopped cabbage. Mix with your hands or a large spoon until the ingredients are thoroughly blended. This mixture can then be used as a filling for dumplings, folded and sealed for boiling or frying.

To boil: Bring 2 quarts of water to boiling in your wok and drop in the dumplings. Stir to make sure the dumplings are not sticking together. Boil for 10 to 15 minutes, adding additional water as needed. Serve the dumplings hot with the soy sauce and vinegar dip.

To fry: Place 2 tablespoons of oil into the wok and swirl it about. Place the dumplings, pleated side up, into the wok and cook until the bottoms brown lightly (about 2 minutes at low heat). Add the chicken broth, cover tightly, and cook until it has been absorbed (about 10 minutes). Add the remaining 1 tablespoon of oil and fry each dumpling at least another 2 minutes. Serve the fried dumplings hot with the soy sauce and vinegar dip.

Cantonese Steamed Pork Dumplings

Yield: About 48 dumplings

2 stalks bok choy (or Chinese celery cabbage)
1 pound boneless pork shoulder, finely ground
1 tablespoon Chinese rice wine or pale dry sherry
1 tablespoon soy sauce
2 teaspoons salt
1 teaspoon sugar
1 tablespoon cornstarch
¼ cup canned bamboo shoots, finely chopped

With a cleaver or heavy, sharp knife, trim the wilted leaves and root ends from the bok choy. Wash the stalks under cold running water, drain, and chop finely. Squeeze the chopped cabbage in a kitchen towel or double layer of cheesecloth to extract as much of its moisture as possible.

Combine the pork, wine, soy sauce, salt, sugar, and cornstarch and, with a large spoon, mix them thoroughly together. Stir in the cabbage and bamboo shoots. Place a spoonful of filling in the center of a dough circle and fold into a dumpling suitable for steaming.

Pour enough water into the base of the wok to come within an inch of the bamboo steamer and bring to a boil. Place the dumplings into as many steamer racks as are needed to hold them and steam for 30 minutes. Add water as needed. Serve the dumplings directly on the steamer plate set on a platter.

Oriental Firepot

Yield: Approximately 4 servings

1 pound sirloin or flank steak, sliced paper thin across the grain (slice flank steak on the diagonal)
2 chicken breasts, skinned, boned, and sliced very thin across the grain
½ pound red snapper fillet, or sole or haddock, thinly sliced
½ pound chicken livers, sliced
½ pound small spinach leaves, washed and trimmed of stems
¾ pound mushrooms, wiped and quartered
2 cups cubed bean curd or peeled and cubed eggplant
1 10-ounce package frozen snow pea pods or frozen Italian-style beans, thawed
2 cups cherry tomatoes
1 bunch scallions, trimmed and cut into 2-inch lengths
Chicken broth or stock
¼ teaspoon ginger
Pungent Sweet-and-Sour Sauce (see Index)
Ginger Soy Sauce (See Index)
Hot cooked rice

Prepare the foods as indicated in the ingredient list. This may be done several hours before serving time. The sauces should be prepared well in advance so that the flavors blend well. Keep food and sauces covered and refrigerated.

Shortly before serving time arrange meat, chicken, fish, chicken livers, and vegetables in small dishes or on plates. Set out the sauces and provide the guests with chopsticks or long-handled forks.

If using the Mongolian cooker, place 6 to 8 charcoal briquettes in the bottom section of the cooker, add charcoal starter, and light. On the range, heat enough chicken broth with the ginger added to fill the Mongolian cooker ⅔ full. Pour into cooker when hot. Cover and continue to heat until broth is just bubbling. Or, fill the electric wok ⅔ full with chicken broth. Add ginger. Cover and bring to boiling point. Adjust heat until broth is just bubbling.

Each guest spoons some of each sauce onto his plate, then picks up desired foods with chopsticks or fork, and lowers them into broth to cook. When food is cooked, he lifts it out with a wire ladle and dips each piece into one of the sauces. Do not try to cook too much food in the broth at one time, as the broth must always be bubbling slightly. Serve with fluffly hot rice. Add noodles to the remaining broth and, when they are done, ladle the soup into soup bowls for each guest.

Poultry

Soy Sauce Chicken

Yield: 4 to 6 servings

1 4½- to 5-pound roasting chicken
2 cups cold water
2 cups soy sauce
¼ cup Chinese rice wine, or pale dry sherry
5 slices peeled, fresh ginger root about 1 inch in diameter and ⅛ inch thick
1 whole star anise, or 8 sections star anise

¼ cup rock candy in small pieces, or 2 tablespoons granulated sugar
1 teaspoon sesame seed oil

Wash chicken and dry with paper towels. In a wok large enough to hold the chicken snugly, bring the water, soy sauce, wine, ginger, and star anise to a boil, then add the chicken. The liquid should reach halfway up the chicken. Bring to a boil, reduce heat to moderate, and cook covered for 20 minutes. Turn the chicken over. Stir the rock candy or sugar into the sauce and baste the chicken thoroughly. Simmer 20 minutes longer, basting frequently. Turn off heat, cover the wok, and let the chicken cook for 2 to 3 hours.

Transfer chicken to chopping board and brush it with sesame seed oil. Remove the wings and legs and split the chicken in half lengthwise by cutting through its breastbone and backbone. Lay the halves skin side up on the board and chop them crosswise, bones and all, into 1 × 3-inch pieces, reconstructing the pieces in approximately their original shape in the center of a platter as you proceed. Chop the wings and legs similarly and place them around the breasts. Moisten the chicken with ¼ cup of the sauce in which it cooked and serve at room temperature.

Chicken Bits Oriental

Yield: 3 to 4 servings

2 tablespoons vegetable oil
2 whole chicken breasts, boned and
　cubed
¼ cup chicken bouillon
3 tablespoons sherry
1 tablespoon soy sauce
½ teaspoon ginger
½ cup water chestnuts, drained and
　sliced thin
¼ cup bamboo shoots, sliced thin
½ cup pineapple chunks, drained
1 cup frozen peas
3 tablespoons reserved pineapple liquid
2 teaspoons cornstarch
2 tablespoons hoisin sauce
1 tablespoon scallion, minced

Heat vegetable oil in a wok. Add
chicken cubes and sauté over high heat until
evenly browned.

Add the chicken bouillon, sherry, soy
sauce, ginger, water chestnuts, bamboo
shoots, pineapple chunks, and peas. Stir to
mix well, then cook over medium heat, stirring constantly, for 2 minutes.

Mix the pineapple liquid and cornstarch
together well. Add to the chicken mixture.
Add the hoisin sauce, mix all well, and
cook, stirring constantly, until sauce thickens. Sprinkle on the scallions before serving.

Chicken Wings with Oyster Sauce

Yield: 4 servings

2 pounds chicken wings (tips may be
　removed, if you wish)
3 slices fresh ginger root

1 clove garlic, crushed
3 tablespoons oyster sauce
2 tablespoons soy sauce
1 tablespoon brown sugar
2 teaspoons dry sherry
⅛ teaspoon 5-spice powder (optional)
1 cup chicken broth

Place the chicken wings in the wok and
add remaining ingredients. Bring to a boil
over moderate heat and simmer, covered,
until the wings are tender, about 20 minutes.
Remove lid and boil hard to evaporate all
but about ½ cup of sauce. Eat hot, or chill
and serve cold for a picnic lunch or as a
snack. Yum! Can even be rewarmed.

Javanese Chicken Casserole

Yield: Approximately 4 servings

2 pounds chicken breasts
1 pound chicken livers
1½ teaspoons flour
Salt and pepper
3 tablespoons margarine or butter
1 pound small onions
1 green paprika
½ can bamboo sprouts
3 to 4 slices of canned pineapple
1 teaspoon ginger
2 teaspoons brown sugar
2 teaspoons wine vinegar

Cut the chicken breasts into even pieces. Do the same with the livers. Coat breast and liver pieces in the flour combined with salt and pepper. Brown the pieces in a little more than half of the margarine or butter in a wok. Transfer to a casserole. Brown the onions in the rest of the melted fat, allowing the paprika to fry with the onions for a few minutes, then transfer to the casserole. Stir a small amount of water in the wok to get up drippings and pour into casserole. Add well-drained bamboo sprouts, slices of pineapple, and seasonings. Simmer the dish, covered, for about 20 minutes. Meanwhile, boil rice to be served with the dish.

Chicken with Mushrooms (Moo Goo Gai Pan)

Yield: 4 servings

4 chicken-breast halves, boned, skinned, and cut into ½-inch cubes
¼ cup dry white wine
1 teaspoon salt
2 scallions, cut into ½-inch slices
½ cup celery, cut into ½-inch cubes
1 tablespoon vegetable oil
12 snow pea pods, strings removed
¼ pound mushrooms, sliced into "T" shapes
6 water chestnuts, sliced
½ cup chicken broth
1 tablespoon cornstarch in 2 tablespoons cold water
½ teaspoon salt
Whole, blanched almonds, optional

Combine the chicken with the wine and ½ teaspoon salt. Set aside. Stir-fry the scallions and celery in oil for 1 minute. Push aside. Stir-fry the snow pea pods 2 minutes. Push aside. Stir-fry mushrooms and water chestnuts 1 to 2 minutes. Push aside. Add the chicken and wine and stir-fry 2 to 3 minutes, until chicken is done.

Combine the chicken and vegetables in the wok. Stir together the broth, cornstarch mixture, and another ½ teaspoon salt. Add slowly to the chicken and vegetables in the wok and heat until thickened and clear. Serve over rice and sprinkle with almonds, if desired.

Chicken with Almonds and Mushrooms

Yield: 4 servings

2 tablespoons vegetable oil
¼ cup whole blanched almonds
1 green pepper, cut into ½-inch cubes
1 medium onion, cut into ½-inch cubes
¼ pound mushrooms, sliced in "T" shapes
4 chicken-breast halves, skinned, boned, and cut into ½-inch cubes
4 to 5 water chestnuts, sliced
2 teaspoons soy sauce
2 teaspoons dry sherry (or white wine)
½ cup chicken broth or water
1 tablespoon cornstarch in 2 tablespoons cold water

Heat oil in wok and stir-fry almonds until lightly browned. Remove from pan. Stir-fry green pepper and onion 2 to 3 minutes. Push aside. Stir-fry mushrooms 1 to 2 minutes. Push aside. Stir-fry chicken 3 to 4 minutes, until done. Return the vegetables to the chicken. Add water chestnuts.

In a small bowl, combine soy sauce, sherry, chicken broth, and the cornstarch mixture. Stir and add to ingredients in the wok. Heat until sauce is thickened. Add almonds. Serve at once with noodles.

347

Chicken with Celery and Mushrooms

Yield: 4 servings

2 tablespoons vegetable oil
3 to 4 stalks celery, cut into ¼-inch
  slices
¼ pound whole small mushrooms
1 broiler-fryer chicken, skinned,
  boned, and cut into ½-inch strips
½ cup chicken broth or water
1 tablespoon soy sauce
1 tablespoon cornstarch in 2 tablespoons water
¼ cup dry sherry

Heat oil in wok and stir-fry celery and mushrooms 2 to 3 minutes. Push aside. Stir-fry chicken 3 to 4 minutes or until done. Combine chicken and vegetables. Add broth, soy sauce, cornstarch mixture, and sherry. Heat until sauce boils and is thickened, stirring constantly. Serve at once with rice.

Chicken with Peas and Mushrooms

Yield: 4 servings

4 chicken-breast halves, skinned,
  boned, and cut into ¼-inch strips
2 tablespoons soy sauce
2 tablespoons dry sherry
½ teaspoon ginger root, grated
1 tablespoon cornstarch
2 tablespoons vegetable oil
¼ pound mushrooms, sliced in
  "T" shapes
1 cup peas, fresh or defrosted frozen
¼ cup whole blanched almonds
½ cup chicken broth or water

Marinate the chicken strips in the combined soy sauce, dry sherry, grated ginger, and cornstarch for 20 to 30 minutes. Heat oil in the wok and stir-fry mushrooms for 1 to 2 minutes. Push aside and stir-fry peas 1 to 3 minutes, until they are heated through. Push aside. Stir-fry the chicken 3 to 4 minutes. Combine chicken, mushrooms, and peas. Stir in the almonds and chicken broth. Heat until sauce boils. Serve with rice.

Chicken with Asparagus

Yield: 4 servings

2 tablespoons vegetable oil
1 clove garlic
1 pound asparagus, cut diagonally into
  ½-inch slices (discard tough, white
  portions)
4 chicken breasts, boned, skinned, and
  cut into ¾-inch cubes
1 tablespoon dry sherry
2 tablespoons black bean sauce,
  optional
1 tablespoon cornstarch in ½ cup cold
  chicken broth
1 teaspoon salt

Heat oil in the wok and brown the garlic to flavor the oil. Remove and discard the garlic. Stir-fry asparagus 2 to 3 minutes. Push aside. Stir-fry chicken 3 to 4 minutes, until done. Return the asparagus.

Combine the sherry, bean sauce, cornstarch mixture, and salt. Add to the chicken and asparagus and heat until sauce thickens. Serve at once with rice or noodles.

Chicken with Bean Sprouts and Snow Pea Pods

Yield: 4 servings

4 chicken-breast halves, skinned, boned, and cut into bite-size pieces
¼ cup white wine or dry sherry
½ teaspoon salt
2 tablespoons vegetable oil
2 cups fresh bean sprouts
1 cup snow pea pods, strings removed
½ cup chicken broth
1 tablespoon cornstarch in 2 tablespoons water
Sesame seeds, toasted, optional

Combine the chicken, wine, and ½ teaspoon salt. Let stand about 20 minutes. Heat oil in the wok and stir-fry bean sprouts 1 minute. Push aside. Stir-fry pea pods 1 to 2 minutes, until their green color intensifies. Push aside. Add the chicken and wine mixture and stir-fry 3 to 4 minutes, until the chicken is done. Return the bean sprouts and pea pods to the chicken in the wok. Add the combined ½ teaspoon salt, chicken broth, and the cornstarch mixture. Heat and stir gently until mixture thickens. Serve at once garnished with sesame seeds.

Szechuan Chicken (Kang Pao Chicken)

Yield: 4 servings

4 chicken-breast halves, skinned, boned, and cubed into ¾-inch cubes
1 egg white
1 tablespoon cornstarch
2 tablespoons vegetable oil
1 cup unsalted peanuts or cashews
2 scallions, sliced
2 tablespoons dry sherry
2 tablespoons hoisin sauce
4 tablespoons black bean sauce
¼ to ½ teaspoon chili paste (very hot!)
1 tablespoon vinegar
1 teaspoon sugar

Combine the cubed chicken with the egg white and cornstarch. Refrigerate for ½ hour. Heat oil in the wok and stir-fry the chicken 3 to 4 minutes, until done. Add nuts, scallions, and remaining ingredients. Heat thoroughly and serve at once with rice.

Chicken with Walnuts

Yield: 4 servings

4 chicken-breast halves, skinned, boned, and cut into ¾-inch cubes
3 tablespoons soy sauce
1 teaspoon sugar
2 tablespoons vegetable oil
1 cup English walnuts
1 teaspoon ginger root, grated
1 clove garlic, grated
½ cup chicken broth or water
1 tablespoon cornstarch in 2 tablespoons cold water
1 8-ounce can bamboo shoots, drained and sliced

Marinate chicken in soy sauce and sugar in a small bowl for 20 minutes. Heat oil in a wok and stir-fry walnuts 2 minutes. Remove from pan. Add chicken, ginger, garlic, and the marinade to the wok and stir-fry 3 to 4 minutes, until chicken is done. Combine the broth and cornstarch mixture. Add to the chicken along with the bamboo shoots. Heat and stir gently until sauce is thickened and bamboo shoots are hot. Add walnuts and serve at once with rice.

Chicken with Celery and Celery Cabbage

Yield: 4 servings

1 tablespoon dry sherry
3 tablespoons soy sauce
1 teaspoon sugar
1 teaspoon grated ginger
1 broiler-fryer chicken, skinned,
  boned, and cut into bite-size pieces
2 tablespoons vegetable oil
1 cup celery cabbage, sliced across the
  head into ¼-inch slices
1 cup celery, sliced diagonally into
  ¼-inch slices (leaves may be
  left on)
¼ pound mushrooms, sliced in "T"
  shape
1 cup bean sprouts
2 tablespoons cornstarch
1 cup cold chicken broth
½ cup nuts, optional

Combine sherry, soy sauce, sugar, and ginger in small bowl. Add chicken and marinate 20 to 30 minutes. Heat oil in the wok and stir-fry celery cabbage and celery 1 to 2 minutes or until green color intensifies. Push aside. Stir-fry mushrooms 1 to 2 minutes. Push aside. Stir-fry bean sprouts 1 to 2 minutes. Push aside. Add chicken and stir-fry 3 to 4 minutes, until done. Return vegetables to the chicken in the wok. Stir cornstarch into the broth and add to the combined mixture of chicken and vegetables. Heat until sauce is thickened and clear. Serve at once with rice. Garnish with nuts.

Chicken with Green Pepper and Cashews

Yield: 4 servings

2 tablespoons vegetable oil
1 large green pepper, cut into
  ¼-inch strips
4 chicken-breast halves, skinned,
  boned, and cut into ½-inch strips
2 tablespoons soy sauce
1 tablespoon cornstarch
½ cup cold chicken broth
2 tablespoons dry white wine
½ cup cashews

Heat oil in the wok. Add the green pepper and stir-fry for 2 minutes. Push aside. Stir-fry the chicken 3 to 4 minutes, until done. Return the green pepper to the chicken in the wok. Combine and stir in the soy sauce, cornstarch, chicken broth, and wine. Heat and stir gently until the sauce is thickened and clear. Add the cashews and serve at once with rice.

Chicken with Hoisin Sauce

Yield: 4 servings

4 chicken-breast halves, boned,
  skinned, and cut into ¾-inch cubes
1 tablespoon cornstarch
1 tablespoon dry sherry
1 tablespoon soy sauce
1 green pepper, cut into ½-inch
  squares
1 tablespoon vegetable oil
½ pound mushrooms, cut into
  ½-inch cubes
2½ tablespoons hoisin sauce
¼ cup cashews

Sprinkle the cubed chicken with cornstarch, dry sherry, and soy sauce. Toss to coat well and set aside. Stir-fry the green pepper in the oil for 1 minute. Push aside. Add mushrooms. Stir-fry for 1 to 2 minutes. Push aside. Stir-fry chicken 2 to 3 minutes, until done. Add hoisin sauce and cashews. Reheat and stir briefly. Serve at once.

Chicken with Sweet-and-Sour Tomato Sauce

Yield: 4 servings

2 tablespoons vegetable oil
1 green pepper, cut into bite-size
    squares
1 medium onion, cubed
1 carrot, very thinly sliced
4 chicken-breast halves, skinned,
    boned, and cut into bite-size pieces
1 cup pineapple chunks

Sauce

2 tablespoons vinegar
3 tablespoons orange marmalade
1 8-ounce can tomato sauce

In a small saucepan, heat the combined vinegar, orange marmalade, and tomato sauce. Heat oil in a wok and stir-fry the green pepper, onion, and carrot slices for about 2 minutes. Push aside. Stir-fry the chicken 3 to 4 minutes, until done. Return the vegetables to the chicken. Add the sauce and the pineapple and heat through. Serve with rice.

Pineapple Chicken with Sweet-and-Sour Sauce

Yield: 4 servings

2 tablespoons vegetable oil
1 green pepper, cut into ¼-inch strips
1 broiler-fryer chicken, skinned,
    boned, and cut into ½-inch cubes
1 8-ounce can pineapple rings, drained
    and cut into bite-size pieces

Sauce

½ cup chicken broth
¼ cup reserved syrup from canned
    pineapple
¼ cup dry sherry or white wine
1 tablespoon vinegar
1 tablespoon cornstarch in
    2 tablespoons cold water
2 tablespoons orange marmalade
1 tablespoon soy sauce
1 teaspoon ginger root, grated

Heat oil in wok and stir-fry green pepper 1 to 2 minutes. Push aside. Stir-fry chicken 3 to 4 minutes, until done. Return green peppers to the chicken; add pineapple. Combine sauce ingredients and add to the wok. Heat and stir until sauce is thickened and clear. Serve immediately with rice.

Shredded Chicken with Almonds

Yield: 4 servings

2 tablespoons vegetable oil
¼ cup whole, blanched almonds
1 medium onion, chopped
1 teaspoon ginger root, grated
4 chicken-breast halves, skinned, boned, and sliced into ½-inch strips
2 tablespoons soy sauce
1 tablespoon dry sherry
1 teaspoon sugar

Heat oil in the wok and stir-fry almonds 1 to 2 minutes, until golden. Remove from pan. Stir-fry onion and ginger 2 to 3 minutes. Add chicken and continue to stir-fry 3 to 4 minutes, until done. Return almonds to pan. Combine soy sauce, sherry, and sugar. Pour over chicken mixture. Heat and serve at once.

Stewed Chicken with Pork

Yield: 3 to 4 servings

1 clove garlic
1 small slice of fresh ginger root
8 ounces pork, cut into 1-inch cubes
8 ounces chicken, cut into 1-inch cubes
2 tablespoons cooking oil
4 tablespoons soy sauce
3 teaspoons sugar
3 tablespoons dry sherry
Water—barely enough to cover ingredients
1 tablespoon cornstarch in 2 tablespoons cold water, optional

Brown the garlic, ginger, pork, and chicken in 2 tablespoons of cooking oil over medium-high heat. Add soy sauce, sugar, sherry, and sufficient water to cover meat.

Cover and simmer over low heat for about an hour or until meat is tender. Remove ginger and garlic clove. Serve meat hot with the sauce. If you wish, the sauce may be thickened by adding 1 tablespoon of cornstarch in 2 tablespoons of cold water to the sauce. Heat until the sauce thickens and is clear.

Chicken Livers with Eggs and Noodles

Yield: 4 servings

4 eggs
¼ teaspoon salt
1 tablespoon vegetable oil
½ pound mushrooms, sliced in "T" shapes
2 scallions, sliced
1 pound chicken livers, cubed
2 tablespoons dry sherry
5 tablespoons soy sauce
½ pound thin spaghetti noodles
2 tablespoons chopped parsley

Combine the eggs and salt and pour into an oiled skillet. Cook without stirring over moderate heat until eggs are set. Cut into ½-inch cubes. Heat oil in the wok. Stir-fry the mushrooms and scallions 1 to 2 minutes. Push aside. Stir-fry the chicken livers 1 to 2 minutes. Add dry sherry and 4 tablespoons soy sauce. Combine liver and vegetables and heat through. Add cubed eggs. Prepare spaghetti according to package directions; drain well and gently combine with 1 tablespoon soy sauce. Serve on a platter with the liver mixture. Garnish with chopped parsley.

Deep-fried Chicken with Lemon Sauce

Yield: 4 servings

4 chicken-breast halves, skinned, boned, and cut into ½-inch strips

Frying Batter

1 large egg
¾ cup water
1 cup sifted all-purpose flour
2 cups vegetable oil for deep frying

Lemon Sauce

1 cup chicken broth
¼ cup dry white wine
1 tablespoon soy sauce
1 tablespoon honey
Grated rind of 1 lemon
3 tablespoons lemon juice
1 tablespoon cornstarch
Lemon slices for garnish

Combine the ingredients for the frying batter and allow to stand for 1 hour. Dip the chicken strips in the batter and deep-fry in oil at 400°F a few strips at a time until light golden in color and the chicken is done. Use a deep-fat thermometer and control the temperature of the oil carefully. Remove chicken from the oil with a slotted spoon and drain on paper towels.

Combine the ingredients for the lemon sauce in a small saucepan. Stir constantly and bring to a boil over moderate heat. Simmer 1 to 2 minutes. Arrange chicken in a serving bowl and cover with the sauce. Garnish with lemon slices. Serve at once while batter coating is still crisp.

Chicken and Shrimp with Vegetables

Yield: 4 servings

2 chicken-breast halves, skinned, boned, and cut into ¼-inch strips
1 tablespoon dry sherry
2 tablespoons soy sauce
2 tablespoons oil
2 cups mixed vegetables (green beans, sliced mushrooms, strips of green pepper, shredded carrots, etc.)
½ cup chicken broth
1 tablespoon cornstarch in 2 tablespoons cold water
½ pound cooked whole shrimp
8 ounces thin spaghetti noodles, cooked according to package directions and tossed with 1 tablespoon soy sauce
1 egg, beaten and cooked in a small skillet over moderate heat as an omelette

Marinate chicken in sherry and soy sauce for about 20 minutes. Heat oil in wok and stir-fry vegetables for 2 to 3 minutes. Push aside. Add chicken and stir-fry for 3 to 4 minutes, until done.

Return the vegetables to the chicken in the wok. Add the broth, cornstarch mixture, and the cooked shrimp. Heat until sauce boils and shrimp are heated through. Serve over spaghetti noodles and garnish with the 1-egg omelette cut into ¼-inch strips.

Peking Duck

Yield: Approximately 6 servings

4- to 5-pound duck
6 cups water
¼ cup honey
4 slices peeled fresh ginger root, about 1
    inch in diameter and ⅛ inch thick
2 scallions, including the green tops,
    cut into 2-inch lengths
12 scallion brushes
Mandarin Pancakes

Sauce

¼ cup hoisin sauce
1 tablespoon water
1 teaspoon sesame seed oil
2 teaspoons sugar

Mandarin Pancakes

2 cups sifted all-purpose flour
¾ cup boiling water
1 to 2 tablespoons sesame seed oil

Wash the duck thoroughly with cold water, and dry. Tie a cord tightly around the neck skin and suspend the bird in an airy place to dry the skin (about 3 hours).

Bring to a boil in a wok 6 cups of water, ¼ cup honey, ginger root, and cut scallions. Lower the duck by its string into the boiling liquid and use a spoon to moisten the duck's skin thoroughly. Discard the liquid and suspend the duck by its cord until it is dry (2 to 3 hours).

Make the sauce by combining hoisin sauce, water, sesame seed oil, and sugar in a small pan, and stir until the sugar dissolves. Bring to a boil and then simmer, uncovered, for 3 minutes. Cool and save for later use.

Cut scallions to 3-inch lengths and trim off the roots. Standing each scallion on end, make 4 intersecting cuts 1-inch deep into its stalk. Repeat at other end. Place scallions in ice water and refrigerate until cut parts curl into brush-like fans.

Preheat oven to 375°F. Untie the duck and cut off any loose neck skin. Place duck, breast-side-up, on a rack and set in a roasting pan. Roast the duck for 1 hour. Lower the heat to 300°F, turn the duck on its breast, and roast for 30 minutes longer. Raise the heat to 375°F, return the duck to its back, and roast for a final 30 minutes. Transfer the duck to a carving board.

With a small, sharp knife and your fingers, remove the crisp skin from the breast, sides, and back of the duck. Cut the skin into 2- by 3-inch rectangles and arrange them in a single layer on a platter. Cut the wings and drumsticks from the duck and cut all the meat away from the breast and carcass. Slice the meat into pieces 2½ inches long and ½ inch wide, and arrange them on another platter.

Serve the duck with Mandarin Pancakes, sauce, and the scallion brushes. Dip a scallion brush into the sauce and brush a pancake with it. The scallion is placed in the middle of the pancake with a piece of duck skin and a piece of meat. The pancake is rolled around the pieces and eaten like a sandwich. The mixture of flavors is exquisite.

To make pancakes, prepare a well in the sifted flour and pour the water into it. Mix and knead the dough for 10 minutes. Let it rest for 15 minutes under a damp kitchen towel. Roll to a thickness of about ¼ inch with a rolling pin. Stamp out circles 2½ inches in diameter with a cookie cutter or a glass.

Brush half of the circles lightly with the sesame seed oil. Place an unoiled circle on top of an oiled one and roll flat to a diameter of about 6 inches. Fry each pancake, 1 minute to a side, in an unoiled skillet. As each pancake is finished, gently separate the halves and stack them. Makes about 24 pancakes.

Szechuan Duck

Yield: Approximately 6 servings

4- to 5-pound duck
2 tablespoons salt
1 tablespoon whole Szechuan pep-
    percorns, crushed with a cleaver
    or with a pestle in a mortar
2 scallions, including the green tops,
    cut into 2-inch pieces
4 slices peeled fresh ginger root, about
1   inch in diameter and ¼ inch
thick
2 tablespoons soy sauce
1 teaspoon 5-spice powder
3 cups peanut oil, or flavorless
    vegetable oil

Roasted Salt and Pepper

5 tablespoons salt
1 tablespoon whole Szechuan
    peppercorns
½ teaspoon whole black peppercorns

Wash the duck thoroughly with cold water and dry. Mix the salt, crushed peppercorns, scallions, and ginger. Rub the duck thoroughly with the mixture both inside and out. Place the scallions and ginger inside the duck and refrigerate overnight while covered with plastic wrap or aluminum foil.

Mix the soy sauce and 5-spice powder and rub it over the duck both inside and out.

Place the duck on its back on a platter inside a bamboo steamer, add water to the wok to within an inch of the steamer, and steam for 2 hours. Turn off the heat and let the duck rest in this position in the closed steamer for another 30 minutes. Turn the duck onto its breast, re-cover the steamer, and let it rest for another 30 minutes. Remove the scallion and ginger pieces and let the duck dry for 3 hours.

Pour 3 cups of oil into a wok and heat it to 375°F. Carefully lower the duck into the hot oil on its back and fry it for about 15 minutes. Move the duck periodically to prevent it from sticking to the bottom of the wok. Then turn the duck over on its breast and deep-fry as before for another 15 minutes.

When the duck is a deep golden brown on all sides, transfer it to a chopping board. Cut off the wings, legs, and thighs of the duck and chop them across the bone in 2-inch pieces. Cut away and discard the backbone; chop the breast, bone and all, into 2-inch squares. Serve the duck pieces, attractively arranged, with a dip of Roasted Salt and Pepper.

To make Roasted Salt and Pepper, pour the salt and peppercorns into a hot wok. Turn the heat down to moderate and cook, stirring constantly, for 5 minutes or until the mixture browns lightly. Don't burn it! Crush the browned mixture to a fine powder. Strain it through a sieve.

Seafood

Steamed Sea Bass

Yield: 4 servings

2 sea bass, about 1½ pounds each,
  cleaned but with heads and tails left
  on
1 teaspoon salt
4 mushrooms, chopped
1 tablespoon soy sauce
1 tablespoon dry sherry
1 tablespoon finely shredded, peeled
  fresh ginger root
1 scallion, including the green top, cut
  into 2-inch lengths
1 tablespoon vegetable oil
½ teaspoon sugar
2 whole shrimp

Wash the bass with cold water and dry
with paper towels. With a sharp knife make
diagonal cuts ¼ inch deep at ½ inch intervals on both sides of each fish. Sprinkle the
fish, inside and out, with the salt.

Lay the fish on a heat-proof platter ½
inch smaller in diameter than the bamboo
steamer. Pour the chopped mushrooms and
seasonings over the fish, and arrange the
pieces of ginger and scallion on top.

Pour enough boiling water into the lower
part of the wok so that it comes within an
inch of the bamboo steamer. Bring the water
to a rolling boil and place the platter of fish
into the steamer with the shrimp arranged
around it. Steam the fish for about 15
minutes, or until they are firm to the touch.
Serve at once in their own steaming platter.

Steamed Fish with Black Bean Sauce

Yield: 4 servings

2 tablespoons black bean sauce
1 clove garlic, grated
1 teaspoon grated fresh ginger root
½ teaspoon sugar
1 teaspoon vegetable oil (for non-oily
  fish)
2 cups water
1 to 1½ pounds fish fillets (flounder,
  trout, etc.)
1 scallion, sliced

Combine the bean sauce, garlic, ginger,
sugar, and oil. Place 2 cups water in the wok
and arrange fish on a rack 1 to 2 inches
above the water so the water will not boil up
onto the fish but the steam can circulate
freely around it. Spread the bean sauce mixture evenly over the surface of the fillets.
Sprinkle with scallion slices. Cover wok and
steam until fish separates into flakes with a
fork. Serve immediately. (Rack may be
covered with one layer of cheesecloth before
fish are placed on it. This will prevent fish
from adhering to the rack.)

Shrimp with Lobster Sauce

Yield: 4 servings

Lobster Sauce and Cantonese Sauce are
made with garlic, fermented black beans, and
egg. The sauce does not contain lobster, but
is used with lobster, shrimp, and other seafoods. This is how the name was derived.

2 to 3 ounces minced pork
2 tablespoons vegetable oil
1 pound cooked shrimp, cut into bite-
  size pieces

1 teaspoon grated ginger root
3 cloves garlic, grated
1 tablespoon black beans (dow sei),
    washed and mashed
1 cup chicken broth or water
1 teaspoon soy sauce
1 teaspoon salt
1 teaspoon sugar
2 tablespoons dry sherry
1 tablespoon cornstarch in 2 table-
    spoons cold water
1 egg, beaten
Scallion slices, leaves only

Stir-fry the pork in the vegetable oil until well-done. Add shrimp, ginger, garlic, and beans, Stir-fry briefly. Combine broth, soy sauce, salt, sugar, sherry, and the cornstarch mixture. Stir and add to the wok. Heat until thickened. Remove from heat and pour egg in slowly while stirring with a fork. Serve on rice and garnish with green scallion slices. The sauce must not be hot enough to coagulate the egg as it is stirred in with a fork. The purpose of the egg is to color the sauce and thicken it slightly.

Stir-fried Sweet-and-Sour Shrimp

Yield: 4 servings

2 tablespoons honey
1 tablespoon vinegar
1 clove garlic, crushed
2 tablespoons soy sauce
1 tablespoon tomato paste
Pinch chili powder
12 large shrimp, peeled and deveined
2 tablespoons vegetable oil

Combine the honey, vinegar, crushed garlic, soy sauce, tomato paste, and chili powder in a small bowl. Add the shrimp and marinate in the refrigerator for 30 minutes. Remove the shrimp from the marinade and stir-fry in the oil for 3 minutes. (less if cooked shrimp are used). Add the marinade and heat 2 minutes. Pour shrimp and sauce into a hot serving dish. Stir-fried vegetables may be added if you wish.

Shrimp in Garlic Sauce

Yield: 4 servings

2 tablespoons vegetable oil
1 small onion, chopped
1 teaspoon grated ginger root
4 cloves garlic, sliced
5 or 6 Chinese dried black mushrooms,
    soaked 30 minutes in warm water
    and sliced
1 cup peas, fresh or frozen defrosted
1 pound cooked shrimp
½ cup chicken broth or water
2 teaspoons soy sauce
1 teaspoon salt
1 tablespoon cornstarch in 2 table-
    spoons water

Heat oil in wok and stir-fry onion, ginger, and garlic for 1 to 2 minutes. Add mushrooms and peas and stir-fry 1 to 3 minutes. Add shrimp and continue to stir-fry 1 to 2 minutes. Combine broth, soy sauce, salt, and the cornstarch mixture. Add to wok and heat until sauce boils and has thickened. Serve immediately with boiled rice.

Oriental Shrimp

Yield: Approximately 4 servings

1 teaspoon curry and, perhaps, some
    paprika powder
4 tablespoons margarine or butter
2 red and 2 green paprikas
2 yellow onions or 2 pieces of leek
2 clove garlics or garlic powder
2 pounds shelled and deveined shrimp
6 tablespoons tomato purée
½ cup water
½ cup heavy cream
Salt
2 cups fresh mushrooms

In a wok fry the curry and paprika powder in the margarine or butter, add paprika strips, onions, garlic, and shrimp to soften. Add the tomato purée, water, wine, and cream and let simmer for a few minutes. Heat the shrimp in the mixture, taste, and correct seasoning. Stir in the mushrooms and finish cooking.

This mixture can be served hot in shells or eaten with white bread or rice. The mixture can also be used as a filling in crepes.

Shrimp Egg Roll Filling

Yield: 6 or 8

2 tablespoons vegetable oil
12-ounces cooked shrimp, minced
2 cups Chinese celery cabbage, sliced
    across the head into very fine shreds
8 to 10 water chestnuts, shredded
2 stalks celery, minced
1 cup bean sprouts
1 teaspoon salt
1 tablespoon soy sauce
1 teaspoon sugar

6 to 8 egg roll wrappers (6 × 6 inches
    each)
1 egg, beaten (for sealing)
2 cups oil for deep-frying

Heat 2 tablespoons oil in the wok and stir-fry shrimp, cabbage, water chestnuts, and celery for 2 to 3 minutes, until the green vegetables become brighter. Add the bean sprouts. Stir in the salt, soy sauce, and sugar. Place mixture in egg roll wrappers and seal with beaten egg. Deep-fry a few at a time in oil at 375°F, until brown and crisp. Serve at once.

Deep-fried Scallops with Sweet-and-Sour Sauce

Yield: 4 servings

1 pound scallops (cubed fish fillets may
    be substituted)

Batter

1 cup sifted all-purpose flour
¾ cup water
1 large egg
½ teaspoon salt
2 cups oil for frying

Sweet-and-Sour Sauce

4 pineapple rings, cut into small pieces
Reserved pineapple syrup and water to
    make 1 cup
1 tablespoon cornstarch in 2 tablespoons cold water
2 tablespoons vinegar
¼ cup brown sugar
1 teaspoon soy sauce
1 small onion, sliced
Few strips each of carrots and green
    pepper
2 cups hot boiled rice

Combine the batter ingredients and beat just until smooth. Allow to stand for 1 hour. Dip scallops a few at a time into the batter and deep-fry in oil at 375°F just until golden brown and done, about 3 to 4 minutes. Drain on paper towels.

Combine the sauce ingredients in a saucepan. Stir constantly while bringing to a boil. Heat until thickened and the carrot and pepper strips are heated through.

Place scallops on a bed of boiled rice and cover with the sauce. Serve at once while the scallop batter coating is still crisp.

Lobster Cantonese

Yield: 4 servings

2 tablespoons vegetable oil
2 tablespoons black beans, rinsed and mashed
2 cloves garlic, grated
1 teaspoon grated ginger root
2 to 3 ounces minced or ground pork
1½ to 2 pounds live lobster, cleaned and chopped into 1-inch pieces or 1 pound lobster tails, split lengthwise
1 cup chicken broth or water
1 teaspoon soy sauce
½ teaspoon sugar
1 tablespoon cornstarch in 2 tablespoons cold water
Salt and pepper
1 egg, beaten
1 scallion, sliced

Heat the oil in the wok and brown the black beans, garlic, and ginger briefly. Add pork and stir-fry for 1 minute. Add lobster and stir-fry for 1 minute. Add the broth, soy sauce, sugar, and cornstarch mixture. Cover and heat for 5 minutes. Remove from heat, season with salt and pepper, and slowly pour

in the egg while stirring with a fork. This sauce should not be so hot as to completely coagulate the egg and turn it white. The egg should give the sauce a yellowish color. Serve at once with rice. Garnish with scallion slices.

Red-Stewing

A cooking technique native to the Fukien area of China is stewing in soy sauce. This is called "red-stewing" because of the red color imparted in the stewing process.

Red-Stewed Pork Shoulder

Yield: Approximately 6 servings

6-pound pork shoulder
2 cups water
¼ cup sherry
1 cup soy sauce
4 slices preserved ginger root
4 scallions
1 tablespoon sugar
Hot cooked rice

Wash pork well and pull off any hairs that may be on the skin. Place the meat, skin side up, in a wok with the water. Turn heat high; when water boils, pour the sherry, then the soy sauce, over the pork. Place ginger root and scallions in the liquid. Cover pork, lower heat, and simmer for 1 hour. Turn the meat and simmer for another hour. Turn the meat again, add sugar, and cook for 30 minutes longer. The meat should now be tender enough to give way with chopsticks. Serve on a bed of rice in a deep bowl, with the gravy poured over it.

Red-Stewed Beef

Yield: About 4 servings

1½ pounds beef
Water to cover meat
1 tablespoon oil
1 clove garlic
4½ tablespoons soy sauce
1 tablespoon sugar
1 tablespoon wine
2 slices ginger the size of a penny

Cut the beef into cubes 1 × 1 inch and simmer in a wok with enough water to barely cover for 15 minutes. Drain beef and brown it at medium temperature, using 1 tablespoon oil and 1 clove of garlic. Add soy sauce, sugar, wine, and ginger. Add the drained juice; simmer at low heat until tender. During the stewing process you may add potatoes, turnips, Brussels sprouts, or carrots.

Red-Stewed Shin of Beef

Yield: Approximately 4 servings

2 tablespoons cooking oil
2 pounds shin of beef
⅛ teaspoon pepper
2 slices fresh ginger root
1 clove garlic
1 scallion, halved
1 teaspoon salt
2 teaspoons sugar
¼ cup soy sauce
1 teaspoon sesame seed oil
1 teaspoon sherry
Water to cover the meat

Heat the oil in a wok; when it is hot, add the meat and brown on both sides. Add the pepper, ginger root, garlic, and scallion. Add the salt and sugar and pour the soy sauce, sesame seed oil, and sherry over it. Add enough boiling water to cover meat. Bring liquid to a boil, cover, and turn down heat. Simmer slowly for 2½ hours. Remove meat and cut into slices ¼ inch thick; arrange on a shallow dish. Pour gravy over it and serve at once.

Eggs & Omelettes

Eggs with Bean Sprouts

Yield: 4 servings

2 tablespoons vegetable oil
2 scallions, cut into ¼-inch slices
2 ounces mushrooms, cut into "T" shapes
4 eggs
3 water chestnuts, cut into thin slices
3 ounces cooked chicken meat, shredded
1 tablespoon soy sauce
½ teaspoon sugar
½ teaspoon salt
½ tomato, cut into thin wedges
1 cup bean sprouts

Sauce

¾ cup water
1½ teaspoons cornstarch
1½ teaspoons sugar
1 tablespoon soy sauce

Heat the oil in the wok and stir-fry the scallions and mushrooms 1 to 2 minutes. Combine the eggs, water chestnuts, chicken, soy sauce, sugar, and salt. Add to the scallions and mushrooms in the wok and stir briefly. After the eggs have heated for about a minute, spread the tomato wedges and bean sprouts over the top. Continue cooking until the eggs are browned on the bottom. Do not stir. Carefully turn the eggs over and cook for another minute. Slide the omelette out onto a hot dish and serve with the thickened soy sauce prepared by combining all ingredients and bringing to a boil, stirring continuously. Serve at once.

Egg Foo Yung

Yield: 4 servings

2 tablespoons vegetable oil
½ cup scallions, thinly sliced
¼ cup celery, finely chopped
1 clove garlic, crushed
1 cup cooked shrimp or pork, diced
6 eggs
½ teaspoon salt
¼ teaspoon pepper
1 tablespoon soy sauce

Heat the oil in the wok. Add scallions, celery, and garlic, and stir-fry 2 to 3 minutes. Remove and discard the garlic. Add the shrimp and continue to stir-fry until shrimp are lightly browned. Beat the eggs with the salt, pepper, and soy sauce until frothy. Add to the shrimp mixture and stir until blended. Cook over low heat until the eggs set. Fold over and slide onto serving plate. Serve at once.

Mushroom Omelette

Yield: 4 servings

2 tablespoons butter
¼ cup mushrooms, sliced
¼ cup onions, finely chopped
6 eggs

Salt and pepper
Lettuce or parsley for garnish

Melt butter in wok, and, over a very low heat, stir-fry the mushrooms and onions. (Butter will burn if heated over 225°F.) Remove and set aside. Beat eggs with salt and pepper. Pour into wok and heat slowly. Lift up edges of the eggs as they become set on the bottom and allow uncooked egg to run under. Cook until golden brown on bottom and creamy on top. Place mushrooms and onions in center and roll out on plate. Garnish with lettuce or parsley. Serve at once.

Vegetables & Rice

Stir-fried Chinese Celery Cabbage

Yield: 4 servings

2 tablespoons vegetable oil
1 slice fresh ginger root
1 pound Chinese celery cabbage (bok choy), cut diagonally into ¼-inch slices
3 stalks celery, cut diagonally into ¼-inch slices
½ teaspoon salt
½ teaspoon sugar
3 tablespoons chicken broth
1 teaspoon sesame oil

Heat oil in the wok. Brown and discard the ginger slice. Stir-fry the bok choy and celery for 2 to 3 minutes. Add the salt, sugar, and chicken broth. Cover and heat for 1 minute. Serve at once sprinkled with a little sesame oil.

Stir-fried Broccoli with Shoyu Ginger Sauce

Yield: 4 servings

1 head fresh broccoli or 1 package
  frozen, defrosted broccoli
2 tablespoons vegetable oil

Sauce

½ tablespoon cornstarch
½ tablespoon soy sauce
⅛ teaspoon powdered ginger
½ cup chicken broth
½ teaspoon salt

Prepare the fresh broccoli for stir-frying by breaking off the branches from the main stem and slicing the branch stems very thin. Cut each floret into several bite-size pieces. Heat the oil in the wok and add broccoli. Stir-fry for 1 minute, cover, and steam for 3 minutes. Broccoli should still be bright green in color, crisp, but heated through. Serve at once with the Shoyu Ginger sauce that has been prepared by combining the sauce ingredients and bringing them to a boil, stirring constantly. Sauce may be served separately or poured over the broccoli in the wok just before the broccoli is removed.

Sweet-and-Sour Carrots

Yield: 4 servings

2 tablespoons vegetable oil
1 slice fresh ginger root
1 pound carrots, cleaned and roll-cut
  into 1-inch pieces
½ teaspoon salt
½ cup chicken broth
1 tablespoon vinegar
½ tablespoon brown sugar

2 teaspoons cornstarch in 2 tablespoons
  cold water
½ cup canned pineapple chunks,
  optional

Heat the oil in the wok. Brown and discard the ginger slice. Stir-fry the carrots for 1 minute. Add the salt and chicken broth. Cover and steam over moderate heat for 5 minutes. Stir in the vinegar, brown sugar, cornstarch mixture, and pineapple chunks (if desired). Heat until sauce thickens. Serve at once.

Stir-fried Green Beans with Variations

Yield: 4 servings

2 tablespoons vegetable oil
1 clove garlic
2 to 3 cups green beans, washed,
  stemmed, and cut into 1-inch pieces
½ cup chicken broth
½ teaspoon salt
½ teaspoon sugar
1 teaspoon cornstarch in 1 tablespoon
  cold water

Heat the oil in the wok. Brown and discard the garlic. Stir-fry the green beans for 3 minutes. Add the chicken broth, salt, and sugar. Cover and steam over moderate heat for 3 to 4 minutes, until beans are tender but still bright green and crisp. Stir the cornstarch mixture and add it to the wok. Cook, stirring, until the sauce is thickened. Serve at once.

Variations. Green Beans with Black Bean Sauce: Combine 1 tablespoon black bean sauce, 1 teaspoon dry sherry, and 1 teaspoon sugar and stir into the beans just before serving. Green Beans with Water Chestnuts:

Add 8 to 10 water chestnuts, sliced, to the beans just before the stock is added. Green Beans with Sweet-and-Sour Sauce: Add 2 teaspoons lemon juice and 1 teaspoon sugar to the beans just before serving.

Chinese Mushrooms and Bamboo Shoots with Hoisin Sauce

Yield: 4 servings

2 tablespoons vegetable oil
½ pound fresh mushrooms, cut into "T" shapes
4 ounces bamboo shoots, sliced (½ small can)
½ teaspoon salt
1 teaspoon cornstarch in 1 tablespoon cold water
2 tablespoons hoisin sauce

Heat the oil in the wok. Stir-fry mushrooms for 2 to 3 minutes. Add bamboo shoots and stir-fry 1 minute longer. Combine the remaining ingredients and add to the vegetables. Heat and stir gently until the sauce thickens and the vegetables are coated. Serve at once.

Tossed Spinach with Peanuts

Yield: 4 servings

1 pound fresh spinach, washed and stemmed
¼-cup peanuts (or more)
1 tablespoon vegetable oil
1 tablespoon soy sauce
Salt and pepper

Steam the spinach in a small amount of boiling water for only 2 to 3 minutes. Drain at once, pat dry, and cut into fine strips. Crush half the peanuts with a rolling pin or mince with a cleaver. Heat oil in the wok and add the crushed peanuts, spinach, soy sauce, and salt and pepper to taste. Stir-fry for 1 to 2 minutes. Serve garnished with the remaining peanuts.

Five Precious Oriental Vegetables

Yield: 4 servings

5 to 6 Chinese dried black mushrooms
1 small head of Chinese celery cabbage
1 or 2 bamboo shoots
4 or 5 water chestnuts
2 tablespoons vegetable oil
1 cup bean sprouts
3 tablespoons chicken broth
1 teaspoon salt
2 teaspoons soy sauce
1 teaspoon sugar

Soak the mushrooms in warm water for 20 to 30 minutes; drain, remove and discard the tough stems, and cut the caps into strips. Wash the cabbage well, drain, and cut diagonally into ½-inch slices. Cut the bamboo shoots and water chestnuts into slices. Heat oil in the wok. Stir-fry the cabbage 1 minute, then add mushrooms, bean sprouts, water chestnuts, and bamboo shoots. Stir-fry all together for 3 to 4 minutes. Add broth with the remaining ingredients. Mix well and heat through. Vegetables should be tender but still crisp. Serve at once.

Crispy Fried Vegetables

Yield: 4 to 6 servings

Batter for frying

1 cup sifted all-purpose flour
1 egg
½ cup milk
Salt and pepper
Cut the following vegetables into
   matchstick size strips:
     2 carrots
     2 potatoes
     1 stick celery
     8 small cauliflower florets
     1 sliced onion
     2 cups oil for frying

Prepare the batter by combining the flour, egg, milk, and a little salt and pepper in a small bowl. Mix or whisk until the batter is smooth and lump-free. Batter should be thin. If it seems very thick, add more milk.

Thoroughly mix the cut-up vegetables into the batter. Let stand for ½ hour. Using a slotted spoon, lift out spoonfuls of mixed vegetables and drop gently into deep fat at 375°F. (Use an electric wok or a thermometer to maintain proper temperature of the fat.) Deep-fry for 2 to 3 minutes, a few spoonfuls at a time. Lift out and drain on paper towels. Serve as a vegetable at any meal.

Fried Rice Sub Gum

Yield: 6 to 8 servings

3 tablespoons vegetable oil
1 medium onion, chopped
1 green pepper, thinly sliced
4 ounces cooked ham, diced into
   ¼-inch pieces

4 ounces cooked chicken, diced into
   ¼-inch pieces
4 ounces cooked small shrimp, left
   whole
3 to 4 cups cold, cooked rice
1 to 2 tablespoons soy sauce
2-egg omelette (optional garnish)

Heat oil in the wok and stir-fry the onion until it is translucent. Push aside. Stir-fry the green pepper for 1 to 2 minutes. Return the onions to the wok. Add the meat, shrimp, and rice and stir-fry together for 4 to 5 minutes, until rice is golden. Sprinkle with soy sauce and garnish with ⅛-inch strips of omelette.

Vegetable and Ham Rice Cake

Yield: 4 servings

2 tablespoons vinegar
2 tablespoons sugar
½ teaspoon salt
3 cups cooked, cold rice
2 tablespoons vegetable oil
3 carrots, cut into matchstick-size
   shreds
2 ounces mushrooms, sliced
½ unpeeled cucumber, sliced
3 scallions, sliced
2 tablespoons soy sauce
2 teaspoons prepared horseradish sauce
2 tablespoons light cream
4 slices boiled ham, shredded

Combine vinegar, 1 tablespoon of the sugar, and salt together with the rice. Toss well. Heat oil in the wok. Add carrots and stir-fry 2 to 3 minutes. Add mushrooms, cucumber, and scallions and continue to stir-fry until all the vegetables are very tender. Stir in the remaining 1 tablespoon of sugar and the soy sauce. Set aside.

Grease an 8-inch spring-form pan (or use an 8-inch square baking pan lined with plastic wrap extending well over the sides so the mixture can eventually be lifted out). Pack half of the rice in the bottom. Cover with ¾ of the prepared vegetables, then the remaining rice. Combine the horseradish sauce and cream and spread over the rice. Cover with the remaining ¼ of the vegetables and the ham shreds. Place a piece of waxed paper over the top and weight it down. Chill for 30 minutes. Remove weight and paper, then carefully remove cake from pan. Use a wet knife to cut cake into slices and arrange on a platter. Serve cold with a little soy sauce.

Shrimp and Egg Fried Rice

Yield: 4 to 6 servings

1 slice bacon
2 scallions, sliced
1 clove garlic, minced
3 ounces shrimp, cut into small pieces
2 cups cold, cooked rice
1 egg beaten with salt and pepper
1 to 2 tablespoons soy sauce

Fry bacon in wok until crisp. Remove and set aside. Add scallions and garlic to wok and stir-fry in the bacon fat for 1 to 2 minutes. Add shirmp and stir-fry until pink (if frozen or canned shrimp are used, add while stir-frying the rice). Add the rice and stir-fry 4 to 5 minutes, until rice is golden. Pour the beaten egg into a well in the rice. Stir and heat until all the egg is coagulated. Crumble the bacon and add to the rice with the soy sauce. Combine well.

Dips & Sauces

Hot Mustard Dip

Yield: 2 to 4 tablespoons

2 to 4 tablespoons dry mustard
Sufficient vinegar to make a paste

Combine the dry mustard with vinegar. This makes a very hot dip. Only a small amount should be used on foods.

Soy-Sesame Oil Dip

Yield: ¾ cup

½ cup soy sauce
¼ cup sesame seed oil
1 teaspoon sugar
2 tablespoons dry sherry

Mix all the ingredients together. Serve in dipping bowls. Recipe may be halved, as sauce is thin and small amounts adhere to the food.

Sweet-and-Sour Dip

Yield: Approximately 2½ cups

2 tablespoons cornstarch
¾ cup pineapple juice
½ cup brown sugar
½ cup vinegar
1 tablespoon catsup
1 teaspoon salt
Cup crushed pineapple

Combine cornstarch and pineapple juice in a saucepan. Add remaining ingredients and stir over medium heat until the sauce boils and is thickened.

Ginger Soy Sauce

Yield: About 1½ cups

½ cup soy sauce
1 cup water
2 tablespoons white wine, optional
2 teaspoons sugar
1 teaspoon powdered ginger

Mix together all ingredients and heat gently. Serve warm.

Plum Sauce

Yield: 1½ cups

1 cup plum, peach, or apricot preserves
½ cup chopped chutney or Indian relish
1 tablespoon sugar
1 tablespoon vinegar

Combine the ingredients and refrigerate for 1 to 2 hours. Serve in dipping bowls.

Easy Sweet-and-Sour Sauce

Yield: About ½ cup

1 tablespoon cornstarch
3 tablespoons water
2 tablespoons soy sauce
3 tablespoons sugar
2 tablespoons vinegar
1 tablespoon catsup

Mix cornstarch and water in a custard cup. Mix soy sauce, sugar, vinegar, and catsup in a wok or small saucepan and bring to a simmer. Add cornstarch mixture and simmer until it thickens and clears, stirring constantly. If too thick, thin with water.

Rich Sweet-and-Sour Sauce

Yield: About 1½ cups

½ cup chutney
½ cup plum jam
¼ cup cold water
1 tablespoon sugar
1 tablespoon vinegar

Combine ingredients in a wok or small saucepan; simmer 1 minute. Cool; store in refrigerator.

Pungent Sweet-and-Sour Sauce

Yield: About 1 cup

1 cup bottled sweet-and-sour sauce
2 tablespoons catsup
2 teaspoons prepared mustard

Mix ingredients together and heat gently. Serve warm.

Tempura Sauce for Chicken

Yield: 1 cup

½ cup chicken broth
4 tablespoons soy sauce
4 tablespoons sherry

Combine all ingredients and warm in a saucepan. Serve in dipping bowls.

Tempura Sauce for Seafood

Yield: ¾ cup

½ cup dashi (fish broth) or chicken
broth
2 tablespoons soy sauce
2 teaspoons sugar
1 tablespoon horseradish sauce

Combine all ingredients and serve warm
in dipping bowls.

Desserts*

Mandarin Fruit

Yield: 4 to 6 servings

2 11-ounce cans mandarin oranges
1 1-pound 4-ounce can lychees
(available in Oriental-food stores)
1 tablespoon lemon juice
2 slices ginger root

Combine oranges and lychees with the
syrup from both. Add lemon juice and the
slices of ginger. Chill for a few hours before
serving and remove slices of ginger root.

Peach Coupe with Cherries Jubilee

Yield: About 6 servings

1 can (1 pound 14 ounces) pitted black
Bing cherries
1 tablespoon sugar
1 tablespoon cornstarch
1 cup cherry juice
1 3-inch piece lemon peel

2 tablespoons cherry liqueur
6 canned cling peach halves
1 pint vanilla ice cream
⅓ cup warmed brandy

Drain cherries and reserve juice. Mix
sugar with cornstarch and add 1 cup cherry
juice a little at a time.

Add the lemon peel and cook gently, until clear and thickened, about 5 minutes.
Remove from heat. Take out the lemon peel
and stir in the cherry liqueur and the cherries. This may be prepared ahead.

To serve: Have the dessert dishes ready
on a tray at the table. Place a peach half and
some ice cream in each. Transfer the sauce
to an electric wok and heat gently. Pour the
warm brandy over the hot sauce, without
stirring. Set ablaze and spoon over the
peaches and ice cream.

Almond Cookies

Yield: About 3 dozen

1 cup hydrogenated shortening
1 cup sugar
1 egg
2 teaspoons almond extract
3 cups sifted all-purpose flour
3 dozen blanched whole almonds

Preheat the oven to 350°F. Cream
together the shortening, sugar, egg, and almond extract. Stir in the flour 1 cup at a
time. The dough will be very stiff. Form
dough into round balls the size of small walnuts. Place on a greased baking sheet and
flatten to form thick rounds. Press an almond into the center of each cookie. Bake
for 10 minutes. Remove, and cool on a wire
rack. Store in an airtight container.

*Some of these desserts are not prepared in a wok. However, all go well with the Oriental-style recipes in this chapter.

Deep-fried Date Buns

Yield: About 48 buns

1 pound pitted dates
1 cup shelled walnuts
4 tablespoons frozen orange juice
   concentrate
4 tablespoons grated orange rind
2 to 3 cups oil for frying
Confectioners' sugar

Cut dates into chunks about 1-inch square. Place in blender ¼ at a time, with ¼ of the walnuts. At high speed, blend into finest particles. Turn into a large bowl, add orange juice and rind, and knead into a large ball. Place a spoonful into the center of a dough circle and twist into bun form. Roll in the hands until smooth.

Heat oil in the wok to 375°F. Fry the buns 6 to 8 at a time until just golden brown. Drain well, cool, and sprinkle lightly with confectioner's sugar before serving.

Steamed Date Buns

Yield: About 48 buns

½ cup lard or hydrogenated shortening
2 cups canned red-bean paste
1 pound pitted dates, finely chopped
Red food coloring, optional

Melt the lard in the wok at moderate heat, add the canned bean paste and chopped dates, and cook, stirring constantly, for 8 to 10 minutes. Transfer the contents of the wok pan to a bowl and cool thoroughly.

Place a spoonful of the mixture into the center of a dough circle and twist into a bun form. Roll in the hands until a smooth ball is formed. Steam the smooth buns in bamboo steamer trays above boiling water in the base of the wok for 10 minutes. Serve hot directly in the steamer tray placed on a pan.

Index

Index

Black-Cherry Crepes (Crepe), 38
Blintzes (Crepe), 41
Blueberry
  Cake (TO), 318
  Crepes (Crepe), 37
  Pudding (TO), 319
Bolognese Sauce (Crock), 64
Borscht, Russian (FP), 116
Bouillon with Crepes (Crepe), 10
Bourbon or Rum Balls (FP), 129
Bread
  Apple-Raisin (FP), 120
  Apricot-Nut (Crock), 78
  Banana-Orange Nut (FP), 119
  Boston Brown (Crock), 78
  Brown (PC), 225
  Cottage-Cheese-Dill (FP), 122
  Dark German Rye (FP), 124
  Date and Nut (PC), 225
  Date-Nut-Carrot Whole-Wheat
    (FP), 120
  French (FP), 122
  Garlic (TO), 284
  Light Rye (FP), 122
  Nut and Date (TO), 321
  Pudding (PC), 226
  Pumpkin (TO), 323
  Pumpkin Tea (Crock), 79
  Round Light Rye Sandwich (Crock),
    78
  Round Pumpernickel Sandwich
    Bread (Crock), 79
  Round Raisin Whole-Wheat
    (Crock), 80
  Round Whole-Wheat Sandwich
    (Crock), 80
  Skillet (SK), 233
  Stuffing, Basic (FP), 106
  Swedish Limpa Round Rye (Crock),
    77
  White (FP), 123
Breakfast Casserole (TO), 286
Brioche Rolls (FP), 125
Brisket with Wine (PC), 184
Broccoli
  Casserole (TO), 309
  in Cream Sauce (PC), 209
  Stir-fried, with Shoyu Ginger Sauce
    (Wok), 362
  Soup, Cream of (MW), 136
  Toast (TO), 284
Brown Beef Broth or Bouillon (Crock),
  72
Brown Betty with Hard Sauce (SK),
  277
Brownies (TO), 319
Brunswick Stew (PC), 218
Brussels Sprouts and New Potatoes
  (PC), 210
Bugnes (FP), 125
Butterfish in Sour Cream (SK), 258

C

Cabbage
  with Bacon and Dill (SK), 266

Chinese, with Mushrooms (PC), 210
French-fried (SK), 267
Leaves, Stuffed (MW), 165
in Meat Essence (PC), 210
Red, and Apples (SK), 267
and Rice (PC), 210
Rolls in Beer (Crock), 54
Caesar's Vegetables (SK), 270
Cake
  Apple-Crumb Coffee (FP), 124
  Baked-Apple Crepe (Crepe), 35
  Blueberry (TO), 318
  Chocolate Applesauce (TO), 317
  Chocolate and Molasses (MW), 170
  Chocolate and Orange (MW), 170
  Egg White (TO), 320
  Loaf (TO), 321
  1-2-3 (TO), 322
  Pineapple (TO), 322
  Sugar-and-Cinnamon-Topped Coffee
    (TO), 323
  Victoria Lemon (MW), 171
Calorie-Counters Crepe Batter
  (Crepe), 4
Calves Liver with Bean Sprouts
  (Wok), 338
Calzone Alla Napoli (FP), 95
Calzone Italiana (FP), 95
Cambridge Sauce (FP), 103
Camembert Spread (FP), 88
Cannelloni Alla Siciliana (FP), 129
Cannelloni Crepes (Crepe), 32
Carbonnade of Beef 'n Beer (Crock),
  49
Carp in Red Wine (PC), 200
Carrot
  -Lemon Relish (FP), 105
  Squares (TO), 310
Carrots
  Glazed (SK), 267
  and Raisins (SK), 268
  Raisins and Pineapple (PC), 210
  Sautéed Grated (SK), 268
  Sliced, with Honey and Parsley
    (FP), 100
  Sweet-and-Sour (Wok), 362
Cassata Alla Siciliana (FP), 130
Cassoulet (Crock), 65
Cauliflower
  Casserole (TO), 310
  Crepes with Mornay Sauce (Crepe),
    14
  Sautéed (SK), 268
Celery
  and Amonds (PC), 211
  Braised (MW), 166
  Cabbage and Pork Soup (Wok), 329
  Cabbage and Shrimp Soup (Wok),
    328
  Cabbage, Stir-fried Chinese (Wok),
    361
Champagne—Fruit Cocktail (FP), 88
Cheese
  Bacon and Onion Crepes (Crepe),
    16
  Bake (TO), 286
  and Beef Rolls (Crepe), 9
  Camembert Spread (FP), 88

Cubes (SK), 231
Fondue, Swiss (FP), 95
Fritters (SK), 238
-Olive Snack (Crepe), 9
Pudding (TO), 286
Puffs (TO), 283
Puffs, Surprise (FP), 88
Roll-overs (TO), 283
Yums (TO), 283
Cheesy Dipping Chips (Crepe), 9
Cherry
  and Apple Crepes (Crepe), 37
  Soup, Chilled (PC), 181
Chick Peas and Ham (Crock), 68
Chicken
  à la King (SK), 250
  with Almonds (SK), 250
  with Almonds and Mushrooms
    (Wok), 347
  with Asparagus (Wok), 348
  Baked (TO), 298
  Baked, and Broccoli (TO), 299
  Baked, and Spinach Casserole (TO),
    299
  and Bananas (PC), 192
  Battered (PC), 192
  with Bean Sprouts and Snow Pea
    Pods (Wok), 349
  Bits Oriental (Wok), 346
  Breast, and Ham (SK), 253
  Breasts Baked in Cream (TO), 300
  Breasts with Lemon and White
    Vermouth (MW), 152
  Breasts, Rolled (PC), 191
  Breasts, Stuffed (FP), 96
  Breasts in White Wine (SK), 253
  Breasts in Wine (PC), 192
  and Broccoli Soup (PC), 182
  Broth or Stock (Crock), 72
  Casserole, Belgian (MW), 152
  Casserole, Javanese (Wok), 346
  with Celery and Celery Cabbage
    (Wok), 350
  with Celery and Mushrooms (Wok),
    348
  Chow Mein (SK), 250
  Chow Mein, Simple (TO), 300
  Consommé with Crepes (Crepe), 10
  and Corn Soup (PC), 182
  Crepe Soufflé (Crepe), 23
  Curry (PC), 192
  Cutlets (SK), 251
  Deep-fried, with Lemon Sauce
    (Wok), 353
  Delight (SK), 251
  Dinner with Asparagus (SK), 274
  Dinner, Island (PC), 218
  Divan Crepes, Quick (Crepe), 23
  Egg Drop Soup (Wok), 326
  Enchiladas (Crock), 61
  -Filled Crepes (Crepe), 22
  Florentine (TO), 300
  Fried, with Cream Gravy (SK), 254
  in Fruit Sauce (PC), 193
  with Green Pepper and Cashews
    (Wok), 350

Index

Index

Index